twentieth century thinkers

in adult & continuing education

second edition

edited by

peter jarvis

**KOGAN
PAGE**

First published by Croom Helm Ltd in 1987
First published in paperback by Routledge in 1991
Second edition published by Kogan Page in 2001

Kogan Page Limited
120 Pentonville Road
London N1 9JN
UK

Stylus Publishing Inc.
22883 Quicksilver Drive
Sterling, VA 20166–2012
USA

British Library Cataloguing in Publication Data

A CIP record for this book is available from the British Library.

ISBN 0 7494 3408 2

Typeset by Jean Cussons Typesetting, Diss, Norfolk
Printed and bound in Great Britain by Biddles Ltd, Guildford and King's Lynn

Contents

About the authors

David L Alfred is a tutor-organizer for the South-eastern District of the Workers' Educational Organization (WEA) in the UK. Graduating in government from Exeter University in 1963, he has taught liberal studies and sociology in colleges of further education, and many social science courses as a part-time tutor for the WEA (in conjunction with Oxford's Delegacy for Extramural Studies) and the Open University. A WEA workshop in Hastings that he convened, wrote and produced *The Robert Tressell Papers: Exploring 'the ragged trousered Philanthropists'* in 1982. His article on *The Relevance of the Work of Paulo Freire to Radical Community Education in Britain* appeared in *The International Journal of Lifelong Education* in 1984. He wrote a dissertation on political education in the British Army 1941–1945 as part of the MSc degree in educational studies that he was awarded by Surrey University in 1985.

Brenda Bell is associate director of the Center for Literacy Studies, University of Tennessee, and coordinator for field research for Equipped for the Future – the national standards-based system reform initiative for adult literacy and life-long learning in the United States. She has been a consultant to Highlander's labour program, and has led and participated in workshops there. She once served as regional coordinator of the Amalgamated Clothing and Textile Workers' Union Humanities Education Program; has taught on the Southern Summer School for Union Women; and has work experience in the areas of labour education, social work and community education. She is co-editor of *We Make the Road by Walking*, which is a dialogue between Myles Horton and Paulo Freire.

Stephen Brookfield began his teaching career in 1970 and has worked in England, Canada, Australia and the United States, teaching in a variety of college settings. He has written and edited eight books on adult learning, teaching and critical thinking and is a three-times winner of the Cyril O Houle World Award for Literature in Adult Education. After 10 years as a professor of higher and adult education at Columbia University, New York, he now holds the title of Distinguished Professor at the University of St Thomas in Minneapolis, Minnesota. His latest book (written with Stephen Preskill) is

Discussion as a Way of Teaching, published in the UK by the Open University Press.

Ronald M Cervero is a professor in the Department of Adult Education at the University of Georgia. He earned his MA in the social sciences and his PhD in adult education at the University of Chicago. Professor Cervero has published extensively in adult education, with particular emphasis in the areas of continuing education for the professions and the politics of adult education. Of his five books, three have won national awards including the 1989 Cyril O Houle World Award for Literature in Adult Education (*Effective Continuing Education for Professionals*, 1988, Jossey-Bass). He has been invited to present his work at many national and international meetings for different professional groups, such as pharmacists, nurses, physicians, judges, lawyers and educators, and in several countries outside of the United States, including Russia, England, Finland and Malaysia. He has also written *Planning Responsibly for Adult Education: A guide to negotiating power and interests* (1994, Jossey-Bass) and *What Really Matters in Adult Education Program Planning: Lessons in negotiating power and interests* (1996, Jossey-Bass), which offer a political perspective on planning educational programs for adults. His most recent edited book is *Power in Practice: The struggle for knowledge and power in society* (2001, Jossey-Bass). He has served in a variety of leadership positions in adult education including the editorship of *Adult Education Quarterly* (the major journal for theory and research in the field), the Commission of Professors of Adult Education and the Adult Education Research Conference. He has been a visiting faculty member at the University of Calgary, the University of Tennessee, the University of Wisconsin-Madison, the University of British Columbia and Pennsylvania State University.

John M Crane is a graduate of the University of Saskatchewan (1962, BA and BEd) and of the University of Surrey, UK (MSc in Educational Studies in 1982). He has had a long involvement with adult basic education and has been interested in its background. In addition, he has a particular interest in self-paced, individualized learning, which was the subject of his dissertation. He has published a number of articles on adult education and he is currently an instructor on a self-paced, individualized learning program in Camosun College, Victoria, Canada.

Angela Cross-Durrant started her working life in the National Health Service and began teaching in 1971 at an Institute of Adult Education in Bristol, UK. This was followed by a period at Soundwell Technical College, also in Bristol. Three years afterwards, she moved to Twickenham College of Technology, later Richmond-upon-Thames (tertiary) College, where she was a senior lecturer.

She looks upon herself as a 'lifelong learner', as she studied in her own time for her A Levels, various teaching qualifications, and her first degree (in English literature) which she undertook as an external student of the University of London.

(She had previously completed a Cert Ed on a sandwich course under the auspices of the same university). In 1985, she completed an MSc in educational studies on a part-time basis at the University of Surrey. Her interest in lifelong education was formalized during this latter period of study. She has published a number of papers on the education of adults.

Barry Elsey entered adult education as a mature student after leaving school without any qualifications. First by part-time and then full-time study, he went on to university. He entered university adult education as a research fellow and then as a lecturer at the Universities of Liverpool and Nottingham. He now works in Australia. He has wide experience of university extension work and professional training programmes in adult/continuing education. His research and writing in adult/continuing education have reflected a personal interest in adult students, volunteer tutors, 'second chance' education for adults and the application of social theory to policy and practice in adult/continuing education.

Colin Griffin is an associate lecturer in the School of Educational Studies at the University of Surrey, where he is a member of the Centre for Research in Lifelong Learning. He has worked as an assistant librarian at the London School of Economics and with the Open University as a senior counsellor. In addition, he has been a senior lecturer in sociology at Kingston Polytechnic and senior lecturer in education at Cheltenham and Gloucester College of Higher Education. For many years he worked in adult education as a teacher and teacher trainer at Hillcroft College and the University of London Department of Extramural Studies. He has published several books and articles on the curriculum of adult education and the policy analysis of lifelong learning, which is his particular interest. His latest books are *Training to Teach in Further and Adult Education*, with David Gray and Tony Nasta (Stanley Thornes, 2000) and *Post-compulsory Education into the New Millennium*, edited with David Gray (Jessica Kingsley, 2000)

William S Bill Griffith was professor of adult education in the Department of Administrative, Adult and Higher Education at the University of British Columbia in Vancouver, Canada, from 1977 until his death. He had been chair of the Adult Education Special Field Committee at the University of Chicago for 15 years. Beginning his professional career in agricultural extension, he subsequently earned his PhD in adult education at the University of Chicago. In addition to serving as senior editor of the eight-volume *Handbook of Adult Education* in the United States, he had also been chair of the Commission of the Professors of Adult Education and a member of the Steering Committee of the Adult Education Research Conference. In 1980, he was given the Research to Practice Award of the Adult Education Association of the United States.

Peter Jarvis is professor of continuing education adults at the University of Surrey, UK. He was head of the Department of Educational Studies for a number of years and is now a research professor. He also coordinates the Centre for Research in Lifelong Learning. He has written numerous articles and books, including *Adult Learning in the Social Context*, which won the C O Houle World Award for Literature in Adult Education. He has written and edited over 20 books. His latest include: *The Age of Learning*, which he has edited, and *Learning in Later Life*, which he has authored, both published by Kogan Page. He in the founding editor of *The International Journal of Lifelong Education*, and he serves on the editorial board of *Adult Education Quarterly*. His work has been translated into many languages.

Carol E Kasworm is department head and professor of adult and community college education at North Carolina State University. She has her bachelor's degree from Valparaiso University, MA in higher education administration from Michigan State University and EdD from the University of Georgia. She was associate dean for research at the University of Tennessee from 1992–98. Her current research and publications focus upon adult undergraduate students. She is also a consulting editor for *Adult Education Quarterly, Journal of Continuing Higher Education* and *Assessment and Accountability Forum*.

Mal Leicester is Professor of Adult Learning and Teaching at the University of Nottingham, UK. Previously she was at the University of Warwick. She has taught at all levels of the education system and was Avon's Advisor for Multicultural Education. She has published in the philosophy of education, continuing education, values education and in relation to ethnicity and disability. Falmer Press publish her co-edited six volumes on *Values, Culture and Education*. Having researched aspects of educational inequality, she has established the Education Inclusion Research Centre at the University of Nottingham.

Stella Parker was brought up in East Africa and then studied biological sciences at Imperial College in London. She started her academic career in colleges of further and higher education in London, where she taught life sciences to a wide range of students. Later, she worked at the City University London in the Department of Continuing Education and became head of the department and a Pro-vice-chancellor. She was appointed to the Robert Peers Chair in Adult Education at the University of Nottingham in 1997 and is now head of the School of Continuing Education. Her publications cover topics in educational policy and associated curriculum issues for adult students, access and continuing professional development.

John M Peters is professor of adult education and educational psychology at the University of Tennessee and director of the doctoral program in collaborative learning. He edited *Building an Effective Enterprise of Adult Education* (1980), co-edited *We Make the Road by Walking* (Temple University Press, 1990) – a dialogue between Myles Horton and Paulo Freire – and co-edited *Adult Education: Evolutions and Achievements in a Developing Field of Study* (Jossey-Bass,

1991). He is a former secretary of the Adult Education Association of the USA and executive committee member of the Commission of Professors on Adult Education.

William A B Smith graduated from Georgetown College, Georgetown, Kentucky, with a double major in psychology and sociology in 1968 for his BA degree. He graduated from Southwestern Baptist Theological Seminary with a major in Religious Education in 1972 (MRE degree), and with a double major in Psychology and Foundations of Teaching, 1978 (EdD degree). He has served in the following capacities: minister to the deaf, trainer for deaf ministers and teacher of children with learning disabilities. He served local churches as minister of education for 10 years. He has been associate professor of foundations of education on the faculty of Southwestern Baptist Theological Seminary since 1978. He has authored and co-authored publications in creative methods of teaching, leadership training of volunteer teachers and curriculum design.

Alan Miller Thomas was born in Toronto, Canada, in 1928. He was educated at Upper Canada College, University of Toronto and at Teachers College, Columbia University where he studied the history of education, (MA, 1953) and later social psychology (PhD,1964). He served as executive director of the Canadian Association for Adult Education between 1961–69 and was president of that organization in 1972–78. He taught at the University of British Columbia between 1955–61, where he inaugurated the first full-time graduate programme in adult education in Canada in 1958. He was second chair of the Department of Adult Education of the Ontario Institute for Studies in Education 1971–1979. He also served as executive assistant to the Federal Minister of Communications, 1970–71 and on the OECD review team for Finland, 1981. His recent book is *Principia Mathetica: The politics of learning*.

Karen E Watkins is professor of Adult Education at the University of Georgia and interim director of the School of Leadership and Lifelong Learning. She is the co-author with Victoria Marsick of four books, including *Sculpting the Learning Organization – The art and science of systemic change* (1993) and *Facilitating the Learning Organization: Making learning count* (1999). She is co-author with Ann Brooks of *The Emerging Power of Action Inquiry Technologies* (1994).

Jacqueline A Wilson is a doctoral candidate in adult education at the University of Georgia. Her focus is human resources and organization development.

Preface

The idea for the first edition of this book took shape over a number of years of teaching the theory of adult education, during which time it became evident that there existed no single book that provided an overview of the development of the variety of approaches to the subject or one where substantial summaries of any of the key thinkers might be easily obtained. This symposium was designed to rectify these deficiencies in part. As we drew to the end of the 20th century, it seemed a good idea to revisit that original book, revise what had been written and include additional thinkers so that it could capture something of the changes that have been occurring in the education of adults, but without producing a completely new volume.

Deciding upon who might be regarded as a major thinker was a difficult process and colleagues in the field might dispute the selection. However, it was decided at the outset that only writers whose work has been published in English would be included in this volume. Limitations of space forbade the inclusion of too many writers, although five new chapters have been added to the original volume. It was difficult to decide precisely where to stop among those scholars who were still writing at the end of the 20th century but it was decided not to include those whose main focus has been about education for adults in the late or postmodern period. Consultations with colleagues in the field guided me in making the final selection.

The preparation of the first edition of this book was not without its hazards for the authors. Three of those who were originally approached were hospitalized within a few months of the request being made. One of those three subsequently withdrew, and so the editor was forced to write a further chapter. No such hazards befell the additional authors approached!

I should like to express my thanks to all those colleagues who have written and/or updated the following chapters and to those who, knowing about my intention to produce this text, have been so encouraging. Finally, I would like to express my thanks to Jonathan Simpson of Kogan Page who has been very supportive, not only in this enterprise, but in a number of writing ventures in recent years.

The first edition of this book was well received and when it was finally withdrawn from publication a number of years ago, many colleagues told me how useful it had been. Consequently, I hope that both students of, and practitioners in, the fields of education for adults will find this new edition as useful.

Introduction: Adult education – an ideal for modernity?

Peter Jarvis

Throw a pebble into a pond and watch the concentric ripples flow outwards. Throw two pebbles into different parts of the pond and watch the ripples come together and those from the larger stone gradually merge with those from the smaller but still continue. This latter illustrates the forces of globalization, with the forces of social change spreading out from one major central point and others from the minor ones, with the USA being the major one and western Europe being the less powerful. Think back to the Reformation, the Industrial Revolution and the Enlightenment and there was only one pebble and the driving forces for change came from Europe. A great deal of the history of adult education is contained within the broad historical period from the Enlightenment, or more precisely the Reformation, to the beginning of the questioning of the Modernity project in the 1970s, which was concurrent with the beginning of what we now call globalization and late modernity.

When this book was first published, there was evidence of some of the major changes that were about to befall adult education but between 1980–2000, the changes have been quite massive in the West as the Modernity project has been questioned. The changes have not been quite the same in other countries although it is unlikely that they will escape from the forces of economic global-ization. A special issue of *The International Journal of Lifelong Education* (2000, Vol 20, Nos 1–2) seeks to document these changes, which are also discussed in Jarvis, Holford and Griffin (1998).

However, in that original volume, the first chapter was entitled *The Development of Adult Education Knowledge* although even then it was recognized that adult education was not a single field of practice. The thinkers included in that volume were those who had influenced, or were still influencing, the tradi-tional field of adult education. Even so, from Dewey and Yeaxlee to Gelpi, life-long education was a major theme. In this volume, however, we have also included those whose influence has been specifically on continuing professional education, or human resource development. Now they all tend to be subsumed under the term of lifelong learning.

Adult education was born as a social movement and many of the early thinkers had embraced its ideals. Their concerns were social and ethical but, as adult educators, they all wanted to see adult education transform national educational systems so that all people had an opportunity to continue their education. In short, they wanted it to become a system of lifelong education. Perhaps they did not foresee quite how this would happen or what its outcomes would be, but this chapter demonstrates the way in which this has occurred. Most of the educationalists who are currently writing about this process have not been considered for inclusion in this volume, since their focus is slightly different, and so we conclude this volume with the research of Donald Schön and Chris Argyris. In the chapters of this book, however, we are seeking to capture the values, theories and ideas of some of the leading thinkers who influenced adult and continuing education throughout the 20th century and who continue to influence it in the 21st century.

In this introduction I want to argue that while the aims of adult education as a social movement have been in some way apparently fulfilled, we are not left with the achievement of the ideal, since they were not achieved by the forces of adult education alone but by those of global capital seeking to use knowledge to exploit a global market.

PART 1: THE IDEALS OF ADULT EDUCATION

The Enlightenment occurred over an extended period in the 18th century and certainly spanned a number of generations of thinkers who began to question the established norms of the day. They emphasized a number of issues, such as: the use of reason, empiricism, science, universalism, progress, individualism, toleration, freedom, uniformity of human nature and secularism (Hamilton, 1992: 21–22). In a sense, the Enlightenment itself was a product of the social conditions that had already been generated through the Reformation and the Industrial Revolution. Nevertheless, because of the growth in scientific knowledge, the changes in the nature of work and the development of the nation state (Green, 1990), the need for a wider educational system was recognized. Before the Enlightenment, the churches founded not only the universities but also many of the schools, and after it, the state and civic authorities established them. Education became a national institution that prepared the next generation for the world of work and transmitted to it that knowledge that the current generation of adults considered worthwhile.

While this was a period of rapid social change, it was not sufficiently rapid for knowledge to be conceptualized as anything other than truth. The Enlightenment was in part about replacing unchanging truth of revealed religion with the truth of scientific discovery. Hence, there was a new truth – a new knowledge to be disseminated, a new secular mission.

While the focus of education was on children, many others sought to spread this knowledge to adults with evangelical zeal. Knowledge societies of all forms grew up throughout Europe and America. There were literary and philosophical societies, debating societies, antiquarian societies, music societies, mechanics institutes and so on. Some like the Lyceum movement in the USA were rather like 'crazes' – they developed rapidly and died within a few years. However, others lasted longer. Here then was adult education, a social movement functioning outside of what was becoming an established educational framework, having loose organizational structures, with all types of spasmodic activity, and seeking to spread the new knowledge to a wider public. It was both norm and value oriented. This was part of the ideal of many early adult educators – to educate the people. However, the high ideals, it appears, were not always sustainable. What becomes clear from both Kelly's (1970) work on Britain and Kett's (1994) study of the USA was that acquiring academic knowledge for its own sake was not always popular and that some of these societies became popularizers of knowledge in order to survive, but were was still no doubt beneficial to the long-term development of adult education. Kett (1994: xvii), for instance, an academic historian, writes about the USA:

> Whereas in the 1820s both Josiah Holbrook and the promoters of mechanics' institutes expected to transfer a replica of the knowledge of the learned to the uneducated, by the 1840s lyceums and mechanics' institutes were popularizing knowledge in novel ways, for example by sponsoring lectures about science rather than scientific instruction... The history of university extension between 1890 and 1910 is that of ever more approaches to popularization and the gradual downgrading of academic education.

Here Kett actually reflects some of the traditional ideas academics have had about adult education. There were, in contrast, other adult educators who retained the high ideals of education and who endeavoured to introduce high-quality educational opportunities to adults: Mansbridge, for instance, with the establishment of the Workers' Educational Association with its high standard courses, tutorial classes and university extramural connections, and so on. There were also significant voices speaking on behalf of those adults claiming that education should be the right of every adult (A L Smith's *Introductory Letter to the 1919 Report*, Nottingham, 1980).

By the start of the 20th century, however, the adult education movement was already achieving some success and becoming accepted within the educational institution. As early as 1905, for instance, there were three-quarters of a million part-time students in local education authority evening classes (Fieldhouse, 1996: 79) and it was estimated that 50,000 students a year attended university extension classes during the first decade (Kelly, 1970: 246). However, it took a long time for adult education to be accepted completely, as the term extramural suggests.

Universities were cautious about changing, as the publication in the USA in 1964 of the famous 'black book' *Adult Education: Outlines of an emerging field of study* (Jensen, *et al* 1964) indicated. Indeed, in the UK, despite the long and proud history of university extension, many universities did not accept the academics working in extramural education as full members of the academic community until the 1970s and 1980s. Indeed, they are still finding it difficult.

Despite this process of institutionalization, adult educators still considered that they were part of a movement; still seeking to offer service meeting the needs of adults who had not had opportunities for, or were unsuccessful in, initial education. Some saw what they were doing within the context of a welfare state. By 1970, the creation of the British Open University symbolized the fact that adult education was finally accepted, even though there was still some doubt about the value of its awards for a few more years. The ideals of adult educators were beginning to be realized and the value of adult education was finally recognized. At the same time, however, questions were beginning to be asked about the nature of modernity itself. Social forces were operating that were to change society and with it destroy adult education, as we knew it.

PART 2: THE RISE OF LIFELONG LEARNING

Modernity itself was being questioned by the 1970s; French philosophers such as Foucault and Lyotard were already suggesting that post-modernity was dawning. A great number of studies were to follow suggesting that while we live with the consequences of modernity (Giddens, 1990), we might be entering a late or post-modern period. The forces of change were the forces of globalization. As the national state emerged with modernity, so in the late modern period the forces of globalization were to weaken it. Beck (2000: 11) actually defines globalization as the processes 'through which sovereign national states are criss-crossed and undermined by transnational actors with varying prospects of power, orientations, identities and networks'. These same forces produced an end of adult education as a separate entity – but not the end of the education of adults – and the emergence of lifelong learning in the West. Globalization is essentially a process whereby the world is becoming more uniform and standardized through the forces of the capitalist market operating on a worldwide basis, utilizing contemporary information technology.

Perhaps one of the easiest ways to illustrate the structural effects of globalization is to use a traditional Marxist model of society to demonstrate the point. In the Marxist model, society has a substructure and a superstructure; the former comprises the economic institutions owned by the bourgeoisie with whom power resides and a superstructure that is controlled by the forces emanating from the substructure. In the global world, there is still a sub-structure that is capital (financial and intellectual) empowered by information technology; but now the power resides not with those who own but with those who control capital. Beck (2000: 2) states that:

> It means that corporations, especially globally active ones, can play a key role in shaping not only the economy but society as a whole, if 'only' because they have it in their power to withdraw the material resources (capital, taxes, jobs) from society.

The extent to which there is now a single standardized superstructure is more debatable. Robertson (1995), for instance, has developed the useful concept of 'glocalisation' to emphasize that culture is still localized, and Castells (1996) has argued that the state still has a place to play in a not-completely free but extremely competitive global market.

The process of globalization, as we know it today, began in the West (the USA followed by western Europe) in the early 1970s. There were a variety of forces at work, such as competition from Japan, the free trade agreements, the creation of the electronic network, the oil crisis which dented the confidence of the West; and, like the ripples on the pond, it has spread. Corporations began to relocate manufacturing and to transfer capital around the world, seeking the cheapest places and the most efficient means to manufacture, and the best markets in which to sell, their products. This resulted in the continued decline in manufacturing industries in much of the First World and the need for new occupational structures emerged. Theorists began to suggest that there is actually a world economy (Wallerstein, 1974, inter alia) based on the capitalist system of exchange.

This global market has generated a great deal of competition between the large transnational corporations which have, in turn, invested vast sums of money in new research and in the new forms of rapidly changing knowledge – Scheler (1980) called these new forms of positive and scientific knowledge artificial because they do not have time to get embedded in a culture before they are outdated. These processes changed the structure of the workforce, with a decline in manufacturing jobs and an increased demand for knowledge-based workers in some countries, but with new industrial workers in others. Indeed, Reich postulated that there would be three major groups of workers – knowledge-based, service-based and routine production. He (1991: 179–80) indicated that the proportion of symbolic analysts (knowledge workers) had increased in the US workforce from 8 per cent in the 1950s to about 20 per cent in the 1980s. He argued that it would continue to increase. Any major changes in knowledge and increases in demand for knowledge-based workers are bound to have an effect on the education system; and since these workers are adults, these changes were to have lasting effects on adult education.

From about the 1960s we began to see changes occurring in the educational system that together indicate the way adult education was being changed; and we see creeping into the system some of the ideals of adult education, but in a slightly modified form. We have traced these elsewhere (Jarvis, Holford and

Griffin, 1998), so I only want to provide a brief overview here in which we see various axes along which education is travelling.

From initial to adult to recurrent and continuing education: In the 1960s there was an idea that people should have an educational entitlement after they left school, and adult education was called recurrent education. The OECD, for instance, subtitled some of its publications in this period (OECD, 1973) as *Recurrent Education – A strategy for lifelong education.* Probably because of the entitlement to education beyond school, this idea of recurrent education did not gain popularity. By contrast, the idea of adult education as continuing education did. It carried no implications of educational entitlements and, not surprisingly, gained political approval in the United Kingdom. Conceptually, continuing education is also potentially lifelong education.

From teacher-centred to student-centred education: In the 1960s some of the more progressive ideas of the US philosopher, John Dewey (1916, 1938), and which had been quite central to the philosophy of adult education, were incorporated in school education; among these was the emphasis on the child and the way that the child developed. Significantly, it was during the same period that Malcolm Knowles (1980, *inter alia*), in the USA, popularized his version of andragogy, which was a student-centred approach to adult education. Many adult educators have rightly claimed that this was no new discovery, since adult education has mostly been student centred. However, after this expressive period ended in the mid-1970s, the values of student-centred learning had become much more widely incorporated into the educational system, both schooling and adult.

The changing status of knowledge: Knowledge was regarded as the fruits of reason and scientific method was necessarily true. However, as early as 1926, the German sociologist, Max Scheler (1980) began to chronicle the way that different types of knowledge were changing at different speeds, with technological knowledge changing much more rapidly than, for instance, folk-religious knowledge, etc. Indeed, he suggested that knowledge seemed to be changing 'hour by hour'. Now technological knowledge is changing minute by minute and second by second. With this rapid change, it is almost impossible to regard knowledge as a truth statement any longer; we are now talking about something that is relative and may be changed again as soon as some relevant new discovery is made. The way that knowledge is changing has been analyzed by Lyotard (1984) who regards a great deal of it as narrative legitimated by its performativity. Foucault (1972), on the other hand, has treated knowledge as ideological discourse and that which becomes accepted as truth is usually the discourse of the powerful. Consequently, the knowledge taught has to be understood more critically than ever before, and critical theory has entered the educational vocabulary. Additionally, teachers now can only act as interpreters of this changing knowledge (Bauman, 1987); learners have to reach their own decisions and truths.

From curriculum to programme: In curriculum theory, there were a number of different curricula formulations, two being the classical and the romantic. The classical curriculum was one that implied that there was only one truth, or interpretation of the truth, to be taught. Such an approach to education was being undermined during this period as it was being recognized that there were more than one possible interpretation of that knowledge and so the 1960s saw the development of romantic-type curricula (Lawton, 1973, Griffin,1987).

Pluralism led to the recognition that it was becoming increasingly difficult to prescribe precisely what should be taught and there was really too much knowledge to be included in curricula so that knowledge was broken down into smaller clusters of ideas and presented as modules, or short courses. Modular courses, without being called that, had often been used in adult education to cater for the contingencies of programming, but now it became central to the development of both liberal adult and also higher education. Now there are programmes of modules, menus if you like, that comprise a bachelors or a masters degree. These modular programmes make studying a topic more manageable, but, significantly, also more marketable.

From liberal to vocational: There has always been a vocational orientation in education, especially in the education of adults. However, a great deal of adult education was liberal, and even the Open University began as a 'liberal arts university'. But now the Open University has become more vocationally orientated and, for a while, it seemed that all liberal adult education in UK would have to be self-funded. It is not only the Open University that is oriented to adults. Campbell (1984) records that since 1974 there have been more adults in universities in Canada than undergraduates. This is true of most North American and UK universities. In the UK, for instance, the Higher Education Funding Council reported that there were many more people studying in universities who were over the age of 21 years than there were traditional undergraduate students in 1993.

But now we are also seeing continuing vocational education courses for the service occupations being run in colleges of further and higher education, which often lead to a first degree. Universities are increasingly offering vocationally oriented first degrees and most of their postgraduate programmes are for mature adults and are vocationally based. However, this expansion of higher education into lifelong learning is not just a trend for taught courses, it is also a trend in research. Increasingly people researching for PhDs are part time; their research is work based and they are often funded by their employers. Practitioner researchers (Jarvis, 1999) are becoming a relatively common phenomenon in the universities of knowledge societies and the concept of research is being redefined and democratized as a result of these changes.

It is clear, however, that a great deal of the demand for this change is coming from the large transnational companies and all the other knowledge-based industries. Clearly, much of this new knowledge is also emanating from them, rather than from the research being undertaken in university and other research centres. This means that a great deal of this high-level information resides in these industries in any case and so other new trends are beginning to occur.

Universities are, therefore, being called upon to adapt to this rapidly changing world. But what happens if they do not? Increasingly, the corporate university (Eurich, 1985) is emerging. These are universities that are created by industries or large transnational themselves, so that both in the USA and the UK large corporations are creating their own universities – from Disney and McDonald's to Motorola in the USA and Body Shop, British Aerospace and British Telecom in the UK. Transnational corporations have the knowledge, the finance and the employees to provide specialized teaching and learning, – but significantly they are training their own employees as well as opening their doors to other learners. This is a new idea, but throughout the history of education, there have been different founders – the church, the state and now the large corporations.

From face to face to distance: Education has traditionally been conducted in the face-to-face mode with either scholars going to where the teachers reside or worked or, in former times, peripatetic teachers, even circulating schools, going to wherever the students were. However, it has only been in extremely large and sparsely populated countries, like the Australian outback and Russia, that this face-to-face tuition could not take place regularly. With the advent of new information technology, all of this was to change.

The birth of the British Open University was to be a catalyst in education for adults in the new information society. Educational courses could be delivered at a distance, through print, radio and television. Still there was face-to-face contact, but it played a less significant role. Students could choose the modules they wished to study, and as associate students, they did not even have to register for a whole degree course. Modules could be bought off the shelf and studied at the students' own time, in their own place and at their own pace. The British Open University was a harbinger of thing to come, and with the rapid development of information technology, distance education has been transformed yet again. Education courses are now being delivered through the World Wide Web, as well as by other means. Time and space have been transformed in education and people can study at any time in any place during their lives.

From education and training to learning: The traditional distinction between education and training has disappeared with the need for all workers to have practical knowledge at the different levels at which they work. The higher status education was a hindrance to the development of high-status training, and so both became merged into learning. It no longer matters how or where the knowledge was learnt, so long as it is learnt. Additionally, education relates to the production and supply of marketable commodities but learning is a process of consumption, and we live in a consumer society.

From rote learning to learning as reflection: Beck (1992: 155) argued that we live in a period of reflexive modernity, when 'the sciences are confronted with their own products, defects, and secondary problems' since science is now an activity without truth. When knowledge was regarded as something true, something that had been verified either by the force of rational logic or by scientific research, then it was to be learnt, that is, to be memorized. Learners were expected to grasp the truth of the scientific discovery and remember it. However, knowledge has now become narrative and even discourse and it has to be treated as such; it has to be considered, criticized, reflected upon in order to ascertain the extent to which it contains any truth. Hence, learning theory has now become reflective (Kolb, 1984; Schön, 1983; Jarvis, 1987, 1992, *inter alia*) but, paradoxically, we have stopped questioning our civilization and the need for radical adult education has already re-emerged.

From welfare needs to market demands (wants/desires): The idea that education is part of the welfare provision of society is disappearing with the welfare state. Once education ceases to be a welfare provision, it can only become a market provision. This was precisely what Bacon and Eltis argued in 1976 – Britain had to transform its welfare provision into wealth production. This is the economics of monetarism, introduced by the US economist, Milton Freidman. Education had to be seen to be a money earner, and this was much more simple after the success of the Open University and the realization that the wide choice of modules that it offered in its prospectus constituted a market for courses that could be bought off the shelf, as it were. Educational needs have turned into a matter of supply and demand – a market. Learning is now a consumer activity, as aspiring groups 'adopt a learning mode towards consumption and the cultivation of a lifestyle' (Featherstone, 1991: 19).

As early as 1929, Yeaxlee wrote about lifelong education, even though at that time adult education was only just becoming established in the United Kingdom. After the Second World War, UNESCO adopted lifelong education (Lengrand, 1975). But what we can see is that that from 1970–2000 a new form of education for adults emerged; not lifelong education but lifelong learning. It contains many of the elements that those early adult educators fought for, but many of their ideals are missing. Adult education as we knew it has been swallowed up in this broader social change. What we have is hardly a movement but a market, and there is no way in which the lifelong learning market can be regarded as a movement.

CONCLUSION

The thinkers in this book reflect the debates of the 20th century and some of the trends discussed above, but as we enter the 21st century, we should not forget the values and ideals that those early adult educators espoused. As Freire (1972) consistently reminded us, education is not neutral and neither is the system within which it has been institutionalized.

REFERENCES

Bacon, R and Eltis, W (1976) *Britain's Economic Problem: Too few producers*, MacMillan, London

Bauman, Z (1987) *Legislators and Interpreters*, Polity, Cambridge

Beck, U (1992) *Risk Society*, Sage, London

Beck, U (2000) *What is Globalization?* Polity, Cambridge

Campbell, D (1984) *A New Majority?* University of Alberta Press, Edmonton

Castells, M (1996) *The Rise of the Network Society*, Blackwell, Oxford

Dewey, J (1916) *Democracy and Education*, Free Press, New York

Dewey, J (1938) *Experience and Education*, Collier Books, New York

Eurich, N (1985) *Corporate Classrooms*, Carnegie Foundation for the Advancement of Teaching, Princeton

Featherstone, M (1991) *Consumer Culture and Postmodernism*, Sage, London

Fieldhouse, R (1996) The Local Education Authorities and Adult Education, in *A History of Modern British Adult Education*, R Fieldhouse and associates, NIACE, Leicester

Foucault, M (1972) *The Archaeology of Knowledge*, Routledge, London

Freire, P (1972) *Pedagogy of the Oppressed*, Penguin, Harmondsworth

Giddens, A (1990) *The Consequences of Modernity*, Polity, Cambridge

Green, A (1990) Education and State Formation, MacMillan, London

Griffin, C (1987) *Curriculum Theory in Adult and Lifelong Education*, Croom-Helm, London

Hamilton, P (1992) The Enlightenment and the Birth of Social Science, in *Formations of Modernity*, ed S Hall and B Gieben, Polity, Cambridge

Jarvis, P (1987) *Adult Learning in the Social Context*, Croom-Helm, London

Jarvis, P (1992) *Paradoxes of Learning*, Jossey-Bass, San Francisco

Jarvis, P (1997) *Ethics and the Education of Adults in a Late Modern Society*, NIACE Leicester

Jarvis, P (1999) *The Practitioner Researcher*, Jossey-Bass, San Francisco

Jarvis, P, Holford, J and Griffin, C (1998) *The Theory and Practice of Learning*, Kogan Page, London

Jensen G, Liverright, A and Hallenbeck, W (1964) *Adult Education: Outlines of an emerging field of study*, American Association of Adult and Continuing Education, Washington

Kelly, T (1970) *A History of Adult Education in Great Britain*, University of Liverpool Press, Liverpool

Kett, J (1994) *The Pursuit of Knowledge under Difficulties*, Stanford University Press, Stanford

Kolb, D (1984) *Experiential Learning*, Prentice Hall, Englewood Cliffs, NJ

Knowles, M (1980) *The Modern Practice of Adult Education*, Association Press, Chicago

Lawton, D (1973) *Social Change, Educational Theory and Curriculum Planning*, Hodder and Stoughton, London

Lengrand, P (1975) *An Introduction to Lifelong Education*, Croom-Helm, London

Lyotard, J-F (1984) *The Postmodern Condition: A report on knowledge*, University of Manchester Press, Manchester

OECD (1973) *Recurrent Education – A strategy for lifelong learning*, OECD, Paris

Reich, R (1991) *The Work of Nations*, Simon Schuster, London

Robertson, R (1995) Glocalization, in *Global Modernities*, eds M Featherstone, S Lash and R Robertson, Sage, London

Scheler, M (1980) *Problems in the Sociology of Knowledge*, Routledge and Kegan Paul, London

Schön, D A (1983) *The Reflective Practitioner*, Basic Books, New York

Wallerstein, I (1974) *The Modern World System*, Academic Press, New York

Yeaxlee, B (1929) *Lifelong Education*, Cassells, London

Part I

EARLY TWENTIETH-
CENTURY ENGLISH
THINKERS

Chapter 1

Albert Mansbridge

David Alfred

The 'Great Tradition' describes a uniquely English form of adult education. According to Wiltshire, it is humane, socially purposive, non-vocational, free from intellectual means-testing and based on the tutorial group, and its incentive is the pure love of learning. More than anyone else, Albert Mansbridge was responsible for popularizing this type of adult liberal education (quoted in Shaw 1959: 187). Born in 1876, the fourth son of a carpenter and leaving school at the age of 14 to work in a succession of clerical jobs in London, Mansbridge succeeded in constructing a unique 'educational alliance' – the Workers' Educational Association (WEA) – between the working-class movement and university extension, between labour and learning, and rose to that social and educational eminence symbolized by the award of the Companion of Honour and a number of honorary doctorates.

The purpose of what follows is to examine the central elements of Mansbridge's educational thought within its social and historical context, and to assess briefly its influence and contemporary relevance. An attempt is also made to bring out some of the contradictions of his educational ideas and practice and to show how they were conditioned by, and subtly articulated, those of the society in which he grew to maturity.

Described as the 'prophet-founder' of the WEA, 'the biggest educational revolution of his generation', and the 'architect of modern adult education', Mansbridge was also responsible for many other educational innovations, generally less well known (Bishop of Chichester, 1952:146; J H Jones and Dover Wilson, quoted in Mansbridge, 1944: xvii, ix). They are the Central Joint Advisory Committee for Tutorial Classes (1908), the Central Library for Students (1916),[1] the Church Tutorial Association (1918),[2] the World Association for Adult Education (1919),[3] the Seafarers' Education Service (1919), The British Institute of Adult Education (1921),[4] and the College of the Sea (1938).

Mansbridge was also involved in British and Australian army education, participated in many official education and church committees and commissions, notably the one that produced the 1919 Final Report that articulated the classic case for the Great Tradition, delivered innumerable sermons, speeches and lectures throughout Britain, the USA, the dominions and on the continent, and wrote a great deal. Mansbridge's educational thought coalesced from three sources, each with its own rich history: Christian, ethical idealism (represented by Westminster Abbey); University Extension; and the Co-operative movement. Mansbridge's influence did not lie in the originality, let alone the translucence, of his ideas, but in the way he integrated them into something new and made them appealing to diverse social groups who, inspired by his sincerity, commitment and enthusiasm, then helped him to put them into action.

In his youth, Mansbridge became deeply religious and turned from the Congregationalism of his parents to Anglicanism, then 'more in harmony with the spirit of the age' than Nonconformism (Halevy, 1961: 183). He was active in religious education and propaganda. Spending much of his free time in Westminster Abbey, Mansbridge heard 'the succession of great Anglican preachers' of the 1890s (1924: 33). Pre-eminent among them was a Charles Gore, an Anglo-Catholic of 'radical temper (who had a) hatred of social injustice... and whose influence on the Church of England was unequalled in his generation' (*Dictionary of National Biography*, 1949: 349, 352).[5] At the age of 18, Mansbridge had occasion to meet Gore who, until he died in 1932, became his 'friend, counsellor and guide' and the greatest of his many and varied heroes (1929: 16).

Gore's main influence on Mansbridge was to reinforce the conviction he had already gained from his parents that Christian belief and practice cannot be dissociated from social issues. Gore was the exemplar of what Kelly (1983) calls 'education for civilisation', a programme that sprang from the social responsibility to working people felt mainly by the Anglican academic section of the dominant class.[6] In the 1850s F D Maurice and Charles Kingsley founded the Working Men's College. A generation later, the early death of Arnold Toynbee inspired the founding of Toynbee Hall, a university settlement. Kelly talks of these and others as seeking to socialize Christianity and to Christianize socialism, ie to preserve the existing social order by reforming it through social reconciliation. Thus Maurice's aim was to unite the classes through the sharing of higher spiritual ideals and Christian fellowship. In *Property: Its duties and rights* which he edited in 1914, Gore advocated moral teaching to counter 'the traditional cry of "the rights of property"' and urged Christians to be 'ready for a deep and courageous... act of penitence and reparation' to the wrongfully dispossessed working class (Smith, 1956: 39). Kelly argues that a crucial feature of 'education for civilisation' was its creation of the distinction between liberal and vocational education, commonly expressed by the slogan that 'education is a means of life, not a means of livelihood'.

Parallel with his religious enthusiasm, Mansbridge became a keen and successful student at extension courses arranged by London University.

University Extension, another part of 'education for civilisation' (which might be characterized as the 'educated man's burden'), provided short lecture courses and other educational activities aimed mainly at workers in urban areas.

Mansbridge was among the quarter or so of about 60,000 extension students throughout the country who were working class but not deterred by cost or by the largely middle-class control of extension centres. He recalled being 'entranced (when) sitting at the feet' of his lecturers at Battersea (1945: 14). They 'demonstrated… the power of trained skill and learning. Above all they opened up vistas of what the universities might mean to men and women who never by any chance could actually study in them' (1929: 17). No doubt, Mansbridge was thinking of his failure to get an Oxford scholarship to study for the priesthood, his great ambition. The older universities, far from being rejected, became all the more the 'land of heart's desire… magnificent expressions of the best in human life and the foundations of inspiration and instruction', even though not always realized in practice (1929).

The extension lecturer who most influenced Mansbridge – 'the great light on my horizon' – was the legendary Hudson Shaw of Oxford who attracted huge, mainly working-class audiences in places such as Oldham and Rochdale where the Co-operative movement was most active (1945: 14). Indeed it was Shaw's 'Housing speech' at the 1898 Co-operative conference at Peterborough that Mansbridge claimed to be the origin of the WEA. Mansbridge's assessment of the significance of university extension was that it 'prepared the way for more effective service' in the co-operative movement' (1929: 16).

Through his mother's active membership of the Co-operative Women's Guild, Mansbridge was already familiar with the ethical ideals and voluntary self-help of cooperation that made it such a strong and distinctive working-class movement. From his father's involvement with the Amalgamated Society of Carpenters and Joiners, Mansbridge gained further understanding of the value of independent and democratic working-class organization. In 1895, his way to Oxford and the Church barred and getting nowhere at work, Mansbridge may have faced a personal crisis (Jennings, 1973: 7). From the following year, when he was 20, he began what was to prove a crucial 10-year association with the Co-operative movement.[7] While working for it as a clerk, then as a cashier, Mansbridge became involved in its educational work in his spare time. He was a teacher, a frequent contributor to its newspaper and in 1898 and 1899 attended its national conferences, a dominant theme of which was the closer collaboration between Co-operation and university extension advocated by Shaw, Robert Halstead, formerly a weaver and then secretary of the Co-operative Productive Federation, and Michael Sadler, secretary of the Extension Delegacy of Oxford University. Mansbridge recalled Toynbee's 'ringing challenge (in 1882)… to meet the passion for Dividend by the passion for Education' (Mansbridge, no date: 10). Co-operation thus forged the link between Mansbridge's socially activist religious faith, his admiration for university education and his conviction that the working-class people, with whom he strongly identified, had as much right to education as anyone else and, furthermore, badly needed it. Combined, these elements led Mansbridge to create a secular 'field of practical idealism' that compensated for his 'frustrated vocation for the priesthood' (Jennings, 1973: 11).

Despite his inauspicious debut at the conferences mentioned above, Mansbridge's own passion for education was recognized by Gore, J A R Marriott (Sadler's successor and, later, a Tory MP) and Canon Samuel Barnett, Warden of Toynbee Hall, who said of him: 'that young man has fire in his belly' (quoted in Smith, 1956: 17).

By the beginning of 1903, Mansbridge was ready for action. An article he had been invited to write for Oxford's university extension journal on *Co-operation, Trade Unionism and University Extension* was published in January and aroused so much interest that he was asked to write two further articles. Shortly after, Mansbridge and his wife, Frances, with two shillings and sixpence (12p) from the housekeeping money, set up An Association to Promote the Higher Education of Working Men (renamed the Workers' Educational Association in 1905) 'primarily by the extension of university teaching, and also by the development of an efficient School Continuation System and the assistance of Working Class efforts of a specifically educational character'.

The question arises as to how Mansbridge, barely known in either the Labour movement or university extension, managed not only to establish but make a success of such an educational innovation as the WEA. However formidable were his personal qualities of commitment, energy and persuasiveness, the explanation must take into account the pattern of social forces at the time. Briefly put, there were considerable class conflict and clear divisions within both the working class and the capitalist and aristocratic classes. In general terms, the former was divided between a section organized through Nonconformism, Co-operation, craft unions and the Radical wing of the Liberal Party, and a newer section of mainly semi- and unskilled workers organized in general unions which, partly through the 'socialist revival' of the 1880s, demanded either separate parliamentary representation for Labour as an interest in existing society or the transformation of the existing social order. By the turn of the century, the compromise arduously reached was that there should be an independent and non-socialist Labour Party. Mansbridge's WEA may be seen as the educational counterpart of these wider political changes. In both cases, minority revolutionary socialist groups criticized these 'broad churches' for being too broad and conciliatory.

Unlike the Labour Party, the creation of the WEA would not have been possible without the active involvement of a small but influential group of religious, educational and social progressives from within the dominant social class. They may be conveniently called the Oxford Reformers, consisting of several overlapping networks of people with whom Mansbridge came into personal contact.

The largest and most significant network of reformers was centred on Balliol College (whose previous luminaries included Jowett and Toynbee): Gore; William Temple, later Archbishop of York, then of Canterbury, and the WEA's first president (1908–1921); R H Tawney, later a leading economic historian and socialist writer, the first tutorial class tutor, and WEA president (1928–1944); and the historian, A L Smith, Master of the college (from 1916), a strong supporter of WEA Summer Schools and chair of the committee that produced the 1919 Final Report. From New College, the group included Alfred Zimmern, an authority on international relations, co-author with Tawney of the 1908 Oxford report, and sometime treasurer of the WEA; H H Turner, professor of astronomy; and (later), Sir Robert Morant, the first Permanent Secretary to the Board of Education (1903–1911). Other Oxford supporters of the WEA included: Sidney Ball, president of the Oxford Fabian Society; Sir William Anson, Warden of All Souls, Unionist MP for Oxford, and Parliamentary Secretary to the Board of Education (1902-1905); and John Holland Rose, historian and editor of the University Extension Journal.

The Catiline Club was a ginger group of Oxford dons – Gore, Temple, Zimmern, Richard Livingstone and others – who shared Mansbridge's criticism of the way the country's leading educational institutions had unjustly excluded the 'generality of the labouring poor' for whom they had often been wholly or partly founded (1929: 17).

Another important network centred on Toynbee Hall, co-founded in 1884 by Samuel Barnett, a Christian socialist, in memory of Arnold Toynbee, as a social and cultural centre in the impoverished district of Whitechapel. Tawney and Morant had served as residents there and William Beveridge as Sub-warden (from 1903 to 1905). Mansbridge traced the WEA's origins to the religious, social and educational principles that had animated Toynbee's short but active and influential life, and which he had articulated in his 'epoch-making address' on 'The Education of Co-operators' at the Co-operative Congress held at Oxford in 1882 (1924: 132).

The WEA–Oxford conference held in 1907 and chaired by Gore on 'What Oxford can do for Work people' constituted the greatest success for both the Oxford Reformers and Mansbridge. Jennings argues that the conference and the report that resulted from it, *Oxford and Working-Class Education* (published in the following year), was part of a planned campaign to reform the university by raising its standards and democratizing its recruitment (1975: 55). The conference was typical of those Mansbridge had organized since the WEA had sprouted in 1903. Among hundreds of 'ordinary' working-class men and women mingled representatives of all wings of the Labour movement, the churches, government authorities and the universities. The most dramatic moment of this conference was the unexpected and electrifying intervention of J M Mactavish, a Portsmouth shipwright and Labour councillor (succeeding Mansbridge as the WEA's general secretary in 1916) who demanded that Oxford give 'all the best that (it) has to give to the working-class, not for their individual self-advance-ment but for the great task of lifting their class', and rhetorically asked whether a university's 'true function (was) to train the nation's best men, or to sell its gifts to the rich', to its own detriment and that of the country and the 'work people deprived of the right of access' (1913: 194).

As a result of the report, Oxford gave its blessing to the tutorial classes that were just starting at Longton and Rochdale, and Morant agreed that the Board of

Education would give them some financial support. An independent Joint Tutorial Committee of the WEA and the University was set up to oversee this type of work, and a Central Joint Advisory Committee for Tutorial Classes was also established to coordinate such courses throughout the country.[8]

Mansbridge saw the tutorial class, a sustained course of university standard over three years, as the pinnacle of working-class educational achievement. Together with the annual summer schools held at Oxford, such education constituted a 'workers' university' (Smith 1956: 90).

The early success of the WEA thus owed much to the support of Oxford, the Board of Education and the church, or, rather, the progressive elements within these prestigious and influential institutions. They cleared the space for Mansbridge and others in the WEA who, while mostly sharing their religious, social, and educational views, possessed the crucial advantage over them of working-class identity. The Mansbridgean WEA offered the perfect channel for 'clerical conscience', overcoming the inherent limitations of the sponsorship 'from above' of 'education for civilisation' (Jennings 1973: 28). The WEA may thus be seen as an original form of 'education from above–from below'.

Freire's (1972: 21) proposition that 'every educational practice implies a concept of man and the world' applies clearly to Mansbridge whose educational ideas were permeated by Christian values. He believed that God created and sustained all matter and expressed will or spiritual power through it. He believed that 'real man is eternal and spiritual', and that his duty is to continue God's work of creation. Whether conscious of it or not, the power of the spirit guides all human life (1940: 227). Since all human beings shared the same creator and had within them the divine spark, Mansbridge believed in the 'essential value of every human being' (1928: 5). Going further, he held the view that 'every man and woman is a genius in some way' (1944: 194). Mansbridge's concept of 'man' was in the tradition of Christian humanism and spiritual egalitarianism.

Mansbridge defined knowledge, not in terms of the common view of 'learning its formulae' or 'mere cleverness', but, following John Henry Newman, as a process of 'inward digestion', ie passing into a person's experience and so transforming their personality and bringing about wisdom (1929: 32). That Mansbridge's perspective was religious, so that wisdom was interpreted as aware-ness of the power of the spirit, does not detract from the important principle that knowledge is of little account unless fused with experience and better action, whatever may be the criterion of 'better'. However, the way he sometimes thought of 'the pursuit of knowledge for its own sake' indicates some ambiguity if not ambivalence about the way he viewed education (1913: 1).

From his religious conviction, Mansbridge believed that the purpose of educa-tion is to help people 'in the power of the spirit, through knowledge and training, to order the material of the world for the welfare of man and the glory of God' (1929: 35). Education is a 'force enabling man to develop to the furtherest limits of his powers... of body, mind and spirit... to reach out the work God intended that he should do' (1920: 54, xv). It was thus 'an affair of the spirit', its end being a 'joyous life for all men' (1928: 13, 16). Observing that spiritual influences on education were greatest in adult education, as exemplified by the work of Grundtvig, Vincent Paton and Masaryk, Mansbridge described adult education as 'la secular gospel' (1920: 65–66).

Mansbridge believed that the 'educated man' was anyone who 'fulfils his allotted task in the spirit and in the act, whether it be the digging of a trench or the writing of a poem' (1920: xv). He did not question the social processes by which people were allocated to different occupations nor why they were (as they still are) so unjustly 'rewarded'. By assuming the harmony of the existing social order and education, Mansbridge could assert that the educated person 'can do no harm to the community' because, not 'merely drifting down the streams of opportunity or aiming at (other) false purposes', he or she uses knowledge only 'for the purpose of ministering to the common good' (1920).

So closely bound in his thought were spirituality, wisdom and knowledge that Mansbridge was convinced that the individual's desire for the latter 'is so uniform as to constitute a law of life' (1920: 8). Although Thomas (1982: 61) states that he looked to 'established traditional education for the model of workers' education', Mansbridge's attitude was again ambiguous. On the one hand, he praised the university tutorial class as the 'most prominent constructive work of the WEA', on the other he emphasized the need to unify the 'practical experience of students' lives with knowledge gained in class' (1920: 40). Although he valued 'humanistic studies', Mansbridge criticized the way they were badly communicated to the majority of people. Hence his insistence that WEA members should say 'how, why, what, or when they wish to study' (1920: xvii–xviii). Moreover, if traditional education involved a certain practice of pedagogy as well as particular types of content, it is clear that Mansbridge was far from being conservative.

He introduced his book on *University Tutorial Classes* in 1913 with two educational maxims: 'How shall a man learn except from one who is his friend?' (Xenophon); 'The lecture is one, the discussion is one thousand' (Arabian proverb). Generally less concerned with defining the content of knowledge, Mansbridge emphasized the importance of satisfying people's need for it, whatever it was. Not only did his research into educational history show him that working people had always produced their own scholars, but he also observed (ironically, in materialist terms) that all music, art and literature was based on or derived from the 'basic and fundamental activities of man' (1929: 32). Mansbridge had a healthy disrespect for the patently false and self-serving notion that culture is confined to the dominant social class (Smith 1956: 58).

The social and political aspects of Mansbridge's educational thought centre on the linked concepts of 'democracy' and 'citizenship'. He applied them to society as a whole and to education in different and sometimes contradictory ways. Mansbridge pictured society, the 'vast body of humanity', as an organism made up of different kinds of 'cells', individuals, each having its own function. Some people, like the heart, provide spiritual sustenance; some, like the brain, mental; and most, like the limbs, provide various forms of labour 'to sustain the state of the world in which the heart and brain may freely work' (1940: 220). Although partly mitigated by his spiritual egalitarianism, Mansbridge's social theory exemplifies the idealist, organicist and functionalist perspective, common at the time, conditioned by the nature of contemporary British capitalism and imperialism.

Accepting that society is inherently hierarchical, Mansbridge defined democracy as a 'state of society in which every individual not only has the opportunity to make the best of his or her own individual gifts, but actually takes advantage of the opportunity' (1944: 76). It was the 'Christian idea of the community', manifesting the 'cooperation of self-fulfilling individuals, each doing well in their own calling or type of work' (and so achieving in the words of T H Green) 'the promotion in a spirit of justice of the welfare of all classes of the citizens' (1928: 10; 1940: 220; undated: 9). Determined by the type of Christian perspective he adopted, Mansbridge's depoliticized definition of democracy proved very acceptable to the majority of the progressive wing of the dominant class represented by the Oxford Reformers. His appeal to them was reinforced by his fulsome 'adulation of university men and university values' (Jennings 1975: 58). Thus, in his 1903 articles, Mansbridge argued that only the 'deep draughts of knowledge' provided by university extension could combat the 'veneer' of elementary education that encouraged the 'unthinking absorption of facts (which rendered men) susceptible to flights of mere rhetoric' (1944: 1). In similar vein, the Oxford report asserted that it would involve a grave loss both to Oxford and to English political life were the close association between the University and the world of affairs to be broken or impaired on the accession of new classes to power' (1909: 48). The early success of Mansbridge's WEA, therefore, owed much to its being seen 'as a politically and socially "safe" movement' and a 'sound political investment' (Jennings 1973: 25, 1975: 58).

Mansbridge's attitude towards individualism was contradictory. Like socialists, he specifically opposed utilitarian individualism and the idea that education should be used for material advancement or as a way of leaving the working class. Nor did he see education as a means of personal cultural development. It is interesting to remember that the WEA was based on group or federal, and not individual, membership. However, Mansbridge was plainly hostile to socialism as an alternative vision and model of society. He thought that social improvement would come about by individual, not social or collective, transformation, because he believed that the source of social injustice and the conflict it generates lay in the failure of the spirit of individuals, not in the failings of the existing social order. Mansbridge represents the ideology that acknowledges the existence of social classes, and indeed criticizes inequalities of opportunities, particularly educational ones, but denies their inherent or structural antagonism, which is rooted in relations of dominance and subordination.

Mansbridge articulated the well-meaning but naive belief shared by Christian socialists and some others with a social conscience that what was euphemistically called 'the social question' could be overcome by Christian faith, goodwill, reasonableness and academic reason, which together would produce 'right thinking'. He was not, therefore, an individualist in the Manchester-Liberal

vein, but rather an advocate of the New Liberalism, the educational philosophy of which was succinctly expressed by the 1919 Final Report (Ministry
of Reconstruction: 27): 'Adult Education rests on the twin principles of
personal development and social service'. Mansbridge specifically argued that
tutorial classes were 'not mainly about the acquisition of knowledge but a
stimulus to perform the voluntary civic work of their (the students') associations
and unions and to spread the desire for education' (1944: 61). It is thus not
wholly true that Mansbridge 'carefully eschewed any idea of social purpose'
(Smith, 1962–63: 48). Of course, it all depends on what is meant by 'social
purpose'.

Radical socialists who were concerned with education (as they had been
throughout the 19th century) defined 'social purpose' quite differently from the
way Mansbridge did. They campaigned for 'Independent Working Class
Education' under such slogans as 'knowledge for action' and 'education for
emancipation'. They argued that existing adult educational provision, including
that of the WEA, was tainted by ideological forms of knowledge and educational
practices, which blunted the spikes of increasing working-class power. When still
a radical, Ramsay Macdonald (later Labour Party leader and Prime Minister) said
that Oxford would 'inoculate the more intelligent sections of the working-
classes... (it) will assimilate them, not they Oxford' (quoted in Fieldhouse 1977:
11). The Central Labour College (set up by the Plebs League after the Ruskin
College student strike of 1908) and the National Council of Labour Colleges
spent many years locked in ideological combat with the WEA.[9] Mansbridge's
position was clear. In his 1903 articles, he quoted the historic Taff Vale industrial
dispute (which ended in punitive restrictions on trade unionism) as an example
of how the lack of education or 'thinking power' can lead workers astray. He
unequivocally blamed 'obstructive, poisonous and wrecking forces' for the
'unrest in British life' (1929: 31). Mansbridge's attitude to the purpose of education in society well exemplifies the valuable distinction made by Williams
between the motive forces of 'social conscience' and 'social consciousness' (1983:
14–15).

Phillips and Putnam (1980) contrast Mansbridge's preference for 'educational
uplift', as an expression of advanced Christian Liberalism, with 'education for
emancipation'. Jennings (1973: 30) neatly summarizes the same idea by saying
that Mansbridge thought that 'education is emancipation'. This did not prevent
others such as Tawney, G D H Cole and George Thompson from bringing to
the WEA far more radical philosophical and political perspectives than those of
its founder.[10] Their involvement was evidence of Harrison's observation that
socialism was replacing or strongly influencing Christianity as a new evangelical
movement for the 'new generation of working men' (1961: 229).

However, there were other aspects of 'democracy' which concerned
Mansbridge and on which all in the WEA could agree. One was the indignation
felt at the 'lamentable... neglect of education for the people' and the way in
which the 'ordinary working man was disinherited' (1920: 55). Echoing this,
Temple said (no date: 13) that the 'whole purpose of the WEA is to claim for

working-class people their place in the whole great national heritage of educational culture'. Mansbridge lambasted the idea and practice of a restricted and ineffective 'educational ladder', which he wished to see replaced by a 'highway' along which anyone can travel, provided only they had the necessary 'mental equipment and high character' (1920: 31). Temple (no date) defended the WEA from the criticism that it accepted without question the dominant class's conception of what constitutes the 'national heritage' by the example of Tawney's work in economic history that changed its received view. Nevertheless, Mansbridge and others tended to accept the conventional definition of the content of liberal or humane education, concentrating their fire instead on the flagrant injustice of the organization of the educational system.

Another aspect of democracy was the belief that education 'unites (people) and does not divide' (quoted in Smith 1956: 45). Mansbridge likened what he called the 'WEA spirit' to a 'new Renaissance', consisting of a 'common hope united in the common activity of unlike people' (1924: 135). He saw education as a means of bringing together all people in fellowship, whatever their social status or political or religious affiliation. Mansbridge expressed pride that the WEA's 1905 conference at Oxford resembled 'a replica in miniature of English life' (1920: 19). However commendable his attitude, Mansbridge avoided facing the question of how knowledge is defined and constructed, how it is used and what its effects are on conserving or changing the existing social order.

The third and probably most innovative democratic principle uniting all in the WEA related to the organization and practice of workers' education, and indeed to education as such. Mansbridge believed that the only way of overcoming 'the distrust of Universities among working people in general' was to avoid the 'education "from above" that had neutralised the good intentions underlying the Mechanics Institutes, Working Men's Colleges and traditional University Extension' (1913: 22). He thus flatly disagreed with Maurice's opposition to 'pupils (having) the least voice in determining what we shall teach or not teach or how we shall teach' (quoted in Smith 1956: 17). On the contrary, Mansbridge claimed as a fundamental principle that the 'education of working people can never develop unless there is frank and free intercourse on the basis of equality between teachers and taught' (1920: 5). He exhorted WEA members to 'Discover your own needs, organise in your own way, study as you wish to study... The initiative must lie with the students. They must say how, why, what or when they wish to study. It is the business of their colleagues, the scholars and administrators to help them obtain the satisfaction of their desires' (1920: 23). Mansbridge's model of relations in a tutorial or any other type of class is one in which the teacher should be 'in real fact a fellow-student, and the fellow-students are teachers' (1913: 1).

Although he had to resign from the WEA in 1915 because of ill health and thereafter had very little to do with its subsequent development, Mansbridge's influence on the course of adult education was considerable. Tawney went so far as to refer to it as the 'Mansbridgean revolution' and stated that its three 'dominant conceptions' were that the majority of ordinary people need humane education as much as the minority, that the intimate and continuous small tutorial group is its proper vehicle, and that the organization of such education should be based on the equal participation of Labour and Learning (Tawney 1966: 89). Real education thus implied both humaneness, emphasizing learning for life, ie wisdom – 'a liberal as against a merely bread-and-butter education' – and democratic organization and pedagogy (*Manchester Guardian*, quoted in 1920: 19). As already mentioned, not everyone who made a significant contribution to the WEA's growth and development shared Mansbridge's ostensibly apolitical interpretation of 'education for emancipation' (of the workers) or his predilection for the company of 'bishops and professors'.

However, the contrast between Mansbridge's cultural purism and others' political realism is not completely accurate because Mansbridge was concerned with education for spiritual wisdom, and not 'for its own sake' (Fieldhouse 1977: 58). With the acceleration of the secularization of social life since Mansbridge's time, much of adult liberal education does seems to have substituted cultural for spiritual enrichment as its main aim. Although both emphasize education's effect on the individual rather than on the collectivity, it should be recalled that Mansbridge's attitude towards individualism was contradictory.

It is impossible to calculate the impact of Mansbridge, directly or indirectly via the WEA, on many people of all sorts.[11] Temple averred that 'he invented me' (quoted in Iremonger, 1948: 77). Mansbridge recalled that George Reuben, who once belonged to the Marxist Social Democratic Federation and later became mayor of Swindon, was 'converted to the idea of the WEA at its 1907 conference' (1944: 191). Taylor *et al* (1985: 176) have unearthed evidence of the WEA's influence on some US adult educationists in the 1920s; for example, Leon Richardson, external director of California University, visited Mansbridge and the WEA in 1921.

To assess the contemporary relevance of Mansbridge's educational thought and practice, it is necessary to separate out some of its constituent elements and to evaluate the way in which society has changed since his time. As for the latter, despite much chattering at various times about the 'quiet revolution', the 'mixed economy', the 'post-industrial society' and nowadays the seemingly unending 'technological revolution', the basic features of the social, economic and political structures of British society are little different today from what they were at the beginning of this century. It is, therefore, still characterized by a number of forms of avoidable social injustice and oppression, even though their outward appearances may differ in some ways from what they were before. Despite changes in the economic, welfare and occupational structures, most people are still 'workers' (whether currently employed or not) or related to them. Therefore, 'education for emancipation' of workers (of either sex and of whatever ethnic background), is as necessary today as it was in 1903.[12]

With the decline of the social influence of religion, few today would share Mansbridge's specifically Christian conception of the good society. Nevertheless, his steadfast defence of 'liberal' education is of enduring value. Mansbridge was not opposed to vocational education, which is necessary if people are to do their work properly. However, he rightly resisted the idea, often advocated by powerful groups, that it should ever be confused with or supplant liberal education, which every person needs and to which all are entitled. Mansbridge saw clearly that the aim of education is wisdom, that is, the integration of knowledge, understanding and action. Its process is that of rational enquiry, which depends on the availability of all pertinent information and the evaluation of all contesting perspectives or theories. Its social implications are far-reaching: mutual respect and toleration between all those engaged in it, acceptance of the uncertainty of its outcome (which is not to be confused with fence-sitting) and freedom from external constraints serving to censor the process.

Mansbridge's concern with democratic education needs to be revived and redefined. The type of religiosity he espoused prevented Mansbridge from confronting the sharp political issues raised when education and democracy are mentioned in the same breath. For example, it is unrealistic to expect future and present citizens, that is, children and adults, to play their full part in a democratic political system (or one that aspires to be so) unless they experience democratic processes in their everyday lives: in their homes, places of work, voluntary organizations and other places (eg hospitals, government offices, etc). Unless its values are practised both within and outside educational institutions, liberal education will either fail or rightly be criticized as a sham. Described as an 'evangelical humanist', Mansbridge recognized and sought to redress the educational injustice suffered by working-class people (Smith 1956: 19). Despite its expansion since his death, most formal education, or rather schooling, at all levels continues to be as competitively individualistic, undemocratic and socially discriminatory in recruitment and in much of its curriculum content as it was before. However imperfect it is, the WEA remains a bastion of an alternative form and vision of education – cooperatively social, democratic in its organization and pedagogy (or andragogy) and free from the distractions of certification and meritocracy. Together with other educational organizations, the WEA is also the protagonist of education for those who are nowadays euphemistically called the 'disadvantaged' or 'deprived', with the aim of maximizing effective social and political participation.

What an anonymous benefactor said of Mansbridge – 'He is the most dangerous man in England. He taught the working people to think for themselves' (quoted in Mansbridge, 1944: xi) – should be the goal and proud boast of all education, particularly adult education. Until now, when workers and others who are oppressed have thought for themselves, they have often been attacked by those who rightly perceive a threat to their domination, however slight in practice, as subversive. If it is merely a code phrase for habitual fence-sitting and the avoidance of what are conventionally thought to be radical or 'extreme' social and political attitudes, in the mistaken belief that knowledge and life or action are incompatible, then 'thinking for oneself' is nothing but intellectual self-deception and moral cowardice.

In assessing Mansbridge's pioneering role in the development of the 'Great Tradition', it may be helpful to put forward a necessarily simplified schema of the different ways in which the idea of adult liberal education has been interpreted. The conservative view is that it is purely a self-contained process of rational enquiry, which is unrelated to specific social practices and so unconcerned with all the ways by which it is restricted by society or the state. The progressive interpretation, though recognizing and ready to counteract social constraints of free enquiry, remains suspicious of the practical social consequences that would be expected to result from its widespread practice. The radical perspective acknowledges that the purpose and values of liberal education cannot be fully realized unless it actively shapes and is supported by congruent social relations, structures and processes. Whereas his interpretation tended to the second type, it is argued that the third is the logical and practical implication of Mansbridge's concept of adult liberal education.

Mansbridge's assertion that 'adult education and the claims of democratic citizenship are inseparable' was, is and always will be valid, provided education is not, as it all too often is, desocialized and thus stripped of its inherent humaneness and political relevance (Smith 1956: 58). Freire put it concisely: 'education is not neutral' (1976: 140). Raymond Williams said recently that adult education is not just determined by social change or is only about extending opportunities; it is about making 'learning part of the process of social change itself' (1983: 9). Cole and Freeman made the same point even more clearly in 1918 when they affirmed that adult education is about the 'creation of a manhood and a womanhood capable of controlling their own destinies in a free and democratic country' (Hughes and Brown 1981: 58).

Mansbridge dedicated his life to an 'adventure' in education. Today, those who think honestly and fearlessly about the nature of people, society, the world and knowledge and what their relations are and should be and who take education, including adult and workers' education, as seriously as he did, can continue to develop his work with an equal passion, enjoyment and commitment.

NOTES

1. Established as a library for adult students in tutorial classes, it became the national Central Library in 1931, and was later incorporated into the British Library, Lending Division. Mansbridge was its chairman until 1931 and thereafter chair of its Board of Trustees.
2. Gore, Temple and Tawney were also associated in this venture. Yeaxlee (1926: 67) records that during 1923–24 there were 13 classes and 3 tutors' courses in progress.
3. Mansbridge was its chairman until 1929 and thereafter its president. Jennings (1984: 62) notes that, of all Mansbridge's projects, the WAAE showed the greatest gulf between aspiration and achievement. It was dissolved in 1946.
4. This was in association with Lord Haldane. The BIKE was the forerunner of the present National Institute of Adult Continuing Education.

5. Born in 1853, Gore was the first principal of Pusey House, Oxford, founded the Community of the Resurrection, was Canon of Westminster (1894–1902) and then Bishop of Worcester, Birmingham and Oxford (until 1919).
6. Kelly's classification includes education for salvation, for vocation, for civilization, for participation and for recreation. He does not mention education for emancipation.
7. Mansbridge continued to be associated with the movement for many years, when he became a director, then president, of the Co-operative Building Society (forerunner of the Nationwide Building Society), about which he wrote a book in 1934.
8. This was the first time that the universities had ever come together about anything.
9. For the views of the radical participants, see Millar (no date) and Craik (1964). See also Corfield (1969) and Phillips and Putnam (1980).
10. George Thompson was the first secretary of the Yorkshire District of the WEA, serving from 1914 to 1945 (including six years in New Zealand).
11. Fieldhouse (1977: 29–31) summarizes some interesting data on this question.
12. The early WEA was actively involved with women's education. Frances Mansbridge helped to initiate, and was a member of, the national Consultative Committee concerned with the education of working women. There were women's sections in three branches by 1910. Margaret McMillan, another of Mansbridge's heroes, was also involved with this early radical development (information given by Linda Shaw).

REFERENCES

Chichester, Bishop of (1952) In Memoriam: Albert Mansbridge, *Highway*, **44**, pp 145–48
Corfield, A J (1969), *Epoch in Workers' Education*, WEA, London
Craik, W W (1964) *The Central Labour College*, Lawrence and Wishart, London
Dictionary of National Biography 1931–40 (1949), Oxford University Press
Fieldhouse, Roger (1977) *The Workers' Educational Association: Aims and achievements 1903–1977*, University of Syracuse
Freire, Paulo (1972) *Cultural Action for Freedom*, Penguin Books, Harmondsworth
Freire, Paulo (1976) *Education: The practice of freedom*, Writers and Readers, London
Halevy, Elie (1961), *Imperialism and the Rise of Labour*, Barnes and Noble Inc, New York
Harrison, J F C (1961) *Learning and Living 1760–1960: A study in the history of the English adult education movement*, Routledge & Kegan Paul, London
Hopkins, Philip G H (1985), *Workers' Education*, Open University Press, Milton Keynes
Hughes, H D and Brown, G F (1981), *The WEA Education Year Book 1918*, University of Nottingham
Iremonger, F A (1948) *William Temple*, Oxford University Press
Jennings, Bernard (1973) *Albert Mansbridge*, Leeds University Press
Jennings, Bernard (1975) The Oxford Report Reconsidered, Studies in *Adult Education*, **7** (1), pp 53–65
Jennings, Bernard (1976a) *Albert Mansbridge and English Adult Education*, University of Hull
Jennings, Bernard (1976b) *New Lamps for Old? University adult education in retrospect and prospect*, University of Hull

Jennings, Bernard (1979) *Knowledge is Power: A short history of the WEA 1903-1978*, University of Hull

Jennings, Bernard (1984) Albert Mansbridge and the First WAAE, *Convergence*, **17** (4), pp 54–64

Kelly, T (1973), Two Reports: 1919 and 1973, *Studies in Adult Education*, **5** (2), pp 113–23

Kelly, T (1983) The Historical Evolution of Adult Education in Great Britain, in *Opportunities for Adult Education*, ed M Tight, Open University Press, Milton Keynes

Mansbridge, Albert (1906) *A Survey of Working-class Educational Movements in England and Scotland*, CWS Annual, Publication no 10, WEA

Mansbridge, Albert (1913) *University Tutorial Classes*, Longman, Green & Co, London

Mansbridge, Albert (1920) *An Adventure in Working-Class Education*, Longman, Green & Co, London

Mansbridge, Albert (1923), *The Older Universities of England*, Longman Green & Co, London

Mansbridge, Albert (1924) The Beginning of the WEA, *Highway*, **16** (3)

Mansbridge, Albert (1928) *The Educated Life*, Ernest Benn Ltd, London

Mansbridge, Albert (1929) *The Making of an Educationist*, Ernest Benn Ltd, London

Mansbridge, Albert (1932) *Margaret McMillan: Prophet and pioneer*, J M Dent & Sons Ltd, London

Mansbridge, Albert (1934) *Brick upon Brick*, J M Dent & Sons Ltd

Mansbridge, Albert (1935) *Talbot and Gore*, J M Dent & Sons Ltd, London

Mansbridge, Albert (1940) *The Trodden Road*, J M Dent & Sons Ltd, London

Mansbridge, Albert (1944) *The Kingdom of the Mind: Essays and addresses 1903-37 of Albert Mansbridge*, J M Dent & Sons Ltd, London

Mansbridge, Albert (1945) W Hudson Shaw, *Highway*, **37** (October)

Mansbridge, Albert (1948) *Fellow Men: A gallery of England 1876–1940*, J M Dent & Sons Ltd, London

Mansbridge, Albert (no date) *Arnold Toynbee*, C W Daniel, London

Millar, J P M (no date) *The Labour College Movement*, NCLC Publishing Society Ltd, London

Ministry of Reconstruction (1919) *Final Report*, Adult Education Committee, Cmd 321

Oxford (1909) *Oxford and Working-class Education*, University Press, Oxford

Phillips, A and Putnam, T (1980) Education for Emancipation: The movement for independent working-class education 1908–1928, *Capital and Class*, **10**

Shaw, Roy (1959) Controversies, in *Trends in English Adult Education*, ed S G Raybould, Heinemann, London

Smith, H P (1956) *Labour and Learning: Albert Mansbridge, Oxford and the WEA*, Basil Blackwell, Oxford

Smith, H P (1962-3) Adult Education in History: A Review, *Rewley House Papers*, **4** (1)

Stocks, Mary (1953) *The WEA: The first fifty years*, Unwin, London

Tawney, R H (1952) Mansbridge, *Highway*, **44**, pp 42–45

Tawney, R H (1966), *The Radical Tradition*, Penguin Books, Harmondsworth

Taylor, R, Rockhill, K and Fieldhouse, R (1985) *University Adult Education in England and the USA*, Croom-Helm, London

Temple, W (1924) The WEA: A retrospect, **16** (3)

Temple, W (no date) *The Place of the WEA in English Education*, WEA NW District

Thomas, J E (1982) *Radical Adult Education: Theory and practice*, University of Nottingham

West, L R (1972) The Tawney Legend Re-examined, *Studies in Adult Education*, **4** (2), pp 105–19

Williams, Raymond (1983) *Adult Education and Social Change: Lectures and reminiscences in honour of Tony McLean*, Workers' Educational Association, South-eastern District, Rochester

Yeaxlee, B A (1926) *Spiritual Values in Adult Education*, Oxford University Press, Oxford

Wiltshire, H (1956) The Great Tradition in Unversity Education, *Adult Education*, 29 (2), pp 88–97

Chapter 2

Basil Yeaxlee and the origins of lifelong education

Angela Cross-Durrant

INTRODUCTION

Lifelong education is generally thought to have emerged as a result of the United Nations' International Education Year (1970), during which the concept was offered for discussion. The United Nations Educational, Scientific and Cultural Organization (UNESCO) adopted the notion in 1972 and decided to clarify the concept, and to pose it as a potential alternative to existing educational principles, envisaged as being better able to prepare people to maintain and improve the quality of life amid change and uncertainty. Shortly thereafter, a comprehensive study was undertaken to form a well-constructed, logically sound and authoritative base of descriptive guidelines for the introduction of a system of lifelong education. The study relied upon the synthesis of philosophical, historical, sociological, psychological, anthropological, ecological and economic considerations, and resulted in a comprehensive collection of studies edited by Dave (1976). The ideas of (among others) Lengrand (1975) and of the Faure Report (1972) set the pattern of thought for this 'European' concept.

The idea of lifelong education is generally regarded, therefore, as being attendant upon modern technological and societal changes, and as such, as being 'new'.

However, although usually associated with UNESCO, the concept first found expression half a century earlier in England, through the vision and intellectual effort of Basil A Yeaxlee (1929). His was the original English 20th-century publication that sought to establish a way of seeing education *in toto*; to

attain... unity of spirit and purpose amidst differentiation of functions (p 124);

recognize the educational value of the unorthodox, and perhaps unsuspected, means of education to which thousands... respond (p 121);

express that activities and organizations 'recreational or... connected with livelihood... must play their part'. (p 122);

point out that 'To ask whether a man should be a student for the sake of the knowledge he acquires or for the sake of the qualities he develops in the course of particular studies is to raise a false dilemma. Each has its own importance but neither is separable from the other' (p 146);

and to assert that 'While... the case for lifelong education rests ultimately upon the nature and needs of human personality in such a way that no individual can rightly be regarded as outside its scope, the social reasons (ie democracy and responsibility) for fostering it are as powerful as the personal' (p 311).

Yeaxlee's publication represents the first formal attempt this century to combine the whole of the educational enterprise under a set of guiding principles with each phase or agency (formal, informal and non-formal) enjoying equal esteem. His idea of lifelong education rested upon integrating learning and living, both horizontally across work, leisure and community 'life spaces'; and vertically from virtually the cradle to the grave. Its area of concern was different from either university tutorial, mainly liberal educational classes, appended to the end of secondary, further or higher education; and from compensatory education for adults. The kind of integration he advocated demanded a degree of cooperation, coordination and sharing of philosophy and resources, which the emergent educational provision (and current provision) was not wont to do.

The backcloth of envisaged social reforms after the First World War and of major changes in secondary education provided the scene for the first major, fully articulated argument for lifelong education in England. Although the 1919 Report had expressed dissatisfaction with the concept of technical and vocational training, and had seen such activity as outside the province of education for adults, one of the contributors to the Report saw the possibilities for new technical and vocational preparation as part of a reinterpretation of education and its relationship to industrial, social, community, professional, private and family life – to the whole of life itself. This was Basil A Yeaxlee, who remained optimistic about the possibilities that he perceived emerging from the great post-war educational debate, and the prevailing 'mood' of social reconstruction. He was as interested in the education of the young as he was in that of the adolescent and the adult.

THE CONTEXT

Basil A Yeaxlee, CBE, MA B Litt (Oxon), BA, PhD (London), was born in 1883 and died in 1967. He was deeply involved in adult education and religious education, as is manifest from the following posts which, among others, he held during his working lifetime: 1915–18, editorial secretary of the National Council of Young Men's Christian Associations; 1917-19, member of the Ministry of Reconstruction Adult Education Committee; 1920-28, secretary, Educational Settlements Association; 1930–35, principal, Westhill Training College, Selly Oak; 1933-57, editor of *Religion in Education*; 1935–49, university reader in educational psychology, and lecturer and tutor in the Department of Education, Oxford; 1940–48, secretary, Central Advisory Council for Adult Education in HM Forces; 1949–51, secretary, Education Committee, British Council of Churches.

It is clear from some of his published work, viz, *An Educated Nation* (1920), *Spiritual Values in Adult Education Vols I and II* (1925), *Towards a Full Grown Man* (1926), and *Religion and the Growing Mind* (1939), that Christianity was the spring from which he drank, the source of his interpretation of life, and the vehicle he used to convey his views about the meaning and purpose of education.

But it is his book entitled *Lifelong Education*, published in 1929, which is one of the earliest expressions of a vision of regarding all of life's resources and experiences (personal, social and work) as playing a related and meaningful part in an individual's education, and of education as being seen as truly life long. Yeaxlee viewed education at school as merely the start of the process, and projected subsequent education for adults beyond an exclusively compensatory, occupationally expedient, abstractly liberal or politically led activity. He did not subscribe to the notion that tutorial classes and university education were the only means of education for adults.

> Neither 'the university of the people' nor 'nightschool' is a sufficient description of what adult education really is. Both ideas may be included, but many other names will be needed as well. One human being may be seeking the philosophic key to the meaning of existence; another may be concerned with political or economic questions; another may be discovering some hitherto unsuspected aptitude for using his or her hands artistically and skilfully. Each is attaining a new understanding of himself or herself and enriching the values of his or her world. (Yeaxlee, 1929: 45)

> Adult education must be more comprehensive than university education. It must teach many things which a university would not include… and by methods which (it) would never dream of adopting… and yet… must maintain the ideals… which we so naturally associate with university traditions (p 152).

Much of education for adults, he argued, should be practical in terms of its relationship to students' experiences and interests, while at the same time it ought to be concerned with 'intellectual authority', so that it would help adults to continue to reflect and to think rationally.

> No man is free so long as he remains… in bondage to intellectual authority, however venerable, or to his own crassness and ignorance, however absorbed he may be in the practical service of his kind (p 50).

He also exhorted his readers to consider new, informal and non-formal methods of learning and teaching, to:

> look about them for new and promising forms of educational life and activity among men and women, and perhaps themselves to take some share in adding to the number (p 100).

In this context, he acknowledged and applauded the educational work carried out over the wireless by the British Broadcasting Corporation. He also looked to 'all kinds of community organization' to play their parts in the educational enterprise, 'recreational or controversial, connected with livelihood or wedded to leisure' (Yeaxlee, 1929: 122). He also wished to unite the efforts of the various 'realms' of education (elementary, secondary, technical, university, adult) in order to embark upon the joint enterprise of education for, through and throughout life.

By the time Yeaxlee had published most of his books, intensification of class consciousness and espousal of a joint cause provided the main impulse for educational reform. Yeaxlee, however, preferred to look to the evolutionary development of each citizen, rather than to a mass, politically led strategy. His religious beliefs convinced him that respect and responsibility emanated outwards from the individual's spirit. On the other hand, however, disillusionment in the (Anglican) Church had resulted from the inescapable recognition of the implications of Christian fighting Christian during the First World War. Some Christian educators recognized and acknowledged the supremacy of the 'humanistic socialism' pervading the day, eg R H Tawney.

> We have to revise the work not of four years but of a century and a half. The quarrel is not merely with the catastrophic changes of 1914–1919, but with the economic order of the age, which began with the spinning-jenny and ended with the great war... Social Reconstruction either means Social Revolution, or it means nothing (Tawney in Hinden, 1964: 103).

These men sought to legitimize large-scale economic and social transformation (which would include education) for economic and social liberty and responsibility.

Yeaxlee, on the other hand, argued for transformation of education to prepare everyone for, and provide everyone with, continued, lifelong education, so that having thereby given human beings their intellectual and, consequently, their spiritual freedom, they would find their way back to the Christian fold, better acquainted with themselves, their fellows, the world and the metaphysical. He saw education as clarifying the image of human beings for themselves; that image not being simply a passive victim of their condition, but rather a vital, responsive, interactive agent capable of generating the right attitudes and future conditions for the flourishing of self-fulfilment and perpetual growth of harmony and of love, until all were united in a 'wholeness' of humanity and Christianity. Only concentrating on the full development of individuals while celebrating collective life, he argued, could human beings hope to seek freedom and claim responsibility. 'The aim, then, is a philosophy and a way of living, an insight and a joyous purpose, with sane power of achieving it.' (Yeaxlee, 1929: 165) He would have everyone develop

> his or her own individuality to the utmost, no longer as a separated and conflicting being but as a part and contribution to one continuing whole (H G Wells in Yeaxlee, 1929: 164).

When referring to Robert Peers' similar views, Yeaxlee wrote:

> There all the distinctive notes of lifelong education are struck – knowledge experience, wisdom, harmony and the giving of self in service. All of them are rooted in the practical affairs of ordinary men and women. Each of them reaches out into the infinite. They are meaningless apart from the growth and the activities of the individual personality. They are impossible unless that personality is in perpetual living relationship to the whole – the whole of truth and the whole of life, immediate reality and ultimate (Yeaxlee, 1929: 165).

It is here that Yeaxlee's concern with the 'ultimate' and 'the whole', of which he would have claimed we are all a part, comes to the fore. While some educators (eg Tawney and Dewey) with strong social consequences and commitment looked to social, politico-economic and educational reform or revolution for the betterment of the human condition, Yeaxlee sought to use educational reform to lead people back to Christian values, thereby putting themselves at the (social) service of their fellows.

In his book *Lifelong Education*, Yeaxlee looked to the education of adults to help the whole nation to 'grow up', to seek the twin ideals of freedom and responsibility. 'We begin to seek quality in living – more life and fuller.' (Yeaxlee, 1929: 23) Based on a notion of 'knowledge as the mother of understanding and thus of creative enjoyment' (p 24), he saw the adult education movement as a means of achieving a harmonized world and a more democratic lifestyle. He would have all adults aware of and responsive to

> industrial disputes and social crises, rather than subject to crass ignorance and culpable narrowness of outlook. They are the fruitful irritant sources of malignant disease in the body politic. The less we are conscious of them the more, like repressions and complexes in the individual personality, they work desperate mischief (p 22).

He pointed to improved and prolonged education for children and young adults as an optimistic and positive step in achieving the wherewithal to generate such understanding and behaviour, and shared the view that 'a great increase in the facilities for higher education given as a right of citizenship, independently of social status or financial circumstances' (p 26) should form part of the new educational structure. He then addressed himself to a question which, it seems, even today has considerable currency – a view that has long influenced the paucity of resources trickled into provision for adult education

> Shall we not then grow out of the need for adult education – and perhaps sooner than we anticipate? Ought we not to avoid exaggerating the importance of it, and to recognize that it is a transitory social phenomenon, a medicine for a social weakness that we are rapidly overcoming rather than a part of 'human nature's daily food'? (p 26)

This was followed shortly afterwards by what could be viewed as the linchpin of the concept of lifelong education in its modern guise also, as outlined, for example, by Dave et al (1976).

> We discover more, and not less need of adult education as we make progress. It will not have a fair chance until better preparation is made for it during the years of adolescence. On the other hand, we are unlikely to achieve a thoroughly sound and complete system of primary and secondary education until the adult members of the community, by continuing their own education, realize how mischievous a thing it is to abbreviate or mishandle the school education of boys and girls. But adult education, rightly interpreted, is as inseparable from normal living as food and physical exercise. (Yeaxlee, 1929: 28)

Yaxlee argued that in as much as people are all involved in political and social strife, changes and reinterpretations, it becomes obvious that we all stand in need of much wider and fuller lifelong education (p 34).

> The enjoyment of expansion, of growth and exercise (he claimed), was to be found in the love of sport, exciting music, dancing, and so on. Education does not imply any extraction of the sparkle and the sting from these expressions of vitality. It sends them on fresh voyages of discovery, with more reliable compasses and with better charts – which they are to take their share in completing. When, therefore, we interpret adult education in terms of life and people, and not merely in those of books and subjects of formal study, we shall see fresh opportunities and stimulating challenges everywhere The distinction between 'highbrow' and 'lowbrow'... will no longer possess meaning (p 39)

As he saw it, everyone had the capacity to continue to grow intellectually long after leaving, and outside, formal education (and he cited Spearman's and Thorndike's work to support his claim); he was at pains to establish the view that adult education ought not to be regarded as compensating for earlier deficiencies, or as a rival to technical education, or as the poor sister of higher education. He did he accept that people received all the education they were ever likely to need or want by the time they left formal education. Incidentally, he was also one of M Knowles' (1978) precursors in drawing attention to activating factors in adult learners. 'It is largely in order that he may answer the questions or satisfy the hungers stimulated by the experience of daily life that he (the adult learner) turns to the resources of class, lecture-room, or library'. (Yeaxlee, 1929: 44)

He also faced the long held assumptions, prejudices and differential esteem regarding vocational and liberal education.

> Clearly, it is not a matter of superiority or inferiority. The two are simply different but also complementary. The consideration of motive and aim is relevant and helpful only when we agree that in both fields the governing impulse may and should be a worthy one, and that in the complete personality, fulfilling a proper function in society, the two will blend harmoniously (p 129).

The solution to this enduring dualism, he argued, was for the agencies of education to 'attain this unity of spirit and purpose (ie the full bloom of personality and growth) amidst differentiation of functions' (p 14). He urged society to keep in mind that in a democratic community, everyone has a distinctive contribution to its well-being and progress; and that difference is not to be equated with inferiority. But he did support the claim that humane studies formed the foundation for all education.

> Humanistic studies must surely include all that for them lends living a deeper significance and a more abiding joy, whichever of the senses or of the areas in the grey matter of the brain may happen to be the gateways whereby it finds entry (p 153).

'Humanistic studies', he claimed, can have no finality.

> If we ask 'When is his (a person's) education complete?' the only true answer is 'Never while he lives'. There all the distinctive notes of lifelong education are struck (p 164).

Yeaxlee made the claim that self-realization (the achievement of continually developing personality as a result of ongoing learning) and social idealism had always been presented as conflicting aims of adult education. This, he argued, was a fallacy, because it was possible to combine both. A lifetime of education, he maintained, would provide mastery of ascertaining relevant fact, the ability and courage to distance and analyze 'one's own views and prejudices, or those of one's party, as well as those of differing or opposed groups' (p 50) lest any group cared overmuch for the immediate success of its cause, at the expense of care for its members. 'At once more critical and more tolerant our corporate life would become, more imaginative and creative, because more scientific in its quality' (p 148). The best preparation for this practice, he argued, was an early and then ongoing liberalizing education (alongside any vocational needs) conducted in a democratic spirit, and he embraced recreational learning activities for adults as well as for children, such as painting and other hobbies, carried out at Working Men's Institutes, for example, as a 'not less important or fruitful' nor 'less truly a part of the adult education movement'. (Yeaxlee, 1929: 114–15).

> To stereotype adult education is to arrest, if not to kill it. But the real issue is whether we shall be sufficiently alert to recognize the educational value of the unorthodox, and perhaps unsuspected, means of education to which men and women respond in thousands – books, plays, music, the cinema, wireless, the Press, travel, political and religious activities, and a dozen others. If we recognize their potentialities in self-education by such means, are we going to help them to strive for high standards and encourage them to maintain a level of excellence that does not depend upon being academic and conventional?
>
> Moreover, no aspect of community life and human growth must be over-looked or excluded. Recreational or controversial, connected with livelihood or wedded to leisure, all the forms of community organization must play their part (pp 121–22).

For the construction of a bridge between technical and liberal education, he suggested that 'sociology, broadly interpreted, is the proper bridge' (p 130) since it could so readily be made part of both technical and liberal education. To make the bridge, he suggested that not only fundamental connections between the two be made via 'technique and leadership' in teaching and learning, but also through critical contiguity (thus providing an early suggestion of comprehensive education). It is interesting to compare this notion with that of Tawney who, with the backing of the Labour Party, advised different types of secondary education in quite different schools, though, of course, enjoying parity of esteem. It is highly debatable which of the two approaches was the more idealistic in its assumptions. Yeaxlee made the point that what was needed was some common ground or meeting place (for adults particularly)

> where every kind of liberal study and educative activity may be pursued, and where all sorts and conditions of men may interchange knowledge and opinions, experi-ence and ideals. The struggle for freedom and self-government, for a social and international order which will ensure creative and joyous peace, must be carried to a victorious issue in the minds and spirits of men before it can be happily resolved in their political and social organization. More than this, there must be achieved a keenness of insight as only a constructive clash of minds and temperaments in the frankest friendship can give (Yeaxlee, 1929: 116–17) ... and constraining them to judge and choose between the ultimate values by which their lives shall be ordered (p 125).

His vision clearly spanned a much wider horizontal canvas than did that of some other advocates of education for adults; for example, those who leant towards university 'content and style'.

These few extracts serve to illustrate that so far as Yeaxlee was concerned, education was a means of developing personality, of establishing a unity of purpose – a 'wholeness'; each person at one with himself or herself, his or her society, the universe and ultimately with God. He ended his book on lifelong education with a quotation from Middleton Murray, which included the following:

> The soul is simply the condition of the complete Man. And to this completeness in the man, which is his soul, there corresponds a completeness and harmony of the world of his experience; it also, without abstraction or denial of any of its elements, suffers a like transformation and becomes organic, harmonious – it becomes God (Yeaxlee, 1929: 166).

Yeaxlee's thesis was based upon the premise that the fully actualized individual, immersed in a lifetime of learning, was bound to be self-propelled towards Christian values, and it was the resultant quickening of human sympathies that would lead to harmonious, egalitarian social and Christian life. He had not, it seems, fully appreciated the extent of both social and religious disspiritedness.

It is as well to remember, however, that the origins of the WEA were equally 'spiritual', rooted in recognizably Christian socialism, although Albert Mansbridge allied himself particularly to the immediate condition of the working class.

> The appeal of the hour to trade unionists and cooperators is that they make political strikes, promote bills, register protests and send deputations to responsible ministers. The true appeal is that they lift themselves up through higher knowledge to higher works and higher pleasures, which, if responded to, will inevitably bring about right and sound action upon municipal, national, and imperial affairs; action brought about without conscious effort – the only effectual action (Mansbridge, 1964: 2).

> The ground of his hope was spiritual, not political or economic (Harrison, 1961: 263).

Mansbridge himself had written:

> It was quite clear in my mind at that time, (when the ideas of the WEA occurred to him) that education was a reaching out of the soul towards the divine (Mansbridge in Harrison, 1961: 262).

His meeting with the Canon of Westminster, Charles Gore, was significant in the formulation of his ideas of education for working men and women, and as Harrison has noted, it is an interesting feature of the conception of these ideas that Mansbridge was, to a very large extent, self-educated, a Christian, and that the like-mindedness of Anglican bishops and Oxford dons provided the foundation for the WEA. Also, Mansbridge did succeed in bringing together under his educational banner, personalities from the religious, political and educational fields. There may yet be some important lessons to be learnt from such an (originally) holistic effort, especially now in these times when there is much professing of supposed harmony, while the actual practice is polarization. Mansbridge had intended class reconciliation. Gradually, however, the ideology of the workers' educational movement determined that education was to be used explicitly to aid the struggle for a classless society. Yeaxlee's concept of lifelong education supported the potential held in knowledge and education for personal fulfilment and with all subjects considered as equal in value. The workers' movements, on the other hand, decreed that some subjects were of more use than others in the bid for social and industrial emancipation. Thus, the social sciences were placed in highest position and consequently all subjects were not given equal value. Those that were deemed relevant to the class struggle emerged as most important, and a strongly utilitarian or political ethos hung around the education of all those participating. The Labour movement was growing, and since the WEA had become more closely and explicitly allied to Labour's plans, touching as they did upon everyone's day-to day physical and material conditions, it is not difficult to understand why such a movement should overshadow, if not stifle, notions such as those of Yeaxlee.

Religious ideals had, of course, also given rise to Adult Schools in earlier years. These schools, because of their intellectual distance and, therefore, their less intellectual and literary approach, from the universities, and indeed from 'left-wing political overtones' (Harrison, 1961: 301), once again began to appeal to many ordinary working people. They placed great emphasis on community activity and the spirit of fellowship. By 1930, the Settlement ethos found its way to the Adult Schools, which eventually became local 'centres', catering now for somewhat higher academic achievement but coupled with semi-educational and semi-recreational activities. The presiding ethos changed from the religious to the secular (partly due no doubt to the influence of the Board of Education's inspections, which were necessary for financial support) but nonetheless still encouraging a corporate life ideology. In this instance, what began as a religious enterprise, gradually became humanistic in design and practice (see Harrison, 1961: chapter VIII).

Nonetheless, the argument for a liberalizing, university-style education found impressive support. For example, writing in a 1914 article in *Political Quarterly* Tawney pointed to the inescapable fact that most people lived by working, and that for different kinds of work specialized kinds of preparation were necessary. He turned roundly upon the notion that 'humane education' was suitable preparation only for some who entered a restricted group of professions (eg doctors, lawyers, business managers), 'but that it is a matter with which the manual working classes have nothing to do' (Tawney, 1914 : 71). The following extract is self-explanatory:

Such a misinterpretation of the meaning of educational specialisation is felt to be intellectually an imposture. If persons whose work is different require, as they do, different kinds of professional instruction, that is no reason why one should be excluded from the common heritage of civilization of which the other is made free by a university education, and from which, ceteris paribus, both, irrespective of their occupations are equally capable, as human beings, of deriving spiritual sustenance. Those who have seen the inside both of lawyers' chambers and of coal mines will not suppose that of the inhabitants of these places of gloom the former are more constantly inspired by the humanities than are the latter, or that conveyancing... is in itself a more liberal art than hewing.

It is certainly not the case that the only avenue to humane education of the kind ought to be that which consists of a career of continuous school attendance from 5 to 18... To suppose that the goal of educational effort is merely to convert into doctors, barristers, and professors a certain number of persons who would otherwise have been manual workers is scarcely less unintelligent than... to regard the existence of freed-men as making tolerable the institution of slavery... Universal provision is wanted because society is one... because no class is good enough to do its thinking for another... It is not enough that a few working class boys and girls should be admitted to universities, and that many more will be admitted in the future. We want as much university education as we can get for the workers who remain workers all through their lives. The idea of social solidarity, which is the contribution of the working classes to the social conscience of our age, has its educational as well as its economic applications... Perhaps our educationalists have not hitherto allowed sufficiently for the surprising fact that there is no inconsiderable number of men and women whose incentive to education is not material success but spiritual energy, and who seek it, not in order that they may become something else, but because they are what they are (Tawney in Hinden, 1964: 71–73).

These magnificently articulated sentiments also serve to illustrate that there was considerable agreement with Yeaxlee's notions of spiritual gain from education in adult years. They were both concerned with the quest for self-fulfilment. Tawney, however, preferred the tellurian idiom. He had looked to the specifically human condition first, and clearly to 'university type' education, rather than to Yeaxlee's expansive, 'pluralistic' notions of educational activities.

Yeaxlee's proposal was to induct children into metaphysical thinking (ie to direct them away from just the 'here and now' and the obvious and physical), and to make explicit the metaphysical or spiritual enquiry in adult education. He claimed that what was wrong with the world was that it had 'lost sight of spiritual values' (Yeaxlee, 1925: 8); that 'we have not found, or even set ourselves to find, that philosophy which sees everything as part of one harmonious whole', using education to help young people and adults alike to develop personalities 'rightly and consciously related to society and the universe' (Yeaxlee, 1925: 7). This philosophy, or metaphysical quest, he argued, was a natural goal of every person – 'In the depths of every mind there is a philosophy' (G Gentile, in Yeaxlee, 1925: 9).

According to Yeaxlee, then, philosophy or seeking answers to metaphysical questions about the purpose, meaning and value of life, was not beyond the 'shop and market place', nor 'beyond the ken of the common people' (Yeaxlee, 1925: 8–9). In psychological terms, he spoke of this capacity as an integral part of personality.

The problem of knowledge, the problem of thought, the problem of unified moral action, are all problems that spring out of the greater problem of the nature of personality. How do we remain ourselves and yet go out of ourselves? How can we retain our identity and yet enter into innumerable relationships with others? To this Bergson offers an answer: 'obviously there is a vital impulse... something which ever seeks to transcend itself, to extract more from itself than there is – in a word to create. Now a force that draws from itself more than it contains, which gives more than it has, is precisely what is called a spiritual force' (Yeaxlee, 1925: 21).

It is this imminent force that Yeaxlee sought to uncover and develop throughout life (in the way that Dewey (1916: chapter 4) explored 'growth'), in order to have it propel humanity towards values that would interpret and ennoble all of life and place each individual, society and nation in a universal setting, thus enabling understanding of what makes life worth living.

Why should we make any leap (in any one particular direction) at all; why not confine ourselves to the little bit of reality we have seen? The answer is that we are not only spectators of reality, we are also makers of reality. When we act, we create a new bit of reality. The movement of time compels us, whether we want to or not, to act. But for action we need to form some hypothesis as to the universe in which we act, as to what lies beyond the range of previous experience. (Mackenzie in Yeaxlee, 1925: 35)

Yeaxlee argued that education could not escape the universal, the metaphysical dimension to the quality and meaning of life; questions such as: What is personality? How is each person related to other persons and to the universe? What are the meaning and purpose of human life? Where can we find a scale of values that is ultimate and universal? (He did not question that there was such a universal and ultimate 'scale'.) Education, he claimed, 'being inevitably concerned with them, should both implicitly and explicitly direct enquiry and thought towards them' (Yeaxlee, 1925: 54). On this point, he argued further that adult education could be appropriately envisaged as a kind of spiritual activity because earlier schooling had failed to remove most people from the 'here and now'. Adults were capable of re-evaluating their lives. 'Education as a weapon, or as an elevated form of recreation, appeals readily to many a man who has never conceived it as integral to life itself. The revelation of spiritual values and the adjustment of personal and social life to them' had not been seen as the 'supreme gains' of education (Yeaxlee, 1925: 57). However, as adults, bringing with them wider experience of the rigours and practical wisdom of, say, adult social and working life, such enquiry acquired relevance and perhaps urgency.

For Yeaxlee, citizenship was not merely an expression of Christian life, it was the Christian life. By comparison, 'Tawney never sought to blend socialism and Christianity together into a civic religion. A just social order, Tawney implied, will be a better garden for the flowering of Christian life. But a just social order is not itself the Kingdom of God' (Terrill, 1973: 178). 'In Tawney's terminology the "vacant throne" of religious authority was occupied by totalitarian power, theories and the secular messiahs who incarnated them' (p 140). Tawney, according to Terrill (p 193), was more interested in 'right relationships' than in control and saw himself as socialist rather than proletarian.

Both men proclaimed an innate spirituality of humankind, both began with the individual; 'the individual is an end in himself' (Tawney, in Terrill, 1973: 215). Tawney could not agree that socialism was predicated on saintly conduct, though he fully assented to the importance of 'spiritual edification'.

> Opportunities for spiritual edification are more important than mere material environment. If only the material environment were not itself among the forces determining men's capacity to be edified (Tawney in Terrill, 1973: 164).

There are those today who, to an extent, would echo Yeaxlee's sentiment with regard to 'religious studies' forming an important part of individual cognitive development. See, for example, Jarvis' exposition of the questions of meaning of human beings changing as they advance from childhood to youth to adulthood, and the way that changed circumstances or 'biography' can produce a situation 'in which the individual recommences his quest for meaning' (Jarvis, 1983a: 22).

> Since man's religious quest begins with the individual, then the aims of an adult education course (in religious studies) should relate to the facilitation of the growth of the... participants and to assist them in discovering or re-discovering beliefs and ideas that they regard as relevant to their question of meaning. In no way should the educator seek to inculcate ideas. Finally, this approach recognizes no conflict between the process of exploring knowledge discovered in different disciplines and exploring beliefs articulated by various religions. Hence, the more we explore the meaning of life the more we may grow and develop – and that, surely, is an aim of adult education (Jarvis, 1983a: 22-23).

Yeaxlee went further and said that the

> relationship between adult education and religion is not only close, but organic. Either the relationship follows directly from the nature of personality, the meaning of spiritual values and the necessities intrinsic to the educational process, or it is indeed negligible (Yeaxlee, 1925: 60).

On the other hand, it is equally indisputable that a spiritual attitude towards life and the universe does not necessarily imply possession of definite religious faith (Yeaxlee, 1925: 62).

Yeaxlee did claim, however, that Christianity may be used as a vehicle for formalizing the relationship between education and religion, because, he argued, it was less open to superstition and misunderstanding than, say, Stoicism or Buddhism.

Thus, Yeaxlee claimed that by reflecting purposively upon the nature of human beings, the purpose of life 'and the nature of the power that controls the universe' (1926: 27) each individual would become 'full-grown', by having 'felt desperately the necessity and gained some glimpse of the possibility of such a view of life – nay, until he has begun to test it, and found that he can live by it. His philosophy must become his religion' (1926 : 28). This could be achieved, he argued, by referring to gestalt psychology. Perceiving outward objects, action, etc, in patterns 'each part of which owes its significance to its relationship to the other parts, while the whole is more than the sum of the parts' (Yeaxlee, 1952: x) was the start.

'Furthermore, we are constantly aware of incomplete patterns and we find ourselves impelled to try to complete then by insight.' This is how a person might perceive the 'wholeness' or the 'universal'. This process, Yeaxlee argued, should begin in childhood, with education aimed at developing to the full the sentient and sentimental (in the truly psychological sense) personality or disposition of every child, and was best achieved by including Christian religious study in the school curriculum to provide the best model for understanding and for behaviour.

This, then, was the religious inspiration of Basil Yeaxlee. In a world far more secularized now than at the time of his earlier writing, his inspiration might appear somewhat confined. On the other hand, there are those who would commend a 'philosophical' stance (as opposed to a religious one) in education, on the grounds that 'philosophy ought to transform those who pursue it. People ought to be better, by being philosophical' (Sprague, 1978: 5). The point might be said to be made, admittedly grandiloquently, by Sir Thomas Browne: 'The world was made to be inhabited by beasts, but studied and contemplated by man'. Contemporary philosophers might enlarge upon this by explaining the world, philosophically, at any rate, as all that

> anyone might perceive. The effect… is to bring out what we can expect to get in touch with, the sum of all that is, by perceiving what we can of it and understanding that there is still more to it than we can perceive at any one time. These considerations will lead one to say that we do not see the world, but only bits of it; so the world is not a perceptible thing, but a notion we have that there is a system that contains all we have seen, and can see, and more (Sprague, 1978: 84).

This enquiry and perception have then to be made meaningful.

> Generally, things become meaningful to us as we attach values. Family, community, church, nation are meaningful to us because they represent certain values. Would that be equally true of mankind? Is not mankind meaningless to most of us because we do not attach any particular value to it? This may be a matter of indifference rather than intent. Some may also question whether the survival of mankind is worth the effort involved. But suppose we had determined that civilization must not perish, that we want to make a better world for our children if not for ourselves, that through education we must try to create a better understanding of our world. Would mankind not then became meaningful? (Hirschfield in Ulich, 1964: viii).

Unfortunately, the irrational behaviour of man is caused not only by his psychological limitations; it has its cause also in our intellect itself. For purposes of clarity, the intellect has to isolate the object of its attention from the whole within which it stands. Even when we try to extend the span of our interest as far as possible, the whole is beyond our grasp; it exists only in our vision, or intuition. Yet without a picture of the whole we cannot even comprehend the single. Behind every person is also his or her society, his or her nation, and its history, mankind, and finally the universe. It is good to remind ourselves from time to time of all this infinity in order to acquire this healthy relativism, which should prevent us from idolizing ourselves and our nation, our creeds, our truths, and our little knowledge (Ulich, 1964: 22–23).

Though secularized sentiments, there is much in these views that is in sympathy with Yeaxlee's ends.

Whereas Kekes (1980) looks to philosophers to interpret, criticize, defend or develop 'world views', Yeaxlee would have argued that, with appropriate education, everyone could contribute to that process. Others might well point to the fact, however, that 'in the face of violence and destruction that have come upon us this century, a philosophy based on the fundamental goodness of man seems altogether 'naïve' (Kitwood, 1970: 86). It is salutary to reflect that the quest for meaning and purpose has endured throughout time, in all segments of the globe. Sometimes it has been conveyed or interpreted through myths, through religions or through philosophy. The questions remain; they remain unanswered yet seemingly pertinent to each generation. (Perhaps the reason we are now particularly failing to answer questions about our humanity is because, tied as we are to 'the scientific method' and to 'objectivity', we cannot cope with questions that concern us most, and in which we are inextricably and deeply involved.) However, 'we must... try to understand what is human for the very simple reason that we have a human life to live' (Kitwood, 1970: 8).

Religion as an educative vehicle gradually lost its supremacy as secularization increased and the state gained more control over educational provision. Perhaps this is why a writer so committed to religious inspiration and design was lost to a society increasingly looking to human beings and 'humanness' as opposed to 'superman' and the religiously metaphysical. Nonetheless, a metaphysical perspective on human life still has currency – albeit largely but not exclusively in the philosophical realm. Many people would prefer, perhaps, to use the term 'philosophical' rather than 'religious', but Jarvis (1983b) makes the point that religion is one element in the response of human beings to the process of questioning, that the questioning endures and has endured throughout time. In his sociologically slanted discussion on religiosity, he makes a case for regarding any process of the questioning for meaning as 'religious':

Religion is, therefore, regarded as an element in the response of human beings to this fundamental process of questioning. The provision of answers to questions of meaning suggests, at the very least, that the person has pondered upon the problem of human existence and may thus be described as being religious. (Jarvis, 1983b: 55)

Human beings have always sought universal meaning beyond merely detailed, documented knowledge. The language or medium of religion, once popular and arguably misused, employed to convey the collective and personal search, may seem inappropriate now, but the process – as argued for example by Jarvis – when analyzed, can offer great insight into personal development and the realization and nourishing of 'self'.

Yeaxlee attempted a plan to draw upon the inherent quest of human beings (in a process of lifelong education), to help to equip themselves with the intellectual and affective instruments to guide them to a truly democratic, benevolent society, committed to Christian values. While some looked to government and political activity for potentially sweeping changes in society, Yeaxlee focused his attention on each individual in a universal setting. He would have had everyone understand him/herself and the concept of the universe, in order to unite collective effort towards an ultimate goal. He was not alone in expecting that each individual could reach out beyond his/her inheritance to seek out the question of meaning and quality of life and explore their possibilities.

Whether a religious, philosophical or ideological perspective is used to 'examine' life, the one linking strand is that education sets the sights, and that a lifetime of education ensures continuous examination.

CONCLUSION

It needs to be borne in mind that Yeaxlee's views were being published at a time when the Board of Education was strengthening its control over church schools, because, it was argued, religious dogma adversely influenced the standards in these schools; as highlighted by Simon, 'that other lion in the path of educational advance, the interest of the Churches in many elementary schools and in most of the worst of them' (Simon, 1974: 149).

There was general dissatisfaction with church elementary schools on the part of many local education authorities. It was recognized also, by Labour Party supporters, that unless the church improved the standards of teaching and learning conditions and the buildings, many children would be doomed to failure, regardless of the proposed secondary schools, because of inadequate earlier learning opportunities. In this climate, when the general public and many educators were disenchanted with the church's relationship with education and suspicious of religion generally, there was probably only a minority who would have accepted all that Yeaxlee had to suggest. Also, a disastrous general strike had recently occurred in a desperate bid to improve the lot of the workers materially. To these exhausted, and probably hungry, people, it could be argued, the ethereal, metaphysical or spiritual assumed low priority in their pressing concerns.

Whereas Yeaxlee was wise in seizing the opportunity to ask that education for adults be considered at the same time as secondary education for all was being established (for he saw the one being inextricably linked to the other), he was clearly fighting a losing battle. It is hardly surprising that government policy concentrated first and foremost on establishing national secondary education. The organizational task involved was obviously of immense magnitude, and it seems likely that the Board of Education was only too happy, for that moment, to allow the universities and voluntary bodies to continue the major overseeing of education for adults – such as it was.

In any event, by 1924, the Board of Education agreed to 'separate' liberal adult education from technical and evening classes. The decision was reached after consultation with the Advisory Committee on the Liberal Education of Adults and this effectively cemented the gap between liberal adult education and all other forms of education. Thus, for another 50 years the idea of integrated life-long education lay dormant and almost forgotten. The concept and its practice are beginning to be found in some of the initiatives of community and tertiary colleges, in new means of accreditation, access, mature student programmes in polytechnics, colleges and universities, taught collaborative degree schemes, 'flexistudy' and open learning. Its future rests in the intellectual and active efforts of those who acknowledge that the late-20th century manifested features that demand complex and systematic reappraisal of the nature, purpose and duration of education – a reappraisal begun in the 1920s by Basil Yeaxlee.

REFERENCES

Dave, R H (1976) *Foundations of Lifelong Education*, UNESCO, Paris

Dewey, J (1916) *Democracy and Education*, Collier-Macmillan, New York

Faure, E (1972) *Learning to Be*, UNESCO, Paris

Harrison, J F C (1961) *Learning and Living 1790–1960: A study in the history of the English adult education movement*, Routledge & Kegan Paul, London

Hinden, R (1964) *Tawney: The radical tradition*, Allen & Unwin, London

Hirschfield, G (1964) The Council for the Study of Mankind, in *Education and the Idea of Mankind*, ed R Ulich, University of Chicago Press

Jarvis, P (1983a) The Lifelong Religious Development of the Individual and the Place of Adult Education, *Lifelong Learning: The adult years*, **5** (9), pp 20–23

Jarvis, P (1983b) Religiosity – A theoretical analysis of the human response to the problem of meaning, *Bulletin for the Institute for the Study of Religious Architecture*, University of Birmingham, pp 51–66

Kekes, J (1980) *The Nature of Philosophy*, Blackwell, Oxford

Kitwood, T M (1970) *What is Human?* Intervarsity Press, London

Knowles, M (1978) *The Adult Learner: A neglected species*, Gulf Publishing Co, Houston

Lengrand, P (1975) *An Introduction to Lifelong Education*, Croom-Helm, London

Mansbridge, A (1964) *The Kingdom of the Mind – Essays and addresses*, Dent, London

Ministry of Reconstruction (1919) (reprinted 1980) *Final Report of the Adult Education Committee*, University of Nottingham

Simon, B (1974) *The Politics of Educational Reform*, Lawrence & Wishart, London

Sprague, E (1978) *Metaphysical Thinking*, Oxford University Press, New York

Terrill, R (1973) *R H Tawney and his Times*, Andre Deutsch, London

Ulich, R (1964) Education and the Idea of Mankind, University of Chicago Press

Yeaxlee, B A (1925) *Spiritual Values in Adult Education* (2 vols), Oxford University Press
Yeaxlee, B A (1926) *Towards a Full Grown Man* (The John Clifford Lecture), The Brotherhood Movement, London
Yeaxlee, B A (1929) *Lifelong Education*, Cassell, London
Yeaxlee, B A (1952) *Religion and the Growing Mind*, Nisbett & Co, London

Chapter 3

R H Tawney – 'patron saint of adult education'

Barry Elsey

This short biography of Richard Henry Tawney (1880–1962) deals mainly with his extensive and significant contribution to the 'heroic age' of adult education. This means making only passing reference to the many other important activities of Tawney's creative and crowded life. But for him adult education was a matter of great personal commitment, where he worked out his values and used his position as a teacher, organizer, executive, advocate, reformer and writer to give expression to the many other avenues of academic life and social affairs where he excelled.

It has to be acknowledged that it is virtually impossible to say anything new about him for Tawney has been canonized in at least six biographies, which amply testify to the volume, scope and significance of his impact on adult education, economic history, social and political philosophy, government policies in education and industry, educational journalism and the development of the Labour Party (see References at end of the chapter). Nonetheless, from the standpoint of the gloomy and cynical 1980s, it is difficult to be objective, but possible to attempt some assessment of his continued influence on British adult education.

Before detailing Tawney's contribution to adult education it is necessary to outline the origins and destinations of his life and career. Tawney was born in Calcutta into the folds of the privileged upper class where his progress in life was mapped out by private education, first at Rugby and later at Balliol College, Oxford. His father was a distinguished Sanskrit scholar and after service in the Indian Education Service became a professor and head of Presidency College. Such a background would have moulded most into a comfortable acceptance of privilege but Tawney was made of different metal. Tawney's early life has been described as a mixture of the breeding of a gentleman fired by the instincts of a social democrat and the leaning towards service to the community as a duty of the high-born. It seems that Oxford made sense of these strands embedded in Tawney's life for during his undergraduate days a view was emerging that the right to influence the values of society should be based on an individual's contribution and service to the community, not just from the ownership of property or high social status. This led Tawney to turn his back on the 'call of India', characteristic of his Oxford contemporaries, and seek instead an understanding of poverty by becoming a social worker at Toynbee Hall in the East End of London. It should be noted, though, that Tawney learnt his trade as a professional scholar at Oxford, as well as his abiding taste for social reform through active involvement. His subsequent career is marked by an outstanding capacity to combine scholarship with practical actions on a wide variety of educational and political fronts.

Today, some of the work Tawney did at Toynbee Hall would be regarded as non-formal adult education, closely allied to the ideas and practices of community development. In his time, university settlement work was seen as a mission to the poor, by providing a taste of edifying culture laced with a strong sense of paternalism under the leadership of Canon Samuel Barnett (Preston 1985: 27–32). Tawney made his own special contribution by emphasizing the importance of social investigation and giving regular classes on literature, religious topics and political economy. These were the embryonic beginnings of Tawney as an adult educator. His view that the purpose of his lectures was to help the workers gain political power through knowledge put him at odds with Barnett's cultural vision of adult education. Tawney's views attracted the notice of Albert Mansbridge, founder of the Workers' Educational Association (WEA), and therein began a very long partnership. (See the first chapter of this book for a full discussion on Mansbridge.)

In 1903, the year Tawney took up residence at Toynbee Hall, the WEA was founded, a movement pioneered by Mansbridge to promote the higher education of working people. Tawney met Mansbridge at the instigation of Canon Barnett. Mansbridge was impressed by his enthusiasm and energy. Soon afterwards William Temple was attracted to the WEA by Tawney, cementing the Balliol–Toynbee Hall connection and bringing together three illustrious figures that gave the Association such an impressive early start (see Styler, 1985: 590–91). As Terrill (1974: 37) remarks:

> For Tawney it began half a century of institutional connection (he was on the WEA executive for 42 years, and president, 1928–1945) that for many years meant more to him than even his connection to the Labour Party, the London School of Economics, or the church. He had come to think that education, not charity, was what workers needed. And he chose the WEA, rather than academia, as the arena for his first sustained phase (seven years) of teaching and research. Life in the WEA made him a socialist; work in the WEA made him an economic historian. In turn, he gave tutorial classes in England; the spirit of comradeship in study was their genius.

The decisive development for the WEA, and for Tawney, was the setting up of university tutorial classes. For Mansbridge, the cultural enlightenment of the working classes depended upon the acquisition of properly taught and rigorously learnt knowledge. Tawney shared the same view, except for him the road to working-class power and socialism lay through political education. These two outlooks sometimes led to clashes between Mansbridge and Tawney but this emerged sometime after university tutorial classes were fairly well established. The real achievement of the WEA was to bring together in a working partnership traditionally conservative, yet socially conscious, universities with the trade unions and cooperators, representing working-class educational aspirations. Thus in 1908 these interested parties gathered together in an historic assembly to consider the prospect of a university-level adult education for the working class. The tutorial class movement that sprang from the conference and report *Oxford and Working-Class Education*, which was largely written and inspired by Tawney, was founded on the idea that a sound education was more than the outpourings of occasional lectures. Mansbridge believed passionately in the virtues of sustained and regular study involving class discussion, private reading and essay writing in the manner of the highest education of university standards. These were the highways to individual development, cultural emancipation and class equality. Tawney worked within the broad framework of these ideas and provided the additional dimension of a scholarly based education to the ideas of political theory and economic history. He also put into effect the idea of adult education as 'the spirit of comradeship in study'. This contribution warrants more detailed description.

Tawney had accolades heaped upon him in just about every avenue of his glorious career, especially as an adult educator. It was Mansbridge, in offering to provide Rochdale with the first university tutorial class, who described Tawney as the 'best tutor in England' on the understanding that 30 worker-students pledged themselves for two solid years of study under his tutorship. Longton in Staffordshire soon became the base for the second tutorial class under Tawney and the sponsorship of Oxford university.

Tawney's workload would cripple most WEA and University Extension tutors today. Tawney would set off by train from Glasgow (where he was a part-time lecturer at the university), and later from his marital home in Manchester, for Longton on Friday for an evening class. Spending the night at a local pub, he would travel to Rochdale for an afternoon class, returning on Sunday. Tutorial classes by modern standards were large, between 30 and 40 hungry and relatively untrained adult minds. A lengthy lecture was followed by an hour of discussion, which often spilled over in an informal and relaxed way to free-ranging exchanges over matters of philosophy, history, religion, politics and literature. Over tea and biscuits Tawney showed himself as more than just a teacher and he revelled in the unique opportunity to rub shoulders with ordinary men and women fired with the thirst for knowledge. It was an experience that opened doors of the mind for those special few who shared the fellowship of learning. Tawney acknowledged the benefits of this experience in some of his later writings. In the meantime, he slaved over the essays laboriously produced by students. In one session of nine weeks he marked and made elaborate comments on over 500 essays.

The images of Tawney as a lecturer are well worth quoting:

> To all students he was a fine lecturer. He always had a script, done in his cramped handwriting, all loops and hooks, sometimes on the back of notepaper picked up in hotels, and he would declaim its rolling phases with quiet intensity. He would steer gargantuan sentences to harbour because he had an unerring sense of the geography of a sentence, revealed in his meticulous punctuation. At the lectern, ash would drop onto his papers, and sometimes he would, when transported, thrust his still burning pipe into a pocket of his tweed jacket (Terrill, 1974: 65).

The admiration of his biographer is obvious but even more so is the image of Tawney as an adult teacher, in the days when the didactic style of lecturing was considered quite normal and credit was given for knowledge distributed and lubricated by clever phrases and learned wit. Such a style has all but disappeared from adult education and although there might be some regret at the passing of the scholarship that went with it, few would wish to resuscitate such an old-fashioned method of enabling adults to learn. In Tawney's day, it was the accepted and admired method of teaching adults.

Tawney was probably a better teacher when he was off the pedestal of the lectern and the formally prepared lecture. Indeed biographers have noted his liking of questions from students and the opportunity to talk over ideas in an informal manner. Tawney, like all good adult educators, learnt from his students and in recognition of their valuable insights into everyday economic and social life he readily acknowledged their wisdom and contribution to his own thinking. It is held that Tawney's excellent contribution to economic history as an academic subject grew out of his involvement with working-class adult education, and his classic book *The Agrarian Problem in the Sixteenth Century* is dedicated to the WEA. Tawney (1912: ix) wrote paying tribute to:

> members of the Tutorial Classes conducted by Oxford University, with whom for the last four years it has been my privilege to be a fellow-worker. The friendly smitings of weavers, potters, miners, and engineers, have taught me much more about the problems of political and economic science which cannot easily be learned from books.

Tawney's career as a teacher, in the narrow sense of being involved in conducting university tutorial classes, was a relatively short seven years Of course, he taught for many years at the London School of Economics (LSE) but that was not the same experience as the education of working adults, which was his first calling. In a wider sense Tawney continued as an adult educator throughout his long life. His involvement was cemented throughout half a century with the WEA. For over 40 years he served on the WEA executive and was president for 17 years. During those years, Tawney undoubtedly stamped his mark on the educational and social ideals of the WEA. He once claimed that his experience of the WEA made him a socialist and economic historian. In return Tawney insisted that the WEA honour, in form as well as spirit, its commitment to high intellectual standards and to working-class education. This insistence sometimes put him at odds with Mansbridge who occasionally resented Tawney's sharp criticisms about declining standards and demands for better facilities to enhance the 'tutorial' side of classes.

Good teaching and high intellectual standards were for Tawney essential complements to the ideas of equality of opportunity for workers and the use of education for political ends. He spent his life teaching these ideas at a time when the dark forebodings of totalitarianism were gripping the world and suffocating democracy. Intelligent citizenship had to spring from a sound education of adults and he regarded a slackening of intellectual standards as a disservice to the ideals of social democracy and moral reasoning. It was Tawney's moral passion and academic respectability that played such a decisive part in building solid foundations for the WEA and its partnership with the universities. Tawney sustained and advocated these beliefs on a much wider and significant canvas thereafter.

In later years, Tawney expressed some disquiet about the WEA, fearing that it had lost sight of its original purpose. He was critical of the WEA's attempt to broaden and popularize its programme and lamented the decline of the tutorial class movement. Tawney was caught out of step with the times as his vision of workers being challenged by education was being superseded by a 'cafeteria diet' of more easily digested fare. More significantly, the idea of education for socialism had all but vanished as a moving force in the WEA and adult education generally.

During his zenith as the WEA president, Tawney devoted great energy to its executive affairs and was in every sense a working leader. His involvement ranged from political infighting within the executive of the WEA to the details of staff appointments. His main struggles were to keep the WEA's commitment to working-class education and avoid splinter groups forming for the purposes of serving wider, apolitical cultural interests. This line of thought reflected the earlier version of Mansbridge and was taken up by Richard Livingstone, who in 1941 wrote the definitive account of liberal adult education ideals and values. Tawney was in these matters an astute strategist and a ruthless side to his otherwise generous nature showed through. By skilled manipulation he successfully shunted the idea into a harmless non-providing role. His attempts were in the long run only partially successful for the WEA was turning itself into two organizations. The traditional commitment to an intellectual education service for working-class adults was giving way to provision for recreational and leisure-time pursuits. Tawney was witness to the gradual waning of his ideas but for most of his active years he maintained a strong stand between adult education and the social emancipation of the working class.

Alongside his executive role and an earlier teaching one with the WEA, Tawney lubricated its ideas and development through the power of his writing.

He wrote frequently for the WEA journal *Highway* and essays in other publications of the organization. His writing output for the WEA is modest compared with his enormous contribution to educational reform and ideas as a correspondent for the then *Manchester Guardian*. Through his writings Tawney was in turn advocate, critic and teacher. Simultaneously, he continued to produce a steady stream of high-quality academic scholarship on economic history, social and political philosophy and other matters. This output was combined with membership of government committees of inquiry where both his ideas and writing skills were deployed.

His reputation as a teacher, organizer and charismatic leader drew him into the ambit of policy making, mainly in education but also in other spheres of government activity through committees, commissions and quango bodies. In adult education Tawney is best known, in this particular context, for his membership of the Ministry of Reconstruction, which produced the famous 1919 Report (reprinted in 1980), still regarded as the foremost document of philosophical and practical insights into the provision of an education service deliberately designed for adult purposes and needs. The report has served as a model for other official committees that periodically examine the nature and future directions of adult education. Tawney undoubtedly exerted his influence throughout the committee's proceedings, as he did with so many others (notably the Royal Commission on the Mining Industry). He wrote two sections of the 1919 Report: on the supply of teachers and the organization and the finance of adult education. Even with the driest subject matters Tawney had the literary skills to elevate thought to a high level of lucidity and comprehension.

This short biography has dwelt on Tawney's life in general and his involvement with adult education in particular. Attention shifts now to his visionary philosophy and the moral values that underpinned his actions throughout his life and career. Indeed it is the bequest of the ideas that he gave to adult education that warrants his inclusion as a great contributor to the movement. It is the abiding good fortune of adult education, certainly in the past and to a considerable extent today, that his ideas reached, permeated and were consistently expressed through his teaching, writing and organizing in a movement that grew into a significant range of learning opportunities for millions of adults throughout the 20th century. Undoubtedly, adult education today would be poorer, both as a service and a movement of ideas, without the continuing influence of Tawney's thinking, which he so vigorously stamped during the long years of his reign.

There are four pillars of thought that Tawney inscribed onto the heart of British adult education. The first may be termed the fellowship of learning, reflecting the humanitarian spirit of adult education. The second is the idea of liberal education expressed through the great art of teaching adults. The third is the belief in adult education as a purposeful means of ensuring the survival of a democratic citizenship based on educated and critical minds. Finally, there is the link between adult education and the values of socialism. These ideas are, and were for Tawney, interrelated values that he so eloquently expressed through adult education.

With regard to the idea of fellowship of learning, passing mention has been made of Tawney's impact on the adult students attending university tutorial classes. The key idea is the belief that in all regards other than knowledge and scholarship the relations between the tutor and adult students is based on mutual respect. Adult education offers little room for punditry or tyranny, which are the temptations inherent in the teaching and control of compulsorily educated schoolchildren. Tawney, along with other early adult educators, established the legacy that teaching is founded upon informal and friendly relations. This idea is just as valid today in teaching adults, most of whom in returning to learning experience the feeling of uncertainty about abilities and other self-doubts. At its best adult teaching is a delicate balance between sympathetic empathy, the skills of the adult tutor in communicating knowledge and the capacity to enable students to learn. Through his example set in university tutorial classes Tawney has handed down a model for teaching and learning which is more than trained skills and academic knowledge and is just as much about rapport and understanding of adults as learners and individual people. It is to Tawney's credit that he related education to ordinary adults and broke through the pomp and arrogance of university teaching. Reduced to essentials, adult education is a profoundly humane experience and Tawney was amongst those who demonstrated this simple value.

Closely related to his legacy of the fellowship of adult learning is the ethos of liberal education. Tawney was a passionate advocate of the liberal ideal at a time when adult education was still struggling for a place in the educational system, and during the dark years of encroaching fascism and precarious democracies. Given Tawney's scholarly erudition and socialist beliefs it would have been easy to slip from education to indoctrination in pursuit of his political views. Tawney steadfastly avoided that pitfall into arid polemic without compromising his passionate zeal for social reform and equality. Instead, Tawney stuck to the practice of examining ideas from different perspectives and treating them to a fair-minded yet critical analysis. He upheld the virtues of dispassionate inquiry and was reportedly very stern with adult students, some of whom in their conversion to left-wing views were impatient with him for his moderation and tolerance.

Liberal education is more than a balanced approach to rival political ideas. It is also a belief in the value of knowledge for its own sake, without regard to its vocational purposes and means of occupational and social mobility. It is not clear where Tawney exactly stood in relation to this idea. As suggested earlier he was sometimes at odds with Mansbridge and his cultural view of the purpose of adult education. Tawney regarded adult education as a means to working-class political power. In that sense education was not just for personal cultivation but for political emancipation. Thus Tawney's view of liberal education was focused on an approach to learning and an emphasis upon a knowledge of political economy as an avenue of class liberation. But that does not mean he was against the exploration of religious ideas, the arts and literature. Clearly not, for Tawney was a man of learning and religious conviction. Liberal adult education was for him the pursuit of knowledge for social purposes and personal development based on an ideal of intellectual excellence and the inquiring mind. His struggle was against blind beliefs and trivial pastime learning masquerading as adult education in the corridors of the WEA. His views of recreational learning in the developing adult education services provided by local education authorities in the inter-war years is less well known. It is likely that he viewed it as irrelevant to the really important task of education as a means of political consciousness. But this is mere speculation.

It is clear that Tawney passionately believed in adult education as an arm of democracy. This belief goes beyond his partisan political values expressed through his educational activities and involvement with the Labour Party. Tawney's brand of socialism, fused with his religious values, humane sympathies and liberal education practices made him an ardent social democrat. On that basis, he regarded adult education for working-class people as a vehicle for various forms of emancipation – intellectual, cultural and political. But this was not to create an hegemony of the working class, replacing one tyranny of class domination with another, but as a means of fostering a genuine pluralist society founded on secure democratic principles. Tawney's adult education work testifies to the practice of sharing knowledge and ideas through reasoned argument and discussion with people of mixed abilities and background. This is the stuff of a basic 'grass-roots' democracy, equipping adults with the tools and knowledge for a fairer society. This kind of social democracy arises from real experience rather than an imposed version handed down by political leaders. In its essence democracy is built upon adult education and active involvement in learning experiences which are meaningful to ordinary people.

This idea certainly took root, surprisingly, during World War Two with the setting up of the Army Bureau of Current Affairs. ABCA, as it was known, established the principle and the practice of the open-minded discussion of political ideas and invited undereducated servicemen and servicewomen to pool their thoughts about the social reconstruction of Britain after the war. This was the practice of the idea of democratic citizenship through discussion. The antecedents of this approach to adult education can be traced to the splendid example set by the WEA and university tutorial classes, which Tawney so indelibly stamped with his values.

Tawney's ideas have certainly been an inspiration to many people in adult education, without them necessarily sharing his political beliefs. As a practitioner, through the several avenues of creative expression in adult education, Tawney has been a shining example. Few could fail to be inspired by his teaching, scholarship, humanity and capacity to lead a major adult education provider of this century. Of course, he is not the only inspiring example, as this book and *The International Biography of Adult Education* (Thomas and Elsey, 1980) amply testify.

It is Tawney's political beliefs and the communication of these through adult education that are for me his abiding contribution. Therein lies the nature of his inspiration. Adult education, like other branches of the educational system, is so easily dominated by the passion for bureaucracy, matters of technique, regulation of behaviour, allocation of resources and all the other tedious (but necessary) elements of the everyday business of management and organization. Tawney's work is a constant reminder of the vitality of far-reaching ideals and political vision that gives the movement its dynamic thrust and wider social purpose.

The heroic age of adult education is just about spent. Today, adult education is managed little enough by inspiration and too much by careerists. Adult education with a fiery will is a thing of the past and with each year beginning to radiate a romantic glow. Tawney is part of the romantic heritage of adult education and a British style of socialism that has long since faded into glorious memory.

It would be foolish to expect adult education and the socialism of Tawney to make a comeback. In any case his style of teaching would be old-fashioned and his liberal, democratic beliefs largely unheeded in the scramble to survive through the contingencies of vocational training and cafeteria-style programmes. Nonetheless, if only for the sake of history some explanation of Tawney's socialism and its relation to adult education is useful.

The socialism of Tawney was based on two ideas. First, he was a man of deep religious conviction and Christianity was in his view founded on a belief in a common humanity; this common humanity derived from a recognition of God as the Father of human beings. It does not matter whether Tawney's God was 'out there' or an internal spiritual force that men and women discover for themselves in the light of life experiences. For Tawney, God represented a moral basis to the human condition that had to be achieved through personal awareness and collective action. The means to establishing a social order properly recognizing the moral basis of our common humanity is the idea of equality of worth.

Human beings have qualities that go beyond individual differences. These qualities of humanity express the potential for individual contributions for the common good. This idea is underpinned by a belief in the ultimate moral goodness of human beings and, in more concrete terms, the capacity of people to recognize their obligations towards others freely. The route to this essentially moral view of human beings is through a proper recognition of the equal worth of people and the need for equal treatment. By such means social relations and social order rest on a commonly accepted consensus of values.

Tawney in his role as an adult educator gave expression to the idea of treating people equally, as he did in his personal life too. He crossed the boundaries of a class-ridden society, with its deep, inbuilt inequalities of a material and cultural kind, through the simple act of treating others as equals and raising their self-esteem. He enabled the teaching of adult students by the moral principle of regarding them as worthy people with skills to unfold to make valuable contributions to a more just society. Equality is more than the distribution of power and wealth in this approach for it demonstrates the humane quality of egalitarianism through social relationships. This is socialism as fellowship, just as there is morality through fellowship, and these constitute the bedrocks of our common humanity.

The second dimension of Tawney's socialism, closely linked to the first, is the idea of equality as a means of personal freedom and development. This is not the same thing as greedy, self-seeking individualism for it involves a sense of obligation and the urge to do one's duty for the common good. Again, this is an essentially humane aspect of socialist beliefs, not slide-rule socialism with its concern for distributional equality.

Freedom arises from within people who are given the opportunity to explore their capabilities and develop themselves. This is the ideal ethos of liberal adult education and the pursuit of knowledge and learning for its own sake, that is, without regard to vocational or certification purposes. Adult education was for Tawney an inalienable right and a means of self-fulfilment through the struggle for knowledge by sustained learning. But adult education used in that way is also the route to a more equal society. In this regard adult education enables talents to develop and become available for the common good of society. The socialism in this view rests on a belief in the desire of those who have benefited from access to educational opportunities to serve the community through their abilities. Self-fulfilment, therefore, is linked to the ideal of service that in the long run reduces inequalities in society.

Central tenets in Tawney's socialism are the belief in morality and serving the needs of a common humanity. It is an essentially human doctrine derived from the experience of fellowship. The allusion to basic Christian doctrine expressed through the ideas of morality, service and fellowship is very strong. His classic book on the subject of equality (Tawney, 1952) is rich with the thinking of a socialist guided by a concern for the quality of social relationships as much as political and economic analysis. Tawney's ideas of common humanity and fellowship were formed in part from the experiences of his high-born family background. Just as significant, though, were the deep impressions derived from the experiences of mixing with ordinary working people in the East End of London and, undoubtedly, through the exchanges and insights of teaching adults in university tutorial classes. In this sense Tawney's experience of adult education provided a real basis for his personal convictions and political beliefs.

An assessment of Tawney's standing today is bound to be subjective. He is still a shining beacon for a particular kind of British socialism with its leaning towards Christian morality and community service. In my early years as a mature student at the LSE the ghost of Tawney stood behind the earthly powers of people like Richard Titmuss who combined academic intellectualism with a real concern to help adult students come to grips with social policy and administration. Titmuss and others like him impressed upon idealistic adult students destined for careers in social welfare the need to combine the rigours of the intellectual-rational tradition with humane feelings and practical common sense. This is the spirit of Tawney and a legacy of British socialism and social welfare that has largely faded, just like fond memories of the past always do.

Adult education as a form of social welfare in the widest sense has just about let go of the Tawney legacy. There are still faint echoes, as in some of the romantic enthusiasm for the fellowship of learning through some aspects of community-based adult education. In small measure, too, the liberal adult education ethos lives on through some forms of university education and WEA teaching. But time is not on the side of Tawney's kind of adult education. Undoubtedly adult education is a more professional service than in his day and it is much better resourced and established, in spite of prevailing policies of financial restriction. Yet somehow the moral passion and sense of purpose, the idealism of adult education, have given way to a far less spirited form.

ACKNOWLEDGEMENT

I am indebted to Professors Gammage, Stephens and Thomas of the University of Nottingham for their valuable comments on earlier drafts of this chapter.

REFERENCES

Brooks, J R (1974) *R H Tawney and the Reform of English Education*, unpublished PhD thesis, University of Wales

Hinden, R (1964) *The Radical Tradition*, George Allen and Unwin, London

Jennings, B (1985) Mansbridge, Albert, in *International Bibliography of Adult Education*, eds J E Thomas and B Elsey, Department of Adult Education, University of Nottingham

Livingstone, R W (1941) *The Future of Education*, University of Cambridge Press, Cambridge

Preston, P (1985) Barnett, S A, in *International Bibliography of Adult Education*, eds J E Thomas and B Elsey, Department of Adult Education, University of Nottingham

Ryan, A (1980) R H Tawney – A socialist saint, *New Society*, 27th November

Smith, H P (1962) *R H Tawney*, Rewley House Papers, Oxford

Styler, W E (1985) William Temple, in *International Bibliography of Adult Education*, eds J E Thomas and B Elsey, Department of Adult Education, University of Nottingham

Tawney, R H (1912) *The Agrarian Problem in the Sixteenth Century*, Longmans, London

Tawney, R H (1952) *Equality*, 4th edn, George Allen and Unwin Ltd, London

Terrill, R (1974) *R H Tawney and his Times: A socialism of fellowship*, Deutsch, London

The 1919 Report (1980), Department of Adult Education, University of Nottingham

Thomas, J E and Elsey, B (eds) (1985) *International Bibliography of Adult Education*, Department of Adult Education, University of Nottingham

Williams, J R et al (1960) *R H Tawney: A portrait by several hands*, Shenval Press, London

Part 2

EARLY TWENTIETH-CENTURY AMERICAN THINKERS

Chapter 4

John Dewey and lifelong education

Angela Cross-Durrant

INTRODUCTION

John Dewey, born in Vermont in 1859, was one of the USA's foremost pragmatists. Pragmatism as a philosophy emerged in the early 19th century in the USA at a time when many opposing views pulled public opinion and action in different directions. The new scientific world view opposed the religious; romanticism faced positivism; democratic ideals challenged the aristocratic reactionary stance. Pragmatism developed as a unifying or mediating philosophy (Scheffler, 1974), trying to link science and religion, speculative thought and analysis, knowledge and action, and to highlight the responsibilities for the initiation and the consequences of such a unifying theory or philosophy of life. Dewey wrote profusely on 'traditional' philosophical problems of ethics, metaphysics, aesthetics, etc, and on 'applied philosophy', such as that expressed in his educational writing. He also published comments and analyses on prevailing social conditions and on politics. His holistic and unifying philosophical ideals may be readily traced in any of his works.

So far as his educational writing is concerned, Dewey is primarily associated with the education of the very young, but he has been described as the 'major philosophical founder father' of the 'alternative' ideas found in the lifelong or recurrent learning movements (Flude and Parrott, 1979: 21). This is because the movements propose reform of education to allow a new way of perceiving education, *in toto*, with each phase as one small step in a longer coordinated lifelong journey, and they all advocate an holistic view of learning and living.

Before proceeding with the discussion, something needs to be said about 'alternatives' to the prevailing educational enterprise.

Recurrent education is one of several potential alternatives, born of adult educators, and is usually synonymous with a way of seeing education *in toto*, with learning occurring at intervals throughout life, alternating with normal life activities; the unifying of all stages of education; accepting formal and non-formal patterns of education; and embracing education as an integral – not peripheral or separate – part of life. It also subscribes, to a significant extent, to 'de-schooling' (OECD, 1973). It differs from, say, permanent education, continuing education or the notion of alternance, in that these ideas suggest refresher and 'topping up' programmes (semantically, more of the same, so to speak, implying former education to a particular standard as a prerequisite for continuing) and retraining; whereas recurrent education, or Boshier's learning society, or lifelong education, suggest a complete 'shift of paradigm' (Houghton and Richardson, 1974: ix). The approaches of permanent education and of continuing education, even when they mean different things to different people, usually imply a considerable expansion of existing services that form part of the general adult education provision, and as such are concerned primarily with post-compulsory (or post-initial) education. They may be viewed as tinkering with an existing engine.

The approaches of recurrent education, a learning society or lifelong education, on the other hand, involve the fitting of an entirely new engine to drive the educational bus. Implicit in these notions is the view that reform in compulsory education is more significant to post-compulsory learning than any reform or improvement of, addition to, or financial injection into, adult education could be, and this is in harmony with Dewey's thinking.

However, proponents of recurrent education, rather than of lifelong education, suggest that a 'certain amount of "deschooling"' is required (OECD, 1973: 25), which denotes a significant departure from Dewey's adherence to schooling – though very much reformed in terms of methodology and curriculum – as an important vehicle for education. Thus, Dewey's ideas may be seen as closer in spirit to lifelong education in that this latter concept is radical in reappraisal, but reformist in strategy.

Each of the alternatives has its own nomenclature, criteria, principles and strategies, and using the various terms interchangeably (eg Flude and Parrott, 1979: 16) can throw the differences out of focus. They all aim to maintain and improve the quality of life; to help the individual contend with a kaleidoscopic future – though some concentrate on a 'working' future more than a 'personal' future. But lifelong education, as will be discussed, most clearly reflects John Dewey's vision of education.

Although he did not write specifically about adult education, Dewey did explicitly refer to adults learning, and to the fact that all adults would continue to learn throughout life if their earlier education had sown the seeds for continuity of the learning process, thus giving everyone 'a fair chance to act as a trustee for a better human life.' (Dewey, 1922: 97) According to Dewey, this continuity, or lifelong learning, would be achieved through his notion of growth.

This chapter briefly discusses Dewey's theory of growth as it appears in a selection of his works during the period 1886–1938, the last being the year in which his publication *Experience and Education* appeared, in an attempt to view his educational philosophy (culminating in this publication) from a lifelong education perspective.

LIFELONG EDUCATION AND DEWEY'S THEORY OF GROWTH

Because Dewey is so closely associated with the earliest phase of the educational enterprise, his views and potential influence in later phases are rarely given the attention they deserve. Yet pervading his works is the belief that education, being concerned with growth, is truly lifelong, since humans are capable of 'growing' intellectually throughout life, and that whereas schooling is a prerequisite for efficient and effective early learning, all of life's experiences and resources, from preschool to old age, in and outside the school, could play meaningful parts in an individual's education. As a pragmatist he emphasized the empirical basis of knowledge. He believed that continuity involved connectedness and that it was folly (in educational and humane terms) to separate a phase in life from the whole of life itself:

> Education should not cease when one leaves school… The inclination to learn from life itself and to make the conditions of life such that all will learn in the process of living is the finest product of schooling (Dewey, 1964: 51).

Underpinning this sentiment is a recognition that we cannot receive all the education for life during the few years traditionally devoted to compulsory schooling, and a belief that there is immanent in everyone an ability to grow personally, intellectually and, as a result, socially, during and well beyond school years.

Dewey wrote over 700 articles, books, abstracts and lectures on philosophy, democracy, learning and education during his lifetime and it is generally agreed that during the period 1882–1939 he revised and restated more clearly some of his ideas in the form of 'rejoinders' (Schilpp, 1939). This revision of his ideas is often referred to. However, an all-pervading and unchanging theme running through his educational writings is that of growth as a result of educative experiences, which enables an individual to assimilate something from each new experience, add it to the next, and thus change and improve his or her views and actions as a result of this ongoing, lifelong process. *Experience and Education*, for example, published in 1938, is a result of being personally aware of this process, plus a response to critical analysis that distanced and revealed the strengths and weaknesses of his ideas. In 1938 the idea of growth is still central to his theory of education, and rather than being a complete reconstruction of his earlier ideas, the publication is a logical evolution of his thinking. He practised what he preached.

> I seem to be unstable, chameleon like…; struggling to assimilate something from each (influence) and yet striving to carry it forward in a way that is logically consistent with what has been learned from its predecessors (Dewey, 1979e: 22).

It is less important that we all believe alike than that we all alike inquire freely and put at the disposal of one another such glimpses as we may obtain of the truth for which we are in search.

Criticism by means of give and take of discussion is an indispensable agency in effecting (this) clarification (Dewey, 1939b: 607).

LIFELONG EDUCATION

The lifelong education movement is usually associated with the United Nations Educational, Scientific and Cultural Organization (UNESCO). It makes a plea for regarding all of life's resources and experiences, from preschool to the grave, as playing a meaningful part in an individual's education. This education, it claims, should be lifelong since we face a lifetime of novelty and uncertainty as a result of the 'knowledge explosion' and its effects, not only on the role but on the number of roles an individual will have to adapt to in order to contend with accelerating social change. It is an all-pervading theme running through each phase of an unfolding educational process. The theme originates in the adult education phase, but it is not envisaged as that part of the present educational enterprise devoted to the correction of earlier educational deficiencies; nor to the carrying of a few forward from the educational point reached, in 'chaste isolation' from the rest of the educational enterprise (Paterson, 1979: 38); nor indeed as a movement established to solve problems of access to existing provision, as, say, continuing education is largely expected to do (Griffin, 1979: 81–85). It is a (speculative) idea for a completely different way of educating not only adults but children and young adults too. It offers a unifying philosophy for education to be seen as a whole, with each phase working in collaboration with another. This does not, however, imply uniformity of strategy but rather unity of purpose, since much will depend upon local and individual circumstances. Its ultimate aim is to maintain and improve the quality of life – in the face of change and uncertainty – and it wholly recognizes that such a process cannot but be begun during school years. Lifelong education does not, therefore, seek to provide a service appended to the main educational provision as an:

> intermittent peripheral activity only engaged in by people with the necessary time, money and energy. The major purpose of education cannot remain the inculcation of knowledge and skills, but should become the development of intellectual and psychological capacities that enable people to learn continuously for the rest of their lives. (Boshier, 1980: 2)

Lifelong education is thus opposed to the isolated development of the academic mind, of abstract intellectualism to the exclusion of virtually all else. Unlike the Greek school, advocates of lifelong education are concerned with the potency of mind – all minds – with the directive, regulative and disciplinary aspect of intelligence. It does not begin with absolutes or end with ultimate truths. It does not seek separatist educational and social aims. It is in the business of affording everyone the power to achieve a sense of self-actualization, a strong sense of identity, and recognizes fully that the intellect does function effectively throughout life (vertical integration).

> As a result, it is seen as serving to facilitate psychological development throughout life, and lifelong education is proposed as the organizing principle which will make it possible for education to function in this way. (Cropley, in Dave 1976: 196)

On the other hand, lifelong education does not abandon the purely 'academic', but rather embraces it, as for some it will be the means or end of self-actualization. It recognizes the legitimacy, for any individual, of academic, vocational, professional, recreational, community pursuits, etc, with parity of esteem, regarding them all as potentially instrumental in achieving the goal of identity and self-actualization. It demands equality of access to a fully horizontally and vertically integrated process of education throughout the whole of life.

The concept of lifelong education embraces the basic notion of relating school (and later, college, university, etc) learning to the whole sphere of life, but, of course, makes the significant leap of recognizing all of life's situations, institutions, professions, etc, as strategically potential educational agencies (horizontal integration), thus formalizing the notion.

The concept, says Suchodolski, is based 'on the idea that the continuous development of man forms an integral part of his existence' (in Dave 1976: 65). This is in complete harmony with Dewey:

> To prepare him (the child) for future life means to give him command of himself:…
> so that he will have the full and ready use of all his capacities (Dewey, 1966a:27).

A living creature lives as truly and positively at one stage as at another, with the same absolute claims. Hence education means the enterprise of supplying the conditions which ensure growth, or adequacy of life, irrespective of age (Dewey, 1964: 51).

Although the notion of lifelong education has been embraced by adult educators, the problem of dissatisfaction with the quality of compulsory education, because it breeds difficulties for later learning, is the same problem over which Dewey took issue. He, however, viewed it from the early end of the life spectrum.

GROWTH

Growth, according to Dewey, is the reward of education. 'The criterion of the value of school education is the extent to which it creates a desire for continued growth and supplies means for making the desire effective in fact' (Dewey, 1964:

53). His definition of growth was 'a general and persistent balance of organic activities with the surroundings, and of active capacities to readjust activity to meet new conditions. The former furnishes the background of growth; the latter constitute growing' (Dewey, 1964: 52). This concept rested on forming the disposition – through democratic teaching methods based on sequential problem solving rather than on isolated subjects – to be ever ready for new (educative) experience, able to learn from it and from life itself. This disposition was to be established for every child. An educative experience, selected responsibility by teachers, produced a situation of 'undergoing', and 'trying to transact' (practical and active solving) a problem. Reflecting upon these two aspects of a problem (the one passive and the other active), then perceiving relationships, recognizing significance and being changed by the whole experience, enabled the individual to be prepared to bring the findings of that experience to the next. (This, he asserted, was the way to establish meaning). Thus, he saw a kind of chain reaction set up which, in his view, ended only when life ended, since the habit or disposition would have been set in motion, propelling the individual to go on learning indefinitely from, and modifying, subsequent experiences. If it had been educative, previous experiences would change the objective conditions under which subsequent experiences would occur. At school the experiences would have been contrived by teachers but linked to life outside school also, and others would occur naturally in everyday life, throughout life.

Dewey's notions of growth have been criticized because some would argue that whereas growth is taken as the basic value and result of education, Dewey did not specify the direction or ultimate goal of growth – save itself. But, as Scheffler has pointed out:

> the ideals of intelligence, growth, and freedom, open-ended as they are, are not amorphous or directionless; they make the most stringent of demands upon those who would embody them in human institutions and strive to rear their young by their light. (Scheffler, 1974: 247).

It is clear that Dewey would judge any institution or process according to how far it had succeeded in enabling individuals to develop their innate powers of awareness and analysis. These powers might well differ, depending on each individual's capacity, but the disposition to continue their exercise, indefinitely, in order to bring past experience to bear upon new experience, conditions or problems, was never to be abbreviated. Since this disposition could and should be activated throughout life, something would, Dewey insisted, be learnt as a result of each activation. Thus, experiences become educative, and individuals can learn from life, throughout life. In this way, growth becomes a means and an 'end-in-view' (Dewey, 1938: 225). In other words, growth as a process or means becomes growth as an end, and is called into play again each time this process is required to contend with different (problematic) aspects of life. These would include those associated with personal, vocational, leisure and social life, or with disinterested interest. (There is much to bind Dewey's philosophy and pedagogy to Knowles' andragogy (1978), and perhaps further comparisons might well illuminate the similarities found in the methodology of elementary education and in education for adults.) This is not to say that life would consequently be perfect – he well recognized life's hazards, which have to be confronted, as well as the enrichment which life's experiences can bring.

> The more an organism learns the more it has to learn, in order to keep itself going; otherwise death and catastrophe. If mind is a further process in life, a further process of registration, conservation and use of what is conserved, then it must have the traits it does empirically have: being a moving stream, a constant change which nevertheless has axis and direction, linkages and associations as well as initiations, hesitations and conclusions (Dewey, 1979c: 20).

According to Dewey, therefore, armed with the capabilities for intelligent enquiry and solution, (which are the properties of effective growth) no one would be debarred from being intellectually and personally developed to act confidently, discriminating and acting from a position of wisdom, at every phase of adulthood, and to learn 'from life itself' (Dewey, 1964: 51). This was necessary in order to negotiate life's contingencies, and on a grander scale, so that human beings would be able to select that which contributes to the quality of (all) life. Elitist education for the few was, therefore, dismissed by Dewey. To him, the 'educated person' was one whose innate analytical powers were developed sufficiently to enable him or her to be effective in all aspects of life and work. 'This is what Dewey meant when he said that habits, which are the outcomes of educative experience, are ways or arts for dealing with the environment' (Wingo, 1974: 173). Thus, 'ways of knowing' rather than 'states of knowledge' were of primary importance to Dewey.

These views are similar to those expressed by advocates of lifelong education. For example, Cropley says: 'What is needed is a system in which adult and school learning are seen as part of a continuous fabric' (in Dave, 1976: 209). And 'lifelong education squarely recognizes that learning occurs throughout life' (Dave, 1976: 196). Similarly, Janne writes: 'In lifelong education, learning... becomes a normal, constant dimension of man's entire life' (in Dave, 1976: 129). Not only are these writers describing lifelong learning, they are arguably describing Dewey's view of growth.

To understand Dewey's faith in growth, intelligence and behaviour (all interconnected) they have to be seen in terms of power to reason, which underpins his insistence on problems or practice or tensions to be resolved.

> It (reasoning) begins in tensional situation, and its validity is tested by the pertinency of the plans it develops for the resolution of the conditions that create the tension, or problem' (Dewey, 1939a: 430).

Reasoning, Dewey claimed:

as such, can provide means for effecting the change of conditions but by itself cannot effect it. Only execution of existential operations directed by an idea in which ratiocination terminates can bring about the re-ordering of environing conditions required to produce a settled and unified situation (Dewey, 1939a : 430).

He wished to acknowledge that there is an active as well as a passive dimension to reasoning and intelligence. It is suggested that the controversy is not so much over whether Dewey belittled the 'intellectual' or 'educated' person as over the nature of intellect or intelligence and the method for its nurture. For Dewey it was relative, not fixed, and therefore education was not simply in the business of realizing pre-existing abilities, but rather the reaching out of minds to points which they had not previously touched. It rested on a belief that a person's intellectual power and practice could continue to grow throughout the whole of life, so long as the 'habit' of reasoning, or of intelligent appraisal, or of exercising intellect, or whatever other name is given to clear, potent thinking, was formed and nurtured through applicative learning in early schooling.

Dewey has sometimes been criticized for on the one hand expounding the theory and virtues of limitless growth, and on the other for apparently contradicting himself by seeming to confine his idea of growth through learning experiences to those that concentrate more on the practical and utilitarian than on the intellectual or academic. But it needs to be borne in mind that Dewey suggested that practical and active occupations should be adopted as only the first stage in the learning process. Familiarity and practical pursuits may then lead on to social communication; the exchange of ideas in a social content, guided or facilitated by a teacher, for example. The third stage is a growing ability to organize, analyse and to synthesize, all of which underpin mastery of knowledge – however defined (see Dewey, 1964). It is not so much 'subject matter' that Dewey rejected as the manner in which it was used or communicated – usually in terms of the teacher's experience. This meant (and to an extent still means) that children have to identify themselves and their activities in terms of other people, associations, and so on. Children were regarded as 'inexperienced', and particularly because of the US essentialist tradition, this largely remained so for much of their learning lives. Common practice was to begin with the teacher's experience in order to broaden (vicariously) the pupil's experience. The pyramid process in the United Kingdom has long been designed to introduce, at the age of about 11 years, probably the widest subject-based curriculum that learners are ever likely to meet. It is gradually whittled away until 'interest' or 'ability' is discovered in a number of subjects to be taken at, say, General Certificate of Secondary Education Ordinary Level examinations. Those who are 'unmotivated' are led back to what does interest them (hardly surprisingly, the quickest way out of the pyramid) and to find an exit at the top by way of employment, a Youth Training Scheme or a college vocational course. It is perhaps salutary to reflect upon the possibilities of turning the traditional pyramid over, resting it on a corner, and beginning with a pupil's interest, allowing other interests to develop out from there. There may be a case for gradually widening rather than reducing the angle of the pyramid.

Dewey's critics would claim that by confining his idea of growth to practical pursuits he narrowed his field of vision to the parochial, while professing the adoption of a very wide, universal vision. He did indeed advocate a practical, scientific and active approach to learning, which was consistent with his pragmatic philosophical stance. Also, his critics might argue that unless lifelong education is purely utilitarian or vocational in direction (which, since it embraces all kinds of education, it is not), Dewey's notion of growth would not bear comparison with the ideas found in lifelong education.

Poole (1975: 138–49), for example, has criticized Dewey for his remark that 'the simple facts of the case are that in the great majority of human beings the distinctively intellectual interest is not dominant. They have the so-called practical impulse and disposition' (Dewey, 1966c: 98). However, Dewey qualified this by highlighting the fact that most US children left school as soon as they had acquired the rudiments of learning sufficient to get them employment, because they had to. 'While our educational leaders are talking of culture... as the... aim of education, the great majority of those who pass under the tuition of the school regard it as only a narrowly practical tool with which... to eke out a restricted life' (Dewey, 1966c : 98). He did not, however, advocate the removal of all that is cultural but rather the marriage of both 'cultural' and 'technical' in the curriculum, with parity of esteem. His practical approach to learning may be translated into a 'relating' or horizontally integrating approach – as found in lifelong education.

> To realize what an experience, or empirical situation, means, we have to call to mind the sort of situation that presents itself outside of school. And careful inspection of methods which are permanently successful will reveal that they depend for their efficiency upon the fact that they go back to the type of situation that causes reflection out of school in ordinary life. They give the pupils something to do, not something to learn; and the doing is of such a nature as to demand thinking, or the intentional noting of connections; learning naturally results (Dewey, 1964: 154).

> If we were to introduce... the activities which appeal to those whose dominant interest is to do and to make, we should find the hold of the school upon its members to be more vital, more prolonged, containing more of culture (Dewey, 1966c; 99).

Poole also claims that Dewey decried the use of textbooks because of the non-active process of acquiring knowledge therefrom. Poole argues: 'Is thought inactive?... What is wrong with absorbing through a book accumulated knowledge?... Books can engage a reader actively giving him a knowledge of things which his own practical experience cannot provide' (Poole, 1975: 143). However, Dewey has again qualified what he meant by such statements as: 'Most objectionable of all is the probability that... the book or the teacher, will supply solutions ready-made' (Dewey, 1964: 157–58). What Dewey is at pains to point out is that the content of a book should not necessarily be an end in itself, but rather used for 'suggestions, inferences, conjectured meanings, suppositions, tentative explanations; ideas, in short... The data arouse suggestions... Inference is always an invasion into the unknown, a leap from the known' (Dewey, 1964: 158). He censured the use to which books were put, ie meaningless regurgitation, particularly rote learning for 'pupils who have stored their "minds" with all kinds of material which they have never put to intellectual uses are sure to be hampered when they try to think' (Dewey, 1964 :158). 'A book (or a letter) may institute a more intimate association between human beings separated... from each other than exists between dwellers under the same roof' (Dewey, 1964 :5). And it can be argued that there is an instrumental aspect to the study of literature, for example. As Dewey said in *Lectures for the First Course in Pedagogy:*

> Literature as a key to life behind it, or as a mode of interpretation, deserves all that has ever been said in its favour... It is the record of his consciousness of the value contained in that (social) experience. There comes a time when experience is so laden with meaning, that... this meaning breaks through the outer form in which that meaning is bound up. It becomes possible for men to see that their experiences have a value that goes beyond momentary occurrence (Dewey, 1979a: 172–73).

Then there is Peters' (1977) point that much is lost in the purely theoretical sense if our cultural heritage is introduced to children only by stressing its relevance to current practical and social situations. He claims that what is not immediately relevant is deemed by Dewey to be unworthy of inclusion in the educational experiences designed to help people to grow. Dewey did say, however, 'culture is also something personal; it is cultivation with respect to application of ideas and art and broad human interests' (Dewey, 1964: 121). What Dewey was pointing to here was the application, rather than just the passive storing, of the ideas and interests introduced through education. As a humanist he was primarily interested in what education could actually do in 'liberating human intelligence' (Dewey, 1964: 230).

> Social efficiency as an educational purpose should mean cultivation of power to join freely and fully in shared or common activities. This is impossible without culture, while it brings a reward in culture, because one cannot share in intercourse with others without learning – without getting a broader point of view and perceiving things of which one would otherwise be ignorant. (Dewey, 1964: 123)

He argued for a synthesis, for reflection on human methods and interests; that the present should be reflected upon by recapitulating the past and anticipating the future.

By 1925 Dewey said, 'those who start with a coarse, everyday experience must bear in mind the findings of the most competent knowledge, and those who start from the latter must somehow journey back to the homely facts of daily existence' (Dewey, 1979c: 21). Dewey's view of culture was a personal one as opposed to one of 'ism'. 'And there is perhaps no better definition of culture than that it is the capacity for constantly expanding the range and accuracy of one's perception of meanings' (Dewey, 1964: 123). It is a matter of common sense that this cannot be achieved by ignoring the 'theoretical'. All that Dewey is doing is to couch his definition in an active rather than a passive context. 'Learning is active. It involves reaching out of the mind' (Dewey, 1966b: 127). And in response to the accusation that there is little room for the speculative and imaginative in Dewey's practical approach, by 1938 he was able to say, 'the environment, in other words, is whatever conditions interact with personal needs, desires, purposes, and capacities to create the experience which is had. Even when a person builds a castle in the air he is interacting with the objects which he constructs in fancy' (Dewey, 1971: 44). Thus, imagination and creativity, as well as utility, have a meaningful place in Dewey's theory.

The foregoing sentiments signify a far wider perspective on Dewey's part than has been suggested by either Poole or Peters. They also emphasize his view that mastery of the learning process – 'learning to learn' – is more important than the 'encyclopaedic' content of learning, and is in complete accord with lifelong education's call for reform of compulsory education, as outlined by Janne (in Dave, 1976: 152–3).

Dewey's idea of growth emerges also in his views on secondary and further/higher education.

> After all, the period from, say, fourteen to twenty-two is a comparatively short portion of a normal lifetime. The best that education can do during these years is to arouse intellectual interests that carry over (Dewey, 1979b: 212).

He called for education to 'awaken some permanent interest and curiosity' (Dewey, 1979b: 212). So far as the quality of the educational experiences during those years is concerned, be had this to say:

> Its freshness and vitality may be restored by making it what it should be, the renaissance of the individual mind, the period of self-consciousness in the true sense of knowledge of self in relation to the larger meanings of life (Dewey, 1979b: 225).

It could be argued that it is precisely because this has not materialized that few are able to 'learn from life itself', and that a significant part of adult education is beleaguered by the need to fulfil a remedial rather than an augmentative and enhancing role.

Dewey is not, of course, unique in his view that early education 'sets the scene' for effective learning throughout adolescence and beyond, but most comparable theories (eg those of Rousseau, Pestalozzi or Froebel) associate an end of education with mature adulthood. It is this (seemingly) generally accepted view today that weakens the case for provision of adult education. Implicit in Dewey's idea of growth, however, is the notion that curiosity and a disposition to learn can carry over into adult life, and that people would want to learn more as their lives progressed once that disposition had been established. Thus he claimed that 'education as growth or maturity should be an ever-present process' (Dewey, 1971: 50).

Whereas this may not lay the only foundation for lifelong learning and education it is clear that in spirit there is a very strong affinity between Dewey's philosophy and that of lifelong education. Dewey's notions do more than suggest that a mature adult, having experienced appropriate early education, has received all the education he or she will need for his or her future. In the late 1980s, Dewey's earlier ideal of promoting ongoing learning changed to an imperative, if only in socio-economic terms. It becomes clear, therefore, why he is regarded as the philosophical founder-father of lifelong education.

Dewey's wish that an adult would no longer review his or her life and see it as a 'scene of lost opportunities and wasted powers' (Dewey, 1964: 51) is pertinent to any discussion about adult education. His plea for a reformed educational enterprise to equip its wards with the capability to fashion for themselves (through growth) a way of life for which they have respect and conjoint responsibility, his belief in the continuity of learning, his acceptance of a wide spectrum of educational activities cutting across the traditional academical-vocational divide, his faith in the educational value of a broad horizontal integration of school and community, his egalitarian outlook and strongly pragmatic, holistic philosophy, stamp his educational works clearly with the spirit of lifelong education.

CONCLUSION

It is argued that Dewey's theory of growth could have been written for lifelong education.

> What he has learned in the way of knowledge and skill in one situation becomes an instrument of understanding and dealing effectively with the situations that follow. The process goes on as long as life and learning continue. (Dewey, 1971: 44)

> In a certain sense every experience should do something to prepare a person for later experiences of a deeper and more expansive quality. That is the very meaning of growth, continuity, reconstruction of experience. (Dewey, 1971: 47)

This is in complete accord with Suchodolski:

> Man can find his vocation and his happiness only by constantly exceeding the boundaries of what he has already achieved. New horizons of cognition and new spheres of activity are made the source as well as the consequences of lifelong education (Suchodolski, 1976: 64).

The spirit of lifelong education may be traced in Dewey's thought from the late 1890s through to 1939. (Leaders in the adult schools movement, in the cooperative colleges, mechanics' institutes, people's colleges, working men's colleges, etc, had religious, philanthropic and/or intellectual ideals for adult education, but tended to express them either in compensatory terms, or as extra to the main provision. They tended not to demand reform of all education – as does lifelong education.)

References to the growth of the individual can, of course, be found in earlier writings, eg Comenius, Kant, Pestalozzi and Froebel. Dewey's view of growth, however, was not the same as Pestalozzi's, or as Froebel's 'unfoldment'. Earlier views of development or growth were finite. The seedling grew into a plant (a popular analogy) and there the process eventually ended – in full-bloom adulthood. For Dewey, however, growth was not finite; his philosophical stance was pragmatic but humanist rather than Christian-idealist, and his psychological outlook was organic but non-finite. For him, development and learning were able to continue throughout adult life.

Dewey's thorough analysis, and call for reform, of the nature, purpose and methodology of initial education, found especially in *Democracy and Education* can, it is posited, be regarded as the trans-Atlantic origins of 20th-century lifelong education thought. (Yeaxlee, 1925, may be regarded as his British, spiritual/Christian counterpart.) His pragmatic philosophy with its unifying and mediating perspective, striving to weld theory and practice, to hold an holistic view of the problems posed by human life, continually informed and influenced his educational theory, and is easily traced in his attempts to integrate learning and living, school and life, and in his views on learning throughout life. It is impossible in a brief space to do more than suggest that Dewey's thinking is as important to lifelong education as it is to initial education. His writings certainly bear comparison with the many descriptive details, strategies, analyses and discussions of lifelong education.

As R J Roth has expressed it, 'future thought in America' (and for the purpose of this discussion, in lifelong education) 'must go beyond Dewey… though it is difficult to see how it can avoid going through him' (in Scheffler, 1974: 190).

REFERENCES

Boshier, R (1980) *Towards a Learning Society*, Learning Press, Vancouver

Cropley, A J (1976) Some Psychological Reflections, in *Foundations of Lifelong Education*, ed R H Dave, Pergamon Press, London

Dave, R H (1976) *Foundations of Lifelong Education*, Pergamon Press, London

Dewey, J (1922) *Human Nature and Conduct: An introduction to social psychology*, H Holt & Co, New York

Dewey, J (1939a) Logic: The theory of inquiry, in *The Philosophy of John Dewey*, ed P A Schilpp, George Banta, Wisconsin

Dewey, J (1939b) Experience, Knowledge and Value: A rejoinder, in *The Philosophy of John Dewey*, ed P A Schilpp, George Banta, Wisconsin

Dewey, J (1964) *Democracy and Education*, Macmillan, London

Dewey, J (1966a) My Pedagogic Creed, in *John Dewey: Selected educational writings*, ed F W Garforth, Heinemann, London

Dewey, J (1966b) The Child and the Curriculum, in *John Dewey: Selected educational writings*, ed F W Garforth, Heinemann, London

Dewey, J (1966c) The School and Society, in *John Dewey: Selected educational writings*, ed F W Garforth, Heinemann, London

Dewey, J (1971) *Experience and Education*, Collier-Macmillan, London

Dewey, J (1979a) Lectures in the First Course in Pedagogy, in *John Dewey as Educator*, ed A G Wirth, R E Krieger, New York

Dewey, J (1979b) Are the Schools doing what People want them to do? in *John Dewey as Educator*, ed A G Wirth, R E Krieger, New York

Dewey, J (1979c) Experience and Nature, in *John Dewey as Educator*, ed A G Wirth, R E Krieger, New York

Dewey, J (1979d) The Way out of Educational Confusion, in *John Dewey as Educator*, ed A G Wirth, R E Krieger, New York

Dewey, J (1979e) From Absolutism to Experimentalism, in *Doctrines of the Great Educators*, ed J Scotland, Macmillan, London

Flude, I R and Parrott, A (1979) *Education and the Challenge of Change*, Open University Press, Milton Keynes

Garforth, F W (1966) *John Dewey: Selected educational writings*, Heinemann, London

Griffin, C (1979) Continuing Education and the Adult Curriculum, *Adult Education*, **52** (2), pp 81–5

Houghton, V and Richardson, K (1974) *Recurrent Education*, Ward Lock, London

Janne, H (1976) Theoretical foundations of lifelong education, in Foundations of *Lifelong Education*, ed R H Dave, Pergamon Press, London

Knowles, M (1978) *The Adult Learner: A neglected species*, Gulf, Houston

Organisation for Economic Cooperation & Development (OECD)/CERI (1973) *Recurrent Education: A strategy for lifelong learning*, OECD, Paris

Paterson, R W K (1979) *Values, Education and the Adult*, Routledge and Kegan Paul, London

Peters, R S (1977) *John Dewey Reconsidered*, Routledge and Kegan Paul, London

Poole, R H (1975) The Real Failure of John Dewey, *Education Review*, **23**, pp 138–49

Scheffler, I (1974) *Four Pragmatists*, Routledge and Kegan Paul, London

Schilpp, P A (1939) *The Philosophy of John Dewey*, George Banta, Wisconsin

Scotland, J (1979) *Doctrines of the Great Educators*, Macmillan, London

Suchodolski, B (1976) Philosophical Aspects, in *Foundations of Lifelong Education*, ed R H Dave, Pergamon Press, London

Wingo, G M (1974) *Philosophies of Education: An introduction*, D C Heath & Co, Massachusetts

Wirth, A G (1979) *John Dewey as Educator*, R E Krieger, New York

Yeaxlee, B A (1925) *Spiritual Values in Adult Education*, Vols I & II, Oxford University Press

Yeaxlee, B A (1929) *Lifelong Education*, Cassell, London

Chapter 5

E L Thorndike

W A Smith

INTRODUCTION

There are few theories of learning that have had as marked an effect upon US educational practice as Thorndike's. Much of this was due to his prodigious volume of writing. An unusually creative scholar, he was author or co-author of more than 500 books and articles. His influence on psychological and educational thinking has been worldwide. Much of his time and attention was devoted to theoretical aspects of learning, but even more to the applied aspects and classroom situations. The specificity of Thorndike's theory contributed much to its applicability.

Thorndike suggested that the learner was an individual ready to make certain responses, capable of varying those responses, and attempting to respond to the aspects of a stimulus situation that appeared familiar to previously successful responses in similar situations. In order to develop the learner's potentials efficiently, he suggested the following teacher tasks:

1. to determine the particular response desired to a given stimulus;
2. to develop an orderly progression of the parts of the task from simple to complex; and
3. to identify the specific elements of a learning task and present them in a way providing the most favourable opportunity for eliciting the correct response, which could then be rewarded (Thorndike, 1917: 7–10).

As the learner experienced repetition and reward to the correct responses, he or she would cleave to those that were desired and gradually eliminate those that were inappropriate. While Thorndike did not deny that insightful learning occurred, he believed it to be a most infrequent form of learning. Therefore, McClusky has suggested that his theory of learning is a much better explanation of the quasi-mechanical learning of early childhood than it is of the more complex learning of the adult years (Grabowski, 1970: 80–95).

BRIEF HISTORY

Edward Lee Thorndike was born at Williamsburg, Massachusetts, USA, in 1874. He was educated at Wesleyan (Conn), Harvard, and received a PhD from Columbia University. His career of 42 years, was spent at Teachers College, Columbia University, save for one year at Western Reserve University, Cleveland, Ohio. James E Russell, then dean of Teachers College, brought Thorndike to the faculty at Columbia, where he remained until his death. His two brothers were also professors at Columbia: Ashley Horace Thorndike (1871–1933) was an authority on Elizabethan drama, Lynn Thorndike (1882–1965) a medieval historian. Thorndike died at Montrose, New York, in 1949.

The emphasis upon the scientific method at the beginning of the 20th century resulted in making Thorndike a transitional figure in the history of education. He represents a transition from the philosophical approach in the association of ideas to the experimental approach in association through physiological stimulus-response observations.

Thorndike was responsible for many of the early applications of psychology to such fields as arithmetic, algebra, reading, handwriting, and language. Other major contributions include works on the theory of psychological tests and compilations of the words occurring most frequently in English reading matter.

Best known is his three-volume work *Educational Psychology* (1913-14). For our purposes, his work *Adult Learning* (1928) is of major importance. Additional works of special interest treat the behaviour of animals; prediction of vocational success; wants, interests, and attitudes; and principles of education. Some of the better-known publications include *The Psychology of Arithmetic* (1922), *The Measurement of Intelligence* (1926), *The Fundamentals of Learning* (1932), *A Teacher's Word Book of 20,000 Words* (1921, later revised), and *Thorndike-Century Junior Dictionary* (1935).

EARLY INFLUENCES

The events of the late 19th century and the early 20th century, which led to the 'new psychology' movement, greatly influenced Thorndike. Darwin published his *Origin of the Species* (1859) just 15 years before Thorndike was born. Thorndike was five years old when the first experimental laboratory for the study of psychology was established at Leipzig by William Wundt. Ebbinghaus was just a young man when Thorndike was born. G Stanley Hall established the first psychological research laboratory in the USA at Johns Hopkins while Thorndike was a teenager. By the time Thorndike was doing his early work there were only 26 of these laboratories in the United States.

The journals that were to carry Thorndike's reports were just beginning to be published. Hall founded the *American Journal of Psychology* in 1887. Cattell, Thorndike's professor at Columbia, founded P*sychology Review* the year he left Wesleyan and went to Harvard. The American Psychological Association was founded in 1892. This was one year before Thorndike entered college. Thorndike himself helped establish the *Journal of Educational Psychology* in 1910.

He became identified as an experimenter in psychology at the time in which the philosophical associationism of Hobbes, Locke, Hume, Hartley and Mill was accepted. The more scientific studies of Wundt, Ebbinghaus, Morgan, Hall, James and Cattell were just beginning to gain attention. Though he was influenced by both streams of thought, he preferred to be identified with the latter. He said 'it is the vice or misfortune of thinkers about education to have chosen the methods of philosophy or of popular thought instead of those of science' (1917: 164).

Evolution as stated by Darwin was one of the strongest influences from the historical tradition upon the thinking of Thorndike. Joncich (1962: 5) observes that it was through Darwin's influence that Thorndike placed human beings 'squarely in the animal world', making psychology an important avenue in the study of human behaviour and learning. As early as 1909 Thorndike (1909: 65–80) stated that Darwin had shown psychologists that the mind has a history of thousands of years. The mind could be understood only when one understands its past.

Evolutionary views form the basis of his descriptions of mental life. This can be found in the summary work *Selected Writings from a Connectionist's Psychology* published in 1949, the year of his death. Thorndike (1917: 77) suggests that the intellect is developed in the same way the animal or plant kingdom has developed. The difference between animal and human learning is a matter of quantity (Thorndike, 1931: 168). He compares human and animal learning by saying 'no new kind of brain tissue is needed... nothing save a mere increase in the number of associative neurones' (Thorndike, 1931: 181). Human beings are considered nothing more than a superior animal.

At the point of acceptance of evolution and the scientific method, the old associationism of the earlier philosophical associationists ends and the new physiological associationism begins to influence Thorndike. Perhaps William James influenced him more than any of the others. He encountered the work of James as a student through reading *Psychology*. He later acknowledged this to be the most stimulating book he had read (Thorndike, 1935: 263). Indeed, he used the James home for his early chick experiments. He consistently followed the James approach. He freely acknowledged this in *The Human Nature Club* (1901: vi).

Thorndike emerged from the early period of his life as a part of the 'new psychology' movement. He pioneered in extending the descriptive method of research from animal experiments to human learning, thus applying the new psychology to education.

CONNECTIONISM

In an abbreviated account of Thorndike's approach, the impression could be given that he was a very systematic writer. His 'system', with the exception of a few persistent preferences, is in fact a rather loose collection of rules and suggestions. What Thorndike called a 'law' at any one time was a statement that at the time appeared to have some general application. 'No effort was made to retain internal coherence among the concepts used, or to establish any genuine relationship of coordination or subordination among the laws' (Hilgard, 1956: 21).

The physiological nature of human beings underlies the psychology of connectionism and forms the basis for Thorndike's pedagogy. Thorndike said the mind is the 'sum total of the connections between situations which life offers and the responses which the man makes' (1914: 199). Physiological motivation and satisfaction of human wants become of primary importance in the system (1913: 309). Purposiveness in learning is explained as a matter of the superior connection system of human beings. Thorndike said, 'Purposes are as mechanical in their nature and action as anything else' (1931: 122).

Thorndike's S-R formula is derived from this view of the nature of human beings. The changes that occur in behaviour become a matter of changes in the bonds of neurones. He said:

> A man's nature and the changes that take place in it may be described in terms of the responses – of thought, feeling, action, and attitude – which he makes, and of the bonds by which these are connected with the situations which life offers. Any fact of intellect, character or skill means a tendency to respond in a certain way to a certain situation – involves a situation or state of affairs influencing the man, a response or state of affairs in the man, and a connection or bond whereby the latter is the result of the former (1913a).

The primary and secondary laws of learning follow from this physiological view of situation–response–connection.

Humans do not possess at birth all the connection systems they will have later in life. They do have the potential for these connection systems (1917: 2). However, individuals are born with certain connections that form a fund of learnt tendencies found in the 'original arrangement of the neurones in the brain' (1913a: 3) These original connections form the reflexes, instincts and inborn capacities which are classified by Thorndike as unlearnt human behaviour.

The unlearnt human behaviour systems are then classified. From these classifications Thorndike concludes that the 'basic aim of human life' is the 'improvement and satisfaction of wants' (1913a: 123). Humankind changes their environment by eliminating those things that fail to give them satisfaction and by developing those things that give them pleasure. The satisfaction of wants becomes the basic aim for education (1920: 11), the ultimate source of value (1929: 19), and forms the point from which the laws of learning are developed.

The law of readiness

Thorndike says the first guides of learning are certain original satisfiers and annoyers (1913a: 123). He identifies the most characteristic form of learning of both lower animals and human beings as trial-and-error learning, or as he preferred to call it later, learning by selecting and connecting (1913b:11). Satisfaction and annoyance as principles of learning were observed in the animal experiments.

Thorndike said a satisfying state encourages the development of a 'conduction unit (but) an annoying state prevents the development of a conduction unit' (1913a: 124). A conduction unit is whatever makes up a path that is ready for conduction. Hilgard (1956: 1019) argues that Thorndike did not pay much attention to neuroanatomical details and that he talked about neurones to be clear that he was talking about direct impulses to action and not about 'consciousness' or 'ideas'. Hilgard also suggests that it should be remembered that Thorndike's system antedated behaviourism and that physiological language was the most available vocabulary for the objectivist prior to the rise of behaviourism. Actually, Thorndike's 'conduction units' have no precise physiological meaning. If the term 'action tendency' were substituted for 'conduction unit', the psychological meaning of Thorndike's law of readiness would become clearer. 'Readiness thus means a preparation for action' (Hilgard, 1956: 18).

The law of readiness is stated in terms of satisfaction, annoyance and conduction units:

1. When a conduction unit is ready to conduct, conduction by it is satisfying, nothing being done to alter its action.
2. For a conduction unit ready to conduct not to conduct is annoying, and provokes whatever response nature provides in connection with that particular annoying lack.
3. When a conduction unit unready for conduction is forced to conduct, conduction by it is annoying (Thorndike, 1913a: 128)

Thorndike was careful to point out: 'To satisfy is not the same as to give sensory pleasure and to annoy is not the same as to give pain' (1913a: 124). Among humans, satisfaction and annoyance may be emotional and subjective. Also, it should be pointed out that Thorndike's law of readiness was a law of preparatory adjustment, not a law of growth.

The law of exercise

The law of exercise has a history as old as learning. The early associationist thought repetition had something to do with fixing ideas in the mind. The work of Ebbinghaus on memory indicates this approach.

At first, Thorndike called this law the law of habit (1917: 166). In 1911, he changed the wording of his statements and called it the law of exercise (1911: 244). In 1913, the law of exercise was subdivided into the laws of use and disuse (1914: 70). The law of use is stated in relation to a situation. Thorndike says: 'A modifiable connection being made by him between a situation S and a response R, man responds originally, other things being equal, by an increase in the strength of that connection…' (1914).

The law of disuse is similarly stated in relation to a situation. He says: 'A modifiable connection not being made by him between a situation S and a response R, during a length of time T, man responds originally, other things being equal, by a decrease in the strength of that connection' (1914).

Hilgard suggests that in *The Fundamentals of Learning* (1932) and *The Psychology of Wants, Interests, and Attitudes* (1935) Thorndike renounced the law of exercise as a law of learning in his later revisions (1956: 25). However, Thorndike had much earlier stated that he did not believe that frequency alone would produce improvement and retention. As early as 1912 he said, 'mere practice does not make perfect' (1956: 11). He continued to say that repetition must be accompanied with interest and zeal (1914: 12).

The law of effect

Alexander Bain is credited with having first formulated a law of effect in 1877 (Pax, 1937: 117). James (1893: 549) modified the view of Bain by relating the pleasure–pain principle to idea-motor action. Thorndike (1911) developed his own conclusions from the experiments done on animal intelligence.

Satisfaction and annoyance combine with the idea of the possibility of human modifiability in their relation to the law of effect. The original satisfiers and annoyers provide the source of human desires and aversions furnishing the guides for learning. Satisfaction and annoyance also lead to the development of reflexes, instincts and capacities in humans (Thorndike, 1914: 69). These form the basis for human modifiability.

Human behaviour, like animal behaviour, is modifiable because bonds between a situation and a response grow stronger when accompanied by satisfaction. They weaken when accompanied by annoyance (Thorndike, 1913b: 11–12) Thorndike stated the law of effect in these terms:

> When a modifiable connection between a situation and a response is made and is accompanied or followed by a satisfying state of affairs, that connection's strength is increased; when made and accompanied by an annoying state of affairs, its strength is decreased. The strengthening effect of satisfyingness (or weakening effect of annoyingness) upon the bond varies with the closeness of the connection between it and the bond (Thorndike, 1913: 4).

When he published his major work on educational psychology in 1913 these three primary laws of learning were considered as being complete. He said: 'One form of misunderstanding these laws consists in supposing the necessity of additional factors' (1913b: 21). He also felt the law of effect was primary and irreducible to the law of exercise. The two together were considered the moving force in all learning (1913a: 192).

One of the major events in Thorndike's career was the revisions he made in his laws during the later period. He launched a series of experiments in the second decade of the 20th century on the modification of human behaviour. When he announced the results of this work, some significant revisions in the statement of the laws came forth.

Thorndike claimed at the Ninth International Congress of Psychology in 1929 that he had been wrong about the law of effect. Materials written from 1932 to 1935 indicate this revision, plus others regarding the influence of punishment upon connections.

He no longer considered satisfaction and annoyance as being a complete and exact parallelism (1949: 37). He said:

> In general, punishment compares very unfavorably with reward in dependability. Unless it is a means of inducing a person to shift then and there to a right connection that is then and there rewarded, it may involve waste or worse (1949: 56).

> Rewards in general tend to maintain and strengthen any connection that leads to them. Punishments often but not always tend to shift from it to something else, and their educative value depends on what that something else is... (1949: 38)

These statements on punishment indicate quite a revision of the earlier statements made in connection with the law of effect. Thorndike interpreted his findings when he suggested: 'The results of all comparisons by all methods tell the same story. Rewarding a connection always strengthened it substantially; punishing it weakened it little or not at all' (1932: 58).

While doing these later experiments in human behaviour, Thorndike derived a new principle that relates to the law of effect. He called it the principle of belongingness.

Belongingness

Thorndike asked the question: 'In particular, what results in respect to the probability that A therefore will evoke B?' (1932: 63). He concluded that mere sequence and repetition would not cause A to evoke B.

These later experiments led him to believe that sequence should be accompanied by belongingness. He decided that the sense of belonging need not be 'logical or essential, or inherent, or unifying.' He said 'any "this goes with that" will suffice' (1949: 68). According to this principle, a connection is more easily learnt if the response belongs to the situation, and an after-effect does better if it belongs to the connection it strengthens. The belongingness of a reward or punishment depends upon its appropriateness in satisfying an aroused motive or want in the learner, and in its logical or informative relationship to the activities rewarded or punished (Thorndike, 1935: 52–61).

Thorndike also developed secondary laws of learning that were derived from the study of animals. He says they are 'secondary in scope and importance only to the laws of readiness, exercise, and effect' (1913b: 12).

Secondary laws of learning

Five secondary laws of learning are stated. They are:

1. multiple response to the same situation;
2. multiple response to varied reaction;
3. set, attitude, or adjustment, or determination;
4. assimilation or analogy;
5. associative shifting (Thorndike, 1913b: 12–15).

The first law relates to the multiple responses made by animals in the open. The law of multiple response and varied reaction relates to human learning. When a learner faces a new situation he or she will try one thing or another. The response that brings satisfaction or success will eliminate the other responses.

The law of set, attitude, or adjustment, or determination suggests that the total set of the learner serves as a guide for learning. Thorndike says: 'Consequently it is a general law of learning that the change made in a man by the action of any agent depends upon the condition of the man when the agent is acting' (1914: 144).

The law of partial or piecemeal activity states that the learner can pick out the element of a situation and base his or her response on it. Humans are better than other animals at eliminating features of situations that do not relate to the desired response (1914: 145). This law explains analytical and insightful learning, according to Thorndike (Hilgard, 1956: 23).

Explanation of how human beings react to a novel situation is set forth in the law of assimilation or response by analogy. New responses can be explained in terms of past learnt experiences plus the original nature of human beings. Thorndike says: 'To any new situation man responds as he would to some situation like it, or like some element of it' (1914: 148).

The law of associative shifting relates to the idea of conditioned response. Thorndike said that a response series may change to a new stimulus by successively dropping and adding new elements to it (1914).

Thorndike's connection model of education begins with the human organism in a situation. The primary and secondary laws of learning were developed from the principle of the organism being placed in a situation to respond originally from its satisfiers and annoyers. The satisfaction of human wants provides the basis for motivation leading to both motor and mental activity.

LEARNING IS CONNECTION

Thorndike views mental functions as biological connections. When human biological wants are satisfied, biological connections are formed in the brain. He says that learning is connecting, and human beings are great learners because they can make so many connections (1914:174).

Connections account for the range of learning from the most concrete to the most subtle and abstract. This view of learning led to the early development by Thorndike of a connectionist description of the cognitive process.

He outlined much of *Principles of Teaching* in terms of the cognitive process. Thorndike said one learnt through instinct, attention, habit, memory, correlation, reasoning and ideation (1917: 105–64). A few years later, he described the cognitive process in somewhat different terms. Two general principles were introduced at that time. They are analysis and selection. Thorndike stated:

> We roughly distinguish in human learning:
> 1. connection-forming of the common type, as when a 10-month-old baby learns to beat a drum;
> 2. connection-forming involving ideas, as when a two-year old learns to think of his mother upon hearing a word or to say candy when he thinks of the thing;
> 3. analysis or abstraction, as when the student of music learns to respond to an overtone in a given sound; and
> 4. selective thinking or reasoning, as when a school pupil learns the meaning of a Latin sentence by using his knowledge of the rules of syntax and meanings of the word-roots (1914: 138).

Regardless of the level of learning the major characteristic of it is connecting. Thorndike held this view to the end of his career. As late as 1931 he said expectations, intentions, purposes, interests and desires are explained by the same type of mental connection system as hearing four times five and thinking twenty (1931: 120). Thorndike, 1931:122, says:

> I read facts which psychologists report about adjustments, configurations, drives, integrations, purposes, tensions, and the like, and all of these facts seem to me to be reducible, so far as concerns their powers to influence the course of thought or feeling or action, to connections and readiness. Learning is connecting. The mind is man's connection-system. Purposes are as mechanical in their nature as anything else.

Mental connections in the brain provide the necessary equipment in the organism for analysis and selection of common elements in a situation.

ADULT LEARNING

The descriptions of learning as found in the connectionist model of Thorndike hold true for his concepts of adult learning. During the decade from 1925 to 1935, Thorndike did a great amount of research on adult learning. Most of the work was done for the Carnegie Corporation as recommended by the American Association for Adult Education.

Irving Lorge (1974: 778) summarizes the thinking about the adult learning processes before Thorndike's research:

> Previous to 1925, much of the theory for adult pedagogy either was transferred from the known facts about learning established by studies of children, adolescents or college students, or was based upon anecdotal evidence from the learning experiences of able and successful older men and women. Thorndike's *Adult Learning*, in a sense, was a pioneering effort to determine how and how much adults learn.

Thorndike compared adult with youthful learning. He also compared adults of superior and inferior intellect. His conclusion was that adults can learn. Concerning the modifiability among adults he said:

> On the whole, it seems reasonable to state the case concerning sheer modifiability as follows: The general tendency from all our experiments is for an inferiority of about 15 per cent as a result of 20 years from twenty-two on. Learning representing an approximation to sheer modifiability unaided by past learning shows considerably more inferiority than this. Actual learning of such things as adults commonly have to learn shows considerably less (1928: 106).

Later, Thorndike modified this, indicating that adult learning ability decreased slowly after the age of 25 at the rate of about one per cent per year. He summarized the relationship of learning ability to age:

> In general the testimony of this group indicates:
>
> 1. that almost anything is learnable at any time up to age fifty;
> 2. that the experience of these individuals leads them to expect more difficulty in learning from forty on than from thirty to thirty-nine, except with making and breaking food habits;
> 3. that the difficulty expected from thirty up to forty is no greater than for childhood or adolescent years in the case of intellectual acquisition pure and simple, and;
> 4. that, in general, age seems to them to influence the power of intellectual acquisition very much less than it influences motor skill.
>
> There is evidence also that:
>
> 5. the difficulty expected in learning at late ages is in part due to a sensitiveness to ridicule, adverse comment, and undesirable attention, so that if it were customary for mature and old people to learn to swim and ride bicycles and speak German, the difficulty might diminish (1928: 124).

Intelligence loss, he found to be slight from age between 22 to 42 in the case of strength, speed and skill (1928: 158–59).

Intelligence

There have been two types of data used to deal with the issue of adult intelligence; one is cross-sectional and the other is longitudinal. The research that supported the everyday notion that 'what goes up must come down' was cross-sectional in nature. The researcher administered intelligence tests to people of various ages at a given point in time and compared the performance levels of the different age groups. The first of the cross-sectional type was administered by Thorndike and the results of the research were reported in his volume on *Adult Learning* (1928). Numerous studies of this type were conducted following his work. All led researchers to believe that intelligence increases up to early adulthood, reaches a plateau, and begins to decline in a regular fashion around the fourth decade of life (Baltes and Schaie, 1974: 35).

The first doubts about these intelligence studies arose when the results of longitudinal studies began to be available. In this type of study the researcher observes a single group of subjects for a period of time, often extending over many years, and examines their performance at different ages. Longitudinal studies suggested that intelligence during maturity and old age did not decline as soon as people had originally assumed. In contrast to Thorndike's view that aging is equated with a decline in intellectual capacity is the following 1971 *Recommendation to the White House Conference on Aging* from the American Psychological Association Task Force on Aging:

> Many studies are now showing that the intelligence of older persons as measured is typically underestimated. For the most part, the observed decline in intellectual functioning among the aged is attributable to poor health, social isolation, economic plight, limited education, lowered motivation, or other variables not intrinsically related to the aging process. Where intelligence scores do decline, such change is associated primarily with tasks where speed of response is critical (Eisdorfer and Lawton, 1973: lx).

Baltes and Schaie (1974: 35–36) found that longitudinal test scores reflected four general, fairly independent dimensions of intelligence:

1. Crystallized intelligence which encompasses the sorts of skills one acquires through education and acculturation, such as verbal comprehension, numerical skills, and inductive reasoning;
2. Cognitive flexibility that measures the ability to shift from one way of thinking to another;
3. Visuo-motor flexibility that measures a similar, but independent skill, the one involved in shifting from familiar to unfamiliar patterns in tasks requiring coordination between visual and motor abilities; and

4. Visualization which measures the ability to organize and process visual materials, and involves tasks such as finding a simple figure contained in a complex one.

There was no age-related change in cognitive flexibility. For the most important dimension, crystallized intelligence, and for visualization as well, there was a systematic increase in scores for the various age groups, right into old age. Even people over 70 improved from the first testing to the second. The only decline on the four measures was visuo-motor flexibility. The results of longitudinal studies indicate little, if any, decline in intellectual abilities with age (Botwinick, 1973; Knox, 1977).

Memory

Thorndike conducted memory experiments among adults. He found that adults' immediate memory ability is much better than young children's (1928: 160). The ability for memory over longer periods was less conclusive. He also felt his experiments in retention among adults were to be considered inconclusive (1928: 159–65).

Recent research on short-term and long-term memory, as summarized by Botwinick (1973) and Woodruff and Birren (1975), indicates that young people and old people do not differ in short-term ability. However, there is apparently a decline with age in the rate at which information can be retrieved from short-term memory. With regard to long-term memory, recent investigations have found that older adults perform more poorly than young adults in this ability.

The results of recent research also suggest that loss of speed is one of the most important factors affecting learning. Older adults do poorly on rapidly paced learning tasks because of insufficient time to respond, rather than as a result of learning ability that is impaired (Knox, 1977 and Woodruff and Birren, 1975). Knox (1977) states that older adults tend to do best when they set their own pace, and also that they tend to reduce speed of learning and to give greater attention to the accuracy of their response. In summary, age differences in learning performance can be reduced by giving older adults more time and by slowing the pace.

THEORETICAL APPROACHES TO ADULT EDUCATION

Theoretical approaches to learning can be divided into two main groups: those that can be classified as objective theories and those that can be classified as relational theories. The connectionism of Thorndike falls within the objective classification. Objectivism sees the human being as a passive organism governed by stimuli that are produced by one's environment. Based on this assumption, the objectivists feel that human beings can be controlled or manipulated by structuring their environmental stimuli. Therefore, strict objectivism is only interested in the observables of behaviour (ie, stimuli and responses). It avoids any attempted speculation about the internal complexities of human beings (Dubin and Okun, 1973: 3–19).

Some of the behaviourists (also objectivists) criticized Thorndike, saying his language was too subjective. On close examination, however, one finds that Thorndike said nothing about the feelings of learners; he concerned himself only with what the learners did (ie, their overt behaviour). When addressing this particular point, Hill (1979: 59) stated: 'His language may sound subjective, but his meaning is as objective as Watson's.' Goble (1971: 17–18) states that:

> Nearly all American behavioral scientists since 1920, and frequently much earlier have adopted their study of human behavior to the 'scientific' model. Their basic assumption was that the scientific approach, so tremendously successful in the solution of physical and technical problems could be equally successful in the solution of human problems. The behavioral scientist has believed he must study man as an object – an object to be observed but not questioned.
>
> Subjective information, the opinions of human beings about themselves and their own feelings, desires, and wants were to be ignored.

Alonzo, La Cagnina, Giula and Olsen, (1977: 137) have suggested that even though the individual objective theories might differ somewhat, there are common identifiable characteristics that are associated with and incorporated into each particular theoretical variation, be it Watson's, Thorndike's, Hull's, Dollard's, Skinner's or any of the others.

In contrast to the objectivists who choose to study only extrinsic or external and environmental determinants, the relationalists believe a comprehensive theory of behaviour must also include the internal or intrinsic determinants. The relationalists feel that learning theory has to be much more than just an objective science. To understand completely human behaviour, they believe, the subjective must also be considered (ie, the feelings, desires, hopes and aspirations of human beings). 'To them everyday phenomena of life such as experiences, feelings, meanings, and humor are psychologically relevant' (Milhollan and Forisha, 1970: 82).

It is important to note that the relational orientation considers the whole greater than the sum of its parts. Relational psychology is extremely critical of objectivist scientists who utilize the atomistic approach, attempting to isolate independent drives, urges and instincts, and study them separately. The relationalists indicate that each individual part of human beings is related to the others, and unless you study them as a whole, the answers will be insufficient. Consequently they 'desire a science which considers the whole person and which elevates this prerequisite over any particular concern for method' (Milhollan and Forisha 1970: 97).

The relational approach rejects the objectivist's strong dependence on animal psychology. Although animal psychology can be useful in describing those learning characteristics human beings share with all primates, in their view it ignores those unique characteristics of human beings. Therefore, rather than studying cats, rats, pigeons or other lower animals, the relationalists have chosen to deal with humans themselves. Parker J Palmer (1983: 34–35), writing about adult education, has said:

> In the conventional classroom the focus of study is always outward – on nature, on history, on someone else's vision of reality. The reality inside the classroom, inside the teacher and the students, is regarded as irrelevant; it is not recognized that we are part of nature and of history, that we have visions that are of our own... If we believed that knowing requires a personal relation between the knower and the known (as some new epistemologies tell us) our students would be invited to learn by interacting with the world, not by viewing it from afar. The classroom would be regarded as an integral, interactive part of reality, not a place apart. The distinction between 'out there' and 'in here' would disappear; students would discover that we are in the world and the world is within us; that truth is not a statement about reality but a living relationship between ourselves and the world. But such an epistemology is rarely conveyed by our teaching; instead, objectivism is.

Maslow (1970: 150), one of the most distinguished relational scholars, determined that the goal of learning or education should be self-actualization, that is, 'the full use of talents, capacities, potentialities, etc'.

Rogers found from his experience in psychotherapy that when the human being is functioning freely, he or she is constructive and trustworthy. And it is when the human being is in closest touch with the bedrock of him- or herself that he or she is functioning most freely. It is Rogers' contention that if a learning climate conducive to trust and openness has been successfully created, the learner will make decisions most appropriate to his or her particular stage of growth as a learner (1969: 290).

McClusky mapped out directions for the development of a 'differential psychology of the adult potential' in which the concepts of margin (the power available to a person over and beyond that required to handle his or her load), commitment, time perception, critical periods and self concept are central (Knowles, 1973: 34–35). McClusky suggested that 'the mistake of the original S–R formula has been its reductionist oversimplification of the highly complex nature of the learning process. By overemphasizing both stimulus and response as well as their external character, it has reduced, if not ignored, the unique importance of the person as the agent receiving and often originating the stimulus as well as the one giving the response' (Grabowski, 1970: 80).

The andragogical model of Knowles, in *The Adult Learner: A neglected species*, is a process model, in contrast to the content models employed by most objectivists. Knowles (1973: 45) speculates 'with growing support from research (see Bruner, 1951; Erikson, 1950, 1959, 1964; Getzels and Jackson, 1962; Bower and Hollister, 1967; Iscoe and Stevenson, 1960; White, 1959) that as an individual matures, his need and capacity to be self-directing, to utilize his experience in learning, to identify his own readiness to learn, and to organize his learning around life problems, increases steadily from infancy to pre-adolescence'. Adults are seen as much more problem-centred in their orientation to learning.

While the relational approaches to learning can be applied at any level of learning, they are especially applicable to adult education (Rogers, 1969; McClusky, 1971; Knowles, 1973). The distinction made between these two major approaches might seem to suggest that one should:

1. pick one approach over the other;
2. pick one approach for training and one for education; or
3. take the best from each approach and structure teaching around the one most successful for particular kinds of learning (Knowles, 1973: 93–101).

It is suggested here that the two basic approaches are really two expressions or modes of a singular human learning process and this is depicted in the following diagram.

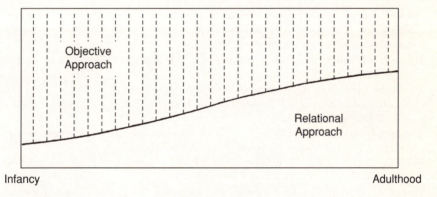

Figure 5.1

The speculation is that children predominantly work out of the mode of objectivism while having some tendency (though less than adults) to learn through relational approaches. As the child moves toward maturity, it is speculated that a shift occurs so that the adult learner works predominantly out of the mode of relationalism while retaining a tendency (though greatly diminished) to learn through the mode of objectivism. If this is true, then an integration of methods for both modes should be developed as one progresses from childhood education to adult education.

Thorndike would have great difficulty with this type of integrated thinking. For him (1931: 122) all of these thoughts could be 'reducible, so far as concerns their powers to influence the course of thought or feeling or action, to connections and readiness. Learning is connecting. The mind is man's connection-system'. For Thorndike, purposes are as mechanical in nature as anything else.

CONCLUSION

Indeed, it may be said of Thorndike that he offered the psychological world of education the first miniature system of learning. This system, however loosely organized, has had a profound influence on the course of learning theory even until this date. His pioneering efforts rank among the greatest in the history of learning. Whatever the ultimate status of Thorndike's basic laws, his theory of learning inaugurated the rise of modern learning theory. His objective approach has generated many questions for the adult educator therefore giving rise to much research in adult learning.

REFERENCES

Alonzo, Thomas M, La Cagnina, Giulia R and Olsen, Bob G (1977) Behaviorism vs. Humanism: Two contrasting approaches to learning theory, *The Southern Journal of Educational Research*, **11** (Sum), pp 135–51

Baltes, Paul B and Schaie, K Warner (1974) The Myth of the Twilight Years, *Psychology Today*, March, pp 35–40

Botwinick, J (1973) *Aging and Behavior*, Springer, New York

Dubin, S S and Okun (1973) Implications of Learning Theories for Adult Education, *Adult Education*, **24**, pp 3–19

Eisdorfer, C and Lawton, M P (eds) (1973) *The Psychology of Adult Development and Aging*, American Psychological Association, Washington, DC

Goble, F G (1971) *The Third Force: The psychology of Abraham Maslow*, Pocket Books, New York

Grabowski, S M (1970) *Adult Learning and Instruction*, ERIC Clearinghouse on Adult Education, Syracuse

Hilgard, Ernest R (1956) *Theories of Learning*, Appleton-Century-Crofts, Inc, New York

Hill, W F (1979) *Learning: A survey of psychological interpretations*, rev edn, Chandler Publishing Co, Scranton

James, William (1893) *Psychology*, Henry Holt Co, New York

Joncich, G M (1962) Selected Writings of Edward L Thorndike: *Psychology and the science of education*, Teachers College Columbia University, New York

Knowles, Malcolm (1973) *The Adult Learner: A neglected species*, Gulf Publishing Company, Houston

Knox, Alan B (1977) *Adult Development and Learning*, Jossey-Bass, San Francisco

Lorge, Irving (1974) Publications from 1889 to 1940 by E Thorndike, *Teachers College Record*, **XLI** (May), pp 778–88

Maslow, A H (1970) *Motivation and Personality*, Harper & Row, New York

Milhollan, F and Forisha, B E (1970) *From Skinner to Fogern: Contrasting approaches to education*, Professional Educators Publication, Inc, Lincoln

Maclinson, C (1936) *History of Psychology in Autobiography – E L Thorndike*, Clarke University Press, Worcester

McClusky, H Y (1971) *Education: Background and issues*, the Fourth White House Conference on Aging, Washington DC

Palmer, Parker J (1983) *To Know as We are Known*, Harper & Row, San Francisco

Pax, W T (1937) *A Critical Study of Thorndike's Theory and Laws of Learning*, Catholic University of America, Washington

Rogers, C R (1969) *Freedom to Learn*, Charles E Merrill Publishing Co, Columbus, Ohio

Thorndike, E L (1901) *The Human Nature Club*, The Chautauqua Press, New York

Thorndike, E L (1909) Darwin's Contributions to Psychology, Chronicle, **XII**, University of California

Thorndike, E L (1911) *Animal Intelligence*, Macmillan & Co, New York

Thorndike, E L (1913a) *Educational Psychology, Vol I: The original nature of man*, Columbia University, New York

Thorndike, E L (1913b) *Educational Psychology, Vol II: The psychology of learning*, Columbia University, New York

Thorndike, E L (1914) *Educational Psychology, Vol III: Mental work and fatigue and individual differences and their causes*, Columbia University, New York

Thorndike, E L (1914) *Educational Psychology: A briefer course*, Columbia University, New York

Thorndike, E L (1917) *The Principles of Teaching based on Psychology*, A G Seiler, New York

Thorndike, E L (1920) *Education: A first book*, Macmillan & Cox, New York

Thorndike, E L (1928) *Adult Learning*, Macmillan & Co, New York

Thorndike, E L (1929) *Elementary Principles of Education*, MacMillan Co, New York

Thorndike, E L (1931) *Human Learning*, Century Co, New York

Thorndike, E L (1932) *Fundamentals of Learning*, Columbia University Press, New York

Thorndike, E L (1935) *The Psychology of Wants, Interests and Attitudes*, Appleton-Century-Crofts, Inc, New York

Thorndike, E L (1949) *Selected Writings from a Connectionist's Psychology*, Appleton-Century-Crofts, Inc, New York

Woodruff, D S and Birren, J E (eds.) (1975) *Aging: Scientific perspectives and social issues*, D Van Nostrand, New York

Chapter 6

Eduard Lindeman

Stephen Brookfield

At the occasion of a testimonial dinner for Eduard Lindeman in 1953, the last year of his life, a letter of tribute from the American Civil Liberties Union declared that 'a catalogue of Dr Lindeman's activities during his first seventy years might lead a careless visitor from Mars to believe that he was not a man but a syndicate'. On the same occasion a letter on behalf of the Adult Education Association of the United States written by Malcolm Knowles, then the Association's administrative coordinator, addressed the Association's tribute to Lindeman with the words 'you have been the one "elder statesman" in the field to whom the younger organizers of the new Adult Education Association have consistently and confidently turned for inspiration, moral support, and wise guidance'. Letters of tribute for this dinner were also received from organizations as diverse as the American Labor Education Service, the International Ladies' Garment Workers' Union, the League for Industrial Democracy, the Society for Ethical Culture, the Planned Parenthood Federation of the USA, the Association on American Indian Affairs, the National Child Labor Education Committee, and the Women's Trade Union League.

The breadth of interests represented in these tributes, and the fact that Lindeman never held an academic appointment as a professor or lecturer in adult education, make it all the more surprising that he should still be regarded as the major philosopher of adult education in the United States. He wrote, after all, only one major work on the field, *The Meaning of Adult Education* (Lindeman, 1926a) and that in the early stages of his career. Yet though his writings on adult education (scattered through these may be and representing only a fraction of his total work), and through his active involvement in adult education committees, associations and programmes, he both articulated and implemented a vision of adult education which still constitutes the conceptual underpinnings of the field of theory and practice in the United States. This can be interpreted both as a testament to the accuracy and power of his vision and as a depressing verdict on the paucity of philosophical analysis that has characterized the US field since his death.

LIFE

Eduard Christian Lindeman was born in St Clair, Michigan, in 1885, one of 10 children of Danish immigrant parents. Orphaned at an early age he worked in a series of labouring jobs in agriculture, shipbuilding, and construction attending formal schooling only intermittently. At 22, however, he managed to gain admittance to a special programme for 'sub-freshmen' at Michigan Agricultural College, later Michigan State University, in East Lansing. Biographers such as Gessner (1956), Konopka (1950) and Rielly (1984) all agree that on his entry to college Lindeman was, if not illiterate, at least well below the average in terms of reading and writing abilities. With the help of a sympathetic college secretary, and a series of jobs on the college farm, however, Lindeman persevered with his studies to the extent that while an undergraduate he authored essays, poetry, editorials for the college newspaper and a four-act play. While at the college he met and married (in 1912) Hazel Taft, the daughter of the chair of the Horticultural Department.

For nine years after his graduation, from 1911 to 1920, Lindeman was employed in a series of different jobs. For a time he was editor of a Michigan agricultural journal, *The Gleaner*, in which some of his earliest published writings are contained. He was assistant to the minister of the Plymouth Congregational Church in East Lansing, 4-H Club extension director based at Michigan Agricultural College, and instructor at the YMCA George Williams College in Chicago. In 1920, however, he obtained his first university teaching post (at the North Carolina College for Women) and he was to stay in university life, apart from the interruption caused by World War Two, until his retirement. Moreover, he was to serve nearly all his time as a professor at only one institution, the New York School of Social Work (later the Columbia University School of Social Work), which he joined as professor of social philosophy in 1924.

It was soon after joining the New York School of Social Work that in 1926 he published his major work on adult education (actually his fourth book) titled *The Meaning of Adult Education*. According to Rielly's biographical sketch (1984), in the 24 years between *The Meaning of Adult Education* and his retirement in 1950, Lindeman published approximately 204 articles, 107 book reviews, 5 books, 16 monographs, and 17 chapters in other works. He edited 4 books, shared joint authorship of another, and gave at least 44 talks of which some written record remains. He was a close friend and advisor of Leonard and Dorothy Elmhirst during their establishing of Dartington Hall in Totnes, the progressive experimental school; in fact the Elmhirst's held the mortgage on the Lindemans' home in New Jersey where the family lived until 1942.

Rielly (1984) records that Lindeman served on the National Child Labor Commission, was education director of the Workers' Education Bureau (of America) from 1926 to 1937 and editor of the journal *Workers' Education*. He was both a lecturer and trustee at the New School for Social Research in New York City, and held visiting professorships at Temple University (1934–35), the University of California (1936 and 1938), Stanford University (1941), Columbia University (1941–42) , the University of Wisconsin (1943) and the University of Delhi, India (1949–50). He was advisory editor to Mentor books (a series he conceived), educational advisor to the British Army of Occupation in Germany (1946), and chair of the American Civil Liberties Union Commission on Academic Freedom (1949). After retirement from the New York School of Social Work in 1950, he undertook numerous speaking engagements in locations as far afield as Texas and Oregon, gave occasional lectures at the New School for Social Research (New York), formed a consultancy group, and served as president of the National Conference of Social Work. He died in New York City in 1953, after an illness.

The breadth of his activities, both intellectual and organizational, means that nowhere in his writings after the early statement in *The Meaning of Adult Education* did Lindeman undertake a sustained elaboration of his ideas on adult education as a field of theory and practice. Indeed, many of his ideas concerning the field are to be found in writings on apparently tangential issues, such as his voluminous pronouncements on the workings of democracy, his work for the birth control organization Planned Parenthood, and his analyses of the pernicious and insidious influence of propaganda in US life.

Nonetheless, it is possible to discern four recurring preoccupations, which engaged his attention as an adult educator throughout his life:

1. his attempt to articulate a clear conceptualization of adult education;
2. his elaboration of appropriate curricula for adult learning groups arising out of this conceptualization;
3. his concern to develop methods of group learning, which he saw as fundamental to adult education as properly conceived and practised; and
4. his belief that adult education was a force for constructive social action.

In addition, he made some telling comments on two important sub-themes in his work: the influence of the capitalist system on education, and the need to reconceptualize the whole educational system in terms of a lifelong learning enterprise. It is to these themes and preoccupations that we now turn.

CONCEPTUALIZATION OF ADULT EDUCATION

In a recent essay on *The Meaning of Adult Education* Stewart (1984: 1) identified as a major omission from the book, a succinct definition of the concept of adult education. The book identifies central principles that are argued as endemic to adult education, but does not articulate a crisp and clear definition. This is surprising since in a paper published the year previously entitled *What is Adult Education?*, Lindeman describes adult education as:

> a co-operative venture in non-authoritarian, informal learning the chief purpose of which is to discover the meaning of experience; a quest of the mind which digs down to the roots of the preconceptions which formulate our conduct; a technique of learning for adults which makes education coterminous with life, and hence elevates living itself to the level of an experiment (Lindeman, 1925: 3).

In this paper he warned against the dangers of faddism and linguistic debauchery, which he felt were confounding attempts to define adult education. A discussion of workers' education and public libraries published in the next year (Lindeman, 1926b) afforded him the opportunity to differentiate adult education from other forms of education. Adult education was held to emphasize the primacy of personal experience. It had as its aim the interpersonal exchange and exploration of such experience, and it relied on discussion methods for this pursuit. The leader of the adult learning group was to be thought of as guide and stimulator, rather than as lawgiver; an early statement of a conceptualization of the educator's role that is now known as that of facilitator. This theme of adult education as the collaborative exploration and interpretation of experience was repeated in his writings and gave rise to the methodological imperative that 'adult education must be confined to small groups and that lectures and mass teaching are automatically eliminated' (Lindeman, 1926a: 11). To Lindeman the current interest in adult education using distance teaching methods and educational broadcasting (as in the Open University in the United Kingdom), or through individual computer usage, would have been not only inexplicable, but a contradiction in terms. These activities would have been scorned as mass instruction or programmed instruction, rather than the collaborative articulation and interpretation of experience claimed by him as the quintessential adult educational activity.

In a later digression on conceptualizing adult education, Lindeman (1938) identified two opposing paradigms of thought within US adult education concerning what educators felt to be the proper realm of practice. The first of these, what he called the mechanistic school, viewed adult education as the extension of existing forms of education to the illiterate and underprivileged. To Lindeman this approach was naive, instrumental and essentially static. He contrasted its truth with what was called an organic conception of adult education. In the organic conception adult education was not seen as an extension of existing privilege to a new population, but rather as 'a right, a normal expectancy' (1938: 3). The idea that adult educators were bountiful philanthropists, bestowing their intellectual gifts on a disadvantaged but eternally grateful population, was repugnant and arrogant.

The single, best-known statement of his ideas on the nature of adult education is contained in the four principles argued as endemic to the field in *The Meaning of Adult Education* (1926a). Education was, first and foremost, conceived as a lifelong process, and to regard it as preparation for an unknown future was to condemn teachers and students to intellectual stasis. Second, adult education was held to be unreservedly of a non-vocational character. He wrote that 'adult education more accurately defined begins where vocational education leaves off' (1926a: 5) and condemned the fact that 'the possibilities of enriching the activities of labor itself grow less for all workers who manipulate automatic machines' (1926a). In his view, for workers to experience 'the good life, the life interfused with meaning and with joy, opportunities for expressing more of the total personality than is called forth by machines will be needed' (1926a). It was the task of adult education to assist these workers to find meaning and creative fulfilment in the areas of their lives separate from the factory and to counter the development of fractional personalities seen as the inevitable consequence of a highly specialized division of labour. This defiant rejection of adult education having any involvement with vocational training was characteristic of all his writings. Indeed, in one of the last pieces he published he reaffirmed his conviction that adult education 'is wholly lacking in coercive or compulsive elements' and that it is 'an act of free will' (1953: 18). Such unequivocal declarations concerning the centrality of voluntary learner participation in adult education have provided valuable sustenance for current opponents of mandatory continuing education in the United States (Rockhill, 1983).

The third principle of adult education – that we emphasize situations, not subjects, in our teaching – calls to mind the progressive educators' epithet that 'we teach children, not subjects'. Lindeman was a personal friend and occasional intellectual collaborator of John Dewey, and the emphasis on situations not subjects evidently owes something to Dewey's influence. Lindeman wrote that adult education began at the point at which adults found themselves needing to adjust to new situations, and in this stress on the educational potential inherent in adults' attempting to make sense of, and come to terms with, changed realities at work, in the family or in society at large, there are echoes of the ideas of later theorists of adult learning. The idea pre-dates Havighurst's (1952) notion of the developmental tasks of adulthood and the teachable moment represented by adults having to adjust to changed work, or familial, social and economic conditions at different periods in their lives. Knox's (1977) more recent elaboration of change events as triggers for significant adult learning is also anticipated in this third principle of adult education as elaborated by Lindeman.

Finally, adult education was held to place primary emphasis on learners' experiences. In a passage evoking the ideas of educational praxis explored by Rogers (1961) and Freire (1970) among others, Lindeman asserted that 'all genuine education will keep doing and thinking together' and that 'experience is the adult learner's living textbook' (1926a: 7). The importance of grounding curricula and methods in the experiences of adults is now something of a self-evident truism in adult education, enshrined as it is in the concept of andragogy (Knowles, 1984) and in Kolb's (1984) experiential theory of adult development. What remains distinctive about this, however, is Lindeman's constant attention to the connection between individual realization through experience, and the need for adults to be involved in social change movements. To him, a major learning need in adulthood was 'to change the social order so that vital personalities will be creating a new environment in which their aspirations may be properly expressed' (1926a: 9).

One aspect of Lindeman's conceptualization of adult education that has largely been ignored by commentators to date is the manner in which he outlined the beginnings of what is now called (in the work of later writers) a critical theory of adult education. In one of his earliest pieces he offered a critique of institutional education which predates Freire's work on 'banking' education (1970) by some 40 years. Lindeman condemned the 'merely additive process' of school education whereby the teacher 'gets from his students what he has already imparted out of his academic repository' (1925: 2). Adult education was the antithesis of this additive process representing as it did 'a new technique for learning… a process by which the adult learns to become aware of and to evaluate his experience' (1925: 3). The adult learner was not viewed as 'merely engaged in the pursuit of new knowledge; he is, in short, changing his habits, learning to live on behalf of new motivations' (1937: 6).

In these passages adult education is charged with assisting adults to understand and interpret their experiences and to make explicit the preconceptions underlying their conduct. This idea has similarities to Freire's (1970) notion of dialogic education as the antithesis of the additive style, banking system. There is also a philosophical congruence (though not necessarily a direct causal link) between these ideas of Lindeman and Mezirow's critical theory of adult learning and education. To Mezirow a central task of adult education is that of 'bringing psychocultural assumptions into critical consciousness to help a person understand how he or she has come into possession of conceptual categories, rules, tactics and criteria for judging implicit in habits of perception, thought and behavior' (1981: 20).

Another point of similarity between Lindeman and Freire is the emphasis both placed on the futurist aspect of adult education. In *Pedagogy of the Oppressed* (1970) Freire constantly affirms the 'revolutionary futurity' (p 72) of education, writing that 'problem-posing theory and practice take man's historicity as their starting point' (p 71). A similar emphasis is evident in a paper Lindeman wrote toward the end of World War Two in which he declared that 'adult education is always futuristic' (1944: 116) and 'a daring challenge to life that is to come'. Adult educators were described as 'heralds of the future' (p 117), rather than as commentators on history, and the starting point for any analysis of the educational needs of adults was 'not history but rather the contemporary situation' (p 116). In adult learning groups members would analyse how present circumstances resulted from historical antecedents, would realize the culturally constructed nature of individual lives, and would thereby be encouraged to re-shape the future according to their own wishes and visions.

The final aspect of Lindeman's conceptualization of adult education to be discussed is, in many ways, the most unwarrantably neglected. The term 'andra-gogy' is probably the most common of adult educator's shibboleths. As a term summarizing a number of central beliefs concerning the unique character of adult learning and the implications for practice which flow from these, it is undeniably the most important concept in the field to many practitioners. Introduction of the term into adult education is generally credited to Malcolm Knowles who, in correspondence with Merriam-Webster dictionaries (Knowles, 1980: 253–54) could find no previous use of the term in the English language. Until recently (Brookfield, 1984) Lindeman's treatment of this concept remained undetected.

In the 1920s Lindeman, together with Martha Anderson, undertook an interpretative translation of various articles describing the folk high school system in Germany. Under the title *Education through Experience* (Anderson and Lindeman, 1927) the authors described the activities of the Academy of Labour in Frankfurt-am-Main. Early in their report is a section headed 'Andragogy' in which they declare that 'Andragogy is the true method of adult learning' and that 'life itself is the adult's school' (1927: 2–3). Adult experience is located within the realm of action, so that 'between the child and the adult lies the field of action. The adult enters history and becomes a link in the chain of guilt entanglement, want and pain'. In this same section the process of adult learning is described as 'an effort toward self-mastery' (1927: 3) and the realization of adulthood is signalled by a developing awareness of self and a readiness to make existential choices. Endemic to this process is the adult coming into conflict with previously untested conceptions and exploring oppositional viewpoints. In the emphasis on opposition, conflict and critical discussion as central to andragogy Lindeman formulates the concept in a way quite different to Knowles's later work. The language used by Lindeman in the description of adults entering history and becoming a link in a chain of guilt, entanglement, want and pain is imbued with a form of existential angst very different to Knowles's practice injunctions. For the student of Lindeman's work his lack of any further attention to a concept that was to exercise such an influence on the minds of adult education theorists and practitioners in the 1970s and 1980s is one of the most frustrating aspects of his intellectual activities. We can only speculate on how he would have regarded Mezirow's (1981) charter for andragogy, emphasizing as it does the development in adults of habits of critical reflection, and the fostering of the willingness to change uncongenial aspects of their worlds.

METHODS OF ADULT EDUCATION

Throughout Lindeman's writings on adult education there is a constant preoccu-pation with method, deriving partly, perhaps, from his own pragmatic orientation to changing the world rather than merely analysing it. The stress on the discussion method as the educational method derived from, and uniquely suited to, the effective facilitation of adult learning was a theme he emphasized until the end of his life. Not for him an acknowledgement of the virtue of flexibility and eclecticism in choosing appropriate methods; computer-assisted instruction, educational broadcasting and lectures would all have been condemned as inherently anti–adult educational.

Although the stress on the importance of discussion method was evident throughout his work, it can be seen at its strongest in *The Meaning of Adult Education* (1926a). He advised adult educators to ignore questions of curriculum development and 'to devote their major concern to method and not to content' (1926a: 114). Such an oppositional dualism of content and method would be rejected by analytic philosophers of adult education such as Paterson (1979) and Lawson (1979), both of whom argue that an activity can only be considered educational if the curriculum comprises knowledge deemed intrinsically worthwhile. They would agree with Lindeman, however, that educational activities must also be characterized by morally acceptable pedagogic procedures. The separation of content and method is also criticized by Freire (1970) who regards a collaborative analysis of individual and collective experience to be essential to problem-posing education and to the bringing of assumptions into critical consciousness. Central to conscientization is the nurturing of an awareness of power discrepancies within society.

The distinctive purpose of adult educational method, according to Lindeman, was the inculcation in learners of a set of analytical skills that could be applied to understanding a range of different situations. He wrote that 'education is a method for giving situations a setting, for analyzing complex wholes into manageable, understandable parts' (1926a: 115). This idea of adults developing a set of analytical procedures applicable to a variety of settings is, perhaps, a conceptual precursor of the notion of mathematics, of learning how to learn, as developed in adult education by R M Smith (1982). To Smith, the chief purpose of adult education is to help learners to understand their idiosyncratic learning styles and to develop skills of inquiry, analysis and synthesis, which can be adapted to different intellectual pursuits.

The medium through which these replicable, analytic skills would be developed among adults was the discussion group. Lindeman wrote enthusiastically of the use of discussion groups within the Danish Folk High School and the Workers' Education Association, and he argued his case for the appropriateness of this method for adult learners in the following way:

> Small groups of aspiring adults who desire to keep their minds fresh and vigorous; who begin to learn by confronting pertinent situations; who dig down into the reservoirs of their experience before resorting to texts and secondary facts; who are led in the discussion by teachers who are also seekers after wisdom and not oracles: this constitutes the setting for adult education, the modern quest for life's meaning (1926a:7).

This theme of adult learning groups comprising small numbers of individuals involved in articulating, reflecting upon and analysing their experience (and not relying on textbooks and secondary facts) has, if anything, even greater relevance in the 1980s than the 1920s. In the growth of the women's movement, and in a range of other consciousness-raising groups, we can see a direct realization of his ideas. The stress on teachers and learners using their experiences as educational material, rather than being constrained by pre-defined curricula, is at the heart of the encounter group movement and can be seen in the recognition by many colleges and universities of prior, experiential learning as being as meritorious and valid as institutionally sponsored learning. The most definitive statement regarding, the inherent suitability of discussion to adult education was contained in his entry to the *Encyclopedia of Social Sciences* in which he declared that 'if there is anything distinctive about method in adult education, it is derived from the growing use of discussion' and that 'the discussion method has come to be the accepted learning process for large numbers of adult classes' (1930: 465). At the end of World War Two he proposed the widespread use of discussion groups as a force for societal rejuvenation. In a paper (somewhat grandiosely) titled *World Peace through Adult Education* he wrote that 'if we genuinely want understanding and a good peace, we must quickly bring into existence an adult education movement which springs from the "grass roots" of American life' (1945b: 23). This movement would be based on neighbourhood discussion groups since such groups were held to be 'essential for democratic life' and 'the finest available medium for dealing with controversial issues'. Such groups would combat propaganda, develop flexible modes of thought, and encourage the emergence of 'natural' leadership qualities in its members as a challenge to 'artificial' and 'arbitrary' leadership so characteristic of modern society.

In stressing the importance of discussion method Lindeman is reflecting the central importance accorded to this medium by adult educators throughout the world. In US adult education it is the Junto groups, the Lyceums, the Farm Forum, and living-room learning initiatives such as the Great Books programme in the 1950s that come closest to constituting a distinctive adult education tradition. The Danish Folk High School relied on the use of discussion, and the culture circles used by Freire (1970) are a form of learning group as conceived by Lindeman. In Britain, Paterson (1970) has commented that advocacy of the discussion method is one of the chief articles in the catechism of liberal adult education, and it has certainly been the focus of the tutorial group movement in the extramural movement in that country. It is also, as Elsdon (1975) notes, the major training method used to prepare adult educators for their professional duties.

A CURRICULUM FOR ADULT EDUCATION

In the previous section it was pointed out that Lindeman, in his early writings, was somewhat disparaging about what he saw as an unhealthy preoccupation of adult educators with questions of curriculum. On the whole, it is this element in his writings that has been emphasized by latter-day interpreters such as Knowles (1980), whose andragogical tenets imply that questions of appropriate curricula are to be decided by learners' wishes and interests. In *The Meaning of Adult Education* (1926a), Lindeman expressed a disapproving surprise that 'schoolmen now find their center of interest in curriculum-making' (p 11), an activity he regarded as 'the process of transforming the school into a department-store bargain counter'. To him, the preoccupation with curriculum development sprung from the unfortunate centrality of subject teaching in US schools, a practice he attacked as 'compatible with a shallow and perverted pragmatism and profitable to an industrial order which requires technicians, not educated men and women' (p 15).This repugnance for developing curricula grounded in, and suited to, the unique concerns of adulthood has, in general, typified the writings of adult educators since that time. Studies of participation, programme development manuals and descriptive surveys of practice predominate within the literature of the field. Those seeking to maintain the a-curricular nature of adult education provision (saying, in effect, that it is up to educators to give learners what they say they want), frequently quote Lindeman in their defence. This is because his articulation of such a view is contained in his best-known and most widely circulated work, *The Meaning of Adult Education* (1926a). As will be seen presently, his reversal of position on this to the extent that in the 1940s he was making very specific curriculum suggestions for adult education classes, is one of the most neglected aspects of his work.

One curricular mission that was emphasized in *The Meaning of Adult Education*, however, was his idea that adult educators should work towards making all forms of artistic endeavour more democratic in their creation and dissemination. His comments in the book on what he regarded as the sterility of highbrow culture are scornful and contemptuous. He condemned the kind of artistic snobbery that led many poorly educated people to believe that artistic appreciation 'remains the inherited prerogative of a coterie of so-called cultured people' (1926a: 66) and he was highly critical of universities trying to indoctrinate students with preconceived notions of correct criteria for judging 'good' music, painting or literature. We can only speculate on how his early exclusion from formal education was partly responsible for this attitude of contempt toward the cultural values and standards perpetuated in formal educational institutions.

Lindeman urged adult educators to reject formal ideas concerning what comprised 'worthwhile' art and he wrote that such a rejection would 'aid greatly in the much-needed procedure of transforming a growing artistic snobbery into an indigenous folk-expression... In short, adult education may justly be expected to do something toward democratizing art' (1926a). Adult educators, in his view, were champions of popular culture and populist art forms. They were urged to oppose vigorously the academic sterility regarding the enjoyment of 'good' art, and thereby to give US art a new impetus. Central to this opposition was to be a rejection of criteria of good taste and standards of excellence derived from European cultural circles. Much as the Welsh and Scots are wary of the cultural imperialism of the English, or the Canadians of the United States, Americans were urged to be wary of contributing to the maintenance of a European cultural hegemony. Only if ideas of discrimination and artistic appreciation derived from European art were abandoned could the United States develop an indigenous artistic culture, grounded in, judged by and reflective of the US experience.

One aspect of tying adult education to the emergence of an indigenous form of US folk art was the need for adult educators to 'teach people how to make their thinking glow with the warmth of honest feeling' (p 67). One result of too great a respect for European cultural forms and artefacts was a marked unreadiness to express honestly and spontaneously feelings of warmth or approval toward works of art, lest these be considered too lowbrow. Americans had gained the habit of repressing their instinctive reactions to art forms until they were sure that these forms were culturally sound according to the dictates of high culture. One task of adult education was to 'aid in delivering us from that abject fear of expressing our quick and enthusiastic enjoyments – the fear to which we have become habituated under the discipline of professional criticism' (1926a: 70). Life itself could to considered a work of art with its creative constituents being the adding of a new dimension to one's experience. His advocacy of a fusion of art and life was expressed as follows:

> A well-organized and adequately expressed life deserves to be called beautiful no less than a well-conceived statue. Aesthetics suffers by reason of its artificial isolation, its exclusiveness. Beauty is not discovered solely by contemplation of beautiful objects; beauty is experiencing (p 55).

It was not until World War Two, nearly 20 years after the publication of *The Meaning of Adult Education*, that Lindeman's ideas on suitable curricula for adult education classes were more fully developed. At the end of the war, he wrote several pieces in which he proposed a curricular agenda for the neighbourhood discussion groups that he felt so strongly were vital to the maintenance of democratic societies in the post-war years. In *New Needs for Adult Education* (1944) he stated that adult education should be seen as a mode of social adaptation, which would assist adults 'to learn how to make important choices reflecting the issues they are obliged to confront' (Lindeman, 1944: 115). The liberal arts were felt to be in need of a severe and critical review, and much greater attention had to be paid to education within labour unions, one of the most vital and significant settings for adult learning. The central curricular question that had to be discussed concerned the form of economic arrangement that Americans believed was best suited to a democratic society. He suggested that a network of discussion groups consider the merits of the free enterprise system, socialistic ownership of the means of production, and a form of mixed economy. Implicit in his criticism of the kinds of discussions in which people were forced to choose between free enterprise capitalism and socialism, is his own preference for a mixed economy in which the benefits of individualistic enterprise were seen as married to an expanded welfare state. He argued that adult education and higher education were charged with fostering a more pluralistic and tolerant conception of economic affairs than had been the case up to that time.

A further elaboration of his curricular ideas was contained in a piece on the sociology of adult education (Lindeman, 1945a). In addition to the need to discuss the form of economic arrangement suitable to democratic societies, he identified three additional issues – 'what is to be done about our deep-seated habits of racial discrimination, how we are to democratize our vast educational equipment, how we are to play an appropriate role in world affairs' (1945a: 12). Discussion of these topics would 'furnish adult education with its program and its mission' (1945a: 13). If living-room learning groups across the country of 10 to 20 Americans were talking freely about these issues under the guidance of a skilled leader, then 'there would be no cause to fear for the future of democracy'. Such an avowedly political curriculum for adult education classes is very different to that currently pertaining in US adult education where concern for personal fitness, economic well-being and recreational diversion is paramount, in non-credit adult education at least. Debate on questions such as the merits of free enterprise capitalism, socialism and the mixed economy, or on how best to combat racism, are rare indeed in public adult and continuing education. The question of how best to democratize education is rarely raised in an era when public provision is being severely cut and attention is being refocused on the 'back to basics' movement for the rote learning of literacy and mathematical skills.

Finally, the discussion of foreign policy and the role of the United States in world affairs can hardly be said to be a central curricula concern of adult and continuing education. Initiatives along the lines of those envisaged by Lindeman, such as the recent experiment in developing a study circle movement in New York state to discuss questions of public policy (Osborne, 1981) are the exception rather than the rule.

ADULT EDUCATION AND SOCIAL ACTION

Throughout his writings, the social nature and purpose of adult education were a constant theme. In *The Meaning of Adult Education* (1926a) he urged that education orient itself as much to the social reality in which an adult lived, as much as to the individual person. Individuals were seen as caught inextricably within social milieu and forced to live collectively, so that 'collectivism is the road to power, the predominant reality of modern life' (1926a: 43). Adult education served as a catalyst to collective enterprise by revealing the nature of the social process, by replacing destructively warring interests with creative conflict, and by 'making the collective life an educational experience'. Distortions of reality could only result from viewing individual conduct as somehow separate from social behaviour. Moreover, such a view encouraged and justified a selfish pursuit of individual desires without regard to broader social concerns.

The replacing of warring interests by creative conflict was seen as most necessary in the arena of industrial relations. Through adult education, workers and managers would become aware of the socially created nature of individual conduct and would cease to be as secretive and combative as was customary. Concealment and conflict would be replaced by open democracy – 'the assumption that what we want is worth wanting, possesses sufficient integrity to stand comparison and is capable of making its way on merits and not through coercion' (1926a: 102). Lindeman was scathing on the effects that unbridled capitalism would have on social relations and regarded nationalism and imperialism as 'merely outward manifestations of this 'pseudo-power' which degrades us all' (p 26). He viewed 'the pervading economic structure of our civilization' as being based on 'a doubtful competitive ethic and avowedly designed to benefit the crafty, the strong and the truculent… warfare is the rule of the game'. Taken along with his comments on the debilitating dualism inherent in capitalism – 'that my advantage must mean your disability; that efficacy for me can exist only through your disqualification' (p 28) – his condemnation of capitalism stands as the most vigorous statement on this theme by a mainstream US adult educator.

Of greatest concern to Lindeman was the insidious infusion of capitalist ethics into the educational system. He wrote:

> We may, for example, so far exaggerate the incentives and motives which are derived from capitalism and profit production as to cause the entire educational system to become a direct response to this system and to lead to its further emphasis… If this system, both on its economic and educational sides, becomes too rigid and too oppressive and incapable of sincere self-criticism, nothing short of violent revolution will suffice to change its direction' (p 49).

This apocalyptic vision was speculation, not prediction. It was based on an assessment of what might happen within US society if certain perceptible trends became ossified into institutional forms. Revolutions were, in fact, fundamentally anti-educational, signalling that the society concerned had suffered a collective loss of faith in the power of learning and the use of intelligence. In puzzling contrast to the force of this critique, however, were Lindeman's ideas on industrial reform. He hoped for 'a revolution of the mind' (1926a: 27) that would develop 'cleaner motives, sharper intellectual insights and finer wills' among workers. His belief was that through workers' education (the most vital sector of the adult education movement) workers would came to displace force by intelligence and thereby discover 'better motives' for production. Trade unions would be turned into creating rather than fighting organizations.

As is evident from these comments, Lindeman stopped short of advocating a fundamental restructuring of society in his prescriptions for reform. The worker–employer divide remained intact, with reform occurring within the free enterprise, capitalist framework. Production was seen as becoming more participatory and collaborative, so that managers' 'power over' workers was transposed into 'power with' them. The contrast between the full-blooded critique of capitalism and the muted timidity of the reforms suggested above (a revolution in workers' minds to find finer meanings in, and better motives for, production) is puzzling. As Rockhill (1985: 192) points out, however, the fusion of ideals of political democracy with free enterprise production is so strong in US culture, that socialist or even social democratic proposals for industrial reform are likely to be instantly condemned as examples of totalitarian communism. For making comments as mild as the above, Lindeman was publicly condemned at different times as an atheist and subversive communist.

In *The Meaning of Adult Education* (1926a: 105) the following summation of the social role of adult education is given: 'adult education will become an agency of progress if its short-term goal of self-improvement can be made compatible with a long-term, experimental but resolute policy of changing the social order'. The form of this experimental policy was discussed in a number of works in the 1930s and 1940s, in which Lindeman wrote on the irreducibly social nature of adult education. He declared that 'adult education is learning associated with social purposes' (1937: 6) and that 'the complete objective of adult education is to synchronize the democratic and the learning processes'. The goals of adult education were 'social in nature' (1938: 5) and the distinctive feature of adult education was 'the fact that its purpose is definitely social' (1945a: 9). This purpose was increasingly interpreted in an unequivocally political manner. Adult education was 'the operating alternative for dominance, dictatorship, and violence' (1937: 6) of the sort afflicting fascist dictatorships in Italy, Spain and Germany. He perceived democracy as under threat from forces of dictatorship and demagoguery and wrote that 'adult education is the answer to blind prejudice and demagoguery' (1944: 115). In commenting on the outbreak of World War Two he wrote that widespread political illiteracy among the peoples of Western nations had made them susceptible to the diversionary stratagems of skilled politicians. To combat this danger a nation's citizens must be politically sophisticated and used to participating in democratic groups. Since adult learning groups were of this nature, they were a crucial training ground for democratic participation. For these reasons 'the only reliable instrument for establishing confidence among nations is adult education' (1945b: 23); hence, adult education was 'integral to the democratic struggle' (1945a: 10). A network of neighbourhood discussion groups exploring issues such as those identified in the previous section, and characterized by shared authority and democratic collaboration, would be the most effective hedge a society could evolve against the danger of creeping totalitarianism.

In this repeated emphasis on adult education as a force to counter the threats of demagoguery and totalitarian dictatorship, Lindeman anticipates some of Freire's ideas. In his description of how education might combat the process of massification in Brazilian society, Freire wrote that 'a critical education which could help to form critical attitudes' (1973: 32) would assist people to resist the diversions and myths peddled by the mass media. Only through participation in democratic learning groups (within unions, councils, associations, churches, schools and community groups) would people assimilate democratic habits. Freire wrote of the Brazilian people that 'they could be helped to learn democracy through the exercise of democracy: for that knowledge, above all others, can only be assimilated experientially' (p 36).

Almost three decades prior to these comments, Lindeman had declared that the participation of citizens in informed social action was the hallmark of a democratic society. Social action was, after all, essentially a forceful activity, hence it was important that the application of force and coercion occur only after the application of reason and intelligence. To make sure that social action was authentically democratic, it must be preceded by adult education. This meant that 'adult education thus turns out to be the most reliable instrument for social actionists' (1945a: 11). In his most unequivocal mood, Lindeman wrote on the irreducible connection between social action and adult education as follows: 'every social action group should at the same time be an adult education group, and I go even so far as to believe that all successful adult education groups sooner or later become social action groups' (p 12).

SUMMARY

In recent years, there has been something of a revival of interest in Lindeman's ideas. A Delphi study among professors of adult education in US universities (Ilsley, 1982) found that *The Meaning of Adult Education* (1926a) was chosen as the most important book in the field, along with Malcolm Knowles's (1980) programme development manual. Despite it having been out of print for several years the book commanded a revered status in the minds of adult education professors. Brookfield (1983) has examined it as a visionary charter for contemporary adult education and Stewart (1984: 97) describes it as 'the best and most cogent synthesis of adult education as a living activity that has been written to date'. In a re-review of the book Stewart points out that it is 'virtually the only volume written in the generative period of adult education in the 1920s that is still read by Americans today' (1984: 1) and that 'the nation's entire structure of adult education practice has largely been built upon Eduard Lindeman's 1926 philosophical base'. Although Hesburgh *et al* (1978: 38) point out that US continuing education has developed in a manner contrary to Lindeman's strictures concerning the need for it to remain non-vocational, Jarvis (1984: 59) regards this claim as somewhat naive when Lindeman's ideas are considered in their cultural and historical context. Rockhill (1985: 203–07) has also re-examined Lindeman's ideas recently, this time for their articulation of 'the social reconstruction stance in adult education' (Rockhill, 1985: 202).

As Stewart (1984: 1) points out, a characteristic feature of *The Meaning of Adult Education* (1926a) is its rambling, lurching narrative, in which 'ideas popping up within the text, sometimes have only tenuous connections to the announced subject matter'. This same comment might be applied to Lindeman's intellectual effort as a whole, characterized as it was by a diversity and inchoateness to be expected of a renaissance liberal progressive thinker in the early part of the century. His adult educational writings are often to be found in pieces that, at first glance, might appear to have little to do with the field. In addition, his writing style was one characterized by spontaneity, so that articles and speeches would assume the format of his thinking out loud to his audience. Consequently, many issues were raised and claims made that were not fully developed or thought through. This is perhaps a partial explanation of his enduring influence; the questions he asked are ones perennial to the practice of adult education, yet his answers were often given in outline form only. Hence, contemporary readers can interpret his sometimes quasi-mystical language to conform to their own expectations, and can flesh out the outlines of his skeletal schemes for reform with their own substantive, concrete detail.

Six important themes have been identified in his work as regards the theory and practice of adult education. First, there is the conceptualization of adult education as a collaborative, informal, yet critical activity of a determinedly non-vocational character. Judging by current practice in the United States at least, this aspect of his thought has little contemporary relevance. Vocational education, in-service development, training in business and industry, and continuing professional education are all seen by, for example, the American Association for Adult and Continuing Education, as legitimate areas of practice. In addition, those interested in the workplace as a setting for meaningful and critical adult learning (and not just mechanistic instruction in psychomotor competencies), would criticize the separation of work and non-work contexts for learning.

Second, the critical theory of adult learning in which the task of adult education is seen as prompting in adults an awareness of their historicity and of the culturally constructed nature of their environment, is reflected in recent contemporary critical theorists such as Freire and Mezirow. Assisting adults to reflect critically on their internalized values, beliefs and assumptions, is a thread common to all these thinkers. Freire and Mezirow did not, however, use Lindeman's work as a conceptual foundation for their theoretical edifices. There is no necessary causal connection between Lindeman's ideas and those of these other writers just because his work was the first to appear.

Third, it was Lindeman (together with Martha Anderson) who introduced the concept of andragogy into the literature of US adult education. As with so much of his work, however, after introducing the idea he did not attempt to explore it very completely. It was not until the 1970s that Knowles took the idea as a conceptual anchor for a number of assumptions about adult learning and prescriptions for facilitating learning.

Fourth, Lindeman argued repeatedly and firmly that, through practical necessity and moral imperative, adult education was a social effort. Adult educational goals were irreducibly social in nature, and in its practice of democratic collaboration adult education was a training ground for democratic participation. Through participation in adult learning groups Americans would cultivate a degree of political literacy that would serve as a shield against the propaganda and seductive appeal of simplistic solutions and convenient scapegoats offered by totalitarian demagogues.

Fifth, he wrote extensively on questions of method, emphasizing throughout how small group discussion was the distinctive and quintessential adult education format. Sixth, he outlined a curricular programme for adult education that focused on social and political issues such as the form of economic arrangement most appropriate to an industrial democracy, how to combat racism, the international role of the United States, and how to democratize educational resources.

In a field characterized by a preoccupation with technique, it is heartening to record the contemporary influence of a writer who was neither a professional adult educator nor concerned chiefly with questions of technique. His ideas and the words used to express them continue to inspire successive generations of students and professors of adult education, to the point where *The 1984 Adult Learning Review of Books* (Collins, 1984: 1) headed its reassessment of *The Meaning of Adult Education* with the phrase 'possibly the greatest book of the century'. Lindeman's ideas may have been scattered, and his articulation of them may have sometimes been brief, but their contemporary relevance and the force with which they are expressed, continue to affect fundamentally how many adult educators practise their craft.

REFERENCES

Anderson, M L and Lindeman, E C (1927) *Education through Experience*, Workers' Education Bureau, New York

Brookfield, S D (1983) Adult Education and the Democratic Imperative: The vision of Eduard Lindeman as a contemporary charter for adult education, *Studies in Adult Education*, **15**, pp 36–46

Brookfield, S D (1984) The Contribution of Eduard Lindeman to the Development of Theory and Philosophy in Adult Education, *Adult Education Quarterly*, **34** (4), pp 185–96

Collins, M (ed) (1984) *The 1984 Adult Learning Review of Books*, Learning Resources Network, Manhattan, Kansas

Elsdon, K T (1975) *Training for Adult Education*, Department of Adult Education, University of Nottingham, Nottingham

Freire, P (1970) *Pedagogy of the Oppressed*, Continuum Books, New York

Freire, P (1973) *Education for Critical Consciousness*, Continuum Books, New York

Gessner, R (ed) (1956) *The Democratic Man*, Beacon Press, Boston

Havighurst, R J (1952) *Developmental Tasks and Education*, McKay, New York

Hesburgh, T M, Miller, P A and Wharton, C R (1978) *Patterns for Lifelong Learning*, Jossey-Bass, San Francisco

Ilsley, P J (1982) *The Relevance of the Future in Adult Education: A phenomenological analysis of images of the future*, unpublished doctoral dissertation, Northern Illinois University, DeKalb, Illinois

Jarvis, P (1984) *Lindeman Revisited: Continuing professional education and the meaning of adult education*, paper presented to Standing Conference on University Teaching and Research in the Education of Adults, University of Bristol, July

Knowles, M S (1980) *The Modern Practice of Adult Education*, Cambridge Books, New York

Knowles, M S (1984) *Andragogy in Action*, Jossey-Bass, San Francisco

Knox, A B (1977) *Adult Development and Learning*, Jossey-Bass, San Francisco

Kolb, D A (1984) *Experiential Learning: Experience as the source of learning and development*, Prentice-Hall, Englewood Cliffs, New Jersey

Konopka, G (1958) *Eduard C Lindeman and Social Work Philosophy*, University of Minnesota Press, Minneapolis

Lawson, K H (1979) *Philosophical Concepts and Values in Adult Education*, Open University Press, Milton Keynes

Lindeman, E C (1925) What is Adult Education?, unpublished manuscript, Lindeman Archive, Butler Library, Columbia University, New York

Lindeman, E C (1926a) *The Meaning of Adult Education*, New Republic, New York

Lindeman, E C (1926b) *Workers' Education and the Public Libraries*, Workers' Education Bureau of America, New York

Lindeman, E C (1930) Adult Education, *Encyclopedia of the Social Sciences*, **1**, Macmillan, New York

Lindeman, E C (1937) Introduction, in *Adult Education for Social Change*, ed T K Brown, Swarthmore Seminar, Philadelphia

Lindeman, E C (1938) *The Need of Prepared Leaders in Adult Education*, unpublished manuscript, Lindeman Archive, Butler Library, Columbia University, New York

Lindeman, E C (1944) New Needs for Adult Education, *Annals of the American Academy of Political and Social Science*, **231**, pp 115–22

Lindeman, E C (1945a) The Sociology of Adult Education, *Journal of Educational Sociology*, 19, pp 4–13

Lindeman, E C (1945b) World Peace through Adult Education, *The Nation's Schools*, **35**, p 23

Lindeman, E C (1953) Evaluating Your Program, *Adult Leadership*, **4**, pp 13–20

Mezirow, J (1981) A Critical Theory of Adult Learning and Education, *Adult Education*, **32**, pp 3–24

Osborne, K Q (1981) Informal Adult Learning and Public Policy Issues: The study circle approach, in *Continuing Education for Community Leadership*, ed H W Stubblefield, Jossey-Bass, San Francisco

Paterson, R W K (1970) The Concept of Discussion: A philosophical approach, *Studies in Adult Education*, **1**, pp 28–50

Paterson, R W K (1979) *Values, Education and the Adult*, Routledge and Kegan Paul, London

Rielly, E J (1984) Eduard Lindeman: Self-directed learner, *Proceedings of the Adult Education Research Conference*, no 25, North Carolina State University

Rockhill, K (1961) Ideological Solidification of Liberalism in University Adult Education: Confrontation over workers' education in the USA, in *On becoming a person: A therapist's view of psychotherapy*, ed C R. Rogers, Houghton Mifflin Co, Boston, Massachusetts

Rockhill, K (1983) Mandatory Continuing Education for Professionals: Trends and issues, *Adult Education* (USA), **33**, pp 106–16

Rogers, C R (1961) On becoming a person: *A therapist's view of psychotherapy*, Houghton Mifflin Co, Boston, Massachusetts

Taylor, K, Rockhill K and Fieldhouse, R (1985) *University Adult Education in England and the USA*, Croom-Helm, London

Smith, R M (1982) *Learning How to Learn: Applied learning theory for adults*, Cambridge Books, New York

Stewart, DW (1984) Eduard Lindeman and the Idea of Lifelong Learning in America, Lifelong Research Conference Proceedings, No 4, Department of Education (E C Lindeman) in *The 1984 Adult Learning Review of Books*, ed M Collins, Learning Resources Network, Manhattan, Kansas

Part 3

THEORISTS OF ADULT AND CONTINUING EDUCATION

Chapter 7

Robert Peers

Stella Parker

INTRODUCTION

Robert Peers was the first professor of adult education to be appointed at the University of Nottingham (then the University College) in 1923. His chair was established in the wake of the College Council's decision to offer provision for adult students and to put this under the charge of a head with professorial status. Peers thus became not only the first professor of adult education in the UK but also the first in the world, and Nottingham University gained another first when it created a second chair of adult education in 1976 (Thornton, 1977). The department started by Peers is still in existence although now called the School of Continuing Education and as such, it is the longest established of its kind in the UK. It has been recognized as a pioneer in the development of university adult education and many of the practices initiated by Robert Peers are still apparent in the work of the school 80 years after its inception.

Within a short period of taking up his post, Peers had developed a thriving and flourishing activity with hundreds of working people studying part time on a regular basis. The school still has about 6000 adult students who live all over the East Midlands attending over 650 courses annually, most of which lead to certificates, diplomas and degrees. Even today, the East Midlands has an unusually high number of adults enrolled on educational programmes of all kinds, with 50 per cent of adults participating in some form of learning. In the UK, the lowest adult participation rate of 35 per cent is in the West Midlands and the North West of England and the highest is in Yorkshire with 52 per cent (Sargeant *et al*, 1997).

There are few clues as to why the East Midlands of England has proved to be such fertile ground for the development of education for adults. It has been suggested that the reasons are historical and that the region, and the city of Nottingham in particular, have always had a history of radical opposition to the status quo and somehow this has given rise to a thirst for knowledge. This connection may be tenuous, but in common with their compatriots in industrial cities in England, the people of the city of Nottingham do seem to have been rather radical, particularly at the beginning of the 19th century. For example, they recorded their opposition to the bills against sedition and treason, petitioned for the reform of parliament in 1817, protested at the Peterloo Massacre, and petitioned for the establishment of reform schools for young criminals instead of incarcerating them in prisons. In 1856, the city petitioned for entry to the civil service to be open to all by competition (Edwards, 1966) thus breaking the link between a privileged upbringing and access to lucrative jobs in public service.

As to whether or not this radicalism was linked to a thirst for knowledge through education is questionable, but certainly the city corporation in the last century was supportive of educational reform. It granted land for the development of voluntary schools and in 1829 it bought two £100 shares in the University of London. But perhaps more importantly, there seems to have been in the last century in the city of Nottingham lively self-help movements for working people. There were public libraries that held books and pamphlets and where political discussions and debates took place. Of the seven working men's libraries in Nottingham at that time there were six located in public houses where men congregated to drink ale after working all day mostly in manual trades.

In the last century, the people of Nottingham seemed to have been literate by the standards of the time – for example, in 1857, the police recorded that of the 1105 people apprehended in that year, only 411 could neither read nor write (Edwards, 1966). While we may think that any level of literacy is better than none, the respectable classes of Nottingham probably might not have agreed, their argument being that the reason such people got into trouble in the first place was because they could read and write, consequently filling their heads with all sorts of seditious nonsense put out by the radical press that was active in the city at the time. Exactly how such numbers of ordinary working people learnt to read and write in Nottingham is not clear. There was then no regular educational provision funded by the state or by any public agency, and at the beginning of the 19th century over half the children did not attend formal schooling. But there was a plethora of educational providers – informal, non-formal and formal – the latter including adult day schools. There is some evidence suggesting the adult day school that opened in Nottingham in 1789 was a pioneer – it was regarded as revolutionary because as well as teaching people how to read the bible, it also taught arithmetic. Later in the century other forms of education for adults developed in Nottingham, such as the Mechanics Institute, a People's College and the University Extension that had its origins in the two ancient English universities – Oxford and Cambridge (Kelly, 1992).

Oxford and Cambridge were at that time elitist and inward looking, much to the chagrin of some of the social reformers of the day. To counteract this introversion there developed the University Extension movement which had its origins in the more enlightened elements of Cambridge University. University Extension was an attempt to take the University of Cambridge beyond it walls – extramural – and to give lectures on circuit to various parts of the country. These included one-off lectures delivered usually to packed halls and meetings places of full of working people as well as longer courses delivered on a more regular basis.

Nottingham was on the route of the Cambridge Extension circuit but soon broke out and a local loop was formed, linking Nottingham to Derby and Leicester. Cambridge no longer controlled the circuit but the courses belonged to the University of Cambridge for many years. Towards the end of the 19th century typical Nottingham Extension classes were as follows:

- English literature and geography for young women;
- force and motion and astronomy for young men of the middle class;
- political economy and constitutional history for working men.

Although this gender segregation and social class division would not be tolerated today, the labelling of extension classes then did send out a clear message that women and working men were welcome in what otherwise was a middle-class male preserve.

Within the seeds of these extension courses lay the foundations of the present-day University of Nottingham. The early courses were so successful and so popular that eventually a permanent building was acquired for them, together with a free library and a museum. This building was located in Shakespeare Street and became known as the University College. It opened in 1881 and these first courses were later added to so that eventually engineering and science subjects as well as the arts and humanities were offered. Many years later, having outgrown itself, the (then) University College was relocated on to University Park campus and became a fully-fledged university in its own right in 1949. Robert Peers was still working at the University College and (as acting head) he was responsible for steering it through its transition to university status.

In the first few years of the 20th century, the University College was flourishing in the centre of the city in Shakespeare Street. Its University Extension classes were heavily dependent on student fee income for their financial support; the fees were high and out of the reach of many working people and so University Extension became the preserve of the middle classes. Because Extension classes were so expensive to maintain, the usual means of delivery was by lectures to large groups. Students who were keen could find these lectures stimulating but dissatisfying if they wished to study more deeply. These difficulties led to the development of new educational methods, both in terms of course organization and of delivery. The originator of these innovations was Albert Mansbridge who in 1905 launched the Workers' Educational Association (WEA) that pioneered the development of tutorial classes for adults (Peers, 1958). These were a new form of educational provision for adults because they were based on a partnership between working people (represented by the WEA) and universities/university colleges. The partnerships resulted in courses that were fashioned on the needs of working people (articulated by the WEA) but delivered through an academic framework (articulated by the universities/university colleges). A plethora of WEA tutorial classes was in existence in Nottingham when Peers took up his post in 1923. Four years previously the government's Education Act of 1919 had recommended the setting up of university departments of adult education and Peers arrived at University College with an agenda to build on and further extend the established educational movements in the city.

HIS LIFE

Robert Peers was born in 1888 into a working-class family in Liverpool and became an apprentice at the Camel Llaird shipyards as a teenager. He attended night classes at an adult school and won a mature student's scholarship to the University of Liverpool from which he graduated with a first-class honours degree in economics at the age of 25. The following year he held a postgraduate studentship at the University of Heidelberg but then war broke out in 1914. He completed his war service, rose to the rank of captain and won the Military Cross. At the age of 31, he was appointed as lecturer in economic history at University College in Exeter. He worked at the University of Exeter for a short time before applying for and being offered the chair at Nottingham – a steep career rise that would not be possible today! He was then completely unknown as an adult educator and this is perhaps significant of the uncertain status of adult education at University College, Nottingham – it was not sufficiently prestigious to attract well-known and established figures to apply for the post. However, within a very short period Peers had established a significant student body – about 2000 enrolments within a few years studying on a range of courses. Peers' vision and planning probably helped the remarkable growth of the department in its earliest days. By 1928, it had 12 full-time academic staff and there were 63 tutorial classes that covered such subjects as economics and economic history, literature, philosophy, religion, art and political theory.

Robert Peers worked with the Nottingham WEA from the start of his employment at the University College, but his relationship with it was distinctive. Peers was sensitive and responsive to requests for courses from the WEA, but he had the final say. He controlled and administered all the university classes and he did this because he believed it enabled him to provide unified planning of the department's work as a whole. He developed progression routes for students so that the department's one-day courses linked into termly courses, which in turn linked into tutorial classes.

Peers extended his comprehensive programme across the East Midlands into small villages and rural communities and he was able to do this because of the college's unusual right to provide some courses that normally would have been provided by the WEA. At least some of this particular provision was subjected to questions about its quality and standards (Fieldhouse, 1998).

Peers' espoused aim was to teach working people about the world, how it was organized and how it was controlled to enable them to play a wider role in society (Peers, 1958). He also devised a diploma for teachers of adults and many international visitors came to learn about this from him. Although it was pioneering in its beginning years, the department gradually succumbed to the developments that overtook extramural adult education in the UK, including the gradual replacement of working-class students by the middle classes (Fieldhouse,1998).

In this brief and partial story about Robert Peers and the early days of the department at Nottingham, I have touched upon some of the history of the education of adults in England. There are some excellent texts that describe this history fully – for example see Fieldhouse (1998) and Kelly (1992) – and this chapter will not cover that same ground. However, it is important to note that the historical roots of the education of adults in England lie in the developments of civil society. Around 200–300 years before Peers' time, the church in England had initiated some of the earliest recorded examples of education for adults. These examples included informal education for adults by Puritan ministers acting as proselytisers for the salvation of those they taught to read, using the bible as their text. These particular forms of education for adults were organized from above – by one group of adults providing learning opportunities for another group. Later examples included the Mechanics Institutes that developed in the middle of the 19th century, where public lectures by specialists and university academics were delivered. These and other similar examples can be regarded as education organized by one group of people 'in the know' for the benefit of another group.

In contrast, there were in London about 200 years ago coffee houses where people congregated to participate in the debates of the day and occasionally lectures were delivered where public opinion was formed. Arising from these were various loosely organized movements of working people – study circles, self-help groups and the like. Gradually these loose movements became more institutionalized into adult schools, church schools, some earlier forms of university extension and so on. Although different in structure these forms of education for adults had one aspect in common – they all sprang from civil movements of people with their own ideas of what they wanted to know about. In other words, this was education by the people for the people. I refer here to this model as adult education.

This particular model – with its roots in learner autonomy and self-direction – is a major distinguishing feature of adult education. Contrast this with the education of children and of young people. Their teachers are adults who design and deliver what children and young people are taught. Their teachers have specialist knowledge and choose to teach from within the boundaries of knowledge that they deem to be suitable. Their knowledge is, to a varying degree, specialist and more or less confined to certain limited areas – these are the academic fields and disciplines defined by the universities. These academic fields and disciplines have a dominant influence on what is taught to young people throughout all stages of their education. As a young person in the UK ascends the educational ladder, his or her education becomes more and more specialist as he or she moves from school into college or university, and all the time he or she is on the receiving end of education from above – from specialist professionals. I refer to this model of education as schooling. I contend that this model of education is not confined to the education that takes place in schools and that it was the model delivered in the Mechanics Institutes and in the later forms of University Extension that were so well patronized by the middle classes.

Robert Peers inherited the traditions of these two models – one with its underpinning ideology of autonomy (adult education) and the other rooted in an ideology of conformity and control (schooling). In keeping with these traditions, Peers was responsible for designing and delivering a model of educational provision that was a hybrid – giving rise to university adult education. The model was a hybrid of schooling and adult education because it took the needs of adults (expressed with the support of the WEA) and put them into the framework of academic disciplines. In theory (at least) this led to the development of a 'university adult curriculum' and a curriculum is here referred to in Young's terms (Young, 1998). Young defines the curriculum as the conscious or unconscious selection of bodies of knowledge from the knowledge that is available at a particular time. The methods of delivery of any curriculum reflect the ideologies underpinning concepts of learning held by those who are responsible for providing learning opportunities.

PEERS AND THE UNIVERSITY ADULT CURRICULUM

Peers has written extensively about the practice of the delivery of a university adult curriculum and in *Adult Education in Practice* (1934) he provided a lucid account. Here he described how he was required to work within the regulations laid down in 1924 by the (then) Board of Education. The Board was a state-supported organization that contributed towards drafting a national code of practice for adult education. The Board's membership was heavily influenced by supporters of adult education and its regulations laid down the foundations of the participatory teaching methods that have influenced much of British adult education ever since. Universities and other organizations (such as the WEA) were able to obtain state funding on the condition that they (as responsible bodies) adhered to the Board's code of practice, as enshrined in its regulations.

The regulations were singular and unusually tight, spelling out the types of courses that were eligible for financial support from the state. The list of prescribed courses below indicates the level of detail contained in the Board's regulations (Peers, 1934):

● preparatory classes;
● three-year tutorial classes;
● advanced tutorial classes;
● tutorial class vacation courses;
● university extension courses.

These five levels were differentiated academically, and so preparatory classes required less academic application whereas the more advanced extension courses were more rigorous. For each type of course, the Board prescribed general aims and then went into some detail regarding course length, the number of students permitted to enrol and restrictions on the grant available. The regulations clearly stated that courses were to be for the liberal education of adults, but that they were not to be conducted by means of lectures and were to be recognizable as higher education. Certain subjects were not eligible for funding such as work-related subjects, domestic arts, handicrafts and recreational activities. The regulations prescribed the provision of learning resources (in this case, books), the professional status of tutors, the keeping of student registers and so on. In accordance with the Board's regulations, Peers was explicit that there was no need for formal assessment of the students' work (whether this was essays or other evidence of learning). University adult classes were inspected at regular intervals by the state-funded inspectorate of the day (His Majesty's Inspectors – HMIs) and reports were compiled on all completed provision; all planned provision needed to be approved by HMI.

Despite these externally imposed restrictions on practice, Peers dismissed the Board's regulations as mere administrative details. So when writing about the methods of teaching available to the teacher of adults he proclaimed the virtue of there being no standard teaching methods. In other words, he highlighted the autonomy available to adult practitioners and emphasized this by stating that the 'dead hand of tradition' was not apparent in university adult education as it was 'in other branches of education' (Peers, 1934). Although lectures were an acceptable form of teaching, he recommended class discussions and the tutorial method as preferable and superior. He described the latter as a technique found to be particularly successful with experienced classes where each student pursued his/her own line of study, the role of the tutor being a facilitator and a coordinator of student' lines of study.

Peers explained that the Board's regulations did not cover the content of courses or the methods of teaching, so tutors were not expected to work to prescribed syllabuses but rather to construct their own. He regarded the best syllabuses as those prepared in consultation with the class of students. The implication was that the content of university adult courses was different – 'neither glorified school work nor debased University work' (Peers, 1934).

Peers made a virtue of the qualities of adult tutors. He attempted to distinguish adult teachers from others in higher education by claiming that they needed 'special qualities' not required elsewhere in the academy. However, he stated that these 'special qualities' were in fact personal qualities – and as all educators know, these are not often developed through formal training. Nonetheless, Peers initiated programmes of training for Nottingham's adult tutors and developed a diploma in adult teaching.

Peers extolled the benefits of university adult education in terms of its potential to advance social progress, inculcate citizenship, remedy educational deficiencies, lead to personal fulfilment and advance knowledge, *inter alia*. He provided evidence that showed how his courses were accessible to a wide range of students (see Table 7.1).

Table 7.1   *Occupational distribution of adult students in Nottinghamshire (1933)*

Social class	%
B	9
B/C1	16
C1	10
C2	9
C2/D	22
Other	4
Housewives	31

Adapted from Peers, 1934

This gave credence to the belief (espoused by the WEA in particular) that working people who had not been able to attend university in their youth were eager and capable of succeeding in university education.

Peers appears not to have questioned the reasons for the tight control of university adult education or to have been daunted by it. The Board's regulations and the surveillance afforded by HMI appeared to have been acceptable to him, perhaps as a form of protection. Without such protection, there was always the possibility that the fledgling form of university adult education could be submerged by the schooling model that dominated the remainder of university education. So, Peers' position within his institution was conserved by the Board's regulations, but he needed to maintain his credibility with the HMI and the paymasters too.

Through the descriptions of his teaching methods it is possible to deduce that Peers' view of student learning was radical for his time. Firstly, he used evidence from empirical studies, in particular Thorndike's work (1928) on the psychology of adult learning to justify his claim that adults over 25 years of age were still capable of learning (Peers, 1934). Secondly, he espoused a model of participative learning that resonates closely with models of learning that became more accept- able in higher education many years later (see for example Atkins, 1993, Laurillard, 1996).

In Peers' time, students on university adult education could not effect direct transfer on to traditional undergraduate degrees because adult courses were regarded as being different and not equivalent. Notwithstanding this, several universities of the time had arrangements for the matriculation of adult students and some recognized certain of the more advanced forms of university adult education as suitable preparation for entry. Undaunted by the implication that 'different' meant 'inferior' Peers loudly proclaimed the superior qualities of university adult education and in particular its contributions to the development of society and of citizenship. In other words, he did not even pretend that university adult education was equivalent to the remainder of university education (in those days it focused unashamedly on an elite). Instead, he claimed to be operating in a different arena (social justice) that was of no concern to the elitists and where he had no competition.

His evidence for this claim is shown in Table 7.1 and certainly the social mix was unusual for university education of the day, as was the high proportion of women students. In terms of providing access to a form of university education for disadvantaged groups, Peers' contribution is remarkable but in line with other providers of his time. Today this social mix is not apparent in university adult education where recent figures indicate that the majority of students on university adult courses are drawn from the most affluent social groups (Dearing, 1997). However, women students are now well represented in higher education, forming over half the student body.

Despite his claims for the distinctive qualities of teachers of university adult education, Peers relied on part-time tutors (generally untrained as adult educators) for the bulk of adult teaching especially for the elementary classes (which were questionable in terms of quality) and for University Extension (which were less questionable). In this way he attempted to raise the professional status of university adult teachers but, paradoxically, the training of university adult teachers was unique at that time when teacher training was not a requirement for university teaching. By virtue of their need for training, university adult educators became closer to primary school teachers of the day who were trained and whose establishments and practices were subjected to external inspection at regular intervals. Nonetheless, the training for adult tutors introduced by Peers' added to his esteem as an educator and helped him gain renown and status as a leading-edge adult educator. In other words, he played the game of acquiring national and international recognition for his area of work – this is and always has been one important route to gaining personal status in the academic community and for raising the academic standing of a field or discipline.

But it is possible that Peers' claims about the virtues of university adult education were based on an underlying unease about its status and its future. Questions had been posed as to the academic credibility of at least some of the elementary courses in the department, particularly those in the rural areas that would normally have been provided solely by the WEA. Moreover, the future of university adult education depended on continued financial support from the state, and Peers knew that this support was by no means guaranteed, especially if the department's practices did not conform to the criteria of quality as laid down in the regulations of the Board.

In essence, university adult education at University College was part of a state-mediated social intervention that aimed to provide educational opportunities for adults from lower socio-economic groups. As such it enabled universities to claim (in addition to educating an elite) that they were acting as agents of social justice. But as we have seen, this social justice was conducted very much in isolation from the remainder of the university. This isolation was further amplified because funds for university adult education had conditions attached, so that its distinctive practice was tightly regulated and subject to the requirements of the state. In contrast, the state's attitude to higher education elsewhere and in the University College was *laissez faire* and remained so until the late 1980s. Regardless of adult education's distinctiveness within an elitist and status conscious occupational area, Robert Peers was able to raise its profile and maintain its credibility as *bona fide* higher education.

TODAY

Almost 80 years have elapsed since Peers took up his chair at Nottingham. During this time, there have been many changes in all sectors of education in the UK, and in higher education the majority of students now are adults, 55 per cent of them women (HESA, 1999). Another major change is the relationship between higher education and the state. In Peers' time, the state intervened very little in higher education, with university adult education being the one exception. Today the state's intervention in the totality of higher education is great and (broadly speaking) the purpose of intervention has been to ensure accountability. Universities now undergo state-controlled audits and inspections of their financial business, their research output and their teaching and they are required to return strategic plans and annual reports to state funding bodies. So, in many respects universities have now succumbed to the same type of control that was so familiar to university adult educators at the time of Peers. As would be expected this tightening of control has not been well received by the majority working within this sector – a sector that has enjoyed relative autonomy for such a major part of its existence.

However, within the sector, adult education (as practised by Peers) has no history of autonomy from the state and indeed until 1989 HMI continued to conduct their inspections of university adult provision. But in the wake of the 1992 Act, the state began to introduce procedures for evaluating the effectiveness of university provision and introduced procedures for the inspection of teaching and learning alongside financial and other forms of audit. Adult education in universities became subjected to this same regime and thus the distinctive and somewhat protective boundary line that had (for so many years) separated this form of adult education from the remainder of higher education was removed by means of 'mainstreaming'. In effect, this meant that the content of university adult education became indistinguishable from other forms of higher education which (under pressure from government) has become increasingly vocational. So within two years or so in the mid-1990s the concept of university adult education that had been glorified by Peers was officially expunged. Nevertheless, departments of adult education in universities continued to exist although some have begun to disappear as they have been absorbed into the mainstream.

In 1997, there was a general election and a Labour government came to power with a mandate to improve education as a whole. In reality, this new government focused much of its regenerative energy on the education of young people in schools and colleges, but it also introduced the notion of lifelong learning, signalling that the education of adults was not forgotten (DfEE, 1997 and DfEE, 1998). Running as a thread through all policy changes planned by this new government is a clearly articulated commitment to making higher education (in particular) less exclusive, less elitist and more effective as an agent of social justice. The increasingly tight controls that the state now has on the operational activities of universities can provide it with levers to make them conform to this new agenda; but is this agenda so new?

It is not, and if Robert Peers were alive today he might find it familiar, but would undoubtedly be surprised that social justice had become the aim of all academia rather than being the aim of university adult education alone. He would find the regulation of educational provision familiar, too, but it is questionable whether he would dismiss as 'mere administration' the bureaucracy of the state's new procedures for ensuring the uniformity of standards in higher education. On the other hand, he might welcome the introduction of training for university teachers although he could question the content of some of these training programmes.

As a pragmatist, he would be sympathetic to the state's need to regulate the practice of university educators, whose experience of higher education (both as students and teachers) is grounded in a sector that has inherited many elite traditions. The elite tradition is nested within the schooling model, where students are expected to be recipients of knowledge selected for them by experts. If he were to be asked for his advice (based on his experience) of how to make universities less exclusive and more accessible Peers would probably indicate that they need to rethink the way they teach (Daniel, 1993) and adopt some of the principles of good adult teaching. While universities have traditionally coped well with younger students who defer to the authority inherent in schooling, they are less practised in providing for students who believe they know what they want and who seek to fulfil these wants in partnership with the academy. Peers ensured that the principles that underpin this form of teaching were passed on through the programmes he devised for teachers of adults and if there is any one aspect of his work that ranks as his most important contribution to adult education, then it is surely this.

REFERENCES

Atkins, M (1993) *Assessment Issues in Higher Education*, Department for Employment, Sheffield

Daniel, J (1993) The Challenge of Mass Higher Education, *Studies in Higher Education*, **18** (2), pp 197–203

Dearing, R (1997) *Higher Education in the Learning Society*, National Committee of Inquiry into Higher Education, Norwich

DfEE (1977) *National Advisory Group for Continuing Education and Lifelong Learning for the 21st Century*, Department for Education and Employment, London

DfEE (1998) *The Learning Age: A renaissance for a new Britain*, Stationery Office, London

Edwards, K C (1966) *Nottingham and its Region*, Derry and Sons Limited, Nottingham

Fieldhouse, R and associates (1998) *A History of Modern British Adult Education*, National Institute of Adult Continuing Education, Leicester

HESA (1999) *Undergraduate Enrolments in 1998/99 with a Model Age of 21 Years and Older*, Higher Education Statistics Agency, Cheltenham

Kelly, T (1992) *A History of Adult Education in Great Britain*, National Institute of Adult Continuing Education, Leicester

Laurillard, D (1996) *Rethinking University Teaching*, Routledge, London

Peers, R (1934) *Adult Education in Practice*, Macmillan and Co, London

Peers, R (1958) *Adult Education: A comparative study*, Routledge and Kegan Paul, London

Sargent, N *et al* (1997) *The Learning Divide*, National Institute of Adult Continuing Education, Leicester

Thorndike, E L, Bergman, E O, Tilton, J W and Woodyard, E (1928) *Adult Learning*, Macmillan, New York

Thornton, A H (1977) *Introduction in the University in its Region*, Department of Adult Education, Nottingham, pp 3–6

Young, M F D (1998) *The Curriculum of the Future*, Falmer Press, London

Chapter 8

Cyril O Houle

William S Griffith (updated by Peter Jarvis)

If a man does not keep pace with his companions, perhaps it is because he hears a different drummer. Let him step to the music which he hears, however measured or far away (Thoreau, no date: 311).

INTRODUCTION

Cyril Orvin Houle was an adult educator who was never concerned with keeping pace with his colleagues. Instead, he has marched to a different drummer all his professional life. The purpose of this chapter is to review his career, identify some of the influence he has exerted on adult education through his writings, his students and colleagues, and his associated activities. Finally, several of his seminal ideas that have not yet been fully exploited will be discussed, leading to a summary assessment of the contributions of his scholarship to the field of adult education.

BIOGRAPHICAL SKETCH

He was born in Sarasota, Florida, in 1913. Upon graduation from Sarasota High School in 1929, he was granted a state scholarship to the University of Florida. Houle applied himself to his academic work systematically and fruitfully, receiving both his bachelor's and master's degrees in education in 1934, three years after he had matriculated. This remarkable pace of work characterizes his career, impressing all who knew him for his amazing self-discipline and productivity.

Following graduation, he took several jobs, among which was that of administering a statewide programme for the Federal Emergency Relief Administration for training out-of-work teachers to teach adults. Within a year, he had committed himself to a career in adult education and sought an appropriate place to pursue doctoral study.

Floyd W Reeves, who was to become Houle's mentor at the University of Chicago, had been involved in the study of higher education there and had became deeply interested in the work of the Tennessee Valley Authority, which was intended to employ education in the improvement of the human and material resources of the river region. On the basis of his experience in the innovative programming of that organization, Reeves modified the focus of his academic work at the university in 1935 and arranged to offer a graduate degree programme in adult education. This was a pioneering move as only Columbia University had established such a department in the United States. Reeves's influence on Houle's perception of adult education has not been established, but it is interesting to note that for the last 12 years Houle spent at the University of Chicago, he was responsible for leading the graduate programme in higher education, further strengthening the bond between it and adult education.

Houle was Reeves's first doctoral student and through their association, Houle was involved in state and national projects. When Reeves undertook his study of adult education in the State of New York, he involved Houle. Out of that collaboration came the report, *Adult Education: The Regents' inquiry into the character and cost of public education in the State of New York* (1938), regarded by many as the first major study of a state system. At the national level, Houle served as a staff member of President Roosevelt's Advisory Committee on Education in Washington, DC.

In 1939, a year before he had completed his dissertation, Houle was appointed an instructor in adult education at the University of Chicago, beginning a period of employment that would last until 1979, the year of his retirement. In 1940, his PhD was conferred for his dissertation entitled *The Coordination of Adult Education at the State Level*. It may be noted that his co-authorship of the Regents' inquiry had occurred prior to his completion of his dissertation, an experience that may have been instrumental in developing his self-image as a writer and scholar.

In 1942, Houle was named assistant professor; in 1945, he was promoted to associate professor; and in 1952, he became a full professor. From 1945 to 1952, he served as dean of the University College, the adult education division of the University. His imagination in programming and his general administrative competence came to the attention of people on and off campus so that in 1947 he was named Outstanding Young Man in Chicago by the Chamber of Commerce, a rather remarkable accomplishment for a scholar. Relinquishing his administrative responsibilities for the University College in 1952, Houle focused his attention on research and teaching in adult education, an emphasis he retained until 1969, when he accepted the responsibility for chairing the higher education special field of study in the Department of Education.

During the time he was at the University of Chicago, he also engaged in a number of significant activities at other locations in summers and during his terms out of residence. In 1940, he was a visiting instructor in education at the University of California, Berkeley. In 1950, he directed the UNESCO seminar on the role of libraries in adult and fundamental education in Malmo, Sweden. In 1950–51 he was a Fulbright Fellow to the United Kingdom, examining education throughout Great Britain. In 1958–59 he visited nine African countries and six in the Caribbean to study extension work at various universities. In the same year, he made a visit to Denmark to study the Folk High Schools. During 1960, he was Knapp Visiting Professor at the University of Wisconsin, Milwaukee. The series of lectures he delivered there were subsequently published as *The Inquiring Mind*, probably the most influential book he produced. The director-general of UNESCO appointed him to the International Committee for the Advancement of Education in 1961. That summer he was a lecturer in education at the University of Washington. He was a visiting senior research specialist at Oxford University in 1968. President Lyndon Johnson appointed him to the National Advisory Council on Extension and Continuing Education in 1965, a position he held until 1969 and in which he helped to shape policy for the implementation of the Higher Education Act of 1965.

Having served as an advisor to the W K Kellogg Foundation for a number of years, and having been instrumental in the development of the Kellogg Residential Center for Continuing Education at the University of Chicago, he began serving the Foundation in a part-time capacity as a senior program consultant in 1976 and continued in that role until his retirement from the university. Since becoming a professor emeritus in 1979, he was employed solely by the Foundation and maintained a residence in Battle Creek, Michigan, the home of the foundation, in addition to his apartment in Chicago. He has also been a special advisor on adult and continuing education for Jossey-Bass Publishers for over a decade.

Only a few of the most notable of his numerous honours and awards will be mentioned here. He was awarded the DHL by Rutgers University, DePaul University, New York University, and Roosevelt University, and the LLD by the Florida State University and by Syracuse University. In addition, Syracuse University presented him with the William Pearson Tolley medal for Distinguished Leadership in Adult Education. His contributions were recognized by his colleagues in the Association of University Evening Colleges in 1967 when they presented him with the Outstanding Achievement Award. In 1968, the National Association for Public School Adult Education honoured his work by presenting him an Award of Merit. He was also named to the National Academy of Education, a recognition that has seldom been given to a scholar in adult education.

INFLUENCE ON ADULT EDUCATION

Assessing the influence of Cyril O Houle on the field of adult education involves an examination of selected publications, a consideration of his impact on his former students and a review of some of his many associated professional activities.

Through writing – selected publications

Houle was a prolific writer with impeccable standards. This examination of selected publications, ordered chronologically, will indicate the breadth and depth of his contribution to the knowledge base of the field.

One of Houle's earliest contributions to the literature was made as a junior author of the Regents' inquiry into the condition of adult education in the State of New York. Houle, whose own doctoral dissertation dealt with coordination, expressed a strong conviction of the need to rationalize the system of provision of adult education. The report notes:

> … adult education in New York is chiefly a group of disjointed and unrelated activities. For the most part, agencies at both the state and the local level pursue their ways serenely unconscious of other closely related programs in existence. When consciousness of these programs exists, it frequently results in bitter jealousy, and coordination is the exception rather than the rule (Reeves, Fansler, and Houle, 1938: 137–38).

It is not certain how influential his involvement in the examination of the panoply of organizations providing adult education in New York State was on Houle's perception of the need for a broad perspective on the field. It is clear, however, that from then onwards he made a point of emphasizing approaches that reflected an awareness of the richness and diversity of the institutional providers of adult education.

In 1947, Houle served as the leader of a team of investigators examining the armed services and adult education. From that inquiry, he devised a typology of adult education providing agencies. (Houle et al, 1947: 226). The first type consists of agencies originally developed to provide adult education as their major function. The second type includes agencies originally developed for the education of children and young people, but which have since taken on the additional function of adult education. (This category includes universities, colleges and secondary schools.) The third group is composed of institutions originally established to serve the whole community, such as libraries, museums and social settlements. The final type was intended to serve non-educational purposes and has taken on adult education functions as a means of achieving its primary functions more effectively. This type includes churches, labour unions, prisons, cooperatives, hospitals and government departments. While subsequent authors have made some modest modifications of the classification of adult education agencies, no superior classification has been proposed.

In concluding the report, Houle called attention to the positive aspects of the educational work of the armed services and its potential benefits to the nation in the future. He said:

> The armed services blazed a tortuous trail toward a great truth, the truth that everybody has a natural desire to learn and can profit from that learning. If civilian society is willing to accept this basic truth and begins to realize its fullest promise, a great good can be said to have come out of the war. Through the very struggle for democracy, a new implement for democracy will have been forged (Houle *et al*, 1947: 252).

This assertion that all persons desire to learn may not seem a revolutionary insight now, but in 1947 it was commonly thought that there were large numbers of people who had no desire to learn. Further studies by Houle continue to support his assertion that all adults desire to learn and that they all engage in same kind of learning, whether or not satisfactory means have been devised to measure their learning.

In his work with UNESCO in directing the international seminar on the role of libraries in adult and fundamental education in 1951, Houle once again held up the standard of learning for all and the need for a supportive network of cooperating agencies. He said:

> If we work together both within the profession of librarianship and as cooperators with other agencies, perhaps we may hope to establish a view which the modern world, with its nervous preoccupation with the immediate, has tended to neglect. It is the idea that education should be a lifelong process, so that the individual develops his potentialities not merely while he is a child but so long as he lives… it is an ideal which has never been realized by more than a few, chiefly for the rich and the leisured… Adult education should become not the province of the few but the democratic hope of the many (Houle, 1951: 28).

The recurrent themes here are those of lifelong learning and of the need to provide suitable supporting structures to enable all adults to participate. Houle enlarged the conception of the participants to include adult education broadly defined and called their attention to the need for cooperative coordinated programming so that all adults can be served.

In 1956, Houle and C A Nelson wrote *The University, the Citizen, and World Affairs*, in which they proposed a typology of adult citizens based on the citizens' knowledge and concern about world affairs (p 34–35). By applying this typology, Houle and Nelson were able to propose a set of principles by which each of the categories of citizens would most appropriately be served. It is typical of Houle's writing that adults are invariably categorized in some manner relevant to the educational objectives of the programmes being considered.

By 1959, Houle had formulated his basic approach to the design of adult education. In a paper entitled *Educational Engineering*, which he had prepared for the Commission of the Professors of Adult Education, Houle outlined 9 'Fundamental Programming Situations' and 10 'Basic Steps of Program

Development.' He argued that 'The competent educator of adults must have a general theory of program in which the various elements of the learning process fit together into a coherent whole' (Houle, 1959). He espoused the idea that adult educators might well borrow a number of insights from other fields of practice, but that unless they had something that was particular to adult education and drawn from reflection on adult education practice, there would not be much basis for a claim of special competence. Thirteen years later, he presented a revised version of the conception of fundamental programming situations and basic steps of programme development in *The Design of Education*.

In 1960 Houle returned to the theme of coordination in reporting on his consultation with the Extra-mural Department of the University College of the West Indies:

> In every kind of society there must be many kinds of agencies to serve the diversified educational needs of adults. For the sake of economy and efficiency, these agencies need to work together, supplementing each others' efforts and preventing gaps and duplication of service. In an underdeveloped country it is particularly necessary that there be proper coordination, partly because of the scarcity of resources, and partly because of the need, as social services are developed, for each one to grow in the right way and not acquire the isolation shown by the large scale enterprises of more sophisticated societies (Houle, 1960a: 25–26).

This persistent faith in coordination and cooperation was a hallmark of Houle's thinking as expressed in the publications included in this biographical report.

Houle's investigations of phenomena others have examined consistently present new perceptions of the nature of the objects. His approach is exemplified by a statement taken from his 1960 publication, *The Effective Board*, which was written as an outgrowth of his having conducted 10 annual board members' training courses sponsored by the University College of the University of Chicago and the Welfare Council of Metropolitan Chicago. He noted:

> … to become properly aware of the real nature of familiar objects and influences, it is necessary to bring them squarely into view, examining them with the same wonder and curiosity with which one would inspect the rare or the previously unknown (Houle, 1960b: 166).

This freshness of approach distinguishes Houle's observations from the bulk of the writing on adult education.

Houle's series of lectures at the University of Wisconsin, Milwaukee, as Knapp Visiting Professor, formed the material for probably his most influential book, *The Inquiring Mind: A study of the adult who continues to learn*. Based on interviews with little more than a score of adults who had been identified as continuing learners, Houle intuitively (without employing any procedures such as factor analysis) grouped the reports of these interviews into three categories, to which he attached the term 'orientations.' Group one consisted of the goal oriented –

those who use education as a means of accomplishing fairly clear-cut objectives. Group two was called the activity oriented, for they seemed to take part in educational activities because of an attraction to the circumstances of learning rather than to the content or the announced purpose of the activity. Group three was labelled the learning oriented because they seemed to seek knowledge for its own sake (Houle, 1961: 15–16).

The most direct influence of the presentation of the three orientations was the stimulation of a number of doctoral students in adult education at the University of Chicago to undertake research that would refine and advance the notions proposed in *The Inquiring Mind*. As this book and the subsequent related dissertations became known, investigators at other institutions began to mine the same intellectual vein, hoping to identify some particular insight that would produce a quantum leap in the knowledge base. A number of well-known researchers applied quantitative methods and a variety of analytical techniques either to test or to refute Houle's categories. It was not surprising that the refined work involving large numbers of subjects produced refinements in the typology, but has not cast doubt on the soundness of the original conception. Houle's students have refined the typology to include eight major orientations, but it is fair to say that there have been no conceptual advances made in the approach to orientations since Houle proposed his framework.

The remarkable aspect of this study is the elegance of the interpretation of a modest amount of data. The slim, 87-page book is not prepossessing, but the freshness of approach that Houle brought to his investigations is the aspect that distinguishes it from ordinary adult education literature.

In 1964, Houle departed from his established pattern of writing and produced a publication designed to serve the adult student who was returning to study after a number of years away from formal education. This book, *Continuing Your Education*, is a compendium of sage, practical advice taken from years of working with adults of all sorts who had committed themselves to advancing their learning. He presents seven keys to effective learning, an approach that the readers would probably anticipate, and he attempted to broaden the readers' vision beyond the narrow confines of their immediate learning tasks. He notes that:

> The values of learning, while personally profitable, are not narrowly selfish. Both knowledge and the continuing growth of the mind are essential to society as well to the individual. Kingdoms and kingly eras were judged by the ability and wisdom of the king. In a democracy, the people themselves rule – and therefore democracies and democratic eras must be judged by the ability and the wisdom of the people (Houle, 1964a: 171–72).

Houle's writing consistently reflects a respect for the individual learner and an appreciation of the responsibility of educators to work toward the improvement of their society.

In 1964 the Commission of the Professors of Adult Education produced a book, *Adult Education: Outlines of an emerging field of university study*, which was intended to explain to those within the field and those who were trying to comprehend it from outside just what it constituted. Houle contributed a chapter, 'The Emergence of Graduate Study in Adult Education,' in which he traced the history of university study and university graduate programs in adult education from 1917 to 1962. He explained why adult education was introduced into universities as a field of graduate study before any undergraduate programs were developed in the field, saying:

> It might seem appropriate that a field should first build its content and then be accepted as a discipline. The reason why this does not happen is because the university itself is the chief pioneer of knowledge. It develops fields after it admits them (Houle, 1964b: 78).

In 1967, Houle, reflecting on the movement of adult education from a craft to a profession, characterized the professionals' approach to practice as highly particular in each case. He stated:

> What the professional does is to face each new practical case with the awareness that it is unique… Each new opportunity for service presents a problem different from any he has ever encountered before. What the professional knows is drawn from several bodies of subject matter, never just one. Medicine rests upon many disciplines, including anatomy, physiology, pathology and biochemistry. Law depends upon political science, economics, ethics and history. Adult education, like medicine and law, is an art based on many sciences (Houle, 1967: 15).

This capacity for viewing each new case as unique is a hallmark of Houle's approach.

In 1971, Houle reflected on the promise represented by the university residential centres for continuing education and expressed disappointment that they were not achieving their grand goals. After noting their potential to serve three functions: (a) to be a major instrument for teaching adults, (b) to provide a means for training leaders of the adult education movement, and (c) to serve as sites for research, he observed that:

> Some progress has been made in achieving… goals: the training of educators of adults and other advanced students and the conduct of studies and research. As yet accomplishments in these two respects have been far less substantial than they should have been. Few centers have continuing budgets for these purposes and must sketchily improvise ways of taking care of them on a hit-or-miss basis, using the marginal time of staff members, the relatively unskilled and unpaid labor of graduate students undertaking projects and theses, and occasional evaluation funds provided in individual contracts for service (Houle, 1971: 81).

In attempting to show how the centres might be made more effective in carrying out all three of their functions, Houle called for 'vivid and dramatic examples of outstanding achievement' (1971: 81). Drawing a parallel to university laboratory schools and hospitals, he expressed the hope that the desired stature of the centres could eventually be established through 'brilliant leadership'.

Thirteen years after presenting his conceptual scheme for programme planning to the professors of adult education, Houle wrote *The Design of Education*, which he said was intended to present a system of educational design that might have relevance to education at any age of life – one which has grown specifically out of an analysis of the organized and purposeful learning activities of men and women (Houle, 1972: 2–3). In this book, he made clear that he had rejected the notion that there should be a cleavage between the education of children and youth and the education of adults. He endorsed the idea that education is fundamentally the same wherever and whenever it occurs. His basic assumption is that the essentials of the educative process remain the same for all ages of life and the basic design of education is identical throughout life. Houle explained that 'if pedagogy and andragogy are distinguishable, it is not because they are essentially different from one another but because they represent the working out of the same fundamental processes at different stages of life' (1972: 222).

In presenting his 11 categories of educational programmes, he noted that the distinction among categories is in the source of authority and direction so far as planning and control are concerned and not in the apparent physical differences among them (1972: 42). The framework for the analysis or the planning of programmes consists of a combination of decision points and components that must be kept in proper balance to achieve optimal programme outcomes.

This concern for balance and for pattern is another lodestar for Houle's forays into various segments of the field. The artistry of adult education seems to lie in the educator's ability to recognize and to devise harmonious patterns and balanced configurations among the diverse elements in any programme-planning situation.

The External Degree is widely recognized as the definitive work on external degrees. In it, Houle traced the development of the extension degree, the adult degree and the assessment degree, pointing out how they evolved as institutions became increasingly aware of the special learning needs of adults. He referred to the assessment degree as the 'third generation external degree' in that it focuses on the actual learning of the student, rather than on the student's completing a number of formal requirements (1973: 14–15). He saw the desirable outcomes of the increasing acceptance of the external degree which enabled the institutions to reach a new clientele and enabled students who otherwise would not have had an opportunity to begin studies, increased the vitality of internal degree programmes through the introduction of new content and methods, and finally, stimulated the instructors by providing them with experienced adults whose knowledge of the world is superior to even the brightest of the young students of traditional university age (1973: 170–71).

Possibly, because of his appreciation of balance, Houle did not join the parade of adult educators who turned their attention to literacy programs in the second half of the last century. Instead, he conducted complementary inquiries, examining the educational pursuits of the most highly educated members of society. In 1980 he wrote *Continuing Learning in the Professions*, in which he drew upon his studies of 17 professions, seeking to demonstrate that the needs, the general objectives, the specific goals and the methods used all have a marked resemblance (1980: 15–16). His analysis revealed three modes of continuing learning in the professions: (a) inquiry – the process of creating some new synthesis, idea, technique, policy, or strategy of action; (b) instruction – the process of disseminating established skills, knowledge or sensitiveness; and (c) performance – the process of internalizing an idea or using a process habitually, so that it becomes a fundamental part of the way in which a learner thinks about and undertakes his or her work (1980: 31–32). Sensing so many commonalities among the professions, Houle concluded that much could be gained through inter-professional cooperative and coordinated planning for continuing education.

In *Patterns of Learning: New perspectives on life-span education*, Houle began to bear all of the previous considerations of what it means to engage in learning at different stages of life and for a panoply of motivations. He introduced the idea that at any one time an adult is likely to be engaged in several different kinds of learning. He sought a pattern that could be discerned only when these learning activities are seen as interwoven life experiences. He used a 'sequential patterns of learning approach', otherwise known as life-span education, to examine the meaning of education and learning in the lives of a number of individuals. From his analysis, he was able to identify five major patterns (1984b: 172–78). He concluded that the 'patterns of learning in the lives of individuals are emerging as still pictures reporting a cluster of activities at a moment in time. As yet, however, the way by which such patterns change during the course of life has not been generally studied nor widely speculated' (1984b: 231).

In 1989, he wrote a book on governing boards of non-profit making organizations and his final book three years later, *The Literature of Adult Education: A biographical essay*, which explored 'the nature and dimensions of the literature' of adult education. He called the work 'a biographical essay' since in it he considered 1241 books that he had 'read and annotated over the years' (1992: xv). This vast undertaking reflects the breadth of his own scholarship, although he deliberately made no attempt to include papers from journals or conferences. After the Introduction, Houle makes no other reference to the fact that the work reflected his own understanding of the field, but he probed deeply in the British literature as well as that from the United States. In this work, he divides the field into:

1. history;
2. overviews of the whole field;
3. philosophies;
4. adult learners and their needs;
5. providers – to educate children and young people;
6. providers which educate all ages;

7. providers of education for adults;
8. goals related to formal systems;
9. goals related to aspects of adult life;
10. theory and programme design;
11. formats and settings.

Having written and commented on all the books, he also recorded their relative status. While the list was by no means complete, and he recognized that his classification of the field really did not provide a clear introduction to it, it was an excellent reference to the literature of the field, and it is perhaps a fitting memorial to one of adult education's finest scholars.

The persistent search for balance, for perspective and for harmony among the elements characterizes Houle's approach to the study of each aspect of adult education. Never content to take the narrow view, he was committed to the notion that perspective is of central importance in establishing the meaning of all of the phenomena he investigated.

Along with this commitment came an appreciation for the practical aspects of adult education. This appreciation is shown by comments such as 'the effect of a method depends not so much on its inherent efficacy as on the intent and the talents of its user' (1984b: 209). Further, his persistent concern for the improvement of practice was reflected in his reminder that 'to be fully successful, therefore, the professional educator of adults must be deeply conversant with the goals and methods of learning, gaining such knowledge from study in university graduate departments, from other organized training efforts, from self-directed programs of study, or from the contemplative examination of his or her own experience' (1984b: 219).

In his overview of continuing professional education that he presented to the 20th annual conference of the Society for Research into Higher Education, Houle asserted that:

The valid but limited view that the purpose of continuing education is 'to keep up to date on the new research' has been supplemented by an increased awareness that the appropriate goals broaden out to include all the needs for the growth of a profession, beginning with an awareness of its appropriate mission and continuing through a mastery of both its knowledge base and its methods of treatment, its internal structuring, its code of ethics, its relationships with allied professions, and its responsibilities to both its clients and its society (1984a: 193).

This enlarging of the scope of the problem under consideration was characteristic of Houle's approach to the examination of most phenomena as he sought to establish a broad perspective in which to view the elements of interest.

One of Houle's many interests was the study of those who participate least in adult education. At the 1983 European Conference on Motivation for Adult Education, Houle presented a paper on structural features and policies promoting or inhibiting adult learning (1985: 64–73). In that paper he made the point that for each learning venture adults have some immediate reason for seeking learning and that this purpose arises from either a sense of desire or from a sense of deprivation. Considering all adults, from the least to the most actively involved in learning, Houle classified them into six categories with sub-categories in some cases. These six classifications of orientations are as follows:

1. the oblivious person;
2. the uninvolved person;
3. the resistant person;
4. the focused participant;
5. the eclectic participant; and
6. the comprehensive learner (1985: 67–70).

He further subdivided the third and the fourth categories, suggesting that if adult educators are to be successful in assisting learning within the far broader span of lifelong education, it will become increasingly important that they study and understand the learning patterns and sequences of individuals (1985: 72).

From this limited report of his writing, Houle's impressive contributions to the literature of academic adult education are readily apparent. Scores of monographs, chapters in edited collections and individual journal articles have not been included. Nevertheless, the reader should have no doubt that they, too, reflect the same freshness, perspective and creative insights as have been noted in the limited literature mentioned in this chapter.

At this point, it is appropriate to turn to a consideration of the influence Houle exerted through his work with graduate students in the 40 years he was at the University of Chicago.

Through students and colleagues at Chicago

At least 130 individuals earned their doctorates in adult and higher education at the University of Chicago while Houle was a member of the faculty of the Department of Education. Among the more prolific writers who have gone through the programme are Allen Tough, professor of adult education at the Ontario Institute for Studies in Education, who began his studies of self-planned learning under the tutelage of Cyril Houle. Probably the most widely known graduate of the programme was Malcolm Knowles, who was professor of adult education at the North Carolina State University. Chicago alumni are conspicuous throughout North America, with a small number making their contributions on other continents. For the most part, the graduates of the programme appear to be performing in administrative roles, ranging from conference managers to chief executive officers of colleges, yet they are also disproportionately represented in the Commission of the Professors of Adult Education. Testimony from a graduate and from a former colleague at Chicago will demonstrate their assessment of Cyril Houle's influence on their lives and on the field of adult education.

When asked what influence Houle had had on him, Malcolm Knowles wrote first about the contribution 'Cy' had made to his self-concept as an author, and then went on in glowing terms to describe the positive effects on his self-esteem during the course of his doctoral programme. But Houle's most profound contribution, in Knowles's opinion, was 'the inculcation of a deep commitment to excellence. Houle has served as a role model for all of us in the field of adult education... and the improvement in the quality of our literature is at least in part a reflection of his influence' (Knowles, 1985).

George Aker, who was assistant professor of adult education at the University of Chicago in 1962–63 and thereafter professor of adult education at Florida State University, commented that 'the writings of Cy Houle contain the most profound, insightful, coherent, rational, and intelligible descriptions that exist about the field of adult education. Houle's genius in extracting meaning from his observations of practice have produced knowledge, theories, hypotheses and typologies that, while under-utilized by practitioners and scholars alike, provide the best frameworks that we have for advancing the field' (Aker: 1985).

The addition of countless other statements by other scholars and administrators whose lives have been changed and enriched and whose appreciation of the field has been shaped by their association with Houle would not alter the prevailing tone of respect and appreciation, so no further testimonials will be reported. It is useful, nevertheless, to consider briefly some of the associated activities and actions that are significant in any consideration of the influence of Cyril Houle.

Through associated activities

In addition to performing his central responsibilities for conducting research, for teaching and advising graduate student, and for administering the office of secretary of the Department of Education at the university for a period, Houle managed to establish, support or work on behalf of a prodigious number of related organizations and programmes, only a few of which will be mentioned here for the purpose of demonstrating the variety of his interests. As a member of the Chicago Literary Club, he sought to broaden his own appreciation of the world of letters and in turn to help others appreciate his field. To increase his understanding of the situations of poor people living in the inner city, he lived and worked part-time for a year at Hull House, Chicago's best known settlement house.

In collaboration with Robert M Hutchins, who was president of the university, and Mortimer Adler, he developed the series of readings and discussion techniques that became the heart of the Great Books Program. The experience of selecting the readings, coupled with his own disciplined yet insatiable reading, helped to develop him into probably the most liberally educated US adult educator (Blakely, 1981: 12).

To encourage the professional growth of adult educators in the Chicago area, he established the Northern Illinois Round Table of Adult Education, an informal organization that met monthly to facilitate communication and cooperation among the administrators of adult education. With the support of the Carnegie Corporation, he mounted and conducted a series of summer workshops for administrators of university adult education, drawing upon creative and effective administrators and scholars for his co-leaders and providing adult education administrators who had been given their positions without having had any academic preparation in their new field, a taste of adult education as a field of study. As would be expected, Houle supported the Adult Education Council of Chicago, the Adult Education Association of Illinois, and the Adult Education Association of the United States persistently, ever prepared with wise counsel and practical advice when it was sought.

The extent of his work in voluntary organizations and on behalf of international, national, regional, state and local causes will probably never be known, for he was reticent to identify or to discuss these, possibly because of a concern that his motivation for involvement would be misunderstood. His entry in *Who's Who* is extremely modest, overlooking what lesser scholars would regard as significant accomplishments.

In 1947, Cyril Houle married Bettie Eckhardt Totten, who is also a serious lifelong learner, having also earned her PhD degree from the University of Chicago. They had one son, David, who agreed with his mother that Cy Houle was the best waterskiing instructor they have ever known. That he should also excel in the teaching of physical skills may come as a surprise to those who consider him to be almost purely a cerebral creature, but it would not be surprising to anyone who has come to understand his commitment to excellence in whatever he undertook.

Seminal ideas not yet fully exploited

If one were to judge the extent of popular acceptance of Houle's ideas on the basis of the number of his publications, his honorary degrees, his appointments to international and national positions and the awards he has been given by practising adult educators and adult education researchers, it would be reasonable to conclude that his ideas are eagerly seized upon and readily become part of the commonly accepted body of knowledge about the field. The situation is not so clear.

Much of the best-selling literature on programme planning in adult education tends to deal with a restricted range of programme forms and situations, possibly because authors find it easier to write prescriptions for behaviour for highly specific settings and purposes. In *The Design of Education* Houle described in precise detail 11 different kinds of programme planning situations, each with its own particular constraints on the planning process. Such a perspective is of great value to a person seeking to analyse a variety of instances of programme planning. It is not highly useful to a harried programme planner, rushing to complete a menu of course offerings in time to meet a printer's deadlines. *The Design of Education* will never become popular as a 'how to do it' sort of manual. Instead, its most appropriate audience seems to be the reflective student of adult education who is prepared to spend the time required to analyse his or her own practices from a new perspective and to seek to develop future programmes that reflect an optimal balance and harmony among their elements.

Houle's monumental work, *Continuing Learning in the Professions*, demonstrated his capacity to perceive commonalities as well as differences among the continuing education practices of the members of 17 professions. Although this work was given the prestigious Imogene Okes Award by the Commission on Research of the Adult Education Association of the United States, his insightful discussion of the modes of inquiry, instruction and performance was known to only a small group of scholars who were seriously interested in the conceptualization of means for facilitating continuing learning. Little has been done to utilize this conception of modes of continuing professional learning, so exploitation of the implications of a coordinated approach, building upon all three modes, is still some time in the future.

The study of adult education participation was a persistent concern of Houle for decades and his approaches to studying it have developed as his conceptualization of the process evolved. Beginning with a unidimensional approach, which counted the number of episodes of different kinds of learning activities, he soon concluded that to make sense of the phenomenon it would be necessary to move beyond the refinement of methods of quantification. In *The Inquiring Mind*, he advanced the notion of orientations to learning and proposed three categories as a tentative classification. As has been noted earlier, graduate students and other researchers expended a great deal of energy refining these initial three orientations to eight through quantitative analytical approaches, but they made no appreciable change in his conceptual approach. Then, in 1984, with the publication of *Patterns of Learning*, Houle shared his latest approach to the study of participation. Although he identified five major patterns, he observed that he had measured a dynamic process by the use of still photographs so that he was not able to examine fully the pattern of activities at various points across the life span. And even though his studies of six notable individuals, living and dead, allowed him to reach some conclusions regarding the use of various methods, he did not have access to information that would enable him to reach defensible conclusions about the succession of patterns of learning across the life span. That task lies ahead and there is as yet scant evidence that it will be undertaken by other researchers.

Even though Houle's ideas have received appreciable recognition by scholars, their influence on the practice of adult education appears to be less than they deserve. Blakely, in attempting to explain why *The Design of Education* and *Continuing Learning in the Professions* have not had their anticipated impact, said:

Perhaps the field of adult education has not yet reached a stage of high enough common awareness to use a design that is at the same time simple and comprehensive. Certainly continuing education in the several professions is not yet sufficiently advanced to accept a scheme based on commonalities. I foresee that both of these books will become increasingly influential as adult education matures into a more self-recognized and self-analytical field, and as continuing education in the several professions, after working through their peculiarities, approaches a point where it can recognize its commonalities (Blakely, 1985: 14).

Houle's work is among the best known in the world of adult educational scholarship; his fullest impact on the practice of adult education may lie with the scholars whose early careers have been stimulated by the awards that bear his name.

SUMMARY ASSESSMENT

Cyril O Houle was widely regarded as a leading scholar in adult education for the better part of his long career. A prolific writer, yet one with the highest of standards, he continued to produce significant books and articles that reflected fresh insights into complex phenomena. His eminence in his chosen field is assured by the quality of his contributions to the literature and to his inculcation of standards of excellence in the hundreds of graduate students he has guided and taught. The fact that the American Association for Adult and Continuing Education established an award, the Cyril O Houle World Award for Literature in Adult Education, and that the Kellogg Foundation has funded a Houle Scholars scheme at the University of Georgia, are both clear testimony to the esteem in which he and his writing are held.

As an individual, he has impressed many of his students and associates with his air of self-restraint, seeming always to be wary of offering unsolicited advice or counsel. Although highly articulate, he was a quiet man, observing and reflecting on those observations. Though admirably self-disciplined himself, he was never harsh in judging the performance of those who are less gifted or organized. His compassionate sensitivity and concern for students, colleagues and other associates often was unsuspected by those who perceived only an austere scholar.

Dedicated to a philosophy that values cooperation, coordination, individual excellence and balance in all aspects of life, Cyril Houle has done more than any other scholar to establish adult education as a legitimate field of university study and professional practice in the United States of America.

REFERENCES

Aker, G F (1985) *Personal letter to W S Griffith*

Blakely, R J (1981) *Cyril O Houle*, unpublished manuscript in the personal files of W S Griffith

Houle, C O et al (1947) *The Armed Services and Adult Education*, American Council on Education, Washington, DC

Houle, C O (1951) *Libraries in Adult and Fundamental Education*, the report of the Malmo seminar, UNESCO, Paris

Houle, C O and Nelson, C A (1956) *The University, the Citizen, and World Affairs*, American Council on Education, Washington, DC

Houle, C O (1959) *Educational Engineering*, unpublished manuscript, a working paper prepared for the annual seminar of the professors of adult education meeting at Madison, Wisconsin

Houle, C O (1960a) *Adult Education in the British West Indies*. Notes and essays on education for adults, No 31, Centre for the Study of Liberal Education for Adults, Chicago

Houle, C O (1960b) *The Effective Board*, Association Press, New York

Houle, C O (1961) *The Inquiring Mind: A study of the adult who continues to learn*, University of Wisconsin Press, Madison, Wisconsin

Houle, C O (1964a) *Continuing Your Education*, McGraw-Hill, New York

Houle, C O (1964b) The Emergence of Graduate Study in Adult Education, in *Adult Education: Outlines of an emerging field of university study*, eds G Jensen, A A Liveright and W Hallenbeck, Adult Education Association of the USA, Chicago

Houle, C O et al (1967) *The Continuing Task: Reflections on purpose in higher continuing education*, Notes and Essays on Education for Adults, No 54, Centre for the Study of Liberal Education for Adults at Boston University, Brookline, Massachusetts

Houle, C O (1971) *Residential Continuing Education*, Notes and Essays on Education for Adults, no 70, Syracuse University Publications in Continuing Education, Syracuse, New York

Houle, C O (1972) *The Design of Education*, Jossey-Bass, San Francisco

Houle, C O (1973) *The External Degree*, Jossey-Bass, San Francisco

Houle, C O (1980) *Continuing Learning in the Professions*, Jossey-Bass, San Francisco

Houle, C O (1984a) *Overview of Continuing Professional Education. Education for the Professions*, papers presented to the 20th annual conference of the Society for Research into Higher Education, The University, Guildford, Surrey, the Society for Research into Higher Education and NFER-Nelson

Houle, C O (1984b) *Patterns of Learning: New perspectives on life-span education*, Jossey-Bass, San Francisco

Houle, C O (1985) *Structural Features and Policies Promoting or Inhibiting Adult Learning: Motivation for adult education*, working papers presented to the European Conference on Motivation for Adult Education organized by the German Commission for UNESCO and the UNESCO-Institute for Education, ed J H Knoll, German Commission for UNESCO, Hamburg

Houle, C O (1989) *Governing Boards*, Jossey-Bass, San Francisco

Houle, C O (1992) *The Literature of Adult Education: A biographical essay*, Jossey-Bass, San Francisco

Knowles, M S (1985) *Personal letter to W S Griffith*

Reeves, F W, Fansler, T and Houle, C O (1938) *Adult Education: The Regents' Inquiry into the character and cost of public education in the State of New York*, McGraw-Hill, New York

Thoreau, H D (no date) *Walden*, Peter Pauper Press, New York

Chapter 9

Malcolm S Knowles

Peter Jarvis

INTRODUCTION

Malcolm Knowles is, for many people, the creator of the concept of andragogy and it is true that much of his work, both in theory and practice, was focused on the concept. But Knowles was around the adult education scene long before the term became fashionable, although the term itself was coined long before Knowles actually learnt it. This chapter will, naturally, focus upon the idea of andragogy as Knowles has conceived it, but it also seeks to examine the development of his thought and will, therefore, include some reference to his career, but only in relation to the way that it influenced his thinking.

Knowles was born in 1913 and intended to enter the United States Foreign Service after he graduated in 1935, but since there were no vacancies that year he took a temporary job as director of related training for the National Youth Administration based in Massachusetts while he waited for a vacancy to occur. The focus of this work was with unemployed young adults. But like many who entered the field of adult education, he had no training for the work that he was to do and neither did he have an occupational identity. It was 1937 before he discovered that he was an adult educator! In those early years, he was unable to discover a manual to guide him in his work. However, he was very fortunate in another way, since the person to whom he was responsible and who became his mentor was Eduard Lindeman. Knowles says that it was the many hours that he spent with Lindeman and also Lindeman's influential book *The Meaning of Adult Education* (1926) that helped to guide his thinking. Yet it is interesting to note that it was not Lindeman who taught Knowles the term 'andragogy'; Lindeman used the word in 1927 but, it was not until 40 years later that the Serbian adult educator, Dusan Savicevic, introduced Knowles to it, since the term has had much more currency in the eastern European countries than it has had until recently in the West. In addition to Lindeman, the local director of adult education in Boston, Dorothy Hewitt, was an influence on Knowles; he said that the book that she co-authored with Kirtley Mather, *Adult Education: A dynamic for democracy*, was one that he continued to read on occasions.

Hence, like many adult educators, Knowles learnt a great deal about his work on the job, a form of experiential learning that appears less popular these days, even though learning in the workplace is becoming a more popular idea! By 1940, Knowles, having long rejected the idea of entering the foreign service, was appointed director of adult education at the Huntington Avenue YMCA in Boston. He claimed that it was during this time he began to read adult education literature and became aware how adult educators generally regarded adults' learning processes to be different to childrens'.

After navy service, Knowles was appointed director of adult education at the Central YMCA in Chicago and, like many Americans, he enrolled in the local university graduate programme – his subject, needless to say, was adult education. It was there that he was to meet and be influenced by another of the USA's leading adult educators, Professor C O Houle. Knowles said that it was both Houle's intellectual rigour and his ability to practise adult education principles in the traditional setting of a university that impressed him. It was also during this period that Knowles became acquainted with the work of Carl Rogers, who was already teaching that learners could and should be self-directed. The culmination of these influences was such that Knowles embarked upon a task for his thesis at the university that was to occupy the remainder of his academic life – that of constructing a comprehensive theory of adult education. This led to the publication of his first book in 1950, *Informal Adult Education*.

In 1951, Knowles became the executive director of the newly formed Adult Education Association of the United States of America. There he remained for nine years, during which he was able to influence the growth and direction of the organization. The history of the organization in this period is well documented in his own writings (Knowles, 1977; 177) but he did point out in the preface to the later edition how his involvement as executive director made his interpretation a little subjective. The book in which Knowles records the growth and development of the Adult Education Association of the United States of America was first published in 1962, just after he had actually finished his term of office in the association. This book, *The Adult Education Movement in the United States*, records the first major attempt to draw the early threads of adult education together in a historical sequence. As such, it provides an overview of the development of adult education, but on no account can it be claimed to be a detailed historical study. Indeed, Knowles (1977: x–xi) stated:

> that while he was seeking to locate adult education within a wider perspective there were many gaps in the historical data that he was able to employ. While Knowles was able to undertake some archival research for this study, mainly in the archives of the Adult Education Association, much of the remaining data were gathered through questionnaire research and wide reading of already published material. However, for more than twenty years this overview was the only major source book

of the historical development of adult education in the United States, and it was not until the 1980s that there was a growth in academic interest in this field of study.

Even in this book, Knowles (p 249–80) was arguing that adult education is a separate field of study. In seeking to describe this field, he suggested that adult education is:

- expansive and flexible;
- taking the shape of a multi-dimensional social system;
- institutional;
- a field that has its own subject matter;
- geographical;
- orientated to specific personnel – both leaders and consumers;
- highly interactive with the social system;
- in the process of developing a distinctive curriculum and methodology;
- becoming delineated as both a field of study and practice.

Throughout Knowles's writings there is a propensity to list characteristics in this manner, as will become clear as this chapter proceeds, and this approach is open to the criticism that it provides no conceptual basis on which to assess the validity of the characteristics listed. It thus becomes possible to add or to subtract any characteristic from the list as any scholar desires without reference to the conceptual basis of the phenomenon being described.

It might be claimed that observation of what is happening is sufficient, but observers do have a tendency to see events differently and also to interpret them differently, so that this was not sufficient grounds for omitting the theoretical underpinning of either the phenomenon or the interpretation. At the same time, it was most significant that Knowles should have been seeking to delineate the parameters of the field of study in this way.

In a similar manner, Knowles indicated in the *Handbook of Adult Education* (1960) and in the historical overview (Knowles 1977: 252–53) that the subject matter of adult education was beginning to appear as programmes developed in the following areas:

- academic education;
- education for ageing;
- community development;
- creative arts;
- economic education;
- fundamental and literacy education;
- health education;
- home and family life education;
- human relations and leadership training;
- inter-group education;
- liberal adult education;

- public affairs education;
- adult recreation education;
- science education;
- occupational education.

While it is undoubtedly true that the provision of adult education relates to the division of labour in society, this list appears to confuse the process of education (the first in the list and maybe the second) with the provision of education for adults (the remainder). In addition to this list of characteristics, Knowles (1977: 257–60) specified some generic principles that appeared to him to guide the development of the field:

- these institutions emerge in response to specific needs;
- that development is episodic rather than consistent;
- institutional forms of adult education survive when they become attached to agencies established for other purposes;
- adult education programmes must appear as secondary within those agencies;
- adult education programmes differentiate into administration, finance, curriculum and methodology;
- adult education emerges in different sub-structures of society without general reference to the general adult education movement.

Thus, without the benefit of an extended knowledge of philosophy or the insights of the sociology of movements and organizations, Knowles illustrated the direction that he thought the adult education movement was taking. His concern for adult education was profound and his understanding of many of its manifestations extremely insightful. He saw that the movement was, in a sense, peripheral to the dominant institutions in society and yet important to it. He recognized that the very disparate nature of the movement prevented its being adequately coordinated from a centralized position. His position has subsequently been described as a free-market needs model of adult education provision (Jarvis 1985: 184–186), and globalization has shown that his sense of future of adult education was correct. It is a position that he maintained (Knowles 1980a: 12–40) even after adult education became much more established and scholars were calling for a more centrally coordinated approach to its provision (Griffith 1980: 78–114). However, implicit within this position was perhaps one of the central planks of Knowles's own philosophy: that adult education must be free to respond to need, wherever it is discovered. Need, however, is a contentious concept in adult education, as a multitude of publications reveal, and the learning market was to introduce a sense of demands education.

While it is not the place to explore those here, it is important to understand Knowles's own approach to the subject. In a later work (1980b: 88), he argued that:

An educational need… is something people ought to learn for their own good, for the good of the organization, or for the good of society. It is the gap between their present level of competencies and a higher level required for effective performance as defined by themselves, their organization, or society.

At least two points arise from the above quotation that require further discussion: what he meant by need and the concept of goodness. In a sense, he was arguing that need is the difference between 'want' or 'expectation' or 'demand' and 'performance'. But what if the expectations are conflicting? What if the demands are unrealistic? What if they are unachievable? If there is no agreement about the former concepts, then the assertion of need becomes meaningless. There are, additionally, problems of deciding who has the right to define need within the organization or society at large. This, then, leads directly into the second problem in this quotation: the concept of good is not self-evident and, therefore, it must be asked whom Knowles considered the decision makers to be in his formulation of needs. Therefore, Knowles did not really do justice to the self-evidence of his own understanding of the service ethic of adult education. In retrospect, it can be seen that globalization has removed the idea of welfare from many educational policies and the intrinsic weakness in his original formulation becomes more self-evident.

However, embedded in this historical study lie the seeds of what was to become a crucial issue for him. He claimed (1977: 273–76) that rapid social change created a whole new set of assumptions about education and these he proceeded to specify:

- The purpose of education for the young must shift from focusing primarily on the transmission of knowledge to the development of the capacity to learn.
- The curriculum of education for the young must shift from a basis of subject mastery to a learning skill basis of organization.
- The role of the teacher must be re-defined from one who primarily transmits knowledge to one who primarily helps students to inquire.
- A new set of criteria must be applied to determine the readiness of youth to leave full-time schooling.

Here, at the start of the 1960s, Knowles' ideas were developing in a specific way which, when combined with his earlier observation that adults learnt differently to children, would lead to his new theoretical understanding of adult education. By the time that this book was published Knowles had left the Adult Education Association and had begun his academic career at Boston University. He claimed (1984: 5) that it was during 'this period that a theoretical framework regarding adult learning evolved'. It was also during this period that the Serbian adult educator, Dusan Savicevic, attended one of his summer schools and introduced him to a concept that he was subsequently to make famous – andragogy.

ANDRAGOGY

The term 'andragogy' was originally formulated by a German teacher, Alexander Kapp, in 1833, who coined it to describe the educational theory of Plato. A few years later, the philosopher, Johan Friedrich Herbart, was the first to dispute the validity of the term and so the word fell into disuse for nearly a century. It was revived in 1921 when the German social scientist, Eugen Rosenstock, used it in a report to the Academy of Labour in Frankfurt and Lindeman employed it in the USA in 1927. Thereafter it appears to have gained some currency in eastern European countries, but Knowles clearly knew little of its history when he first employed the term. Indeed, with characteristic honesty, he later admitted to misspelling it when he wrote his first article about it, entitled 'Androgogy Not Pedagogy' in *Adult Leadership* in 1968 (Knowles, 1978: 4–9). However, it was in this address, first given in 1967, that he claimed that adult education had been 'hamstrung by the concepts and methods of the traditional education of children'. (Knowles, 1968: 350–51).

The title of that article indicated the theme of Knowles's next major publication, *The Modern Practice of Adult Education: Andragogy versus pedagogy*, which appeared in 1970. Here he brought together the fruits of his years in adult education and the book became seminal to the field. It set out to be a complete practical guide for the adult educator and as such, it covered all the ground that he considered should be examined by adult educators. In this book, he suggested that there are two opposing fields of education, andragogy and pedagogy, the former defined as 'the art and science of helping adults learn' and the latter as 'the art and science of teaching children' (Knowles, 1980b: 43). These two forms of education, he thought, were opposed to each other and he depicted this in the following manner (see Table 9.1).

Table 9.1   *Comparison of the assumptions of pedagogy and andragogy*

Regarding:	Pedagogy	Andragogy
Concept of the learner	The role of the learner is, by definition, a dependent one. The teacher is expected by society to take full responsibility for determining what is to be learned, when it is to be learned, how it is to be learned, and if it has to be learned.	It is a normal aspect of the process of maturation for a person to move from dependency toward increasing self-directedness, but at different rates for different people and in different dimensions of life. Teachers have a responsibility to encourage and nurture this movement. Adults have a deep psychological need to be generally self-directing, although they may be dependent in particular temporary situations.

Regarding:	Pedagogy	Andragogy
Role of learners' experience	The experience learners bring to a learning situation is of little worth. It may be used as a starting point, but the experience from which learners will gain the most is that of the teacher, the textbook writer, the audiovisual aid producer and other experts. Accordingly, the primary techniques in education are transmittal techniques – lecture, assigned techniques reading, AV presentations.	As people grow and develop, they accumulate an increasing reservoir of experience that becomes an increasingly rich resource for learning – for themselves and for others. Furthermore, people attach more meaning to learning they gain from experience than those they acquire passively. Accordingly, the primary techniques in education are experiential techniques – laboratory experiments, discussion, problem-solving cases, simulation exercises, field experience, and the like.
Readiness to learn	People are ready to learn whatever society (especially the school) says they ought to learn, provided the pressures on them (like fear of failure) are great enough. Most people of the same age are ready to learn the same things. Therefore, learning should be organized into a fairly standardized curriculum, with a uniform step-by-step progression for all learners.	People become ready to learn something when they experience a need to learn it in order to cope more satisfyingly with real-life tasks or problems. The educator has a responsibility to create conditions and provide tools and procedures for helping learners discover their 'needs to know'. And learning programs should be organized around life-application categories and sequenced according to the learners' readiness to learn.
Orientation to learning	Learners see education as a process of acquiring subject-matter content, most of which they understand will be useful only at a later time in life. Accordingly, the curriculum should be organized into subject-matter units (eg courses) which follow the logic of the subject (eg from ancient to modern history, from simple to complex mathematics or science). People are subject-centred in their orientation to learning.	Learners see education as a process of developing increased competence to achieve their full potential in life. They want to be able to apply whatever knowledge and skill they gain today to living more effectively tomorrow. Accordingly, learning experiences should be organized around competency development categories. People are performance-centred in their orientation to learning.

This rather crude distinction was to set off a debate in adult education circles that was continuing well into the 1980s; the same debate, in fact, that it started in the 19th century when the term was originally used, and one that has apparently been conducted in the eastern European countries if the discussion by Skalka and Livecka (1977: 79–85) adequately reflected the state of the art in those countries. However, before examining that debate in the West, it is necessary to recall that in 1973 another book from Knowles appeared, *The Adult Learner: A neglected species*. This book was also to prove an important one, covering some of the same ground as the first one, but seeking to locate andragogy more specifically in the area of the theory of adult learning, although it did not really expand the andragogy-pedagogy debate. It did, however, raise important questions about the accepted theories of learning, although it did not seek to engage them in academic debate. This book is easy to read and sought to illustrate 'an andragogical theory of adult learning' (Knowles, 1978: 51) rather than seeking to produce a new theory of learning. Reference will be made later to the significance of this.

It must also be noted here that within a very short space of four years Knowles produced two seminal books in the field of adult education that were to be the focus of much debate in the following years. They constituted the culmination of his thinking about the practice of adult education and they are the foundation of the ongoing debate in the field that has enhanced the knowledge base of adult education as an area of study.

THE ANDRAGOGY-PEDAGOGY DEBATE

From the outset, Knowles's theory was not accepted uncritically by scholars in the field. Houle (1972: 221), for instance, was gently critical of the distinction between the two terms, but the main debate did not begin until a few years later. This started when McKenzie (1977) sought to provide Knowles's rather pragmatic formulation about adult learning with a more solid philosophical foundation by claiming that andragogy had an existential basis. He pointed out that since adults are existentially different to children, andragogy and pedagogy must be logically different. However, Elias (1979: 254) responded by claiming that this distinction is not necessarily significant since men and women are existentially different but that nobody claimed that 'the art and science of teaching women differs from the art and science of teaching men'. Feminists now would probably not make this claim! This, however, was not the substance of McKenzie's response; he accepted Elias's point but claimed that this existential difference was insignificant in relation to the lifespan but that the lifespan difference between children and adults was significant to the position under discussion. While there may be some element of truth in McKenzie's position, this may lie in the utilization of experience by the learner rather than age per se. McKenzie proceeded to try to show that andragogy should not be equated with progressivism, since the latter is a more complete philosophical system and that this is something that andragogy has never claimed to be. Indeed, this is true but this is because andragogy had never been sufficiently elaborated in philosophical terms. Neither did McKenzie recognize that children might have the same propensity as adults to learn and a similar orientation to problem solving; rather he concentrated upon the differences in learning between children and adults, as he understood them, but these were perhaps more directed to the nature of the learner than to the learning processes.

In 1979, Knowles chose to re-enter the debate and now he recognized that andragogy and pedagogy are not two discrete processes based upon age; he claimed (1979: 53) that 'some pedagogical assumptions are realistic for adults and some andragogical assumptions are realistic for children in some situations'. In 1980, a revised edition of *The Modern Practice of Adult Education* appeared and this time it was subtitled 'From Pedagogy to Andragogy'.

By 1984 and the publication of another book which he edited, *Andragogy in Action*, Knowles had shifted his position about the distinction between andragogy and pedagogy, so that the child–adult dichotomy was less significant. He now claimed that pedagogy is a content model and andragogy a process model in the design and operation of educational programme (1984: 13–18). This is in the realms of curriculum theory (Jarvis, 1985: 45–55) despite the fact that he once claimed, in a personal communication, that adult education had no curriculum. Indeed, his was a fine distinction, recognizing that adult education offered a menu of courses to its potential students, but perhaps it was because he did not use the term curriculum that some of the debate about the distinction between andragogy and pedagogy was a little problematic at times.

The tenor of Knowles' work always continued to suggest that he regarded andragogy was related to adult learning and pedagogy to child learning, probably since this was how the distinction appeared to him in the practice of education. However, this book contains examples of process-orientated education, rather than adult education, and this is how he regarded the andragogical, a point to which further reference will be made below.

Thus it may be seen that the crude distinction drawn between adult learning and child learning could not be sustained, and this was the crux of the position advocated by Knudson (1979: 261) when he suggested that the variety of terms that were beginning to appear, eg, andragogy, pedagogy, gerogogy (Label, 1978: 261) should be replaced by a single concept, humanagogy, which is a theory of learning that takes into account the differences between people of various ages as well as their similarities. It is a *human* (his italics) theory of learning and not a theory of 'child learning', 'adult learning' or 'elderly learning'. It is a theory of learning that combines pedagogy, andragogy and gerogogy and takes into account every aspect of presently accepted psychological theory.

While Courtenay and Stevenson (1983: 10–11) would have clearly agreed with Knudson that 'gogymania' has to be avoided, they still wanted to retain a 'tenuous distinction between andragogy and pedagogy'. Perhaps Knudson's position is the logical outcome of the debate, but humanagogy is a clumsy word that has not gained a great deal of currency since it was first introduced and, in any case, what makes humanagogy any different a concept from that of human learning?

Knudson's term is probably unnecessary, even though his emphasis on human learning is very important. It was an emphasis that Knowles himself made when he wrote *The Adult Learner.* However, Knowles has also changed his position since then and, indeed, he has added a fifth assumption about andragogy (1984: 12) – that the motivation to learn is internal – which he does not equate with adult learning. In his final book, (1989: 84) he added a sixth characteristic – that learning experiences are organized around life-tasks and problems.

THE CONCEPT OF ANDRAGOGY REVISITED

At the outset, it is necessary to enquire what 'andragogy' meant to Knowles. In the 1984 publication, *Andragogy in Action*, the definition had not changed although the emphasis and the formulation had. There was a certain confusion between it and self-directed learning, although they were certainly not synonymous concepts. It was also more concerned with the process model of programme design than with 'helping adults learn', which is an element within the wider curriculum analysis of adult education. He suggested that it has seven elements:

1. climate setting (physical, psychological and human);
2. involving learners in mutual planning;
3. involving learners in diagnozing their own needs for learning;
4. involving learners in formulating their own learning objectives;
5. involving learners in designing their own learning plans;
6. helping learners carry out their plans;
7. involving learners in evaluating their own learning (1984: 14–18).

In many ways, this was a formulation of the romantic curriculum that was popular in school education in the 1960s and can be traced back to Dewey (Jarvis 1985: 45–55). Indeed, this is what some scholars have claimed for andragogy for a number of years: Day and Baskett for instance, claimed that it was an ideological formulation (1982: 143–55); Boyer likened it to Rogers' student-centred learning, which is not surprising when it is recalled that Knowles admits to having been influenced by Rogers' work many years earlier (1984: 17–20); Yonge suggested that the difference between andragogy and pedagogy lies in the manner by which the learner is accompanied by the teacher through the learning process. Since the child is not yet an adult, the child is accompanied through the learning process by a teacher with whom there is a relationship of trust, understanding and authority, but when the child becomes an adult the nature of the relationship changes and becomes an adult one (1985: 160–67). Many of these later formulations seem to be pointing in the same direction, but it remained a position without a thoroughgoing theoretical underpinning. Hartree showed that andragogy lacked an epistemology and a coherent discussion of the different dimensions of learning (1984: 203–10). She suggested that:

> Whilst in a sense he (Knowles) has done an important service in popularising the idea of andragogy, it is unfortunate that he has done so in a form which, because it is intellectually dubious, is likely to lead to rejection by the very people it is most important to convince (1984: 9).

Hartree wrote before Knowles's 1984 publication occurred but much of what she claimed remains a valid criticism of his work. Indeed, Tennant (1986) also attacked the concept, claiming that in this latest work Knowles implicitly admonishes educators for structuring the content of the course while praising them for structuring the process, which is rather a logical inconsistency. Additionally, he pointed to the fact that there is no distinction made between the need for and the ability of adults to be self-directing. However, Knowles (1984: 7) suggested that there was substantial enough body of knowledge about adult learners and their learning to warrant attempts to organize it into a systematic framework of assumptions, principles and strategies, and this is what andragogy tried to do. But it is evident from this quotation that Knowles had not really broken away from the idea that andragogy is about adult teaching and learning in some way, since he is still relating it quite specifically to adults here. Perhaps this signified the sense in which Knowles had been committed to the cause of adult education and had sought to make it a distinctive discipline. Cross (1981: 227) appeared rather dubious that andragogy could ever perform the function of providing an overarching theory of failure to locate Knowles's work within a wider curriculum theory, especially as the 1984 publication seemed to include examples of andragogy from educators who adopted a broadly similar position to his own. Indeed, all that the volume actually demonstrated is that there are many people utilizing a humanistic, egalitarian approach to education rather than demonstrating the validity of his formulation.

Throughout this discussion, it is clear that Knowles's failure to produce a rigorous and well-argued exposition of his position resulted in some confusion about the concept. Even so, it would be possible to claim that Knowles had been trying to let the theory evolve as a result of observing practice, and because adult education itself is a very young field of study, it would have been quite inappropriate to utilize research from other disciplines, especially child education, in the first instance. It would, however, be difficult to sustain this because he has consistently contrasted the education of children to the education of adults. Hence, such reference to the established research could legitimately have been expected.

Since Knowles had noted a difference between adult and child learning so early in his own career, he had perhaps taken it for granted, rather than trying to demonstrate it. But the correlation that he made then between types of learning and age, which remained with him in part ever since, may be spurious, since it may relate to other factors, such as hierarchical traditions, adult authority, etc. In these instances recognition of the significance of the social setting in which education occurs would have added another important dimension to his thinking and might have, perhaps, led to a slightly different formulation in the first instance. Even so, the formulations of the concept of andragogy have been crucial to the development of theory about the education of adults. The debate led to a broadening of the theory of the field of study and, even, to a re-concep-tualization of the concept of andragogy itself (Nottingham Andragogy Group 1983).

There is a sense in which this debate became history with the development of research into experiential learning and lifelong learning. A the same time, it was a very important step in the development of the education of adults since it popularized a great deal of what was widely accepted about teaching them. However, before any further assessment is made of the work of Malcolm Knowles it is important to recognize that he wrote more widely than in just this area and so it is necessary to examine some of this other work.

OTHER ASPECTS OF HIS WORK

One element of Knowles's work that has not yet been mentioned is that of contract learning; he developed this approach to teaching in a small book published in 1975, *Self-directed Learning*, in which he expanded the idea of the self-directed learners discussing their learning needs with the teacher and then entering into a contract with the teacher to achieve their learning objectives by a specified date. While Knowles clearly saw this as part of the practice of andra-gogy, it was not so clearly spelt out in that earlier publication, but by 1984 it was much more explicit. Here he suggests that this is one way to help students to structure their own learning, which may be seen as a partial response to Tennant's criticism, cited above (1986: 18–20). It is clearly one way in which the learners may be encouraged to structure their own learning, to work at their own pace and in their own time. It is certainly an approach that may be very useful in individualized teaching and learning situations (Jarvis, 1986), but this is perhaps also one of the weaknesses implicit in much of Knowles's work, as Tennant (1986) claims. Learning per se is certainly individualistic, but there is a danger in omitting the social context within which it occurs, and the influence that that environment exerts upon the learning process. However, the question still remains as to the precise relationship between contract learning and andragogy.

Apart from this small study, Knowles co-authored a book with his wife on group dynamics, *Introduction to Group Dynamics* (1959), which also reflected his own approach to teaching through the use of groups. While this is in accord with much of Knowles' other writing and practice, no further discussion will occur about it here since he was not the sole author.

Acting as a consultant to a project on Faith Development in the Adult Life Cycle, Knowles recognized that one of the reasons why there was a poverty of

research related to the interface between the adult life cycle and faith development is because the latter concept has not been operationally defined. He then
went on to write:

> If we could discover what the developmental tasks of faith development are at
> various life stages, we would have some clear guidelines for designing adult educa-
> tional experiences that would facilitate the developmental process (in Stokes 1982:
> 73).

However, if both the structure of the process and the end product are already
determined then this raises major questions about the nature of this process,
whether it is education at all or merely a technique of indoctrination. This position reflected a similar one to that which he produced in another context, where
he suggested that needs refer to meeting the organizational or the societal good as
well as the individual one. Indeed, Knowles changed this position little from the
time when he claimed that while these are all valid sources of objectives, their
differences are often magnified (1957: 237), which really demonstrates an underlying belief in the functional interdependence of society without working out
the implications of holding such a position. A position of indoctrination is
probably far from the one that Knowles would have wanted to adopt, or to be
argued from his writings, but that it can be logically deduced from what he has
written demonstrates his failure to work out systematically the implications of
his position.

   Towards the end of his career, Knowles wrote *The Making of an Adult Educator*
(1989), which was an autobiographical account of his own development. It was
not an autobiography, but it was a glimpse into his life and thought. In these
pages he discussed the questions that he was most frequently asked and
throughout, his own optimism, willingness to embrace the future and ability to
change his perspective are clear. This willingness to embrace the future was also
evident when he wrote the *Epilogue to Adult Education: Evolution and achievements
in a developing field of study* (1992). In this thoughtful but light-hearted chapter, he
gently mocked the scholarly approach of the book since he had always written
for a wider audience and predicted that universities would begin to disappear
into systems of lifelong learning – among other things. He also noted that graduate programmes in adult education would become integrated into wider areas
of professional practice, which is perhaps a far-sighted lesson for those who seek
to 'protect their turf' as universities are forced to reorganize in the face of
mounting social pressures.

CONCLUSIONS

It may be seen from the above discussion that a frequent criticism of Knowles's
writing is that he never sought to develop his ideas fully and that he tended to be
descriptive rather than analytical or critical. This is clearly a valid criticism and a

simple example of this may be seen from the fact that andragogy was still defined in the 1984 publication in terms of helping adults learn, although he had changed his stance twice since the time when he actually did define the concept in this manner. Even allowing for the change in position, a question must be raised about whether andragogy is the art and science of helping adults learn or whether it was his own ideological exposition. In other words, is it a psychological position based on research or is it a philosophy of adult education based on his own humanistic ideals? A similar example might be the fact that Knowles consistently claimed that adulthood is in some way related to autonomy and self-direction. This may be true, but Riesman's classical study *The Lonely Crowd* (1950) showed that there were some adults within his study who were 'other directed' as well as those who were 'inner' or 'tradition' directed. The latter may be construed as self directed but the former cannot be seen in this manner. Hence, it is either necessary to argue that those who are other directed are not adults or that his approach to adulthood is ideological. If it is ideological and every adult should be self-directed, then Knowles had to face the question that Hobbes discussed as long ago as 1651 in *Leviathan*. In any case, his conception was clearly individualistic and as such needs to respond to the types of criticisms raised of individualism by Keddie (1980). However, the frequent exposition of his position led to profound debates within the field of study of adult education, which have resulted in an enriched academic understanding of the process of the education of adults. When a debate convinced him that elements of his position were untenable, then with characteristic openness and honesty he always responded by changing his position, although never changing his value system. This openness and humanity characterize both his writing and his person.

Knowles's writing resulted in many people from different areas of work becoming much more aware of this humanistic approach to adult teaching and learning more than they would have done had he not proclaimed his message so forcefully and so widely.

Malcolm Knowles's formulation of andragogy was the first major attempt in the West to construct a comprehensive theory of adult education, and this has been one of the constant concerns that he held throughout his career. While it was not as comprehensive a theory as he would have perhaps anticipated, he provided a baseline for considerable discussion about the nature of adult education.

As a teacher, writer and leader in the field, Knowles was an innovator, responding to the needs of the field as he perceived them and, as such, he was a key figure in the growth of the theory and practice of adult education throughout the Western world in the last century. Yet, above all, it would perhaps be fair to say that both his theory and his practice embodied his own value system and that this was contained within his formulations of andragogy.

REFERENCES

Anderson, M L and Lindeman, E C (1927) *Education Through Experience*, Workers Education Bureau, New York

Boyer, D L (1984) Knowles, Malcolm and Rogers, Carl: A comparison of andragogy and student-centred learning in lifelong learning, *An Omnibus of Practice and Research*, 7 (4)

Courtenay, B and Stevenson, P (1983) Avoiding the Threat of Gogymania in Lifelong Learning, *The Adult Years*, **6** (7)

Cross, K P (1981) *Adults as Learners*, Jossey-Bass, San Francisco

Day, C and Baskett, H K (1982) Discrepancies between Intention and Practice: Re-examining some basic assumptions about adult and continuing professional education, *International Journal of Lifelong Education*, **1** (2)

Elias, J L (1979) Andragogy Revisited, *Adult Education*, **29**

Griffith, W S (1980) Coordination of Personnel, Programs and Services, in *Building an Effective Adult Education Enterprise*, eds J Peters et al, Jossey-Bass, San Francisco

Hartree A (1984) Malcolm Knowles' Theory of Andragogy: A critique, *International Journal of Lifelong Education*, **3** (2)

Hewitt, D and Mather, K F (1937) *Adult Education: A dynamic for democracy*, Appleton-Century Crofts, New York

Hobbes, T (1968) *Leviathan*, Pelican, Harmondsworth

Houle, C O (1972) *The Design of Education*, Jossey-Bass, San Francisco

Jarvis, P (1985) *The Sociology of Adult and Continuing Education*, Croom-Helm, London

Jarvis, P (1986) Contract Learning, *Journal of District Nursing*, (Nov), pp 13–14

Keddie N (1980) Adult Education: An ideology of individualism, in *Adult Education for a Change*, ed J Thompson, Hutchinson, London

Knowles, M S (1950) *Informal Adult Education*, Association Press, New York

Knowles, M S (1957) Philosophical Issues that Confront Adult Educators, *Adult Education*, **7** (4)

Knowles, M S (1960) *Handbook of Adult Education in the USA*, Adult Education Association of the USA

Knowles, M S (1968) Androgogy Not Pedagogy, *Adult Leadership*, no 16

Knowles, M S (1970) *The Modern Practice of Adult Education: Andragogy versus pedagogy*, Association Press, New York

Knowles, M S (1973) *The Adult Learner: A neglected species*, Gulf Publishing Co, Houston

Knowles, M S (1975) *Self-directed Learning*, Follett Publishing Co, Chicago

Knowles, M S (1977) *A History of the Adult Education Movement in the USA*, Krieger, New York

Knowles, M S (1978) *The Adult Learner: A neglected species*, 2nd edn, Gulf Publishing Co, Houston

Knowles, M S (1979) Andragogy Revisited II, *Adult Education*, 30

Knowles, M S (1980a) The Growth and Development of Adult Education, in *Building an Effective Adult Education Enterprise*, eds J Peters *et al*, Jossey-Bass, San Francisco

Knowles, M S (1980b) *The Modern Practice of Adult Education: From pedagogy to andragogy*, 2nd edn, Association Press, Chicago

Knowles, M S (1982) Faith Development in the Adult Life Cycle: An adult educator's reflections, in *Faith Development in the Adult Life Cycle*, ed K Stokes, W H Sadlier, New York

Knowles, M S (1989) *The Making of an Adult Educator*, Jossey-Bass, San Francisco

Knowles M S (1992) The Epilogue to Adult Education: Evolution and achievements, in *A Developing Field of Study*, eds J M Peters and P Jarvis, Jossey-Bass, San Francisco

Knowles, M S and Knowles, H (1959) *Introduction to Group Dynamics*, Association Press, Chicago

Knowles, M S *et al* (1984) *Andragogy in Action: Applying modern principles of adult education*, Jossey-Bass, San Francisco

Knudson, R S (1979) Andragogy Revisited: Humanagogy anyone? *Adult Education*, **29**

Label, J (1978) Beyond Andragogy to Gerogogy in Lifelong Learning, *The Adult Years*, no 1

Lindeman, E C (1926) *The Meaning of Adult Education*, New Republic, New York

Mckenzie, L (1977) The Issue of Andragogy, *Adult Education*, **27**

McKenzie, I (1979) Andragogy Revisited: Response to Elias, *Adult Education*, **29**

Nottingham Andragogy Group (1983) *Towards a Developmental Theory of Andragogy*, Department of Adult Education, University of Nottingham

Peters, J *et al* (1980) *Building an Effective Adult Education Enterprise*, Jossey-Bass, San Francisco

Riesman, D (1950) *The Lonely Crowd*, Yale University Press, New Haven

Skalka, J and Livecka, E (1977) *Adult Education in the Czechoslovak Socialist Republic*, European Centre for Leisure and Education, Prague

Stokes, K (1982) *Faith Development in the Adult Life Cycle*, W H Sadlier, New York

Tennant, M (1986) An Evaluation of Knowles' Theory of Adult Learning, *International Journal of Lifelong Education*, **5** (2)

Thompson, J (1980) *Adult Education for a Change*, Hutchinson, London

Yonge, G D (1985) Andragogy and Pedagogy: Two ways of accompaniment, *Adult Education Quarterly*, **35** (3)

Chapter 10

Roby Kidd – intellectual voyager

Alan M Thomas

Human beings seem to seek after learning; learning seems to be the condition of a healthy organism. The main task is to provide the climate and the atmosphere and stimulus and self-discipline in which learning is promoted (Kidd, 1974a: 8).

Our first problem is to survive. It is not a question of the survival of the fittest; either we survive together or we perish together. Survival requires that the countries of the world must learn to live together in peace. Learn is the operative word. Mutual respect, understanding, sympathy, are qualities that are destroyed by ignorance, and fostered by knowledge. In the field of international understanding, adult education in today's divided world takes on a new importance. Provided that man learns to survive, he has in front of him opportunities for social development and personal well-being such as have never been open to him before (Declaration: Second UNESCO World Conference on Adult Education, from Kidd (1974a: 35).

In many respects the two preceding statements represent the continuing polarities, the Scylla and Charybdis, of the life and thought of J Robbins Kidd. Both life and thought have to be considered in any appreciation of him. To treat them separately would be to risk failing to grasp the essence of the man, the essence of the 'adult education movement' with which he was so intimately associated, and the character of the relationship between the two.

I have believed for many years that no one learns anything without involvement. I am convinced that when someone has learned something well he ought to express that learning in action. From personal experience I know that learning of depth and power occurs when one takes part in significant action, and reflects, studies, analyzes and observes one's own behaviour and that of others engaged in action. I even see that temporary withdrawal from action, to seek quiet and contemplate, the contribution of Asian scholars in particular, is part of the total process of engagement, not disengagement. (Kidd, b).

The maintenance of a coherent life of thought and action dominated Kidd's writing and speaking – those two activities were never widely separated, revolving constantly on such themes as learning; learning in action; learning with others in pursuit of collective goals; the demands of rational behaviour; and the ability to rise beyond one's own cultural and national limitations. More than anyone else among his contemporaries, Kidd reflected upon, articulated and tried to embody the wonderful and inscrutable relationship between individual learning and the world in which that learning manifests itself. For Kidd, it seems, thinking and learning were virtually indistinguishable, and reciprocal action inescapable. For him, that relationship was compellingly implicit in the practice and advocacy of adult education. Practitioners throughout the world, in the years between 1954 and 1982, came to see him as the embodiment of those convictions.

J Robbins Kidd was born in the small town of Wapella in the Canadian province of Saskatchewan in 1915. Early in his life, following the death of his father, the family moved to Vancouver, British Columbia, where he completed his formal schooling. If the Canadian prairies left their characteristic stamp upon him, even at so early an age, it was not particularly noticeable in his later years, though he remained an enthusiastic admirer of the adult education programmes of the Wheat Pools, those most characteristic of all prairie institutions. However, his informal and perhaps non-formal education was very much more the product of adolescent periods spent in Gibson's Landing, a small coastal settlement north of the city of Vancouver. Like all sea coasts, British Columbia has attracted wanderers from all parts of the world. 'However my old grandfather had built a tall, gaunt, shingled house on a hill at Gibson's Landing, to which seaside village had come the poor and the lost and adventurers from everywhere, including some Finnish communists fleeing from the persecution of Marshall Mannerheim, social democrats from many countries of Europe. It was here in the bush and the fishing boats and the road gangs that I learned economics and Canadian history, this was my real college' (Kidd, 1975a: 228). Kidd's speeches and writings throughout his lifetime were sprinkled with references to his years in Gibson's Landing.

He joined the staff of the Young Men's Christian Association of Canada (YMCA) in 1935 where he was responsible for adult and boys' work. In 1943, he moved to the Ottawa 'Y' where he was involved in adult education, and in 1947 he left to take a position with the Canadian Association for Adult Education (CAAE).

Having moved to Montreal in the service of the YMCA, he completed his BA at Sir George Williams University (1939), his MA at McGill University (1943), both in that city, and his EdD at Teachers' College, Columbia University in New York City (1947). In an address to the first international conference of university evening students in Montreal in 1960, he said, '... let me confess that I was never an evening student. But let me hastily tell you that I have some claim to be here; every part of my undergraduate and graduate work was taken while I was fully employed. That should qualify me in spirit if not in fact' (Kidd, 1969:

189). Long before there was much official interest in the unconventional student, except perhaps at Sir George Williams University, the YMCA university expressly designed for them, Kidd demonstrated personally that an individual could do what he later argued ought to be possible for everyone with the appropriate qualifications and determination.

In the same address, true to his relentless advocacy for adult education, even among those who were both prime participants and beneficiaries, he went on to say: 'The fact is that in almost every single list where the results of evening students are compared with those of regular college students, the older student has a better performance' (Kidd, 1969: 191).

It is not entirely clear just under what circumstances and why Kidd developed his interest in and commitment to the education of adults. Possibly it arose in part from his work with the YMCA programmes for boys and men, an experience denied to most formal educators, which allowed him to witness the precious continuity in the lives of individuals who were, by means of various programmes, engaged in learning of equal significance to anything they experienced in school. In Ottawa, he had been involved in the creation of Carlton College, a new post-secondary institution designed largely to provide university education for fully employed civil servants. In addition, counselling for the New York YMCA had brought him into regular contact with relatively uneducated veterans who were trying to continue the transformation of their lives that military service had begun. Certainly, the 'Y' left its stamp on him as it has, indelibly, on the many Canadians who have passed through its employment. Receptiveness, interest, compassion and a consuming curiosity about other individuals are among those characteristics. But perhaps more than anything else, the 'Y' reinforced his natural optimism about the world and all of its people, an optimism, that despite considerable test, dominated all of his work.

He was aware of the effects of the ethos of the 'Y' on him, especially when he found himself among the somewhat more sophisticated participants in the work of the Canadian Association for Adult Education in the late 1940s.

> The fact that I was a YMCA secretary did not endear me to many... When I joined the CAAE staff, some of the board members exercised tolerance for the rather breezy salutations that I had learned in dealing with boys' gang personnel in Montreal as well as the informality of my dress. But it was an association in which differences were accepted and the tolerance eventually turned to a kind of affection which I may not have deserved, but which warmed me. Neither then nor since have I been able to describe an adult educationist as belonging to a particular type (Kidd, a: 29).

Whatever his preparation, once Kidd found himself in the company of dedicated adult educators, voluntary and professional, there was no turning back.

Kidd became the director of the CAAE in 1951. The post allowed him, indeed insisted on engagement with national Canada. A glance at the geography of the country and a slight acquaintance with its pre-war society will explain why, until then, national experience had been largely the preserve of commercial representatives and politicians. His early responsibility for the Joint Planning Commission, a device of the Canadian Association for Adult Education for developing cooperative relationships between voluntary organizations and government agencies active in adult education of all kinds, introduced him to the complex subtleties of the management of education in Canada where the Federal Government, denied an official role by the constitution, must accomplish its inescapable educational objectives by a combination of stealth and diplomacy. Similarly his work with Farm Radio Forum and Citizens' Forum, the two national public affairs programmes operated by the CAAE, in cooperation with the Canadian Broadcasting Corporation, provided experience in the precarious area of adult education centred on contentious political issues involving wide public concern.

Travelling across Canada several times a year in the following decade, Kidd quickly came to see the tangled multiplicity of voluntary organizations and the tiers of frequently overlapping government jurisdictions as a community open to development, to development on the most humane and rewarding of all imaginable bases, the potential of adult learning. He learnt to exert the type of persuasive, non-threatening, supportive leadership that such a small, threadbare, voluntary vehicle as the CAAE demanded, and exercised those skills with great success everywhere in Canada, with the exception of the province of Quebec. Perhaps it was no more than the problems of the historical moment, characterized by the growing, restless nationalism in that province, but Kidd was never able to establish the rapport and mutual trust with French-speaking, adult educators in Quebec that he maintained so successfully in English-speaking Canada and with adult educators throughout the rest of the world.

Working with all types of public and private organizations, large and small, with respect to any problem or opportunity where adult learning might be involved, Kidd developed the special skills and attitudes appropriate for working on the margins of established interests and organizations. In particular he developed an ability to see large organizations not as impersonal, mostly impenetrable systems, but in terms of particular individuals within those organizations, individuals who could be talked with, who could be both understood and persuaded, and above all who could have an effect on the organizations themselves.

In the late 1940s, Kidd undertook the establishment of national awards for achievement in film and radio. He knew that these achievements were already being much admired outside of Canada and he also understood the powerful educational value of public recognition, no matter how modest the actual prize. At the same time, he demonstrated what became a lifelong interest in and enthusiasm for film and broadcasting as vehicles for artistic accomplishment of the first rank and as educational instruments of immense potential.

Kidd participated substantially in the first two national conferences on education held in Canada in the late 1950s and early 1960; was the first president of Canadian Library Week; and managed to be nearly everywhere in the country where the interests of adult learners needed nurture or protection.

These were not easy years, either financially for the CAAE – it was almost always on the verge of bankruptcy – or for the growth of programmatic or financial support of adult education by the dominant educational institutions. Writing in 1950, Kidd said: 'Even where adult education is well established it has not won a very important place for itself. It may have become the 'third' partner along with the public school and the university, but if so it is most certainly a very green and junior partner' (Kidd, 1950a: 12).

Characteristically, he did not lay all the blame for this state of adult education at the door of the institutions of formal education or of the formal educators. In addition, he cited the failure of nerve and determination among Canadian adult educators themselves. 'We are quite likely to make the claim that adult education is needed to save our society and in the next breath ask for a budget for an entire province that would scarcely run a single public school' (Kidd, 1950b: 12). In the same article, there is a flash of the enthusiasm, generosity and tempered optimism that informed all of his life.

> Adult education in Canada could certainly not be considered very radical or very reactionary, or even very daring. But it is based on a respect for reason and belief, and particularly a respect for people... And what does it mean on balance? A history that is brief but full and rich. A list of remarkable accomplishments already, with present and future opportunities and responsibilities that overmatch anything that came before... Will it be enough? Not that there is any doubt that genuine achievement will come. These are certain. But such efforts may still not equal what could and should be done. Will we muster the vision needed and the resources? (Kidd, 1950b: 23).

In 1961, after 14 years at the CAAE, he left to become the secretary-general of the Humanities and the Social Sciences Research Councils of Canada. But he did not leave his commitment to and participation in adult education.

From the earliest days at the CAAE, Kidd became increasingly involved in international adult education. 'I began to look after the study-observation experiences of foreign educationists in 1947, and went first in 1954 into the Caribbean for field work' (Kidd, 1974b: 8). While his involvement, in retrospect, seems little more than casual, Kidd observed later that for him it had a certain inevitability.

> I was as ready as any lover for an offer of marriage, as any actor for a bit part, or any sailboat addict receiving an invitation to leave his office when the sun is high and the wind is fresh... one of the strongest reasons was that I had not been to war. International development seemed to offer some of the possibilities for service, and some of the adventures I had missed (Kidd, d: 35).

Opportunities and self-incurred international obligations followed relentlessly. In 1953 he was invited by UNESCO to become a member of a committee. In 1959, he was elected the first president of the Adult Education Section of the World Conference of the Organizations of the Teaching Profession. In 1961 he became president of the Advisory Committee to UNESCO on Adult Education, a post he was to hold for five years. In 1965, he conducted a study of university extension for the state of Alaska. In 1965 he left his position with the Canadian Research Councils to spend a year developing a major project in adult education for the Indian state of Rajasthan, a project supported by the Canadian International Development Agency, the University of British Columbia, and the government of India. In 1969, he was appointed a member of the UNESCO jury for the awarding of world prizes for achievement in the development of adult literacy, a position he retained for the rest of his life.

But there can be little doubt that his election as president of the second UNESCO World Conference on Adult Education in the city of Montreal in 1960 both symbolized and established irreversibly his personal and intellectual presence on the world stage. The conference convinced Kidd that world coop-eration was not only a necessity, it was a possibility and that adult education was not only a means but an end in that context.

Considerable doubt and pessimism were expressed about the Montreal conference even before the delegates began to arrive. The time was 1960, the period of the deepest freeze in the cold war; the U-2 incident had just occurred and President Eisenhower's planned trip to Moscow had been abruptly cancelled. Moreover, the Montreal conference was the very first international conference in which Communist countries were represented in force (Kidd, 1974a: 13)

... and

Understanding requires a will for it. The delegates at Montreal came for a serious purpose and were an exceptional group of men and women who were bent on talking and working together and were not easily deterred (p 14).

Kidd's fundamental belief in the final efficacy of individuals talking reasonably with each other in circumstances that permitted, indeed encouraged such exchange, even at a global level, seemed to him to have been confirmed.

Following his year in India, in 1966 Kidd joined the newly created Ontario Institute for Studies in Education (OISE) as the first chair of the Department of Adult Education. The institute was one of the many research and development agencies in education founded throughout the world during the educationally opulent 1960s, but unlike most of the others, incorporated graduate instruction among its functions. That inclusion probably saved it from the loss of support experienced by so many others a decade later, and the combination of the three activities, research, teaching and field development, allowed Kidd to continue the major tasks of his life with only a slightly different emphasis. During his years at the CAAE Kidd worked strenuously for the increase in opportunities for the systematic preparation of practitioners of adult education (see Selman, 1982). Almost every summer Kidd had often taught the first course in adult education at universities throughout Canada. His teaching style never lost the casual, somewhat hurried quality so characteristic of university summer school. With little assistance and ferocious acquisitiveness, he had assembled the best library on adult education in Canada. Within the limits of money and space characteristic of a small voluntary organization, that was no mean accomplishment. The department quickly became one of the strongest in Canada and a beacon for practitioners throughout the world. While concentrating on building up the faculty, Kidd was also able to turn to the natural extension of his international work, the development of comparative studies in adult education.

Nevertheless, his 'trigger-finger' continued to itch and in 1972, with modest support from the Canadian International Development Agency, he launched the International Council for Adult Education (ICAE). Despite criticism from some national adult education bodies that the support of the Council would undermine UNESCO, Kidd persisted and by the time of his death, the council had become a non-governmental organization for adult education of major influence. The need for such a non-governmental organization in international adult education, as a counterpoint to the influence of governments that was growing steadily through UNESCO itself, was a consistent thread in Kidd's beliefs. Just as he had extended his 'community-development' skills from the volatile organizational turmoil represented by Canada to the international stage, so he extended ideas and practices that arose from his Canadian experience. Kidd was intensely aware of the ambivalence with which most governments regard 'learning', however democratic they profess to be. The council represented an alternative world vehicle for the nourishment and protection of the principles of lifelong learning.

In the late 1970s, Kidd was invited to edit the adult education section of the new *International Encyclopedia of Education* to be produced by Pergamon Press. In many respects the planning of that section represented the apotheosis of his life and work. A glance at the range of categories that he believed necessary for the understanding of the scope and importance of adult education, in contrast to coverage in earlier educational lexicons, indicates something of the breadth and depth of his experience and his imagination. Kidd died in 1982 before that work could be completed but the section remains as a monument to his life and work.

INTELLECTUAL FOREBEARS

It is not an easy task to identify Kidd's intellectual ancestors and models. Friends, colleagues and above all his audiences throughout the world, grew accustomed to the frequency and variety of the references with which he populated his spoken and written words. He read widely and had an unerring eye for the statement in any text of any historical period that could be used to justify and expand a commitment to adult education. His imagination seemed to be a sponge for examples, anecdotes and statements about learning in any context.

Nevertheless, some ideas and images repeat themselves with sufficient frequency to reveal a pattern of example and influence. He was particularly impressed by men and women who, in terms of educational achievement, had literally dragged themselves up by their bootstraps. He refers repeatedly to Louis de Wolfe, a Canadian educator who rose to the top of his profession with little early schooling; to Eduard Lindeman, with whom he worked in New York during his years of graduate study, and who seemed to epitomize the self-made scholar with a limited regard for intellectual and academic shibboleths; and to other individuals with similar energy, curiosity, and determination. Perhaps the seeds of Kidd's fascination were supplied by the example of his father, of whom, in one of his rare references to him, he said, 'He never went beyond grade four. Still he served his town as mayor for many years, took an active part in provincial and national politics, started the first insurance business and the first garage and automobile agency in that part of the West' (Kidd, 1966: 17). While often discouraged by what he saw in partisan politics he was an admirer of many of the political leaders he met during his lifetime. Of Julius Nyerere, president of Tanzania, and president of the ICAE, he said, 'he seems to hunger for and need direct physical and intellectual contact with people' (Kidd, e: 11). Kidd might have been describing himself.

He was at Teachers' College Columbia University during the last years of the influence of John Dewey and his colleagues and disciples. Men like Kilpatrick, Child, Countz and others of the optimistic, liberal, developmental school of education were still in the ascendancy. It was an intellectual atmosphere that Kidd was to find when he joined the staff of the CAAE and he often refers to Edward (Ned) Corbett, the original director, as his mentor. But the roots of such attitudes and the corresponding ideas are to be found earlier in Kidd's western adolescence and his experience with the YMCA. While there is little trace of formal Christianity or of any other formal doctrine to be found in his work, he had been deeply influenced by what came to be known as Christian humanism. It represented a belief in human value in both thought and action that characterized the pioneer socialists of the Canadian West. The ideas and example of the Canadian pastor-politician, J M Woodsworth, founder of the first socialist party, and many of his associates, influenced Kidd profoundly and were easily translated to the education of adults and his work at the CAAE. In commenting on the relationship of the social gospel and adult education he said:

> It took effort but it wasn't impossible to bring together in the Joint Planning Commission organizations of churches, social agencies, universities, school boards and libraries, business and professional organizations, corporations, trade unions and cooperatives, and cultural societies, because there were some common bonds. One strand that united most, though not all, was an acceptance of much of the social gospel – albeit often stated in secular terms (Kidd, 1956: 258).

It seems to have been the combination of thought and action, in company with the belief in the self-perfectibility of human beings and society represented in that doctrine, that fused so gracefully in Kidd. In *While Time Is Burning*, a major recapitulation of his thought, he said: 'I believe that guidance may come best from the doers, rather than the critics or theorists, although some of the best doers and critic-theorists turn out to be the same people' (Kidd, 1974b: 30).

Obviously, the roots stretch farther back to the Enlightenment and its liberal thinkers. There was not much of Rousseau in Kidd's thought since he did not believe that institutions inevitably corrupted individuals, despite his frequent impatience with them. Like Locke he believed that democracy was the preferred form of government simply because it worked and because it represented both end and means for learning. Perhaps his closest counterparts are to be found in men like Fourier and Owen, who believed that given the right environment, human beings could move towards perfection, and who set out to demonstrate that their beliefs were true.

IDEAS

There is a perpendicular dimension of learning continuing through the entire life-span and consonant with all of the divisions of education. There is a horizontal dimension of learning penetrating into every form of intellectual and spiritual activity known to man... There is a depth dimension to learning responding to immediate and simple needs, on, up, and in the most sublime search for the truth that makes us free (Kidd 1966: 72).

Learning is the key to the effective response to change. As we shall see, continuous learning as a concept can be both a compass and a gyroscope, both guide and stabilizer (Kidd 1966: 25).

The fascination for the meaning of learning, both individually and in a social context, is the foundation of Kidd's thought. The more visible commitment to the education of adults occasionally obscured his preoccupation, though a brief contact with that vocation indicates the inseparability of both pursuits. Kidd entered the world of adult education at a time when the world, industrial and otherwise, was relapsing into an even more encompassing belief in the education of the young as the principal key to every sort of development than had been the case previously. That relapse was occurring despite the fact that a dependence upon the learning capacities of millions of adults had been the primary factor in the prosecution of a global war. In arguing for the commitment of greater resources to the education of adults, it became immediately necessary to dispel a number of myths and prejudices about the learning capacities and will of adults, but also to develop much more precise understanding of actually how adult learning was best accomplished.

Kidd had begun his interest at least as early as his undergraduate years with his thesis on Henry Marshall Tory, the founder of 'frontier' universities in Canada. In his graduate studies at Columbia University he had been impressed by the work of Thorndike and Lorge and deeply influenced by the life and achievements of Eduard Lindeman.

> One of the greatest needs, at the mid-century, was for a book or series of texts that would bring together the scattered information and make some coherence of what was known as well as identify problems for further study... While I was an admirer of Irving Lorge, I pointed out that his remarkable findings, while important, constituted only part of the story, and that something much more comprehensive was needed... My recommendations were for a statement that would capture what was relevant from philosophy and all the social sciences, would analyze many fields of practice, for example, mass communications, training in industry, and the armed forces, adoption of new farm practices, learning a second language. For several years, I made attempts, none successful, to interest some of our colleagues to undertake the work, but nothing happened. So, with considerable temerity, I decided to bring out a book myself... a practitioner's book, written by a practitioner, with just as much theory as I thought I understood (Kidd, a: 9).

The result of that temerity was *How Adults Learn* (Kidd, 1959). Despite his belief that it was not a textbook, by the time of the revision in 1973, it had become a standard text in the field and had been translated into more than 10 languages.

The book established the canons for the approach to adult education, and while as Kidd himself insisted, it was not based on his own research, it was one of, if not the earliest collection and interpretation of available data to be found in one place. However, it went beyond simply being a collection and representation, since it bore the stamp of Kidd's original approach to adult learning and adult education. Two themes predominate. First, as our opening quotation indicates, Kidd had concluded that learning, not just for adults but for all humans, comes closest to being what earlier social psychologists had termed a 'drive': a wholly natural impulse of the living organism. Individuals do not need to be 'motivated' to learn, that is persuaded, seduced, bullied or tricked, but only into learning certain things, that other individuals or collectivities believe will be good for them. The impulse to learn, to change oneself, is a wholly natural one and is only absent by force of unyielding circumstance, which can be cumulative in its effects. 'Men and women are all different. Each has two kinds of limitation, that imposed by his nature and development and that which he imposes on himself. Usually, if not always, the self-imposed restriction, the shackles each man fixes on himself, are the more binding' (Kidd, a: 9). These arguments in the early 1960s were in considerable contrast to the views about resistance to learning that had arisen from the understandable, if unfortunate, identification of learning with the schooling of children.

The second principal theme is the assertion that since adults learn throughout their entire life, any understanding of the nature of learning must be drawn from the fields of enquiry that deal with all of life, not just that section of psychology and educational theory focused on children and youth. Kidd established the need and the right to draw information from all the exercise of human imagination and study in order to understand learning and adult education truly. This conviction not only involved the inclusion of history, philosophy, all of the social sciences and many natural sciences, it also involved the arts. While his direct experience had been in the utilization of what were occasionally called the 'democratic arts' – film, radio, theatre – he was, throughout his life, a keen observer of paint, music and the crafts. He could easily have written the phrase from the Harvard report he was so tireless in repeating: 'Precisely because they wear the warmth and colour of the senses, the arts are probably the strongest and deepest of all educative forces'.

His arguments, based on the range of his investigation of various literatures, became, in turn, his convictions. Not only could adults learn, but they did, and it was of enormous importance for everyone, and especially adult educators, to accept, in fact welcome, that adults were quite capable of learning independently of their teachers.

A third theme, that appeared throughout the book, and that was to preoccupy Kidd increasingly throughout his life, particularly the years of activity in international development, was that of the inescapable social context of adult learning. Since learning always extends far beyond the limits of education, even with the most generous definition of adult education, its manifestations will always be felt in all of the social, political and economic affairs of humanity. For Kidd, there was a continuing fascination in examining social events for evidence of who had or who had not learnt something of significance in the situation. Colleagues who travelled with him frequently experienced an absorbing analysis of the newspaper from the learning perspective.

Kidd himself acknowledged repeatedly how astonishing it was that these canons of adult learning, almost all stemming from the renewed belief in the autonomy of the learner, became accepted so quickly, in theory, if not always in practice.

Learning is a voluntary act. Kidd's belief about the intimate connection between learning and other actions made him particularly sensitive to that fact. In addition, he believed that the most effective learning arose from the voluntary association of individuals. 'Ideas may come from almost anywhere but shared purposes and the commitment that leads to action seems only to be created in face-to-face meetings' (Kidd, d: 19).

From the commitment to the voluntary, he developed, particularly in the special political atmosphere of Canada, a belief in the efficacy of sensibly designed and administered voluntary organizations. He was not a blind enthusiast, for he knew that voluntary organizations could be corrupt, and wilful and obstructive, but he did develop an abiding conviction of the value of some independence from government. In commenting on the relationship of voluntary activity and government in Canada, in one of his first publications, Kidd observed that, nothing in that experience has caused us to cower before our own government. 'The availability of public funds for these (voluntary) purposes, has brought to adult education a wide variety of film and radio programs that would and could not have been provided in any other way' (Kidd 1950: 22). It was this same belief that led him to the creation of the International Council for Adult

Education in 1972; a voluntary, non-governmental organization that could perform the same role with respect to advocacy, experimentation and coordination on a world scale. Basically, Kidd believed that organized voluntary behaviour allowed for an opportunity for human learning that was denied to government and that every society, and the world, needed both.

For Kidd, the commitment to face-to face environments and to voluntary activity placed considerable emphasis on the 'community' and on community control.

It is the growing realization that the setting 'for adult education is the community itself. While there is nothing novel about such an idea, it never had such widespread acceptance before... in increasing measure then, those working in adult education will have to have knowledge, skill, and insight about the forces affecting community life and the organizations which can be the most meaningful' (Kidd 1950: 14–15).

Written at the beginning of his career and in the 'community enthusiasms' of the immediate post-war years, Kidd was increasingly obliged to work in 'national' and 'international' settings where the notion of 'a community' became increasingly esoteric. Nevertheless, he retained throughout his working life a remarkable ability to create some of the most powerful characteristics of community life under many different circumstances, whether it was in the direction of international conferences, the creation of academic departments or the stimulation of small meetings. All were perceived as essential but not necessarily automatically successful vehicles for learning.

ADULT EDUCATION

In the light of Kidd's public and lifelong association with adult education, it is surprising to discover in his thought and writing that the term is used only as frequently as the two other terms that dominate his thinking – continuous learning and lifelong education. He was uncomfortable with the term 'continuing education' since he believed, correctly in the context of his time, that it was inextricably associated with education undertaken only after the formal period and therefore too restricting for his purposes. In addition, he seems to have been uneasy with the lengthy definition of adult education arrived at by his colleagues at UNESCO in 1976. For him it was too clumsy and he appears to have preferred the simpler ones he used in the works of encyclopaedic character that he edited or to which he contributed. The definition to which he returned repeatedly was 'any activity with an educational purpose, planned and arranged for those who have passed adolescence and are not engaged in full-time study' (Kidd, 1961a: 3). While this definition possessed an admirable simplicity for audiences uninterested in the complicated categories of UNESCO and others, it did eliminate full-time adult students, a group that has been growing in numbers and significance over the past decade.

However, to discover Kidd's complete idea of adult education, it is necessary to go beyond definitions and examine the interpretive comments that can be found throughout his work. First of all, he extended the education of adults beyond the preoccupations of the post-war period when so much development took place, much of it under his leadership. Writing in the *Encyclopedia Canadiana* in 1975, he pointed out: 'Adult Education activities in Canada are usually dated from the time of the first national survey that was completed in 1934. Actually there is a much longer history than this. In Champlain's first settlement at St Croix in 1604, the men kept up their spirits through the first long terrible winter by organizing 'L'Ordre de Bon Temps', a society for debates, good talk, music, drama, and dance' (Kidd, 1975b: 51). One could be forgiven for concluding that 'L'Ordre' was closer to a 'service club' than an agency of adult education, nevertheless, the point about its occurrence much earlier in the history of Canada than generally thought and about the range of activities it included, is not to be overlooked.

Second, Kidd repeatedly extended the area of adult education activities beyond the narrow precincts of formal education.

First comes the realization that adult education is not walled in by the classroom or the institution. It occurs all over the community and not always in groups. There is also a recognition that adult educators have and should collaborate with many others, teachers, librarians, recreation specialists, broadcasters, union and management, civic government, artists and other groups (Kidd, b: 32).

Noticeably absent are politicians. Nevertheless it is clear that Kidd believed that the practice of adult education should be as catholic in its everyday character as should be research on which the practice is based.

Third, he extended its significance in social and political terms. 'The organization of adult education has been fuelled by faiths, by revolution, by immigration, by inventions and renaissances, by nationalist ardour, by international organizations, and now by the demands of high technology' (Kidd and Titmuss, 1985: 94). In this light it is characteristic of Kidd, as the original editor of the adult education section of the Encyclopedia, to include so wide a range of categories as are represented, especially such sections as 'Music and Adult Education' and Adult Education and the Plastic Arts'.

For Kidd, the objectives of adult education included the entire spectrum of human objectives, individual and collective. His early commitment to the liberal education of adults, reinforced by his association in the 1950s with the US 'Fund for Adult Education', and its programmes in liberal adult education, perhaps prevented him from narrowing his concepts and interests as adult education became more specialized and to a degree competitive. Despite his long association with the literacy work of UNESCO and his obvious personal commitment to universal literacy, he never allowed himself to adopt a single focus. In 1950 he wrote: 'However, it is now recognized that such professional men as engineers, and doctors need a program of adult education to give them an understanding of their responsibilities as citizens, as much as any other occupational groups' (Kidd, 1950: 21). Then years later, he said to a group of European adult educators:

No nation is so well developed (not even in North America or Western Europe) that it can neglect fundamental education for children or for undereducated adults... on the other hand, no notion is so backward, so quiescent, so deprived, that it does not require the nurture of all of the most able people it can muster, that it does not depend for its survival upon many forms of adult and higher education (Kidd, 1969: 253).

Kidd believed that adult education was a world movement whose time had come. But it had to be based upon constructive theory, proper and increased training of its practitioners and the development of an appropriate, and to a degree distinct, collection of institutions. For the first objective, his summary of the three international conferences, Elsinore (1949), Montreal (1960) and Tokyo (1972), provides a perspective (1974a).

At Elsinore, so soon after the termination of World War Two, the delegates agonized over the condition of human beings, and wondered if adult education had any answer or could speak to the problems of human beings and human bestiality. At Montreal, the conference and international adult education were threatened alike by the Cold War and power politics, yet not only survived but triumphed. In Tokyo, the prevailing note was that adult education is an established part of the learning system – a system that goes far deeper and far beyond conventional schooling (Kidd, 1974a: 3).

But it was to the Montreal conference that Kidd turned again and again for stimulation and inspiration. It had been a crucial personal event for him, the first major test of the application of his beliefs about learning and 'community' on the international stage. Most of his deepest convictions were represented in the final recommendations of that conference.

1. The conference urges governments to regard adult education not as an addition, but as an integral part of their national systems of education.
2. Economic development programs, both bilateral, multilateral, and through the United Nations and specialized agencies, should include adult education, in order to prepare the minds of people to receive the benefits and participate actively in improving their own conditions.
3. Recognizing that the nature of government participation in adult education will vary according to the different stages of development and educational traditions in countries, this conference nevertheless affirms that it is the duty of governments to create the conditions, both financial and administrative, in which satisfactory adult education can be carried on.
4. The conference urges governments to encourage the development of voluntary organizations since without the freedom, the creative resources, and experimental approach that should characterize such bodies, an essential element in education is lacking.

5. The conference urges all Member States to make provisions for the necessary resources – for example, payment of salaries and expenses for travel and subsistence – to enable adults in all occupational groups, to participate in vocational, civic, social and cultural adult education (Kidd, 1974a: 17).

It would be difficult to find a more concise summary of Kidd's beliefs and to find them stated collectively in so fragile and potentially explosive a setting seems little short of miraculous.

Governments were not the only institutions that Kidd addressed. Next in line were the formal educational agencies whose interest in and support for adult education in Canada and elsewhere had been either limited or entirely lacking. In Canada, he addressed the universities in 1956 (Kidd, 1956) and the local Boards of Education in 1961 (Kidd, 1961b). In each case, he pointed to the existence of a history of support by some of the agencies addressed, to the need among the adult population of Canada and to the reforming impact that a concept of continuing education would or could have upon the practices of those agencies. Kidd took seriously the statement in the 1976 UNESCO statement that one of the functions of adult education was to reform the existing systems of education in the interests of equity and justice. Speaking of the universities he said: 'If we really accept the view that there is a lifetime for learning then it might be possible to teach all vocational courses within a broad humane tradition, helping each student to understand that there are opportunities for further learning and growth open to him later' (Kidd, 1956: 98).

Ten years later in his study of a programme of continuing education for the University of Alaska, he described a 'concept of higher education reaching and permeating every kind of intellectual need; of a university extension system that was planned in relation to the total ecology of the region; of an educational program that reached out to people where they lived and one that was planned for all of life' (Kidd, d: 46).

However, despite his characteristic optimism, which he frequently criticized and then surrendered to, he was constantly ambivalent about the imagination or the will of the dominant institutions. He seemed to believe that adult education in the context of those institutions offered a second chance both for the populations concerned and the institutions themselves. But occasionally the optimism faltered. 'But continuous learning does not depend upon the university. It will come, in any case. It is coming. Without the intellectual leadership of the university, however, growth may be slower, and the vision clouded' (Kidd, 1956: 116).

His optimism was less, too, when he became deeply embroiled in education and development, despite his successes in persuading a variety of formal agencies to support his work. In his major statement to the International Development Research Center in 1974, he said:

It has been difficult to obtain a rational consideration of the role of education in development because of the romantics who favoured any and all forms of education regardless of costs; pessimists have felt that the educational processes were too slow and uncertain of results; and those who consider themselves economic realists, and who deny that education or training is relevant to development (Kidd, 1974b).

But a greater recognition is found in: 'And it is now clear that at least during the present century, these objectives could not be attained by many simply by adding further units of conventional school, not even if the total, or a major share of the gross national product were to be used solely for this purpose' (Kidd, 1974b: 8).

In addition, there seemed to be a growing, perhaps primarily personal, discomfort with the increased participation of the very governments for whose attention and commitment he had so long and aggressively worked. Of the UNESCO World Conference in Tokyo he wrote:

Since 1960 UNESCO had become much more an organization of governments and much less the domain of the individual scholar or academic society. Governments selected and instructed the delegates, yet some of the most colourful or best known personalities or prophetic voices in adult education were not even present or heard (Kidd, 1974a: 26).

For Kidd, a circle had been completed, with mixed and even disconcerting results. The achievement with respect to the inclusion of some forms of adult education in the regular educational systems and providing agencies of most of the world's countries had been rapid and even breathtaking. But that seemed now not to be the solution to the primary problems of the world that he and others had hoped for.

Despite his achievements with the International Council for Adult Education; the academic Department of Adult Education at OISE in which he had been able to strengthen the scientific basis and the training for adult education; his development of the field of comparative studies, which he hoped would primarily be of help to practitioners in developing countries, the goal seemed to have receded just a little to a farther horizon.

Occasionally he raised the question of why the growth in stature of adult education seemed so slow, despite the achievements. For the most part he blamed the lack of vision among adult educators, himself included, for the failure. He was not above the occasional scolding.

... the lack in ourselves is more serious, more debilitating. It is not so much how we are regarded by others but our self-regard that is at fault. Some of us do not seem to value our own calling. The economists and educational planners know we are essential and wonder why we seem so diffident and unsure... We are the future. Yet some of us seem jaded; we hark back to older 'better' days, the days of Comenius, or Froebel, or Grundtvig, or Mansbridge. We talk and act as if opportunity or excitement was found only in the developing countries. One hears such talk even in Europe where such fantastic economic and social changes are occurring daily; where miracles are common place... In what other time did men soberly plan to make education the central motif of life? (Kidd, 1969: 241).

In *While Time is Burning*, Kidd reintroduced a concept that he had first articulated in *How Adults Learn*, that of the learning system and the learning force. Of the learning system he said:

> ...that there exist a totality of planned learning activities for people of all ages including (a) programs organized in institutions such as schools, colleges, universities, libraries and museums, (b) educational activities offered by organizations such as corporations, whose primary objective is something other than education, (c) many non-formal experiences through the electronic media, travel, etc which are planned to have an educational result. These activities are so disparate that many people have failed to consider them a part of a system... The learning force is the totality of individuals who are engaged seriously, albeit recurrently or intermittently, in systematic learning... Unless such a system and such a force is postulated it is not possible to undertake an analysis of systematic learning (Kidd, 1974b: 35).

In the same context Kidd argued that much more could be accomplished in development, but only if 'a coherence, a wholeness, a genuine learning system in which all parts are valued and have their place' was utilized as a basic principle (Kidd, 1974b: 30). Kidd seems to have been re-asserting the value of learning over education, though the ideas were not developed a great deal further. What characterized much of his thought in its development was a long reluctance to accept that separation. In many cases, he used the terms education and learning as though they were interchangeable and much of his view of the nature of learning was drawn from examination of essentially educational environments. He was deeply affected by the work of Allen Tough (see Tough, 1971) and argued that: 'A program of motivation that maximized improvement of performance in self-directed learning may turn out to be the most productive education for development as measured in relation to resource investment and could result in a radical readjustment of traditional inputs to education' (Kidd, 1974b: 37).

In one of his last writings, Kidd summarized the 'paradigm shift' that he believed had taken place with respect to the understanding of 'learning' in the past several decades. He reviewed the various contexts in which the term was being used, 'the learning society', 'life-long learning', self-directed learning', 'learning at a distance', etc, indicating some discomfort with the terms 'andragogy' and enthusiastic support for 'mathetics'.

> The importance of the concept of mathetics is that it is a way of linking together most of the fields from which a data bank about learning is developing. The concept stresses interrelationships at a time when increasing specialization has tended to impede knowledge. It also recognizes that important research about learning may not only be discovered in special applied fields, such as library science, but that it may integrate contributions from the 'regular' fields of scholarship in almost every discipline (Kidd, 1983: 525–42).

But in a section entitled 'Learning as a Human, not just a Cultural Phenomenon', he indicates that he has still not broken entirely from the idea of learning as an individual phenomenon, with education as its collective or cultural counterpart.

Perhaps his claim for the need for coherence reflected the difficulty he was having in finding coherence in his own thought. Just as he had represented and reflected so consistently the development of adult education in his own life, he was reflecting the declining enthusiasm for education of any kind in the world and the rising scepticism about the universal value of the formal providing agencies. The centre showed signs of not holding.

It would be impossible to imagine, and to evaluate, the past 40 years in adult education in the world without taking account of Roby Kidd. He emerged from a small liberal tradition in his own country and remained faithful to it on the broader stage. He appeared to embrace no formal ideology except that associated with learning, perhaps because he believed that any world-view that did not allow for the unsettling factor of unpredictable individual change resulting from unanticipated learning, was simply inadequate. He did believe in the perfectibility of human beings though he knew what traps and accidents lay in the path of anyone. He was a Westerner who learned how to work in the East, even if he did not fully understand it, like most of us. He was a male of his generation, with the result that his writing abounds with the male pronoun, yet he believed that much of his work in adult education was devoted to the liberation of women, as has turned out to be the case. He really tried to model his life on his beliefs at every stage and if these were sometimes at odds and contradictory, he usually acknowledged that fact with both grace and humour.

There was a certain innocence about Roby Kidd but it was not naivety. He knew very well what the stakes and the dangers were, if not before the Montreal conference, then certainly afterwards. The human being who is offered only a minimum of learning, skills enough for drudgery but not for development, may turn on us and destroy us. It is the scarcely literate, the partially educated who are the pawns and dupes of the political adventurers, half-skilled people, scarred with failure and eaten by envy of those who have had greater opportunities. Dangers lurk for all of us when we refuse anyone the chance to develop towards his or her full capacity (Kidd, f: 13).

Dangers were also to be found in the limits, sometimes self-imposed, of the remedy to which Kidd had devoted his life. Kidd saw those limits without the time or opportunity of going beyond them. Nevertheless, human and financial resources are limited so there are finite and practical boundaries to purpose and curriculum, even if there are no theoretical ones. The self-directed learner is more free, but even he or she is for the most part restricted by the availability of library and other learning resources. The participant in organized education experiences can only study what the providers offer. There is a compromise between what the providers wish and what the learners will accept, which is largely determined by the priorities of the former, which in turn are set by the social, cultural, political and economic factors in society as a whole. (Kidd and Titmuss, 1985: 99).

The commitment to learning really only in the context of education led Kidd, in the circumstances of the early 1980s, to some dismay about the future.

Nevertheless, he continued to believe that hope was to be found in the minds, imaginations and hearts of individuals, who were willing and capable of learning beyond their existing limitations. Confrontation and collective ideologies were not his style. Persuasion, argument and demonstration were the markers of the path he preferred. In commenting upon his major published work, *How Adults Learn*, he said:

> I have wished sometimes that I had written with greater lucidity and thought, that I might have chosen other examples and illustrations, but I would not alter the tone or the conclusions, except to accentuate the chief conclusion, that people of all kinds, in all places, and of all ages, have a marvellous capacity to learn, and grow, and enlarge (Kidd, a: 4).

The comment on the book might well serve as a comment on his life. Kidd emerged first as a national figure and then on the international stage on the crest of the contemporary interest in the education of adults. He rode the wave with style and compassion, giving it a shape and substance that will inform the decades during which adult learning is once again incorporated into the everyday affairs of human kind.

ACKNOWLEDGEMENT

The author wishes to acknowledge the permission given to him by the Kidd family to draw from personal papers.

REFERENCES

Allen, R (1975) *The Social Gospel in Canada*, Ottawa National Museum of Man, Mercury Series

Kidd, J R (1950a) Present Trends and Developments, in *Adult Education in Canada*, ed J R Kidd, Canadian Association for Adult Education, Toronto

Kidd, J R (1950b) *Adult Education in Canada*, Canadian Association for Adult Education, Toronto

Kidd, J R (1956) *Adult Education in the Canadian University*, Canadian Association for Adult Education, Toronto

Kidd, J R (1959) *How Adults Learn*, Association Press, New York

Kidd, J R (1961a) *Continuing Education*, Canadian Conference on Education Publications, Toronto

Kidd, J R (1961b) *18 to 80: Continuing Education in Metropolitan Toronto*, Board of Education, Toronto

Kidd, J R (1966) *The Implications of Continuous Learning*, W J Gage, Toronto

Kidd, J R (1969) *Education for Perspective*, Peter Martin associates, Toronto

Kidd, J R (1974a) *A Tale of Three Cities* – Elsinore, Montreal and Tokyo, Syracuse University, Syracuse

Kidd, J R (1974b) *While Time is Burning*, International Development Research Centre, Ottawa

Kidd, J R (1975a) The Social Gospel and Adult Education, in *The Social Gospel in Canada*, ed R Allen, Ottawa National Museum of Man, Mercury Series

Kidd, J R (1975b) Adult Education, in *Encyclopedia Canadiana*

Kidd, J R (1983) Learning and Libraries: Competencies for full participation, *Library Trends*, Spring, pp 525–542

Kidd, J R (a) *The High Road to Learning*, the Kidd Family, Toronto

Kidd, J R (b) *Open Roads*, the Kidd Family, Toronto

Kidd, J R (c) *Roadblocks and Detours*, the Kidd family, Toronto

Kidd, J R (d) *The Road Leading Forth*, the Kidd family, Toronto

Kidd, J R (e) Untitled manuscript, the Kidd family, Toronto

Kidd, J R (f) *The Road to the Indies*, the Kidd family, Toronto

Kidd, J R and Titmuss, C (1985) An Overview of Adult Education, *International Encyclopedia of Education*, **1**

Selman, G (1982) *Roby Kidd and the CAAE (1951–1961)*, Occasional Papers in Continuing Education, University of British Columbia, Vancouver

Tough, A (1971) *Adult Learning Projects*, Ontario Institute for Studies in Education Press, Toronto

Encyclopedia Canadia (1975) Grolier Society of Canada, Toronto

International Encyclopedia of Education (1985) Pergamon Press, Toronto

Chapter 11

K Patricia Cross

Carol E Kasworm

Like ripples on a lake, our influence is never known with its initial creative act of written expression. Our work is best understood in reflective examination – through the historical perspective of its influence on the development of the field and from the individual meanings and insights of those that have read our thoughts and listened to our voices.

K Patricia Cross has been a vital and influential figure in the broad landscape of education and the individual histories of many of us in adult education. She has been a leader and visionary for all who espouse lifelong learning; who believe there should be permeable boundaries and supportive structures for adults across society's learning providers; and who are passionately concerned about adult learner access and success. She has transformed many readers by touching their hearts and minds with elegant metaphors, accessible and informing narrative, powerful syntheses of theory and research and a clear agenda to engage the practitioner in improved action. Through her contributions as an administrator, scholar and professional colleague, she has made a difference for adult learners.

An overview of her key efforts reveals that Cross has always been concerned about developing the broad field of education by acting as a catalyst for improved administrative and instructional professional practice and by advocating for further research of both practitioners and researchers. Most recently, she has inspired higher education reform regarding improved faculty teaching and related classroom research. Her national address on 'Taking Teaching Seriously' and her publications on classroom assessment have critically influenced university discourse on the role of faculty instruction for improved student learning. During the 1980s, she actively pursued intellectual inquiry and synthesis of research on adult learning and participation, as well as the examination of related societal policies and services for adult learners. Through the crucial work of the *Adults as Learners* (1981) and *The Missing Link* (1978b), she opened the doors of educators' minds to the centrality of adult learning and challenges for future practice and research on adult engagement in learning. And her early works, such as *Beyond the Open Door* (1971) and *Planning non-traditional programs* (1975), she presented alternative and provocative perspectives for reframing the role of higher education to serve learners, whether they be labelled as new students, non-traditional students, or under-served learners.

BACKGROUND TO HER CAREER

At the time of writing, Cross is a professor emeritus at the University of California, Berkeley. She forged a career that has spanned roles in university faculty and administration, as well as leadership in research institutes and professional associations. Her formal education reflects a diverse background through a bachelor's degree in mathematics from Illinois State University and Master's and PhD degrees in social psychology from the University of Illinois. In her early career, she served as assistant dean of women at the University of Illinois and dean of students at Cornell University. These formative career experiences are often suggested through her advocacy for learner access, support and success. Her contributions are also reflected in her early career involvement as a researcher, both as distinguished research scientist at Educational Testing Service (1963–66) and as research educator at the Center for Research and Development in Higher Education, University of California, Berkeley (1966–80). These two early professional worlds of student support and of research were the leavening for many of Cross's contributions. They provided the grounding for her writing, her advocacy and her mission of improved practitioner practice, policy development and researcher investment in the fields of adult and higher education. During the past 20 years, she has engaged in leadership roles within the academic arena, including professor and chair of the Department of Administration, Planning and Social Policy at the Harvard Graduate School of Education (1980–88) and professor of higher education, University of California, Berkeley (1988–96). In those roles, she continued to be a key spokesperson for lifelong learning and for the important challenges facing our professional worlds in a learning society. In addition, she has mentored a significant number of graduate students and academic colleagues who have pursued leadership roles in adult and higher education.

Cross is the author of 10 books and more than 200 articles and book chapters. She has been recognized for her scholarship by election to the National Academy of Education and receipt of the E F Lindquist Award from the American Educational Research Association, and the Sidney Suslow Award from the Association for Institutional Research. In addition, she has received the Borden medal from the American Council on Education and the Howard Bowen Distinguished Career Award from the Association for the Study of Higher Education. She was selected by *Change Magazine* in 1975 and 1998 as one of the 'top 40 leaders' in US higher education through a poll of 4000 college and university presidents, foundation executives, journalists and government officials. The 1975 *Change* honour was based upon both the impact of her ideas and writings, as well as recognition of her work as a leading spokesperson for shaping educational programmes for the non-traditional learner. The 1998 *Change* honour noted that 'she has remained a highly respected scholar working on a broad range of academic issues, including adult learners, community colleges, and classroom assessment' (Leaders from inside the Academic Community, 1998: 15–18).

Elected president of the American Association of Higher Education in 1975 and chair of the Board in 1989, she has also received many additional awards for her leadership in education. She was designated as an honouree of the International Adult and Continuing Education Hall of Fame and received the national Leadership Award from the American Association of Community and Junior Colleges. She has been honoured with the Outstanding Service Award from the Coalition of Adult Education Organizations and from the National Council of Instructional Administrators, which recognized her outstanding contributions to the improvement of instruction. She has been awarded 15 honorary degrees and is listed in *Who's Who* in America.

Currently a trustee of the Carnegie Foundation for the Advancement of Teaching, she is also a member of the Board of Directors of Elderhostel and of the Advisory Board for the National Center for the Study of Adult Learning. In addition, she currently serves on the National Selection Committee for the Hesburgh Award and the Visiting Committee for the Harvard Graduate School of Education.

HER INFLUENCE ON ADULT EDUCATION

Cross presents a clear and eloquent voice that has captured the essence of current and future trends, understandings and insights related to adult learners, higher education and societal lifelong learning. Because of her vision, her discourse has presented simply stated concepts through richly descriptive metaphors and elegant analyses. Her writings have reflected a conscious effort to add literature to the field that is interesting to read, easy to understand and practical in its application (Cross, 1976, 1981). From her earliest efforts to her most recent writings in 1996, she also challenged and energized communities of practitioners and researchers to seek new knowledge and to engage in informed new practices for lifelong learning. In retrospect, her leadership has provided four broad influences upon the field of adult education:

• challenging higher education to serve new and diverse students;
• advocating for lifelong learning;
• defining, instructing and serving adult learners;
• creating enhanced learning experiences in the classroom.

Challenging higher education to serve the new and diverse students

In the late 1960s and early 1970s, Cross became a prominent figure in challenging the higher education community and particularly community colleges to consider their future. She spoke of the disjuncture between the influx of new students (1971) with variable academic abilities, and the impact of elitist higher education practices upon these students. She characterized higher education as a revolving door that recruited students with greater diversity, but then quickly pushed them out of that door because of that diversity. She spoke to administrators and faculty who were unable and perhaps unwilling to 'change their beliefs, actions, and programs to serve these students in different and effective ways'(1971: 164). In *The Junior College Student* (1968), *Beyond the Open Door* (1971), *Accent on Learning* (1976) and *Can Higher Education Be Equal and Excellent Too?* (1982–83), Cross marshalled findings from research and theory to help educational practitioners understand and improve their practice with this new and diverse population of students. She noted there was a failure to recognize and accommodate these changing demographics. Most colleges continued offering curriculum, instruction and related assessment targeted to the elite and intellectually strong. As she noted, this new student population represented a more heterogeneous set of skills, motivations, abilities and backgrounds. She asserted that higher education should create high performers of all of their students and provide maximum opportunity for each student to develop fully his or her talents (1976: 6). These individuals should be valued in higher education because they could become vital leaders, workers, family members and citizens. She advocated institutional change to reach these new students. Universities, four-year colleges and community colleges had a major role to play in this egalitarian access to higher education and to create learning environments supportive of lifelong learning.

While others were touting the pivotal role of remediation in higher education, Cross saw it as only one element in a complex and evolving set of programmes and services. She stressed the need for colleges to 'create valid alternatives to traditional curricula', alternatives that could build on students' strengths (McAlexander, 1994: 6). In her writings, Cross explored timely curricular and instructional innovations, such as mastery learning, individualized learning and related learning technologies, to serve the variable learning abilities of these new students. She also suggested that academic learning was more than rote cognitive memorization. Higher education practitioners should consider individually developed learning experiences through cognitive styles, personal development, interpersonal skills and learning with other people. These instructional ideas, which reflected cognitive complexity, experiential strategies, variable time-based learning options and many learning modes, would continue to be important threads of discussion throughout her work (1971, 1976). She would also continue to speak throughout her writings on the nature of equity, equality and excellence in working with disadvantaged, marginalized and under-prepared adult learners.

Advocating for lifelong learning

In tandem with her concerns for meeting the new and diverse needs of these students and the special challenges faced by open access higher education, Cross also looked to adult and higher education through the challenges and context of a learning society. Her early work explored the key themes of egalitarian and non-traditional higher education for providing greater access, learning options and assessment alternatives to learners. Her later work incorporated these ideas with a broader focus upon the nature of adult learning in society and a broader vision of lifelong learning. Cross drew upon UNESCO's discussions of lifelong learning and in particular the ideas of Dave (1976) to inform both herself and her readers. Her writings and contributions through the Commission of Non-Traditional Study, spoke eloquently to the importance of new providers, new learning forms and structures and the new possibilities for continued learning by adults (Commission of Non-Traditional Study, 1973; Cross, 1975, 1978b, 1981, 1984). She opened a number of dialogues that foreshadowed the current complexity of instructional delivery through distance learning and time-enhanced technology systems. She explored learning based in learner conceptualizations through self-directed, experiential engagements beyond the classroom. She challenged educational leaders and policy makers regarding resource support for lifelong learning. In doing so, she questioned the lack of infrastructure and financial support to access learning and to provide options for learning. She also raised serious concerns regarding information and counselling services to adults who require quality assistance when they seek new learning opportunities and educational providers (1978b, 1984).

Her dominant focus upon lifelong learning had its probable roots with her involvement in the Carnegie-funded Commission on Non-traditional Study in the 1970s. In those works for the Commission and in her subsequent writings, Cross espoused a strong belief in lifelong learning as an integral element within higher education. Building upon notions of an egalitarian educational model, she advocated new structures, processes and learning perspectives to meet the growing needs of non-traditional learners (Commission of Non-Traditional Study, 1973; Cross, 1975 Cross, Valley and Associates, 1974). Her work and philosophy emulated the Commission's core vision:

> (The design of non-traditional education is)… more an attitude than a system and thus can never be defined except tangentially. (Nevertheless,) this attitude puts the student first and the institution second, concentrates more on the former's need than the latter's convenience, encourages diversity of individual opportunity rather than uniform prescription, and de-emphasizes time, space, and even course requirements in favor of competence and, where applicable, performance. It has concern for the learner of any age and circumstances, for the degree aspirant as well as the person who finds sufficient reward in enriching life through constant, periodic, or occasional study (Commission on Non-traditional Study, 1973: xv).

In planning non-traditional programmes

An *Analysis of the Issues for Post-secondary Education* (1975) along with a number of other reports, Cross and her colleagues on the Commission of Non-traditional Study offered a set of new possibilities for redesigning higher education. Two key groups were targeted: educators who valued the context of national research to understand their current innovative programmes better and those who desired research and collegial discussion for designing new, innovative programs to meet non-traditional learner needs. These efforts had a variety of important impacts. For example, the commissions study of characteristics of Learners and Would-be Learners (Cross, Valley & associates, 1975) provided substantive discussions that built upon previous participation research in adult education. The findings of this study suggested that adults and non-traditional students were motivated to participate in higher education based on career and practical learning. In addition, it shifted the focus of adult learner access from solely institution-related issues to a more complex set of understandings that incorporated learners' needs, motivations, past experiences and life circumstances. It espoused key precepts and possible alternative models for responsive non-traditional higher education based on the principles of lifelong learning. And it suggested alternative ways to organize higher education toward stated goals and outcomes rather than continuing to use the arbitrary time spans that defined credit and degrees. It pushed away many of the conceptual boundaries that had been pragmatic issues between traditional and continuing higher education for many years and suggested a much broader world of education for adults.

In subsequent work on behalf of the Commission, she and Jones (1977) explored the issues of access and participation, drawing upon the earlier work of Johnstone and Riveria, Knowles, Morton and Moses. In this chapter, they explored the concepts of barriers to learning and participation, shaped by the place and being of the learner, as well as by institutional designs and practices. This early discussion is reflective of her efforts to describe and theorize the nature of adult learning in society exemplified throughout her later works, such as her later discussion of participation and barriers in *Adults as Learners*.

As part of her focus upon lifelong learning, Cross was a key advocate for innovation and adaptation of higher education to serve adult learners. As a keen observer of demographic trends and adult learner actions, she recognized that adults had become a major clientele for higher education and that there was a burgeoning industry of providers for adult learning.

> … the biggest impact on adult learners is the explosive growth in the sheer number and volume of providers of adult education: employers, the military volunteer agencies, and private entrepreneurs, to name a few. Adult learners today are not dependent on any one source for education. In fact, if those alternative providers are not to engage in rather destructive competition, it seems to me there will have to be more co-operation within a network of life-long learning providers (cited in Jean-Louis, 1988: 12.).

During the late 1970s and early 1980s, Cross described a changing society oriented to the primacy of learning. Education and learning had become central to the vitality of both the adult learner and society, as suggested by three key elements:

- lifelong learning will be increasingly necessary for everyone;
- those who lack basic skills and the motivation for lifelong learning will be severely handicapped in obtaining the necessities of life;
- lifelong learning will add personal satisfaction and enjoyment to the quality of life.

Voluntary learning for adult learners is the appropriate goal for the learning society. However, since we know that learning is habit forming and that the more people practise it, the more adept and motivated they become, society has an obligation to provide all citizens with the basic tools for lifelong learning and with an appropriate introduction to the satisfactions to be obtained from it.

Diversity of educational opportunity through multiple providers is a proper goal of the learning society and all citizens should be guaranteed access to the learning opportunities most relevant to their needs at any stage of life (Cross,1981: 48–49). In her examinations of lifelong learning, she was particularly interested in the role of self-directed learning and the diverse roles of learning in adult lives. She noted in an interview that 'some of the most valuable learning experiences are taking place not in classrooms but in all kinds of self- and group-motivated activities' (Jean-Louis, 1998: 14). Because self-directed learning is ubiquitous, she expressed interest in the measurement of competencies, rather than traditional measures of certified learning by units, credits or semesters. She was also intensely curious about the development of learner skills in analysing not only data but also arguments and how to synthesize information within self-directed learning. At the heart of her interests was that society and all of education should develop 'gourmet learners who are able to tailor and utilize the resources in the learning society to their own needs' (1981: 250). She pointed to the contemporary societal ills of credentialism, which placed education into purely an instrumental mode and raised issue with mandated continuing education, which moved education away from one's intrinsic motivation of self-commitment to learning. In these discussions of adult lifelong learning, she raised concern about learning providers who used questionable marketing and recruitment practices and about their varied use and abuse of credit and validation of learning. Self-directed learning should be valued for its flexibility, authentic core of learner engagement and its relevancy in pursuit of lifelong learning in all of its topics, forms and conditions. It should not be modularized and co-opted to sell programmes and courses for educational providers to naive adult learners.

Defining, instructing and serving adult learners

From 1976 through to the mid-1990s, Cross pursued an in-depth examination of adult learners and related topics of importance to lifelong learning. Her goals for this effort were best expressed in *Adults as Learners*:

> I have tried to build a holistic understanding of adults as learners through presenting research findings from varying methodological perspectives and then trying to

develop a framework for understandings and interpreting the research. It is my hope that this approach…will advance the cause of lifelong learning through promoting the deeper understandings that are essential both to the identification of missing blocks of knowledge and to the development of practical programs of action (1981: xii).

For many in the profession, *Adults as Learners* became the key source for advocating that adult learners were different and that practitioners required a different practice mindset in serving and researching adult learners' needs, learning experiences, services and outcomes. It was a significant contribution because it combined the diverse current theory and practice contexts related to adult learning and offered broader frameworks for both future research and practice. And it was embraced by many in adult education and higher education because it was engaging, complex in its coverage of theory and ideas and practical in its focus.

This book also provided a major contribution to the discussion of participation in adult learning. Drawing upon previous work from the Berkeley Center and the Commission on Non-traditional Study, as well as work from adult educators, Cross offered readers a more complex understanding of learner motivations and actions. For example, her analyses of statistics of educational attainment and adult learner participation illuminated the key saying 'Education is addictive; the more people have, the more they want and the more they participate' (Cross, 1981: 15). It also provided clear evidence of the inequities of education among various demographic and sociocultural groupings of adults. This work on adult participation also presented a valued and highly used framework of situational, institutional and dispositional barriers to articulate adult participation in learning activities. Used in both practice and research analyses, it continues to be a key framework for discussion of adult engagement in learning.

Her Chain of Response (COR) model was another important addition to the literature. This beginning conceptual framework identified key variables and their interrelationships in predicting adults' participation in learning. Created through her analyses and critique of major learner participation models to include Miller, Rubenson, Boshier and Tough, she hypothesized this dynamic framework. The model was assumed not to be explanatory or predictive (although others have attempted to use it in those ways). Rather, she saw it as a way to organize practitioner and researcher thinking and action. 'The general usefulness of the model will be judged by its capacity to accommodate existing research and, even more important, by its ability to stimulate new research and, ultimately, to improve practice' (1981: 130–31). Curiously, few studies on further theorization have drawn upon this model. This status of the research may be, in part, a reflection of her warning to those seeking easy answers to why adults do or do not participate in learning. 'The answer to the question of why adults participate in learning activities will probably never be answered by any simple formula. Motives differ for different groups of learners, at different stages of life, and most individuals have not one but multiple reasons for learning'

(1981: 97). Nevertheless, her synthesis of previous participation models, her development of the COR model and her concern for conceptual theory in adult participation have had a significant impact on the field.

Cross offered two other key contributions to the field in her discussions on the nature of facilitating adult learning in *Adults as Learners*. One key area focused upon her analyses of andragogy and pedagogy and the varied current interpretations towards understanding adult learning. As she noted: 'Whether andragogy can serve as the foundation for a unifying theory of adult education remains to be seen…. It has been far more successful than most theory in gaining the attention of practitioners, and it has been moderately successful in sparking debate; it has not been especially successful, however, in stimulating research to test the assumptions' (1981: 227–28). Her succinct presentation provided a reflective stance for many in the field. Should andragogy be the central construct for our research and practice and what are its theoretical base and common conceptual understandings? Her discussion was a touchstone for many to critique and to analyse their assumptions and theory regarding the research and practice of adult learning.

She also provided another related contribution in the Characteristics of Adults as Learner (CALS) model (1981: 235). Noted as a tentative framework to accommodate contemporary theories of adult learning, this model spurred thinking about what and how adults learn. It was one of a few models in the early 1980s that highlighted the key areas of physiological, sociocultural, and psychological theories related to adult learning within one schematic. The CALS model brought together a new spectrum of evidence and ideas. In addition, it suggested the importance of considering the context of situational characteristics, most notably, part-time versus full-time learning and voluntary versus compulsory learning as it influenced adult learning experiences.

Cross offered key contributions in *Adults as Learners* with her critique and analysis of societal beliefs and models for the place and role of education in the adult years. Drawing upon the perspective of the lifespan, Cross examined the relationship of learning to societal defined life roles. She questioned the dominant societal model of the linear life plan, where adults live age-segregated lives as defined by K-12 school, then an adult life of work and then senior years of leisure in retirement. She also questioned the alternative of the cyclical life plan, often suggested through European discussions of recurrent education. In this model, adults return to school and major learning experiences in recurrent patterns. Rather, Cross suggested that we are engaging in a new world of lifelong learning that should not have societal beliefs that limit the time and circumstances surrounding engagement in learning. Adults should live their lives through the 'blended life plan', a tapestry of being and living that blends together three strands of life activities – education, work and leisure – into individual patterns throughout their lives (Cross, 1981, 1984; Jean-Louis, 1988).

In her research and writings on adult learners, Cross has also provided a number of key contributions to policy issues, as well as to delineated key services to support adult learners in society. Particularly in her volume *The Missing Link* (1978b) she suggested that society should help adults to define themselves, their learning skills and their interests better. Society should create mechanisms to link adults to the varied, complex and sometimes obscure learning resources of society. In these discussions, she challenged adult educators to look beyond their missionary zeal towards service; instead, we should focus upon the societal realities of education's current impact. Cross suggested that 'adult education as a whole is more elitist than the more traditional segments of post-secondary education, consisting of community colleges, technical colleges and four-year colleges and universities' (1978b: 14). Adult learning outreach was judged to be elitist because it provided little support of financial aid, it was largely voluntary and it typically recruited the self-motivated and educated adult. Thus, adult education had become the provider for services to the educated and the informed of our society.

With this challenge of preferential support for the educated and self-motivated adult, she examined the current status of all adults and their involvement in learning (1978b). In particular, she considered the necessity for services to the disadvantaged adult, the recognition of non-school learning and the myriad of bureaucracies that have surrounded access to many educational providers. She advocated a range of educational brokering and information services, as well as providers. She advocated lifelong learning goals, supported by society that should serve the self-directed adult to make appropriate and effective choices. In these discussions, she particularly voiced concern about the current lack of state policy and involvement in supporting and broadening adult learner services and programmes. Few states have either grappled with comprehensive planning in support of lifelong learning or comprehensively described and monitored the many diverse agencies that could support lifelong learning and related state policy and funding supports. She suggested that vital future issues for policy development should focus upon providers, access, quality assurance and economic revitalization. Providing a macro perspective on educational policy, she believed that most states had only the vaguest ideas about the educational opportunities available to adults. 'They could profit from more information to determine what is distinctive about the missions of the various providers, the extent of overlap, whether competition for adults is constructive or destructive, and which segments of the population are being served' (1978b: 2). She was prophetic in raising a number of concerns, such as quality assurance for adult learning experiences, the potential for charlatan learning providers, and viewing adult education as a catalyst for revitalizing state economics by developing human resources.

In her later research and writing on adult learning and society's role in lifelong learning, Cross also challenged the field of adult education concerning its base of research and theory. She strongly questioned the focus of much of the literature offering a-theoretical discussions of adult learning.

The pragmatism of adult education can be easily understood and to some extent even commended for its no-nonsense practicality, but lack of theory is easier to explain than to defend... the profession of adult education cannot advance beyond its present stage of development if one generation of adult educators simply passes on what it has learned through experience to the next generation. The systematic accumulation of knowledge is essential for progress in any profession. In an applied profession, however, theory and practice must be constantly interactive (1981: 119).

She observed that adult education has not been highly effective in theory building because of the marketplace orientation of most adult educators, because of the lack of scholars in adult education pursuing empirical research and because of the multi-disciplinary, applied nature of the field. With her observations in 1981, she became one of several key individuals who raised issues with the current applied orientation of the field of adult education. These issues continue to be a pivotal concern for our future.

CREATING ENHANCED LEARNING EXPERIENCES IN THE CLASSROOM

Throughout her years of research and writing, Cross advocated quality adult learning experiences in adult and higher education. In her later years at Berkeley, Cross's writings have focused upon the specific role of improvement of faculty instruction in higher education classrooms. As with several other writers in the field, she desired to reach adult and higher education practitioners, engaging them in reflective learning and action. She was particularly concerned about changing understandings and practice for faculty members ensconced and bounded by their content disciplines. She considered faculty to be adult learners who best learnt about their own professional impact by engaging in research and learning in their practice context, that of the classroom. She suggested that improved instructional practices were based in knowledge of the research on teaching, learning and assessment; upon up-to-date knowledge of their discipli-nary content field; and upon the faculty's ability to conduct classroom research that continuously monitored students' learning experiences. In her handbooks on classroom assessment techniques and classroom research (1988, 1996), she and her colleagues noted various strategies and tools to provide faculty with feedback regarding their own instructional learning effectiveness and also feedback to students as a measure of their progress as learners. These handbooks have become the basis for both nationwide workshops and campus-based discussions within many higher educational institutions. These works also have become the basis at many campuses for advocacy of the scholarship of teaching and vital ways to enhance faculty professional development and teaching evaluation efforts.

The core of these two books and the first book's revision (1988, 1993, 1996) presumed that faculty can best adapt and change their practices by intellectual inquiry into teaching and learning, along with insights and understandings about their own teaching, through forms of learning, assessment, research and reflection (1996). In her earlier work of 1988 and 1993, her focus was solely upon faculty members and their practice. However, in the later work of 1996, she further explored the importance of classroom research to create an institutional collegiate climate that takes teaching and learning seriously. Cross believed that the intellectual challenges of teaching require continuing study and investigation as well as collaborative problem-based discussion. In these key works, she articulated the need to enhance faculty understandings of the diversity of learners through the research literature on learners' characteristics and their learning process. She provided case studies of first-hand teaching experiences by faculty in differing disciplines with different class objectives; experiential inquiry projects; as well as related theories and practical suggestions for learner involvement and success in collegiate classrooms. This final thrust of Cross's work has been continued through national projects on the scholarship of teaching by both the American Association of Higher Education and the Carnegie Foundation for the Advancement of Teaching.

HER CONTRIBUTIONS FROM PERSONAL EXPERIENCES

Much of the discussion in this chapter has been through analyses of Dr K Patricia Cross's research and writings and their impact upon the field. She is, however, more than her writings. She has made a significant impact upon individuals, their hearts and their minds as learners and educators. As noted by one of her students regarding Cross's impending retirement in 1995:

> despite (the high energy and complexity of her) activities, she always seemed to make teaching her top priority. Students such as myself, who have had the enormous good fortune to have had her as our teacher, know this first-hand. We know that she somehow managed her complex schedule – which required extensive travelling – such that she never missed a class. We know that she came to each class well-prepared, and that we treasured our time with her because of the high level of learning that always took place. We know that she provided swift and thorough feedback on our work. I recall how, while I was working on my doctoral dissertation, she was invariably the first to respond with careful, thoughtful, constructive criticism on my research and writing. (Barkley, 1995: 1)

Fortunately, for adult and higher education, thousands of others also have experienced her abilities and commitment indirectly through her writings, workshops and speeches. Like her students, they have been guided by her insights and analyses as well as inspired to create enhanced learning environments on their own campuses. Many adult education researchers and practitioners as well as my own students who have experienced Cross through her books and writings have learnt as much about themselves as well as the broader world of adult learning.

These personal impacts and her broader contributions to our field are her legacies to us.

REFERENCES

Angelo, T A and Cross, K P (1993) *Classroom Assessment Techniques: A handbook for college teachers*, 2nd edn, Jossey-Bass, San Francisco

Barkley, J (1995) *Retirements: K Patricia Cross*, http://www-gse.berkeley.edu/admin/extrel/termpaper/past issues/summer95/cross.html

Commission on Non-traditional Study (1973) *Diversity by Design*, Jossey-Bass, San Francisco

Cross, K P (1968) *The Junior College Student: A research description*, Educational Testing Service, Princeton, NJ

Cross, K P (1971) *Beyond the Open Door: New students to higher education*, Jossey-Bass, San Francisco

Cross, K P (1976) *Accent on Learning: Improving instruction and reshaping the curriculum*, Jossey-Bass, San Francisco

Cross, K P (1978a) The Adult Learner, in *The Adult Learner: Current issues in higher education*, Future Directions for a Learning Society, Washington, DC

Cross, K P (1978b) *The Missing Link: Connecting adult learners to learning resources*, College Entrance Examination Board, Future Directions for a Learning Society, New York

Cross, K P (1979) Adult Learners: Characteristics, needs and interests, in *Lifelong Learning in America: An overview of current practices, available resources, and future prospects*, R E Peterson and associates, Jossey-Bass, San Francisco

Cross, K P (1981) *Adults as Learners*, Jossey-Bass, San Francisco

Cross, K P (1982–83) Can Higher Education Be Equal and Excellent too? Underprepared learners, *Current Issues in Higher Education*, No 1, American Association of Higher Education, Washington, DC

Cross, K P and Angelo, T A (1988) *Classroom Assessment Techniques: A handbook for faculty*, National Center for Research to Improve Post-secondary Teaching and Learning, Ann Arbor, Michigan

Cross, K P and Jones, J Q (1977) Problems of Access, in *Explorations in Non-traditional Study*, eds S B Gould and K P Cross, Jossey-Bass, San Francisco

Cross, K P and McCartan, A (1984) *Adult Learning: State policies and institutional practices*, ASHE-ERIC Higher Education Research Report, No 1, Association for the Study of Higher Education, Washington DC

Cross, K P and Steadman, M H (1996) *Classroom Research: Implementing the scholarship of teaching*, Jossey-Bass, San Francisco

Cross, K P, Valley, J R and associates (1975) *Planning non-traditional programs: An analysis of the issues for post-secondary education*, Jossey-Bass, San Francisco

Dave, R H (1976) *Foundations of Lifelong Learning*, Pergamon Press, Elmsford, NY

Gould, S and Cross, K P (eds) (1972) *Explorations in Non-Traditional Study*, Jossey-Bass, San Francisco

Jean-Louis, M (1988) Major Trends in Adult Education: An interview with Dr K Patricia Cross, *Aurora*, No 1, Athabasca University, Edmonton, Alberta

Leaders from inside the academic community, (1998) *Change*, **30** (1), pp 15–18

McAlexander, P J (1994) *In Search of Mina Shaughnessy: A comparison of Mina Shaughnessy and K Patricia Cross*, paper presented at the Annual Meeting of the Conference on College Composition and Communication, Nashville, TN

Chapter 12

Chris Argyris – the reluctant adult educator

Karen E Watkins and Jacqueline A Wilson

Perhaps no one would be more surprised to find himself in a volume of *Twentieth Century Thinkers in Adult and Continuing Education* than Chris Argyris. Yet, few organizational theorists have had as much influence or have thought more consistently on adult education theory. In these pages, we give a brief overview of his career, summarize his key theoretical work as it is pertinent to adult education and discuss his contribution to adult education theory and practice.

BIOGRAPHICAL NOTES

Chris Argyris was the James Bryant Conant Professor of Education and Organizational Behavior at Harvard University from 1971 to 1997. Prior to that, he was the Beach Professor of Administrative Sciences from 1951 to 1971, helping to found that department at Yale University. Following service in the Signal Corps during World War Two, he received his AB in Psychology from Clark University in 1947, his Master's in Psychology and Business from Kansas University in 1949 and a doctorate in organizational behaviour from Cornell in 1951. His advisor was William Foot Whyte, an early pioneer in action research (Putnam, 1995). Currently, he is working with the Monitor Company, an international management consulting organization.

Argyris was a twin, one of three boys born in the United States who spent their childhood in Greece. They returned to Irvington, New Jersey in time to begin their schooling (Argyris, 1992). He notes that two critical influences from his childhood significantly impacted his later work. First, he did not speak English very well and his teachers made it clear that he was in trouble. He had to learn English and learn it quickly or suffer the consequences. A second influence was that there was a lot of prejudice against his family and Greeks in general. He recalls that the reaction of his family was to expect that he would act in ways that proved others wrong, to show that he could meet and surpass the standards of the majority. He found that his approach to research placed him in the position of a deviant, a minority that took him back to these early incidents. 'It activated my sense of courage to confront resistance to change through the use of evidence. But it probably also activated the sense of frustration, loneliness, and self-depreciation that often goes along with being a minority' (Argyris, 1992: 52).

His position at Harvard illustrates why his work has been significant to adult education. Straddling the disciplines of organizational behaviour and education, he was well positioned to develop a theory that merged learning and organizations. In the official Harvard biographical sketch, his research stream is characterized as focused on the unintended consequences of formal organizational structures, leadership and control, and how individuals adapt to deal with those consequences (Harvard Business School, no date). This led him to ways of changing organizations so that the structures, control systems and leadership might more consciously promote a learning orientation, particularly by changing the executive level's mindset. Argyris (1992) said that the two factors that sustained his scholarly inquiry were that he is problem-centred (vs discipline centred) and theory-oriented. He said: 'I seek to study problems in everyday life that contain puzzles, dilemmas, paradoxes, and all that challenges the status quo. I enjoy working toward producing valid knowledge, enhancing human beings' competence, and strengthening justice' (1992: 51). Theory helps keep him intellectually honest. He has to make his reasoning public and submit it to examination by his peers. Developing theory about interpersonal action, according to him, had its roots in the reason he chose to study organizational behaviour in the first place. He served as a manager in the Signal Corps at the end of the war and one woman presented him with a gift from the staff. Later, he was somewhat at loose ends and went back to visit. A person he spoke with said something critical and Argyris called the woman in to 'testify' on his behalf and she did not defend him. Stunned, he said: 'But you hugged and kissed me and said that you enjoyed working for me?' She said, 'Well, the war was over and we were really glad that things turned out well. But the truth is, we were glad to see you move back into the civilian world'. (Fulmer and Keys, 1998: 31; Argyris, 1992). Argyris found this experience highly significant.

Finally, Argyris has a 30-year interest in advocating social science research that is usable, actionable by those who would intervene in organizations (Argyris, 1980). Like Kurt Lewin, he sees action research as the best blend of rigorous research and practical application. Putnam (1995) states: 'Chris has persistently sought to combine intervention and theory-testing research, clashing both with practitioners who turn away from doing research on their practice and with scholars who see consulting as something one does on the side but as not really serious' (p 254).

While tension between theory and practice is hardly new, Argyris has steadfastly continued to problematize this tension and at the same time to offer an approach to transforming it. One example of theory evolving from practice was the development of a theory of action science from his study of the t-group. Argyris was very involved in the t-group movement during the 1950s and the National Training Laboratory (Putnam, 1995). What he observed there, however, was that there was a fundamental mismatch between what people said and what they did and that they had what he termed a 'master program' (Model I) that prompted them to engage in defensive routines rather than accept responsibility for the consequences they created. This led people to make the same errors again and again and to resist learning and change. From these observations, Argyris began to posit an alternative intervention to the t-group that asked people to collect the kind of directly observable data on their practice that would make it possible for them to see their own culpability for these recurring errors and then to challenge the assumptions embedded in the 'master program' that led them to make the error in the first place. Action science is a variant of action research in which practitioners conduct research on their own practice and, in effect, make a science of action.

Once Argyris developed this theory of interpersonal action, the seeds of organizational learning were born (Caulkin, 1997). He stresses that managers create the environment that they operate in and if it is dysfunctional, then they need to change it. If they keep silent, they reinforce it. Moreover, he feels that people in power have a particular obligation to examine their own practice critically (Argyris, 1992). Needless to say, Argyris has made a lot of people uncomfortable. The kind of courage that he calls on individuals to enact, particularly powerful individuals, is often ignored in the discussions of his work.

Practitioners will often reject action science as unrealistic, arguing in essence that 'the world is Model I, and I am only a pawn in that Model I world, who am I to try to make a difference?' But Argyris does not let them off the hook. In an interview, he suggested that the biggest problem facing human resources staff is the fact that CEOs agree that double-loop learning (Model II) is needed, but they do not believe that HR has the competence to create what they are advocating. Blaming the supervisor is simply another way of HR not taking responsibility for learning and changing themselves (Abernathy, 1999). He remarks that double-loop learning is about solving difficult problems. It involves establishing truth by subjecting our own and others' claims to rigorous tests that allow us to see the causal argument underneath those claims more clearly. This he calls transparency. 'Stewardship is the internal commitment to seek truth, transparency, and personal responsibility in the workplace' (Abernathy, 1999: 84).

Argyris challenges conventional definitions of learning that define it as acquiring knowledge, new perspectives or insights, and asserts that the evidence for learning is when individuals are able to produce the new insights (Pickard, 1997: 35). He says that he likes to ask: "How do you know when you know something?" My answer is when you can create what you say you know' (Fulmer and Keys, 1998: 4). Inherent in these remarks is a standard for learning and changing that many find difficult. On the other hand, Argyris notes that what we are currently doing is not working. Radical problems call for radical responses. Putnam correctly describes Argyris as a provocateur (1995).

During the late 1980s while Watkins was at the University of Texas at Austin, Argyris came twice to help launch a long-term project that led to incorporating action science as a theoretical and curricular anchor for the Adult Education and Human Resource Development Leadership programme. On his first visit, he did a presentation in the Business School for both adult education and business students. One young woman challenged his analysis of a case. When he pressed her for her reasoning, she retorted that it was just her feeling that he had it wrong. He pressed more and continued to get similar responses, with the young woman moving more and more into a Rogerian counselling response. Seemingly exasperated, Argyris pointed out that as long as she held her reasoning in the black box of her mind, they could not engage in a dialogue about the case. At this, she burst into tears. We could see first-hand how counter-cultural the standard of transparency is in action.

At a later time, we ate lunch with a key architect of a computer consortium. The individual proudly described how in this organization, every project had its own leadership. Managers had a free rein to define the culture as they saw fit, with someone from one computer organization running their project the XYZ way and another division more like the ABC way. Argyris interjected: 'Wouldn't it be true then that individuals in the same organization might experience an authoritarian leader while their colleagues next door would have more of a laissez-faire culture?' Still in his frame, the individual nodded. So Argyris asked: 'Doesn't that create an injustice?' What followed was a lively discussion of the unintended consequences of a seemingly creative approach to organizational structure.

In the sections that follow, we explore Argyris's work and then compare it to related theories in adult education.

ACTION SCIENCE

This section examines the theory and concepts of action science and documents how action science has been used in organizational studies undertaken by select scholars. We begin with an overview of action science history, theory and components. Action science is a theory that explains individuals' interactions based on their espoused theories and theories-in-use. Argyris (1982, 1985, 1986, 1990, 1993, 1995, 1997, 2000) developed action science based on Kurt Lewin's (1948, 1951) studies of group development and conflict resolution. Like action research, action science focuses on studying real problems, identifying patterns and helping people improve the quality of their lives. Action science encompasses both theory and practice and may be used as tool for diagnosis or intervention either at an individual or organizational level. Key concepts in action science are theories of action, Model I and Model II behaviours, and defensive routines.

Theories of action

Argyris and Schön (1974, 1978, 1996) have written extensively on the concepts of espoused theories and theories-in-use to interpret dilemmas and contradictions in human interaction. Espoused theories are what we say we value; they can be described as explicit, aware and generally idealistic. Theories-in-use, on the other hand, are tacit, unaware and based on experience. Espoused theories describe the way we would like to be; theories-in-use illustrate the way we really act. These concepts exist in the everyday vernacular when we admonish someone to 'practice what you preach' or when we advise others to 'walk the talk'. Once people are aware of how their actual practice differs from what they espouse, they are in a better position to make the necessary changes to bring the two into alignment. The first step is to understand one's defensive routines, which are an intrinsic component of Model I behaviour.

Model I and Model II behaviours

Argyris and Schön (1974) describe two distinct types of behaviour that they call Model I and Model II. Model I behaviour is based on control, winning, rationalism and self-protective behaviour. Action strategies accompanying Model I behaviour are asserting one's views, taking others' views and feelings for granted (assumptions), inferring what others think or feel without asking them (attributions) and saving face. Model II behaviour is based on sharing thoughts, feelings, information, responsibility, problem solving and learning. Its action strategies include stating one's views, inquiring rather than inferring about another's views and opening problems and dilemmas for discussion.

While Model II represents the ideal behaviour, Argyris (1982, 1990, 1993) concedes that Model I is more prevalent and is, in fact, preferred in a crisis where quick, instinctive action is demanded. Model II, by virtue of its collaborative, reflective nature is slower than Model I. Model I behaviour is associated with single-loop learning, which solves each problem as a separate unit. Model II behaviour relies on double-loop learning in which the underlying assumptions and conditions that created the problem (and potentially others of the same dynamic) are surfaced, examined and corrected.

Defensive routines

Argyris (1957) explores defensive behaviours in his early writings based on his interpretation of Lewin's work and his own research with executives, particularly bankers. With the publication of *Personality and Organization: The conflict between system and individual*, Argyris (1957) initiates a description of behaviours he refers to as defensive reactions. These defensive behaviours are elicited whenever an individual feels anxiety, conflict, frustration or failure and is unwilling to take responsibility for being wrong or to change in order to prevent a recurrence. Argyris acknowledges that Freud was the first to study defence mechanisms systematically and notes that while it is uncertain why people 'pick' a particular defence mechanism, 'past experience is an important factor in determining the choice' (1957: 37).

In *Strategy, Change and Defensive Routines* (1985) Argyris introduces the term 'defensive routines'. He defines defensive routines as 'thoughts and actions used to protect individuals', groups', and organizations' usual ways of dealing with reality' (1985: 5). By labelling them routines, he emphasizes the way in which these are habitual, routine, the way we do things around here. He discusses the types of 'defensive routines' people use to deal with threatening situations. According to Argyris (1985), studies of almost 4000 individuals of both sexes, ranging in age from 11 to 70, from all socioeconomic levels in the United States, Europe, South America, India and Africa, yield similar results, suggesting that Model I behaviour is universal and that we are socialized in it from childhood. He shows that these 'defensive routines', in fact, serve to render the problems that individuals wish to solve 'undiscussable' and perpetuate the status quo. Most important, this is a shared group mindset, like culture, that makes it difficult to challenge.

Defensive reasoning is based on questionable beliefs or opinions that are assumed to be valid. An individual makes inferences that may even be inconsistent with his or her original, possibly flawed, beliefs. Ultimately, a conclusion is reached that appears logical to the individual; however, the conclusion rests on a foundation of beliefs and inferences that have not been tested by anyone. Because the individual is an expert at Model I behaviour, which avoids any dialogue that may be threatening or embarrassing, conclusions are neither confirmed nor disconfirmed by anyone else.

Defensive routines 'create self-sealing patterns of escalating error' (Argyris, Putnam and Smith, 1985: 61). People make decisions based on private reasoning under conditions that do not allow them to be challenged. When mistakes are made, individuals collude with each other (Argyris, 1990) to cover-up or bypass the embarrassment. Both the mistake and the reasoning that led to it become 'undiscussables'. The individual and/or the organization are then closed to double-loop learning, the kind of learning that identifies and changes theories-in-use and is dependant on the exchange of valid information and testing one's attributions and assumptions publicly (Argyris and Schön, 1996).

At the organizational level, maintaining defences consumes time and energy that could be spent more productively. As Watkins noted, defensive patterns lead to 'hopelessness, cynicism, distancing, blame, and ultimately to mediocre performance among all involved parties, both those using defensive routines and those affected by others' defensive strategies' (Watkins, 1995: 79). The solution to overcoming defensive routines lies in learning a different way to interact with others. This is done by making one's dialogue productive: 'Productive dialogue is defined as the dialogue which combines advocacy with enquiry; in other words, which states one's position or needs clearly while inquiring into the other person's response. This fosters learning and interrupts defensive routines' (Watkins, 1995: 80). Argyris's early research to test these ideas involved an action research intervention that spanned several years.

ARGYRIS' EARLY LEADERSHIP RESEARCH

In *Increasing Leadership Effectiveness* Argyris (1976) reports on a three-and-half year research study of six company presidents who wanted to improve their effectiveness. The presidents tape-recorded sessions with their subordinates, segments of which were transcribed for group analysis. Argyris found Model I behaviour in both the transcripts and the in-group analysis; yet, despite having it pointed out to them and expressing gratitude for the critiques, the presidents 'would then return to their competitiveness, unilateral attributions and evaluations, and win–lose dynamics' (1976: 45). Model I behaviour was so ingrained in them that while they could appreciate the concepts of Model II behaviour, they could not produce it at will.

Argyris describes four phases that the executives went through in learning how to learn: discovery, invention, production and generalization. In the discovery phase, the executives uncovered their espoused theories and how these were incongruent and inconsistent with their theories-in-use. They also discovered they had no knowledge of how to analyse or alter their behaviour. In the invention phase, the presidents, with the help of Argyris and other faculty, learnt to redesign their behaviour on paper. The production phase consisted of actual role-play where the executives practised what they learnt. The generalization phase allowed the executives to transfer their learning from one scenario to another.

Argyris found the four phases were not sequential at first and that the executives, though highly successful in their careers, were often frustrated, bewildered, angry, lacking in self-confidence and fearful as they found themselves stuck. This led to more defensive behaviour. As they learnt and practised the techniques of Model II, the executives also reported that their subordinates were suspicious of their new behaviour. One of the dilemmas both executives and subordinates faced was how to express fears and ask for help without appearing weak and incompetent. The presidents had to struggle with relinquishing their power base of control to encourage disagreement, openness and confrontation from their subordinates. Several of the presidents sought expert help in working with their key reports to demonstrate Model II behaviour and set the stage for creating a learning environment in their organizations.

Argyris concluded that while the research contributed to knowledge of double-loop learning and how individuals alter their theories-of-action, he also found that discovery and understanding of new concepts did not always lead to their application. In other words, 'moving toward Model II is a life-long process' (1976: 280). This work is an excellent case study of the iterative process of learning in action. Of particular interest is the learning model that separates invention (strategy) from production (action), and then looks at the causes of the discrepancy between what we intend and what we do.

USING ACTION SCIENCE IN ADULT EDUCATION RESEARCH

A number of studies have examined Argyris's Model I framework with different groups and in different organizational settings. Levine and Rossmore (1993, 1995) interviewed 77 individuals from all levels of management in an organization that was not meeting its deadline in implementing a new information technology project. In constructing key individuals' theories-in-use and through the use of role-play, they found the executives' private values and goals overpowered their publicly espoused goals and led to power struggles, sabotage, abuse of authority and the defensive routines described in Model I behaviour. The managers exemplified Argyris's (1986, 1990) descriptions of skilled incompetence as they maintained surface control and cooperation while keeping disagreements undiscussable, avoiding key issues and failing to examine their role in the problem.

A similar study was conducted by Watkins (1990) who interviewed 57 human resource developers in three organizations to collect critical incidents and discover how their tacit beliefs and assumptions affected their work. Her findings showed that the developers often said one thing and did another and that the resulting double binds (Argyris and Schön, 1974) produced patterns of recurring error and reduced effectiveness. One double bind went as follows:

> The best way to tell if training is effective is to assess what students do in the field later; but if trainers collect data, others will know of their mistakes and mistakes are high profile and costly, especially in terms of trainers' jobs (1990: 265).

From the interviews, Watkins constructed an action science map that illustrated how the human resource developers' beliefs, based on their theories-in-use, determined what they did (their action strategies), and had consequences for both the training function and learning. Drawing on Freire, she differentiated between the action strategies and consequences that followed from beliefs that training was either magical, political or learning.

In another study, Watkins (1995) used the data collected from an action science case written by a supervisor who had a series of encounters with a female employee about her attendance and productivity following the birth of a child. In addition to the six managers who worked the case with the supervisor, Watkins also collected data from 44 other individuals drawn from graduate classes and management development programmes, who analysed the case as a case prompt. The original dialogue was given and the respondents enacted the role of the supervisor and supplied the left column, what they would have thought or felt in the situation and what they would have said next. Watkins analysed the data for defensive reasoning patterns and found 12 bypasses, 8 of which employed a common strategy of passing the problem on to someone else. 20 responses illustrated the defensive routine of being forthright. In half of these the 'supervisor' directly confronted the employee; the other half consisted of mixed messages, placing blame or overt threats (1995: 81). She concluded that management training programs need to go beyond providing policy to the point where they train managers to examine their options, acknowledge that policies often conflict and to produce productive conversations that are 'characterized by setting limits and jointly developing solutions with the employee' (1995: 87).

Action science has been used as a theoretical framework in numerous dissertations and research studies in adult education. For example, Rogers (1989) studied the learning of action science by a group of adult children of alcoholics and mapped their defensive reasoning patterns. Broersma (1992) re-analysed transcripts of air traffic controllers' responses to errors in a simulation to identify Model I and Model II behaviours. Shindell (1993) developed a theoretical model of key constructs in Argyris' theory. Putnam (unpublished) studied an individual learning action science over the course of a number of years and identified the importance to novice learners of 'recipes' or scripts of Model II interventions. Finally, Dickens (1998) described an action research intervention in a high technology corporation and mapped the reasoning of the individuals, the teams and the organization. Argyris's theory of action has enabled scholars to bring a normative frame to individual and organizational events in order to illuminate them. Action science has also served to help adult education scholars operationalize key theories such as perspective transformation and organizational learning.

ACTION SCIENCE AND PERSPECTIVE TRANSFORMATION

Mezirow (1991) has focused more on the theory of transformative learning than on strategies for facilitating it. As Taylor (1997) points out: 'Adult educators are being encouraged to practice a particular approach to teaching toward an outcome (perspective transformation) and with a process that is inadequately defined and understood' (1997: 54). Action science as described and practised by Argyris is a vehicle for transformative learning.

Action science sets the stage for perspective transformation by its method: a group of people challenging one another to examine their assumptions and theories-in-use. It does not force people to change, but it does challenge them to reflect. Critical reflection and critical discourse are at the core of both action science and transformative learning. Particularly when participants are struggling with why their interactions with others are problematic, action science offers a method for exploring in a controlled and safe environment a method to practise alternative ways of acting and a venue for trying new roles. Mezirow (1991) has noted that trigger events that lead to disorienting dilemmas may be 'induced' by an educator in 'a secure "practice laboratory" environment...which can mediate between old perspectives and the application of new ones in everyday situations' (1991: 173). This safe environment of the practice laboratory allows the action science participant immediate feedback from a group of individuals who share the desire to improve their effectiveness. The experience of redesigning one's action is a group effort and enables individuals to build competence through practice. The standard is always the capacity to produce new behaviour.

Undoubtedly, reflection is at the core of both transformation theory and action science. Marsick and Watkins (1997) compared six reflective and transformative learning theories, including Mezirow's and Argyris's and concluded that regardless of whether the triggering event was accidental or constructed by a facilitator, there is a process from the triggering event that leads to 'some sense that how one understood the situation before is no longer adequate, followed by re-evaluating and reconstructing the event' (1997: 302). They also observe that in the case of action science, the trigger events are constructed rather than accidental. Marsick and Watkins (1997) find four commonalities in the transformative process, regardless of the model being used:

- Learners are proactive and open to alternative framings of the problem, competing explanations and trying out new behaviours.
- Reflection is the trigger that leads to challenging assumptions and 'comfortable ways of thinking'.
- To retain the new behaviours, individuals need a support system to accept and encourage them.
- Transformative learning may be catalyzed through expert facilitation (pp 303–05).

Both Mezirow and Argyris acknowledge the necessity for critical reflection as part of the emancipatory process. The process of case writing asks the participant to recall a troubling event and then offers him or her the chance to work on exploring why it happened and to role-play alternative ways of redesigning it. In the process, the participant may discover his or her assumptions were flawed and this can be the disorienting dilemma that leads to perspective transformation.

Both action science and perspective transformation stress the importance of socialization (childhood and cultural) in forming our perspectives and assumptions. These are unconscious until we use inquiry and reflection to examine them. Mezirow sees this examination as the 'major imperative of modern adulthood' (1991: 35).

Action science and transformation theories stress the importance of critical self-reflection on one's assumptions and rely on dialogue/critical discourse to enact change. The action scientist and adult educator have roles that include collaboration and intervention to trigger the learning and empower the learner to take action. Both theories acknowledge the sociocultural impact on our beliefs and values and claim to be universal and emancipatory. The key difference is that action science provides a highly developed methodology for precipitating change. Just as action science is similar to transformative learning at the individual level, the ideas of organizational learning and of the learning organization speak to transformation at the organizational level.

ORGANIZATIONAL LEARNING AND THE LEARNING ORGANIZATION

From Argyris and Schön's (1978) early work on organizational learning to their more recent (1996), they have asked: 'What is an organization that it might learn?' Insisting that individuals learn on behalf of the organization, they agree that this learning must be embedded in order for the organization to be said to have learnt. More important to them is the idea that the organization can change its mental model, its way of being, towards a learning orientation (Model II) from a control orientation (Model I). Building on Argyris and Schön's work on organizational learning, Watkins and Marsick (1993) define the learning organization as one that has an enhanced capacity to learn because it has transformed all of those structures, systems and mental frames that prevent learning and change.

In adult education, Watkins and Marsick's model of the learning organization is one legacy of Argyris's work (Watkins and Marsick, 1993, 1996, Marsick and Watkins, 1999). Drawing on a theory of action perspective, they looked at what needs to change in order to create a learning culture. The learning organization is defined as an organization that has created an infrastructure to support continuous learning and knowledge creation. Their model defines the learning culture at the individual, team, organizational and societal levels. It is characterized by seven dimensions:

1. create continuous learning opportunities;
2. promote dialogue and inquiry;
3. promote collaboration and team learning;
4. empower people towards a collective vision;
5. establish systems to capture and share learning;
6. connect the organization to its environment; and
7. provide strategic leadership for learning.

The dimension of dialogue and inquiry most reflects Argyris's direct influence. On the other hand, the driving assumption behind the theory of a learning organization is that an organization can transform itself in a manner that makes more likely a learning orientation and that, when it does, it will have an enhanced, system-wide capacity to learn its way through to a positive future. This is vintage Argyris.

CONCLUSION

What is the impact of Argyris's work on adult education and where might it lead? With Schön, Argyris helps to crystallize what is meant by reflective practice. His tenacious belief that 'if you can't produce it, you don't know it' calls us to a standard of actionable knowledge. One critique of Argyris's theory is that by Kegan (1994) who argues that this standard places unrealistic demands on people, asking them to 'organize experience at a level of complexity beyond the fourth order of consciousness, something few people are able to do' (1994: 321). He particularly questions Argyris's belief that people can observe themselves behaving in the world, to hold a mirror up to their own practice, view it critically and then change it. Argyris sees Kegan's view as deterministic, self-limiting, and continues to believe in individuals' capacity to learn and to change.

In an interview with Fulmer and Keys (1998), Argyris said that his work was aimed towards justice first and then truth, since truth can serve unjust ends. In a field so closely tied to social action and social justice, Chris Argyris is the organizational equivalent of Myles Horton. While this may seem like heresy, especially given Horton's union activism, Argyris has sought over the course of more than 30 years' work to bring about more just organizations by working with those responsible for defining and changing the organization – top executives, managers, organization developers and human resource professionals. Working from the top rather than from the bottom, the message of justice through learning and action is similar. In both, the call to us is to make the road by walking.

REFERENCES

Abernathy, D (1999) A chat with Chris Argyris, *Training and Development Journal*, **53** (5), pp 80–84

Argyris, C (1957) *Personality and Organization*, Harper & Row, New York

Argyris, C (1976) *Increasing Leadership Effectiveness*, Wiley & Sons, New York

Argyris, C (1980) *Inner Contradictions of Rigorous Research*, Academic Press, New York

Argyris, C (1982) *Reasoning, Learning, and Action*, Jossey-Bass, San Francisco

Argyris, C (1985) *Strategy, Change and Defensive Routines*, Pitman, Boston

Argyris, C (1986) *Skilled Incompetence, Harvard Business Review*, **86** (5), pp 74–79

Argyris, C (1990) *Overcoming Organizational Defenses: Facilitating organizational learning*, Allyn and Bacon, Boston

Argyris, C (1992) Looking Backward and Inward in Order to Contribute to the Future, in *Management Laureates: A collection of autobiographical essays, Vol 1*, ed A Bedeian, pp 42–64, JAI Press, Inc, Greenwich, CO

Argyris, C (1993) *Knowledge for Action*, Jossey-Bass, San Francisco

Argyris, C (1995) Action Science and Organizational Learning, *Journal of Managerial Psychology*, **10** (6), pp 20–26

Argyris, C (1997) Learning and Teaching: A theory of action perspective, *Journal of Management Education*, **21** (1), pp 9–26

Argyris, C (2000) *Flawed Advice and the Management Trap*, Oxford University Press, New York

Argyris, C and Schön, D (1974) *Theory in Practice: Increasing professional effectiveness*, Jossey-Bass, San Francisco

Argyris, C and Schön, D (1978) *Organizational Learning: A theory of action perspective*, Addison-Wesley, Reading, MA

Argyris, C and Schön, D (1996) *Organizational Learning II: Theory, method, and practice*, Addison-Wesley, Reading, MA

Argyris, C, Putnam, R and Smith, D (1985) *Action Science*, Jossey-Bass, San Francisco

Broersma, T (1992) *Organizational Learning and Aircrew Performance*, unpublished doctoral dissertation, the University of Texas at Austin

Caulkin, S (1997) Chris Argyris, *Management Today*, pp 58–59

Dickens, L (1998) *A Theory of Action Perspective of Action Research*, unpublished doctoral dissertation, the University of Texas at Austin

Fulmer, R and Keys, J B (1998) A Conversation with Chris Argyris: The father of organizational learning, *Organizational Dynamics*, **27** (2), pp 21–32

Harvard Business School (no date) Christopher Argyris, Faculty biography, http://www.people.hbs.edu/cormsby/om/cargyris/bio.html

Kegan, R (1994) *In Over Our Heads: The mental demands of modern life*, Harvard University Press, Cambridge, MA

Levine, H G and Rossmore, D (1993) Diagnozing the human threats to information technology implementation: A missing factor in systems analysis illustrated in a case study, *Journal of Management Information Systems*, **10** (Fall), pp 55–73

Levine, H G and Rossmore, D (1995) Politics and the function of power in a case study of IT implementation, *Journal of Management Information Systems*, **11** (Winter), pp 115–33

Lewin, K (1948) *Resolving Social Conflicts*, Harper Collins, New York

Lewin, K (1951) *Field Theory in Social Science*, Harper Collins, New York

Marsick, V and Watkins, K (1997) Incidental learning, in *Management learning: Integrating perspectives in theory and practice*, eds P Burgoyne and M Reynolds, pp 295–311, McGraw-Hill, London

Marsick, V and Watkins, K (1999) *Facilitating Learning Organizations: Making learning count*, Gower Press, London

Mezirow, J (1991) *Transformational Learning*, Jossey-Bass, San Francisco

Pickard, J (1997) A Yearning for Learning, *People Management*, **3** (5), pp 34–35

Putnam, R W (1995) A Biography of Chris Argyris, *Journal of Applied Behavioral Science*, **3** (3), pp 253–55

Putnam, R W, An unpublished doctoral dissertation, Harvard University

Rogers, R (1989) *Reflective Learning of Adult Children of Alcoholics*, an unpublished doctoral dissertation, the University of Texas at Austin

Shindell, T (1993) *Modeling Argyris' Action Science*, an unpublished doctoral dissertation, the University of Texas at Austin

Taylor, E W (1997) Building upon the theoretical debate: A critical review of the empirical studies of Mezirow's transformative learning theory, *Adult Education Quarterly*, **48** (1), pp 34–59

Watkins, K E (1990) Tacit Beliefs of Human Resource Developers: Producing unintended consequences, *Human Resource Development Quarterly*, **1** (3), pp 263–75

Watkins, K E (1995) Changing Managers' Defensive Reasoning about Work/Family Conflicts, *The Journal of Management Development*, **14** (2), pp 77–88

Watkins, K E and Marsick, V J (1993) *Sculpting the Learning Organization*, Jossey-Bass, San Francisco

Watkins, K E and Marsick, V J (1996) *In Action: Creating the learning organization*, American Society for Training and Development, Alexandria, VA

Chapter 13

Donald Schön

Ron Cervero

After completing his PhD dissertation on John Dewey's theory of inquiry at Harvard's philosophy department in 1954, Donald A Schön produced a prolific number of publications in a wide range of disciplines, having edited, authored or co-authored several books and over 160 articles (Newman, 1999). He considered himself a 'transplanted philosopher' (Newman, 1999: 10). As he was the Ford Professor of Urban Studies and Education in the Department of Urban Studies and Planning at the Massachusetts Institute of Technology from 1972 until his death in 1997, others would consider him an educator. Although he obviously was involved in many adult education programmes and research efforts over his 43-year career, he certainly would not have considered himself to be, or perceived to be, an adult educator. So why does Donald Schön merit a chapter in a book on *Thinkers in Adult and Continuing Education?* This chapter will show that Donald Schön has indeed been a major influence on the field of adult and continuing education in the 1980s and 1990s, through his two books on the reflective practitioner. Although he published two later books on this same theme (Schön, 1991; Schön and Rein, 1994), his initial presentation in *The Reflective Practitioner: How professionals think in action* (1983) and *Educating the Reflective Practitioner: Toward a new design for teaching and learning in the professions* (1987) was the foundation of his influence.

My first encounter with Schön, like most others in adult education, was through reading *The Reflective Practitioner* (hereafter, RP) in 1983 and assigning it for the graduate course I taught on continuing professional education (CPE). *Educating the Reflective Practitioner* (hereafter, ERP) had just been published when I spent three days in Boston meeting with Schön and Chris Argyris as part of my own continuing education. Because of these meetings and the influence of Schön's ideas on my own thinking that were to be published in *Effective Continuing Education for Professionals* (Cervero, 1988), he agreed to write its foreword. Also, in the early 1990s, he and I were among the faculty for a new

Leadership Institute on Continuing Professional Education that was sponsored by Harvard's Graduate School of Education. We helped design and teach in the 1991 Institute, which was my last personal contact with him. The focus of this chapter is not so much on his personal biography, but rather the influence of his ideas about both reflective practice and the types of education required to improve professional practice. After providing a brief exposition of the genealogy of Schön's idea of reflective practice, I explain why his ideas became so pervasive in adult and continuing education and then show four major areas in which his ideas have had an influence, concluding with my own view of his possible enduring influence as a thinker in this field.

DONALD SCHÖN AND REFLECTIVE PRACTICE: A GENEALOGY OF THE CONCEPT

Although Schön's influence is clearly marked from the publication of two books within a four-year span focusing on reflective practice, this theme can be seen as early as his doctoral dissertation. He argued that the 'question of rationality in the practical decision-process needs to be re-examined' (Schön, 1954: 101, cited in Newman, 1999: 16). He presented Dewey's theory of inquiry as an alternative form of rationality, where the 'stimulus to inquiry is the problematic situation itself' (Newman, 1999: 16). We see here then, in embryonic form, Schön's critique of technical rationality as inadequate for explaining how people solve practical problems in the real world and his argument for a different account. He reasoned instead that people's decision-making processes should be rooted in Dewey's conception of rationality. The dissertation also made extensive use of case studies and examples of the practical problems facing people, such as two managers trying to resolve a strike and a doctor attempting to interpret X-rays. This methodology was to be a hallmark of Schön's work and one that figured prominently in RP and ERP. Newman (1999) provides an extensive biography and a complete list of Schön's publications, showing that he continued to explore this theme individually and with co-authors until his death.

Schön's most well-known collaborator was Chris Argyris, with whom he wrote about many of the same issues (Argyris and Schön, 1974; 1996). Indeed, their *Theory in Practice: Increasing professional effectiveness* (1974) deals explicitly with the same two issues as the reflective practice series, namely, how to understand professional action and how to design education to train professionals effectively. They set forth the problem: 'All human beings – not only professional practitioners – need to become competent in taking action and simultaneously reflecting on this action to learn from it' (1974: 4). They go on to present a model that distinguishes between professionals' espoused theories and theories-in-use, the latter being actually used to solve problems in practice. Education, they argue, ought to allow professionals to identify these theories-in-use in order to evaluate their effectiveness and open them to modification. Whereas Schön incorporated this theme into his books on reflective practice starting in 1983, Argyris did the same with his work on action science (Argyris, Putnam, and Smith, 1985). Together, they also explored the concept of organizational learning (Argyris and Schön, 1978; 1996), which has made a significant impact on adult and continuing education as well. However, Watkins and Wilson (in another chapter) explore the impact of Argyris's work and thus this chapter focuses specifically on Schön's influence in the area of professional practice and education.

As I showed above, dominant and continuing themes in Schön's work address the practical problems that people face in the world, how they learn to resolve them and how to design educational interventions based on these realities. His books on reflective practice specifically focused these themes in the area of professional practice. As in his previous publications, RP and ERP identify a prevailing theory that does not really account for the kinds of knowledge that distinguishes excellent practitioners from merely adequate ones. He argues that this theory, Technical Rationality, assumes that 'professional activity consists of instrumental problem-solving made rigorous by the application of scientific theory and technique' (1983: 21). This account, he believes, makes the grave error of separating knowing from doing, means from ends and research from practice. This view of practice is misguided and his main task is to offer a new 'epistemology of practice' that integrates these dichotomies, which he names reflection-in-action (1983: 49). As with many of his other writings, he based his model of professional practice on detailed studies of several professions, including architecture, town planning, management and organizational consulting.

Schön's starting point is that professional practice is characterized by in-determinate situations that must be transformed into determinate ones (that is, situations that the practitioner knows how to solve). To understand the relationship between professional knowledge and practice, Schön says that 'we should start not by asking how to make better use of research-based knowledge but by asking what we can learn from a careful examination of artistry' (1987:13). By studying professional practice in a variety of fields, he identified two forms of knowing, knowing-in-action and reflection-in-action. Because the latter is central to professional artistry, his new epistemology is called reflection-in-action (RIA). In contrast to the model of technical rationality, which views practice as the application of knowledge, RIA assumes that knowledge is evident in the action of professionals. Most of the actions that professionals take do not stem from a rule or plan that was in mind before acting. Professionals constantly make judgements and, generally, cannot state the rule or theory on which they are based. Schön calls this process knowing-in-action (KIA) and describes it as 'the characteristic mode of ordinary practical knowledge' (1983: 54). This form of knowing has three properties: 1) professionals know how to carry out certain actions without thinking about them prior to or during performance; 2) they are not aware of having learned to perform these actions; and 3) they are unable to describe the knowledge that the action reveals (1983: 54).

Schön's studies made clear that most situations of professional practice are characterized by uniqueness, uncertainty and conflicting values. Therefore, more often than not, knowing-in-action will not solve a particular problem. Rather, one needs to construct the situation to make it solvable. The ability to do this, to reflect-in-action, is the core of professional artistry. Professionals reflect in the midst of action without interruption and their thinking reshapes what they are doing while they do it. The key to completing this problem-setting and problem-solving activity successfully is to bring past experience to bear on current action. This past experience has given professionals a repertoire of examples, images and understandings. When professionals encounter a situation where KIA does not work, they attempt to reframe it as something already present in their repertoire. As they reflect on the situation, professionals ask whether they can frame it in a way to make is solvable and whether they value the results of this solution. This entire process is done in the midst of action: professionals rethink some part of their knowing-in-action, conduct an on-the-spot thought experiment to test its utility, and incorporate this new understanding into immediate action.

Practitioners' knowing-in-action is acquired primarily from the reflection-in-action undertaken in the 'indeterminate zones of practice' (1987: 40). RIA develops new knowledge 'by contributing to the practitioner's repertoire of exemplary themes from which, in the subsequent cases of his practice, he may compose new variations' (1983: 140). Schön is less certain about how the ability to reflect-in-action is acquired and called for more research about why some people learn it better than others. He does argue, however, that to improve this ability, professionals must reflect on the reflection-in-action by describing what they did. To the extent that professionals can more consciously describe how they reflect and what they learn in the process of reflecting, they can more readily employ that form of knowing in new situations. Schön argues that this understanding of how professionals learn should serve to form the basis of how they are taught in pre-service and continuing education programmes. He suggests that: 1) applied science knowledge needs to be taught in a new way if it is to be actually used; and 2) professionals need to be coached in how to reflect-in-action.

Schön believes that the research generated in universities is an important source of information for knowing-in-action. However, this applied science cannot stand alone, but must be incorporated with reflection-in-action. Otherwise, it has little chance of becoming part of a practitioner's repertoire. Thus, professional education programmes should become a place where practitioners learn to reflect on their own tacit theories of the phenomena of practice, in the presence of representatives of those disciplines' that are related to their practice situations. This repertoire-building process accumulates exemplars in ways that are useful to reflection-in-action. Teaching methods that can promote this process include the case method that is used in business education and grand rounds in medicine. Both of these methods connect university-based research and theory into practical ways of knowing. Schön also calls for teaching how to reflect-in-action because it is both a basis of professional artistry and an important source of knowledge for professionals' repertoires. This would be done by examining the 'ways in which competent practitioners cope with the constraints of their organizational settings' (1987: 322). Professionals would reflect on the frameworks they bring to their practices. Instructors would teach like coaches, explaining how they would perform under these conditions, demonstrating their own approaches to skilful performance and reflecting with learners on the frameworks that underlie their work.

REFLECTIVE PRACTICE IN ADULT AND CONTINUING EDUCATION

There is no doubt that the vocabulary of reflective practice and, indeed, Schön's particular articulation of the concept have been accepted in the lexicon of adult and continuing education literature over the past two decades. In assessing Schön's impact on the field, however, it is important to remember that major elements of reflective practice have a long-standing lineage in adult education, particularly in the writings of John Dewey and Eduard Lindeman. Thus, it would not be fair to characterize his ideas as new to the field of adult and continuing education, but rather a current interpretation of the philosophy of pragmatism. Compare, for example, RIA to Dewey's idea that people learn from life. In this book's Dewey chapter, Cross-Durant (1987: 82) says that 'An all-pervading and unchanging theme running through his educational writings is that of growth as a result of educative experiences, which enables an individual to assimilate something from each new experience, add it to the next, and thus change and improve his views and actions as a result of this on-going, lifelong process'. Lindeman's ideas also anticipated Schön's concerns about the design of education when he says that 'all genuine education will keep learning and doing together' and that 'experience is the adult learner's textbook' (Brookfield, 1987: 125). I would argue that Schön's influence has been so prevalent because his idea of reflective practice was planted on the fertile ground of pragmatism, which has shaped many efforts in adult and continuing education during the 20th century.

This re-emergence of pragmatism in adult education (Wilson, 1992) is part of the larger social movement in philosophy and the social sciences (Bernstein, 1983; Carr and Kemmis, 1986). In a sense, then, Schön's influence in adult and continuing education was part of a much larger trend towards pragmatism. As part of this trend, practical reasoning, which has its basis in Aristotle's notion of phronesis (McKeon, 1947), was re-popularized by a number of philosophers. Compare Bernstein's definition of practical reasoning (1983: 54) to Schön's RIA. Bernstein defines it as:

a form of reasoning that is concerned with choice and involves deliberation. It deals with that which is variable and about which there can be differing opinions. It is a type of reasoning in which there can be differing opinions. It is a type of reasoning in which there is a mediation between general principles and a concrete particular situation that requires choice and deliberation. In forming such a judgement there are no determinate technical rules by which a particular situation can simply be subsumed under that which is general or universal. What is required is an interpretation and specification of universals that are appropriate to this particular situation.

Rather than being the lone voice bringing a new concept for consideration, then, Schön's vocabulary of reflective practice was one of many converging works that have re-defined the basis of practical human action.

Although part of a larger historical and social movement, Schön's singular contribution was to interpret professional practice through the lens offered by pragmatism and, more specifically, practical reasoning. His concept of reflective practice had an impact on many topics in the adult and continuing education literature, which I have grouped into four major areas. If we see professional practice as Schön's unique focus, it is not surprising that his influence was felt most directly in the area of continuing professional education. Secondly, reflective practice has figured prominently in many discussions about professional preparation of adult educators including the relation between theory, research and practice. Thirdly, reflective practice is also seen in many re-conceptualizations of adult education practice in such areas as teaching and programme planning. Finally, Schön's ideas have even moved beyond the limited professional arena and made an impact in the literature about adult learning.

CONTINUING PROFESSIONAL EDUCATION

Houle's landmark book, *Continuing Learning in the Professions* (1980) is seen as a major marker of continuing professional education (CPE), a significant area of adult and continuing education. A number of books and other publications followed, nearly all of which bore the mark of Schön's reflective practice themes. As Jarvis observed in 1995, *The Reflective Practitioner* 'has become a classic, catching the mood of contemporary theory. It is perhaps the most frequently cited book on learning in professional practice and it contains the basis of a theory of reflective learning' (1995: 271). Schön's influence is very clear in CPE, no doubt due to professionals being the focus of both RP and ERP. Although the latter book focused mainly on the reflective practicum as used in pre-service professional education, it was easy enough to transfer these concepts into the goals and designs for continuing education.

We can see the major impact of Schön's ideas in two major texts published in 1988. Nowlen's presentation of the performance model (1988) for continuing education rested on Schön's foundation both in its analysis of practice and its prescriptions for education. As he explains: 'The emphasis on problem-solving, as opposed to problem-definition, is a natural consequence of the positivist model of knowledge. The process of problem definition, is, after all, filled with uncertainty, uniqueness, instability, and values conflict – dimensions better addressed by 'soft' knowledge such as artistry, craft, and wisdom' (p 27). As mentioned earlier, Schön's reflective practice was central to my own book (1988) and subsequent writings (Cervero, Azzaretto and associates, 1990; Cervero, 1992a) in continuing professional education. Not only was reflective practice the cornerstone of my analysis of professional practice and learning, but I also used it to conceptualize the practice of continuing education. In this sense I took to heart Schön's comment in the book's foreword about practitioners of continuing education: 'In their effort to help practitioners become more reflective, they should begin with themselves' (Schön, 1988: xiii).

The influence of Schön's reflective practice themes clearly resonated in the professions themselves, spread throughout the world (Brennan, 1990) and continues to the present. In school teaching, for example, reflective practice has become a cottage industry, leading one observer to say: 'Writers who use the term "reflective" at this time in history of educational research risk the wrath of serious readers, if they do not relate their own conceptualization to that of Donald Schön as presented in *The Reflective Practitioner*' (Roberts and Chastko, 1990: 199). Reflective practice has been discussed as a centrepiece to current books on continuing education for lawyers (Roper, 1999) and teacher education (Newman, 1999), studies of how nurses (Daley, 1999) and teachers (Cochran-Smith and Lytle, 1999) learn, and synoptic views of professional learning (Baskett and Marsick, 1992; Bicknam, 1998). Anyone writing about continuing professional education since the mid-1980s has not been able to do so without reference to Schön's themes of reflective practice. He provided a way to think and talk about the goals and design of continuing education in a way that has clearly made a difference in this area of educational practice.

THE PROFESSION AND PREPARATION OF ADULT AND CONTINUING EDUCATORS

While there was an obvious relevance of Schön's reflective practice themes to the provision of continuing professional education, there was also a sustained effort to use this concept for understanding adult and continuing educators themselves. Given the long-term debate over issues related to adult and continuing education as a profession (Cervero, 1992b; Collins, 1992), it is not surprising that practitioners and scholars alike would reflexively see the connection of Schön's work to the theory-practice relationship and the design of graduate education programmes in our field (Jarvis, 1999). The efforts to build a body of practical knowledge and informal theory (Brookfield, 1992) and to re-conceptualize the relationship between theory, research, and practice (Usher and Bryant, 1989) were major developments of the 1980s and 1990s in adult and continuing education. Without doubt, Schön's ideas were highly influential in these efforts.

Two major textbooks that are used extensively in graduate preparation programmes, one in England and the other in North America, use Schön's reflective practice to describe the knowledge base of the field. In arguing for the importance of practical knowledge in his book's final chapter, Jarvis references the distinction between practitioners' espoused theories and their theories-in-use. He essentially agrees with Schön that 'what the practitioners espouse may relate to what they learn during their professional preparation in the classroom whilst what they practise may relate to what they learn in practice' (1995: 259). In their basic textbook, Merriam and Brockett argue that 'reflective practice is perhaps one of the most exciting directions for the future' (1997: 283). They contrast the formal knowledge base covered in their book with the 'actual practice of adult education', which involves much more than familiarity with the basic knowledge of the field. They explain that this formal knowledge is 'what Donald Schön (1987) calls "Technical Rationality." Rather, effective practice also involves being able to reflect critically upon our practice' (1997: 283).

In addition to re-framing the knowledge base of the field, reflective practice has also formed the basis of a major change in the design of graduate education (Peters, 1991) and professional development (Cranton, 1996) for adult and continuing education. Schön's impact has been so profound that some authors (Usher, Bryant, and Johnston) have even worried about the uncritical acceptance of reflective practice given 'the canonical nature of Schön's works (and) their prominence in postgraduate education curricula' (1997: 143). Some programmes have been completely designed around the reflective practice concept (Brookfield, 1988) and others, such as the University of Georgia, have added a 'Reflective Practice Seminar' to the curriculum. At the University of Tennessee, a course on reflective practice 'has become a core requirement for all candidates of master's degrees and doctorates in adult education, and the idea and spirit of reflective practice are promoted across the curriculum' (Merriam and Brocket, 1997: 285). The entire doctoral programme at Teachers College, Columbia University, is 'based on the orienting concept of the critically reflective practitioner espoused by Schön' (Peters, 1991: 438). Many graduate programmes have taken seriously Peters' suggestion that 'such a model, based on the idea of design as the focus of study and research, should be even more seriously considered in the future as the central organizing construct for the university-based study of adult education' (p 436).

RE-CONCEPTUALIZING THE PRACTICE OF ADULT AND CONTINUING EDUCATORS

Alongside the re-conceptualization of the research and knowledge base of the field was the necessary redefinition of practice. Jarvis (1997: 14) describes this major move made in the 1980s: 'Traditionally it was assumed that practitioners went to training school, learned some professional knowledge and then went into practice and applied it... Now it is recognized that practice itself provides experiences from which practitioners might learn. Practitioners find themselves in situations where they have to think on their feet (Schön, 1983) and have to devise new strategies for dealing with situations'. Thus, the field saw a much greater focus on 'what practitioners actually do in real practice settings' (Donaldson and Kuhne, 1994: 14) in research efforts and other publications. Some research even explicitly used Schön's framework to study the practice of adult educators with findings supporting 'the basic assumption of Schön's theory that reflecting practitioners use a constructivist decision-making perspective' (Ferry and Ross-Gordon, 1998: 98). No longer was research and theory to be prior to and better than practice, but rather should be considered as part of 'a captive triangle' (Usher and Bryant, 1989). Schön's imprint on this re-conceptualization of practice is unmistakable, as his books are often cited as the foundation of this 'reflective turn' (Schön, 1991) in adult and continuing education.

This reflective turn permeated many areas of practice. Prominent among these have been teaching and programme planning. Brookfield (1990, 1995) has done more than anyone in exploring Schön's ideas in relation to the practice of teaching adults. His book, *Becoming a Critically Reflective Teacher* (1995), cites the tremendous literature base on reflection in teaching and offers teachers a way to use critical reflection for continuous development of their craft. Johnson and Pratt (1998) offer the apprenticeship perspective as one of five major ways of teaching adults using Schön's work as a major conceptual foundation. In an apprenticeship, master practitioners coach learners in much the same way as Schön describes the reflective practicum. Likewise, programme planning took a turn toward Schön's reflective practice in the 1980s, as Sork and Caffarella (1989: 243) described the discrepancies between theory and practice in their systematic review for the 1989 *Handbook*. They call for: 'Building a theory that takes into account the exigencies of day-to-day responsibilities of practitioners... Reflective practice, as described by Schön (1983) should reveal the major discrepancies. Only by reducing these discrepancies will theory become more relevant to practitioners and will the complexities of planning as it occurs in practice be understood and appreciated by scholars.' Brookfield (1986) and Cervero and Wilson (1994) developed theories of planning practice based on studies of practitioners' actual work.

ADULT LEARNING

Schön's work also spread beyond the bounds of continuing professional education and adult educators' practice to inform our understanding of adult learning. As Newman (1994: 109) points out, 'In the last twenty years reflection has been accorded an increasingly important place in adult learning, and many adult educators now see their major role as that of helping learners reflect on and learn from events, behaviours and emotions experienced.' Of course, Schön was only one of many writers promoting the importance of reflective learning in the 1980s and 1990s (Mezirow, 1991), nearly all of whom trace their efforts to John Dewey's original concern with reflection. This movement towards learning from life experience, and the centrality of reflection in that process, was certainly fostered by Schön's concept of reflective practice. I believe the reason that Schön's RIA was incorporated into our understanding of how adults learn is that he believed the process emulated abilities that all adults possess to reflect on their experience. Thus, while his case studies were of professionals, his theory could easily be used to account for how all adults learn from experience.

Schön's themes of reflective practice are referenced in many writings about adult learning. For example, Jarvis's model of adults learning from life experience includes non-learning, non-reflective learning and reflective learning (1992). Reflective learning draws directly on Schön, especially the sub-category of reflective skills learning that he also refers to as 'reflective practice' (1992: 77). In their most recent textbook on adult learning, Merriam and Caffarella (1999) devote an entire chapter to 'Experience and Learning' and reference 'two concepts that have influenced greatly how adult educators use learners' experience as a central part of the learning process, reflective practice and situated cognition' (1999: 232). The section on 'Learning from Experience' in Tennant and Pogson's *Learning and Change in the Adult Years* (1995) also relies directly on Schön's reflective practice themes. They show how David Boud, a well-known learning theorist from Australia, actually changed his learning theory to correspond to Schön's. Originally, his theories (Boud, Keough and Walker, 1985) had incorporated reflection after a learning experience. But he later came to believe in Schön's notion that 'we experience as we reflect, and we reflect as we experience' (Boud and Walker, 1992: 167). Reflection has also been used extensively in understanding and promoting workplace learning. As Watkins notes, Marsick's book on *Learning in the Workplace* (1987), 'draws on the work of Schön (1983) and defines informal learning as reflection-in-action…. If adult educators are to influence learners in the workplace, they will need to develop a technology for enabling learners to use job experiences more effectively for learning. Critical reflection is one promising approach' (Watkins, 1989: 428-29). The importance of reflection in how adults learn from experience is now firmly located in most theories in the field, due in no small part to Schön's work on reflective practice.

DONALD SCHÖN'S CONTINUING LEGACY?

One measure of the importance of any concept in the world of research and theory is whether it has been criticized. If a concept has not been critiqued then it likely has not really mattered much. As I have tried to demonstrate, Donald

Schön's themes of reflective practice have resonated throughout the literature of adult and continuing education for the past 20 years. As the idea has become commonplace in the vocabulary of adult education, it has been subjected to a number of critiques from both within the field (Brookfield, 1995; Newman, 1994) and without (Grimmett and Erickson, 1988; Newman, 1999). By this measure, then, reflective practice must have been hugely influential in the field. Newman, for example, concluded that Schön's claim to have developed a new epistemology is not borne out in his case studies and that his account of meaning... was incoherent' (1999: 183). Perhaps the most interesting contradiction in Schön's work is that he was able to study processes of practice and change without reference to any explicit socio-political theory of events. Of the many commentators on his work, Bish Sanyal explains this most clearly. Sanyal was the co-editor with Schön of his final book, *High Technology and Low-income Communities* (Schön, Sanyal, and Mitchell, 1999). In a testimonial after his death, Sanyal wrote:

> We must, however, acknowledge one shortcoming in Don's intellectual approach if we are to build on his ideas. Don was silent about uneven distributions of political and economic power and how this unevenness affects learning and innovation. This omission did not reflect ideological posturing on Don's part. It was a result of his work experience, which was primarily in the private sector... Since Don only wrote about issues that emerged directly out of his work experience, he had very little to say about the effects of asymmetrical political and economic relationships' (Richmond *et al*, 1998: 7).

The ideas that Schön championed were present in adult and continuing education since the early part of the 20th century and hopefully will continue to influence the field in the 21st century. However, Donald Schön's legacy will have been to remind us of the importance of staying focused on the practical and to learn as much as possible from the realities that face us as learners and educators. However, I agree with his collaborator, Bish Sanyal and Michael Newman (1994), that although reflective practice is an extraordinarily useful concept, it must be seen in a larger context. If we are to build on his ideas, we need to do so with a clear-headed understanding of the asymmetrical social and political contexts in which learning takes place and to know whose interests reflective practice is serving.

REFERENCES

Argyris, C, Putnam, R and Smith, D M (1985) *Action Science: Concepts, methods and skills for research and intervention*, Jossey-Bass, San Francisco

Argyris, C and Schön, D A (1974) *Theory in Practice: Increasing professional effectiveness*, Jossey-Bass, San Francisco

Argyris, C and Schön, D A (1978) *Organizational Learning: A theory of action perspective*, Addison-Wesley, Reading, MA

Argyris, C and Schön, D A (1996) *Organizational Learning II: Theory, method and practice*, Addison-Wesley, Reading, MA

Baskett, H K M and Marsick, V J (1992) Confronting New Understandings about Professional Learning and Change, in *Professionals' Ways of Knowing: New findings on how to improve professional education*, eds H K M Baskett and V J Marsick, Jossey-Bass, San Francisco

Bernstein, R J (1983) *Beyond Objectivism and Relativism: Science, hermeneutics, and praxis*, University of Pennsylvania Press, Philadelphia

Bicknam, A (1998) The Infusion/utilization of Critical Thinking Skills in Professional Practice, in *Continuing Professional Education in Transition: Visions for the profession and new strategies for learning*, ed Young, Krieger, Malabar, FL

Boud, D, Keogh, R and Walker, D (1985) *Reflection: Turning experience into learning*, Kogan Page, London

Boud, D and Walker, D (1992) In the Midst of Experience: Developing a model to aid learners and facilitators, in *Empowerment through experiential learning*, eds J Mulligan and C Griffin, Kogan Page, London

Brennan, B (1990) *Continuing Professional Education: Promise and performance*, Australian Council for Educational Research, Victoria, Australia

Brookfield, S D (1986) *Understanding and Facilitating Adult Learning*, Jossey-Bass, San Francisco

Brookfield, S D (1987) Eduard Lindeman, in *Twentieth-century Thinkers in Adult Education*, ed P Jarvis, Routledge, London

Brookfield, S D (1988) *Training Educators of Adults: The theory and practice of graduate adult education*, Routledge, London

Brookfield, S D (1990) *The Skillful Teacher: On technique, trust and responsiveness in the classroom*, Jossey-Bass, San Francisco

Brookfield, S D (1992) Developing Criteria for Formal Theory Building in Adult Education, *Adult Education Quarterly*, **42**, pp 79–93

Brookfield, S D (1995) *Becoming a Critically Reflective Teacher*, Jossey-Bass, San Francisco

Carr, W and Kemmis, S (1986) *Becoming Critical*, Falmer Press, London

Cervero, R M (1988) *Effective Continuing Education for Professionals*, Jossey-Bass, San Francisco

Cervero, R M (1992a) Professional Practice Learning and Continuing Education: An integrated perspective, *International Journal of Lifelong Education*, **11**, pp 91–101

Cervero, R M (1992b) Adult Education Should Strive for Professionalization, in Confronting controversies in challenging times: A call for action, *New Directions for adult and continuing education*, no 54, eds M W Galbraith and B R Sisco, Jossey-Bass, San Francisco

Cervero, R M, Azzaretto, J F and associates (1990) *Visions for the Future of Continuing Professional Education*, Department of Adult Education, College of Education, Georgia Center for Continuing Education, the University of Georgia

Cervero, R M and Wilson, A L (1994) *Planning Responsibly for Adult Education: A guide to negotiating power and interests*, Jossey-Bass, San Francisco

Cochran-Smith, M and Lytle, S L (1999) Relationships of Knowledge and Practice: Teacher learning in communities, in *Review of Research in Education*, eds Ivan-Nejab and Pearson, American Educational Research Association, Washington, DC

Collins, M (1992) Adult Education Should Resist Further Professionalization, in Confronting controversies and challenging times: A call for action, eds M W Galbraith and B R Sisco, *New Directions for adult and continuing education*, No 54, Jossey-Bass, San Francisco

Cranton, P (1996) *Professional Development as Transformative Learning: New perspectives for teachers of adults*, Jossey-Bass, San Francisco

Cross-Durrant, A (1987) Basil Yeaxlee and the Origins of Lifelong Education, in *Twentieth-century Thinkers in Adult Education*, ed P Jarvis, Routledge, London

Daley, B J (1999) Novice to Experts: An exploration of how professionals learn, *Adult Education Quarterly*, **49**, pp 133–47

Donaldson, J F and Kuhne, G W (1994) The Working Roles of Continuing Higher Education Administrators: The case of a geographically decentralized continuing education organization, *Continuing Higher Education Review*, **58** (1-2), pp 14–40

Ferry, N M and Ross-Gordon, J M (1998) An Inquiry into Schön's Epistemology of Practice: Exploring links between experience and reflective practice, *Adult Education Quarterly*, **48**, pp 98–112

Grimmett, P P and Erickson, G L (eds) (1988) *Reflection in Teacher Education*, Teachers College Press, New York

Houle, C O (1980) *Continuing Learning in the Professions*, Jossey-Bass, San Francisco

Jarvis, P (1992) *Paradoxes of Learning*, Jossey-Bass, San Francisco

Jarvis, P (1995) *Adult and Continuing Education: Theory and practice*, 2nd edn, Routledge Press, New York

Jarvis, P (1997) Learning and Reflective Practice in an Organization, *Staff and Educational International*, **1**, pp 11–17

Jarvis, P (1999) *The Practitioner-researcher: Developing theory from practice*, Jossey-Bass, San Francisco

Johnson, J and Pratt, D D (1998) The Apprenticeship Perspective: Modelling ways of being, in *Five perspectives on teaching in adult and higher education*, eds D D Pratt and associates, Krieger, Malabar, FL

Marsick, V (1987) *Learning in the Workplace*, Croom-Helm, London

McKeon, R (1947) *Introduction to Aristotle*, University of Chicago Press, Chicago

Merriam, S B and Brockett, R G. (1997) *The Profession and Practice of Adult education: An Introduction*, Jossey-Bass, San Francisco

Merriam, S B and Caffarella, R S (1999) *Learning in Adulthood: A comprehensive guide*, 2nd edn, Jossey-Bass, San Francisco

Mezirow, J (1991) *Transformative Dimensions of Adult Learning*, Jossey-Bass, San Francisco

Newman, M (1994) *Defining the Enemy: Adult education in social action*, Stewart Victor Publishing, Sydney

Newman, S (1999) *Philosophy and Teacher Education: A reinterpretation of Donald Schön's epistemology of reflective practice*, Ashgate Publishing Limited, Aldershot

Nowlen, P M (1988) *A New Approach to Continuing Education for Business and the Professions: The performance model*, American Council on Education and Macmillan Publishing Company, New York

Peters, J M (1991) Advancing the Study of Adult Education: A summary perspective, in *Adult education: Evolution and achievements in a developing field of study*, eds J M Peters, P Jarvis and associates, Jossey-Bass, San Francisco

Richmond, J E D *et al* (1998) A Life in Reflection: Remarks in memory of Donald Schön, *Journal of Planning Literature*, **13**, pp 3–10

Roberts, D A and Chastko, A M (1990) Absorption, Refraction, Reflection: An exploration of beginning science teacher thinking, *Science Education*, **74** (2), pp 197–224

Roper, C (1999) *Foundations for Continuing Legal Education: A guide to research, theories and underlying continuing education for lawyers*, Center for Legal Education, Law Foundation of New South Wales

Schön, D A (1954) Rationality in the practical decision process, Unpublished PhD thesis, Harvard University

Schön, D A (1983) *The Reflective Practitioner: How professionals think in action*, Basic Books, New York

Schön, D A (1987) *Educating the Reflective Practitioner: Toward a new design for teaching and learning in the professions*, Jossey-Bass, San Francisco

Schön, D A (1988) Foreword, in *Effective Continuing Education for Professionals*, R M Cervero, Jossey-Bass, San Francisco

Schön, D A (1991) *The Reflective Turn: Case studies in and on educational practice*, Teachers College Press, London and New York

Schön, D A and Rein, M (1994) *Frame Reflection: Toward the resolution of intractable policy controversies*, Basic Books, New York

Schön, D A, Sanyal, B and Mitchell, W J (1999) *High Technology and Low-income Communities: Prospects for the positive use of advanced information technology*, MIT Press, Cambridge, MA

Sork, T J and Caffarella, R S (1989) Planning Programmes for Adults, in *Handbook of Adult and Continuing Education*, eds S B Merriam and P M Cunningham, Jossey-Bass, San Francisco

Tennant, M and Pogson, P (1995) *Learning and Change in the Adult Years: A developmental perspective*, Jossey-Bass, San Francisco

Usher, R and Bryant, I (1989) *Adult Education as Theory, Practice and Research: The captive triangle*, Routledge, New York

Usher, R, Bryant, I and Johnston, R (1997) *Adult Education and the Postmodern Challenge: Learning beyond the limits*, Routledge, London and New York

Watkins, K E (1989) Business and Industry, *Handbook of adult and continuing education*, in eds S B Merriam and P M Cunningham, Jossey-Bass, San Francisco

Wilson, A L (1992) Pragmatism and Social Action in American Adult Education, *International Journal of Lifelong Education*, **11**, pp 181–89

Part 4

THEORISTS OF ADULT EDUCATION AND SOCIAL CHANGE

Chapter 14

Moses Coady and Antigonish

John M Crane

Nearly 20 years after his death, in a way that was both symbolic and yet very real, Moses Coady's presence could be felt at the 1978 International Symposium on Human Development through Social Change held to commemorate the 50th anniversary of the Antigonish Movement. Several hundred educators, economists, politicians, labour leaders, development workers and students from around the world gathered at St Francis Xavier, a small, Roman Catholic university in the small Canadian town of Antigonish, Nova Scotia, to attend the symposium. Photographs taken at the event show, looming over their heads, the larger-than-life Karsh portrait of the larger-than-life Monsignor Moses Coady, PhD, DD, priest, philosopher, educator and social reformer, first director of the University's Extension Department and the man who led the Antigonish Movement through its first quarter century, its formative and most dynamic years. Ranging from such world leaders as Sir Shridath S Ramphal, Secretary-general of the Commonwealth, to earnest students from across the Third World, the participants came together because they shared a concern for human development in that Third World and an appreciation for the increasing contribution made by the Antigonish Movement through its philosophy and its training centre for adult education and social action, the Coady International Institute.

Hailed as 'the most outstanding education contribution Canada has made to the world' (Milner 1979: 7), the Antigonish Movement has been described by Alexander Laidlaw (1961: 58), an early associate director of the Extension Department and devoted supporter of Dr Coady, as 'a blending of adult education, Christian ethics and a program of social justice, directed through a university extension department'. As Barbara Ward, the Baroness Jackson of Lodsworth, noted economist and author and renowned as a leading spokesman for Third World development, asserted in the tape recording that introduced her paper (1979: 80), the emphasis that the Antigonish Movement has always put 'upon people and upon what people can do to help themselves and to help each other...' has been a fundamental insight only now beginning to be appreciated by the great institutions like the World Bank and the influential government supported programmes. So hypnotic has been the appeal of the high-science, high technology, big growth, 'trickle-down' theory of development and modernization, Ward argued (1979: 80) , that only now are donors realizing that under that system 'much of the work is just wasted or leads, in fact, to social disruption and dislocation'. They 'are all suddenly beginning to realize that if you don't get to the community itself, that if you don't help men and women to take responsibility, to get the leadership that they can give,... you cannot get basic development. It will escape you' (Ward 1979: 80).

Six years later Wasserstrom (1985: 2) would confirm that the foundation he reported on did not simply focus 'upon transferring money to community groups of one sort or another, but rather upon the more delicate and challenging task of empowerment, of helping poor people to create viable organizations of their own... Social change necessarily requires the extension of effective citizenship'.

Did Coady and the Antigonish Movement really espouse such convictions 50 or 60 years ago, convictions that are now becoming what Ward (1979: 80) characterizes as 'the conventional wisdom of the new economic thinking...?' Certainly Msgr Joseph Gremillion, the man who presented Barbara Ward's paper to the symposium and was at the time the coordinator of the Inter-religious Peace Colloquium in Washington, DC, and a fellow in theology at Notre Dame University, held that belief. In 1928, according to Gremillion (1979: 84), 'the Antigonish Movement began creating, applying, and spreading concepts and methods for human development which have received attention and acceptance by the "development elite" only during our own decade'. 'Echo(es) and counterpart(s)' of some of the characteristics of Coady's philosophy and the 'trademarks' of the Antigonish Movement are turning up now under new names 'amidst other climes and contexts' claims Gremillion (p 84–85) who then lists, among others, such modern approaches as: conscientization, Ujamaa, farmer-fisherman-worker self-determination, leader formation, subsidiarity, solidarity, promocion humana and 'small is beautiful'.

The problem of exaggerated praise and extravagant overstatement by enthusiastic admirers is not a new embarrassment for the Antigonish Movement. In 1938, as Laidlaw (1961: 92) quotes, the October 18 edition of *The Extension Bulletin* editorialized:

Exaggerations concerning the Movement... do no good to the cause... It is not necessary to exaggerate the material achievements of the work – which are considerable. The idea of the Movement, however, the restoration of effective ownership to the people and making clearer their way to participation in the heritage of our age, is one the need of which cannot be exaggerated. But no one should underestimate the difficulties in the way. Wishful thinking is the pitfall of the enthusiast.

COADY'S ROLE

No one appears to claim that Coady founded the Antigonish Movement. That responsibility, as Douglas Campbell of the University of Toronto's Sociology Department records in *The Canadian Encyclopedia* (1985: 1829), is justly attributed to Father Jimmy Tompkins. (see also Boyle, 1953: 209; Laidlaw, 1961: 57–58; Faris, 1971: 18; MacEachen, 1979: 12). Nor is Coady mentioned among the earliest pioneers in adult education at St Francis Xavier. Laidlaw (1961: 61–62) writes that Dr Hugh MacPherson, whom Coady (1939: 6) himself calls 'the 'father of cooperation' as far as St FX is concerned', was engaged in agricultural extension services at the university, organizing a fertilizer cooperative as early as 1912, and a letter exists in which Coady declares that 'the person most responsible for the creation of the St Francis Xavier Extension is, of course, Father Michael Gillis… ' (quoted in Laidlaw 1961: 67). Nor is Coady seen blazing a solo path. Those who recall the events in the Antigonish Movement's history always remember a team at work. Corbett (1953: 65) claims that 'the three men largely responsible for the spectacular success of the St Francis Xavier Movement are Dr James Tompkins, Dr M M Coady, and A B MacDonald'. King Gordon (1979: 164), formerly international relations professor at the University of Alberta and later with the International Development Research Centre in Ottawa, expands the team – the 'remarkable team' – beyond Tompkins, Coady and A B MacDonald to include Sister Mary Michael, Sister Anslem, Kay Thompson and Alex S McIntyre. J R Kidd (1960: 12) also makes a point of mentioning the work of some of the women on the Antigonish team when he writes of 'the talents and incredible devotion of those like Miss T Sears, Mrs K (Thompson) Desjardins, (and) Sister Mary Michael… But larger or smaller, more or fewer, Antigonish was always seen as a team'. The enthusiastic contemporary, R J MacSween, reduces the team to the essential two but, 'What a team they were! Dr Coady, learned, dynamic, impressive, yet humble, zealous and kind; A B, charming, jovial and good natured, but at the same time ambitious, practical, and with a rare genius for organization'. (MacSween, 1953: 93). But even as part of the team, Coady is not remembered as 'the person mainly responsible for getting things done – he usually left that to others – usually A B MacDonald. (Laidlaw 1961: 75). Lotz (1977: 109), in stressing that point, claims that Coady 'never organized a cooperative in his life' and then goes on to contrast that with MacDonald and others like him who 'helped to set up study clubs, showed people how to organize meetings, cooperatives and credit unions, taught them how to read and write, checked the books, and did the thousand and one small, mundane things that are the basis of good organization'.

What then was Coady's role in the 'educational adventure' known as the Antigonish Movement? Alexander Laidlaw, who knew Coady and the other leaders at the Extension Department as a result of his own devoted service within the movement, asks and then answers that very question. In Laidlaw's judgment (1961: 14) Coady was the keystone. He held the diverse parts of the movement together and he integrated the various contributions and resources. 'For about thirty years', writes Laidlaw (1971: 75), Coady was the 'chief guide and mentor of the work…, and he was its ablest interpreter right up to the time of his death'.

> In lesser hands, under less spirited and courageous leadership than his, the Antigonish movement could easily have been a milk-and-water affair with nothing to stir men's hearts and imagination; but with him as a sort of father figure who, by the way, took considerable pride in his guerrilla role in a war for social and economic change, Antigonish came to mean something stirring and dynamic, something that struck at the roots of things while others were hacking away at the branches (Laidlaw 1971: 75).

Coady, it appears, was a charismatic leader. (MacDonald, 1979: 157: Lotz, 1977: 107).

THE MAN

Sooner or later, all who knew Coady, all who speak or write of him, emphasize his physical stature, and in doing so seem to be trying to convey the impact this man had on others. E A Corbett (1953: 63) calls him '… a giant of a man, six feet four with the shoulders, chest and limbs of a wrestler'. Although Lotz (1977: 107) shrinks Coady by an inch, he too describes 'a big man, standing 6' 3", strong, rugged, well-educated, a simple and eloquent speaker who got along well with everyone, a happy-go-lucky person who could laugh at himself'. Joseph Hernon, in extravagant apostrophizing of both the man and his work, calls him the 'Giant of Margaree.' 'Coady was big.' says Hernon (1960: 68,69). 'He thought big and talked big… He was a new and disturbing figure, both on the maritime scene and in the ranks of the Catholic Church.'

But there is something more to this picture. As MacPherson (1979: 169) gently hints, the Antigonish Movement thrived on publicity and 'at the heart of this publicity was Moses Coady, a saintly though forceful figure whose physical presence and searching intellect dominated most meetings he attended'. 'In the Maritimes', declares Hernon (1960: 69) in another extravagant metaphor, Coady 'became the Pied Piper because he was big, he exuded confidence and toughness, he was a learned man who commanded respect (sic)…'. But even Hernon who, after all, was penning an appreciation of Coady only a few months after the great leader's death, even Hernon realized there was something unsatisfactory about the picture he drew. 'Scanning early records', he writes (1960: 69–70), 'could give a picture of Coady as a shouting, arm-waving radical, given to exaggeration and shot with overtones of conceit. Coady consciously created much of that image himself. The times called for it. At heart he was truly a humble giant…'.

Others have also remarked on Coady's speaking style. Often several describe nearly identical scenes. Corbett (1953: 63) relates how Coady 'began haltingly, as though he was not quite sure how he was going to develop his subject. His great hands pawed awkwardly at a few notes; his brow was furrowed and anxious'.

Hernon (1960: 69) describes Coady as he 'stood and flexed his great hands and seemed to grope for words. The first two minutes often left the audience wondering if the man could talk at all'. But soon he seemed to find his theme; the words would come easily. 'Then he used the huge hands daintily and with great effect to emphasize a fact, expose an injustice, ridicule an absurdity or drive home a point' (Laidlaw 1971: 15). And he was a talker far more than he ever was a writer. Although he left one book, *Masters of Their Own Destiny*, which is still in print and has been translated into seven languages, as well as what Laidlaw (1971: 9) describes as a 'mountainous' output of written speeches and short articles, 'only rarely... did he write with the same vigor and imagery as he achieved in everyday conversation and impromptu speeches'.

Although characterized as a deep thinker and intelligent and certainly widely read, Coady's restless, importunate, even dogmatic nature meant that scholarship held no appeal for him. Nor did he write for scholars. Coady's offerings, says Laidlaw (1971: 94–95), are presented 'bluntly and unrefined... with the florid appeal of the idealist rather than the cold analysis of the social scientist'. Indeed, Coady could become 'impatient with the jargon and the 'sociologese' of the theorist' (Laidlaw 1971: 57); his own writing was 'simple, brusque and straight-forward, but often eloquent' (Laidlaw 1971: 94).

COADY'S BACKGROUND

Moses Coady was born in 1882, in the lovely Margaree Valley, in Nova Scotia's Cape Breton Island. He came of hard-working, modestly successful farming folk who nurtured in their children both the strong religious faith of their Irish Catholicism and what Corbett (1953: 64) calls the 'innate regard for education which has always characterized the Nova Scotia people'. Along with these values, Coady absorbed the rich, earthy idioms of his people's speech, a heritage that served him well in the work of his adult years. Often when in need of a telling phrase or a vivid image, Coady was able to reach back to his origins and find an apt metaphor that carried his point or sharpened his message.

A big, strong youth, it was only natural that the farm and its demands made many calls upon his time and his energies. Nevertheless, young Coady pursued his education and immersed himself in reading and study at home. It was at this time that the most significant of the influences that were to shape his life can begin to be traced. In a pattern that was to persist for many years, Coady put first one step and then another upon the path already trod by his cousin – his double first cousin – Jimmie Tompkins. Tompkins, in turn, had been inspired by their uncle, another Moses Coady, who had left the Valley to pursue his studies and to become a priest and had then returned.

Older than his cousin Moses by 11 years and 4 months, Jimmie Tompkins was in many ways his antithesis. Small, even skinny, often in doubtful health, he even lacked the physical magnetism that made it easy for Coady to command the attention of others. But they shared the same ancestry and the same background and they shared their zeal. First the one and then the other, 10 to a dozen years later, they left the Valley to complete high school, to take teacher's training, to teach and then to continue further education, enrolling at St Francis Xavier University. Each, in turn, was selected to go to Rome to the Urban College of the Propaganda; each was ordained priest, Tompkins in 1902, Coady some eight years later, and each returned to join the faculty of St Francis Xavier University.

In countless ways that path that Coady followed had been smoothed by Tompkins's earlier passage. George Boyle (1953: 28), Tompkins's biographer, describes how a steady stream of letters, pamphlets, books and cards poured from Tompkins in Rome 'directed to those whom he had picked out to influence'. 'One of the targets for this shower of ideas', Boyle continues, 'was... young Moses Michael Coady'. Corbett (1953: 65) agreed. He wrote that 'Dr Tompkins, from the very beginning, was always prodding people, opening up their minds and pushing them to a realization of the abilities and problems of society. One of the persons he thus influenced early in life was M M Coady...' The flavour of this smoothing of the way, this pushing forward of his protégées, can be discerned in a selection from a 1931 letter to Archbishop McNeil which Boyle (1953: 170) quotes, where Tompkins writes that '... Dr Coady is fast becoming one of the most influential men in Eastern Canada. Discerning people are beginning to call him one of the great Canadians'.

Was Tompkins as generous of heart as this and similar reports would make him appear? Perhaps there was both a measure of genuine selflessness as well as an innate gift for spotting talent, particularly talent that could produce the results he sought. Boyle (1953: 19) records how, as early as the rugged, lonely, difficult days of Tompkins's first school teaching:

> his discernment widened and deepened. He was conscious of an insight regarding individual pupils which was sometimes as tenuous as an intuition, and frequently turned out so right as to be uncanny. He was quick to discover the personal circumstances and mental capacities of his students, and wherever he noted a trace of talent, this he nourished with lavish praise'.

And Joseph Hernon (1960: 60) recognized that in the later years Tompkins 'worked best in his glebe house with a small group in whom he had cannily spotted the potential for leadership'. Then Hernon goes on: 'There is no question that Tompkins visualized Coady as the heart and voice of any real movement that might emerge from his thinking... And Tompkins kindled the flames of learning and social thought in the brash young giant. He counselled him through youth and during his studies in Rome. He saw in Coady the commanding personality he could never have and he set about to groom him for the future he envisioned'.

THE MIDDLE YEARS

'All in all,' says Laidlaw (1961: 14), 'there was nothing remarkable in (Coady's) career before middle age'. He had returned from Rome with his two doctorates and began teaching philosophy at St Francis Xavier. He did some postgraduate work in education in Washington, DC, and even served as a high school principal for a few years. Nevertheless, some special talent for leadership occasionally showed itself. It was during those years, for instance, that he is credited with being 'chiefly responsible for reviving the Nova Scotia Teachers' Union… when it was in danger of extinction' (Laidlaw 1961: 55). And, too, although Dr Tompkins, Father Gillis, Father MacDonald and others were the originators, Coady was being 'prodded' into more and more participation in such adult education activities as the People's Schools of 1921 and 1922 and the later Rural Conferences.

These early, pioneering ventures reflected an intuition that adult education, to be successful, must be linked with the most concrete reality in people's lives. In Nova Scotia that reality was material poverty. Later, under Coady's inspiration, it came to be understood that relieving the peoples' economic hardships was only the first step in an adult education programme. Addressing the needs of the intellectually starved, the level at which more fortunate institutions could begin, remember that 'Livingstone described adult education in England as having sprung from "the desire to combat intellectual poverty"' (Laidlaw 1961: 59), would have lesser emphasis for St. Francis Xavier. And even that was not the ultimate goal, for true adult education was seen by Coady as embracing the political, the social, the cultural and the spiritual as well as the intellectual and the economic.

Father Tompkins and his early, pioneering associates were keenly aware of another certainty of adult education: the lack of a continuing organization could nullify the good work of their ventures. As Boyle (1953: 84) writes, 'Adult education was not new. Specific projects had been carried on. But the tendency was that after a time they deteriorated and disintegrated. They were sporadic. They did not have the organism of continuation. Tompkins wanted to create that'. Unfortunately, in what seemed at the time a crushing and humiliating blow, he was not to be left to continue his work at St Francis Xavier. A prolonged and, perhaps, intemperate conflict with the hierarchy over a quite unrelated question – the federation of maritime universities – saw Tompkins 'banished to Canso…' (Campbell, 1985: 182; see also Lotz, 1977: 105). His dream of the creation of the Extension Department was not to be easily realized. And in fateful confirmation of their fears, the pioneers of adult education at St Francis Xavier saw Tompkins's People's School – that Nova Scotia reflection of the great Gruntvig's inspiration – leave Antigonish, shifting to Glace Bay, only to be discontinued two years later.

They redoubled their efforts. Father Coady and the others within St Francis Xavier persisted; Father Gillis and, now, Father Tompkins and others, from outside. Numerous influences were focused on the reluctant university. The efforts of the diocesan clergy, the Alumni Association, interested government officials, and strong-willed Protestant friends whose support had begun as early as the People's Schools, were finally successful although it had taken six years to get the Board of Governors' resolution. And even then, it was another two years, the summer of 1930, before a budget was approved and the great work of the St Francis Xavier University Extension Department began in earnest.

Coady, who had been named to head the Extension Department, had, at the same time, become deeply involved in another of Father Tompkins's projects. Outraged by the poverty, squalor and despair, malnutrition, ignorance and apathy that he had found among the fishermen of his parish, Tompkins had tried to improve their condition. However, despite his best efforts, despite his pushing and prodding, despite a few small improvements, he had been quite unable to bring about any major change in his people's lot. But on the evening of July 1, 1927, the 60th anniversary of Canada's confederation, while the rest of the nation was celebrating the jubilee, Tompkins organized a mass meeting. 'By calling in the press and asking "But What Have We To Celebrate?", the fishermen... created a uproar that resulted in that most Canadian of responses to urgent social problems – a Royal Commission of Enquiry' (Crane 1983: 154).

Dr Coady's efforts on the fishermen's behalf resulted in an invitation to present a submission. 'Clearly and forcefully he advocated, first, the organization of the shore fishermen so that they might be able to assist in formulating policies for the industry; second, the promotion of scientific and technical education; third, the teaching to the fishermen of the methods of producer and consumer cooperation.' (Boyle 1953: 142). These recommendations were included in the Commission's final report and in 1929 Coady was asked by the federal government to undertake the organizing of the fishermen along the 8000-mile coastline of the Maritimes and the Magdalen Islands. Boyle (1953: 142) records that Tompkins had pressed the government for Coady's appointment. He continues:

> The choice of this man was fortunate... Dr. Coady, a big man physically, was a gripping speaker at meetings. While he had the same outlook as Father Tompkins and the other Antigonish men whose fund of thought had made the People's School, he had the platform presence... that Father Tompkins lacked. He exuded courage and optimism, grand scale. Master of the humorously graphic and folksy phrase, when he spoke to the fishermen he could invoke the plain and apt illustration that made him famous. He showed the people their lost opportunities, their disunity, their obligations to themselves. Cooperation was the message. He shocked, jolted, and prodded the villages into an awakening (Boyle 1953:142).

Within a year the fishermen, having first gained confidence and experience with small, tentative ventures, had their own packing plants, their own adult education programmes and their own United Maritime Fishermen under way.

THE GOOD YEARS

Coady and the movement never looked back. Their history becomes so inextricably bound together over the next 25 years that the philosophy of the man appears as the philosophy of the movement and its accomplishments are often taken to be the accomplishments of the man.

A dynamo of adult education activity, Coady was often giving over 150 speeches a year in person or over the radio. At first in the Maritime provinces, then throughout Canada, and ultimately across the United States as well, Coady spoke and taught and prodded, exploding his 'intellectual dynamite' (Coady 1939: 30). He stressed his ideas on so many occasions, in so many places, on so many levels and in so many ways that the sheer volume of the material he produced renders it difficult to extract a concise and definitive expression of his principles, theories, and philosophy.

One approach, however, exemplified by A A MacDonald's report to the 1978 symposium, may be to analyse the Antigonish Movement and, therefore, Coady's contribution, in terms of sociological phenomena. Possessing 'all the characteristics of a reform social movement as identified in the sociological literature', according to MacDonald (1978: 157), the Antigonish Movement 'was a deliberate collective effort for social change – an effort which followed a commonly recognized and predictable social pattern'.

The first circumstance of the pattern required 'the existence of social strain which results in mental stress and feelings of relative deprivation' (MacDonald, 1979: 157). Certainly that social strain and those feelings of deprivation existed in Maritime Canada. Visibly less prosperous than many other parts of the country, convinced that 'the economic set-up within Confederation was at fault' (Coady 1943: 2), comparisons, always invidious, were made. As Coady explains, it was not the great economic crash of the 1930s that initiated the movement. The Extension Department had been established before then, in 1928, 'one of the peak years of the so-called prosperity era... the good times of the "twenties"' (Coady 1943: 1), precisely because the farmers and fishermen of the area had been missing out on those good times. 'For decades before this (they) had endured their great depression' (Coady 1943: 1). Furthermore, Coady (1943: 3) argued from his Maritime perspective, 'the old order was simply not... a good order. It was unkind to the great masses of the people even in the best of times. The kind of life it gave... was not good. It was insecure. It engendered a social atmosphere which impeded Christian living for our people'. The perceived inequity of the economic was then deemed to explain any real or imagined educational, social, cultural or spiritual backwardness.

The next step, MacDonald (1979: 157) writes, requires 'the development of a philosophical or ideological belief which categorically defines the causes of the strain and infallibly prescribes the solution for the problem'. For Coady, education was the answer. The 'education of the past', his term for conventional schooling, defined the cause of the problem and 'adult education', lifelong learning, identified the solution. While praising the belief in the western democracies that education is the instrument of human progress, Coady often condemned the 'education of the past', as embodying an elitist philosophy that effectively stripped the ordinary people of their brightest and best, thus depriving them of the energy, brains and leadership that would let them improve their own lot in society. But, Coady noted even sadder than 'robbing our rural and industrial population of their natural leaders' (1943: 20) was an additional phenomenon. Once 'the highly energetic and ambitious escape to the most desirable jobs in the nation (p 1), once the escape mechanism has been activated 'by which the lowly can rise from their class and join the elite' (p 17–18), 'their interests are... different from what they would be back home. They have new masters and if they are to succeed they have to promote the interests of the class which they serve. They thus turn against their own flesh and blood and in many cases are the most bitter enemies of any movement calculated to give the people a chance to rise to a better life' (p 20).

Over 30 years later, another challenging educator would make many of the same observations about his own people (Freire, 1972: 22). And Paulo Freire, just as Coady had done those many years before him, turned to adult education for the solution that would break the cycle.

In part because of his natural impatience but also in part because he could not abandon the poor of his generation to a life without hope of improvement, Coady never pursued the idea of reforming the conventional school system. He chose, instead, to work directly and immediately with the adults in economic need. 'Children do not run society' Coady argued (1945: 10). 'Clearly the techniques by which we can improve the social order and hold an educated generation of our youth must be achieved by the adult population.' And yet, it is a measure of the man that in time his vision broadened. He came to believe in lifelong education, in 'continuous adult learning'. He argued (1943: 16) that it was 'necessary for education to be coterminus with active human life' and, while admitting that Antigonish was not at the stage in its development where it could undertake the whole task, believed that 'any programme of adult education should be for all the people, even the so-called educated classes'.

Over the years Coady and his fellows synthesized into an ideological statement a selection of 'theological, philosophical and behavioural science concepts concerning man and the society in which he lives' (MacDonald, 1979: 157) – a philosophy upon which the Antigonish Movement was built. According to Laidlaw (1961: 97–98) the essence of this philosophy was contained in six basic principles given in several publications of the St Francis Xavier Extension Department.

> The first of these is the primacy of the individual. This principle is based on both religious and democratic teaching: religion emphasizes the dignity of man, created in the image and likeness of God; democracy stresses the value of the individual and the development of individual capacities as the aim of social organization.

> ... social reform must come through education. Social progress in a democracy must come through the action of the citizens; it can only come if there is an improvement

in the quality of the people themselves. That improvement, in turn, can only come through education.

... education must begin with the economic. (Since) the people are most keenly interested in and concerned with economic needs... it is good technique to suit the educational effort to the most intimate interests of the individual or group...

... education must be through group action... man is a social being. Not only is man commonly organized in groups, but his problems are usually group problems. Any effective adult education program must, therefore, fit into this basic group organization of society.

... effective social reform involves fundamental changes in social and economic institutions... real reform will necessitate strong measures... which may prove unpopular in certain quarters.

... the ultimate objective of the movement is a full and abundant life for everyone in the community. Economic cooperation is the first step, but only the first, towards a society which will permit every individual to develop to the utmost limit of his capacities.

According to MacDonald (1979: 157) the next characteristic identified in the sociological literature as illustrative of a reform social movement is ' the activity of charismatic leaders who espouse the belief and instigate a core following'. That leadership and that core following are classically illustrated in Moses Coady and the team that made up the Antigonish Movement.

The fourth requirement, 'physical and social proximity of leaders and potential followers', (MacDonald 1979: 157) is clearly fulfilled as well. As Lotz (1977: 112) exults 'Father Jimmy, Moses Coady and the other leaders were born and raised locally... They were known, trusted, loved and respected... None of the workers was a fuzzy do-gooder, parachuted in to help the local people. They had status, prestige and a base at the university's Extension Department'.

Fifth, writes MacDonald (p 157), is 'the organization of efforts to implement the prescribed solutions'. From their hard-won base within the university, those in the movement strove to achieve their objective of a better life for 'the people of the Maritime Provinces... a better economic status, more culture... greater spirituality... equality of opportunity to achieve the realization of all their possibilities through voluntary action in a democratic society' (Coady 1943: 66).

Financially unable to implement their plans with 'lectures and professors and put(ting) the people back to school... through actual teaching (or) by correspondence courses' (Coady 1943: 66), they found what Coady later judged to be a better technique. The technique was discovered by facing the actual situation and planning a way by which the people of eastern Canada could be mobilized to think, to study and to get enlightenment. 'We found the discussion circle. This did not involve any teachers. It was in line with our whole co-operative idea. We would make education part of the self-help movement. The people would come together by themselves and discuss their problems. The first logical step in this process was for someone to round up the people, so to speak. This involved the mass meeting' (Coady, 1943: 66).

He continues, in that 1943 radio broadcast, to describe the movement's adult education techniques as they evolved. In brief, it was the task of the speaker at the mass meeting to inspire, through his personality and the dynamics of his message, the organization of the community into small groups which they called study clubs or discussion circles. These, as Laidlaw (1961: 116) writes, were 'the key educational technique in the Antigonish Movement… the method of Socrates brought up to date…'. They discussed real, everyday problems in order to solve them. Realistic action was to be the goal. Every month or so all the little groups came together into one large community group to share each other's triumphs or problems, to hear inspirational speakers, and for social, cultural or recreational activities. The Extension Department acted as a resource, providing the literature and the specialized information as the study clubs determined what they needed to know.

In time, Antigonish came to offer leadership schools, specialized training courses on the organizing and administering of cooperatives and credit unions, community refresher courses, industrial study classes, weekend institutes for labour leaders, credit union and cooperative directors and leaders of the ladies guilds. They began a journal; originally the Extension Bulletin, it later became *The Maritime Cooperator*. They branched into radio, at first locally but later with contributions to the national broadcasting system, and in 1955 a start was made in the use of television.

According to MacDonald's reading (1979: 157) of the sociological literature, the sixth point says that a social reform movement requires 'the existence of societal conditions, eg laws, social control, etc which permit the effort to be exerted'. Again, the Antigonish Movement conforms to the pattern. Indeed, in many ways the movement was born and developed in a very positive and favourable environment. Not only had individuals within the government service contributed their support as far back as Tompkins People's School and, later, to the establishment of the Extension Department itself, but in some instances the provincial Department of Agriculture and Antigonish worked together so closely that they appear to be sharing extension personnel and responsibilities. Similarly, Coady's selection by the federal government for the task of organizing the fishermen and, provincially, the role he played in obtaining credit union legislation, both indicate the degree to which the authorities respected and supported Antigonish. In the latter instance, Boyle (1953: 157) bluntly states that 'Dr Coady took measures to have a Credit Union Act passed by the Nova Scotia Legislature' while Laidlaw (1961: 85) quotes a report that says that '… Dr Coady, with the sponsorship of Premier Harrington, had it put through the 1932 session of the Legislature'.

This respect and support for Antigonish continues to present times. As Allan MacEachen, then Deputy Prime Minister of Canada, said at the 1978 symposium: 'Through the Canadian International Development Agency, the Government of Canada is actively supporting the work done by… the Antigonish Movement'.

And beyond governments, the support was real and significant. As early as 1938, Pope Pius XI was indicating his approval and, of course, Coady was eventually honoured by his church with the rank of monsignor. Even in the material realm, early and continuing support came from, among others, such diverse bodies as the Carnegie Corporation of New York, now the Carnegie Foundation, and the Scottish Catholic Society.

In still another sense, societal conditions favoured the Antigonish approach. In both the Protestant and the Roman Catholic communities of rural Maritime Canada in the 1920s and 1930s, the habit of looking to the clergy for leadership was still an almost automatic reaction. If Antigonish could win the influential local leader to the movement, their parishioners could be expected to follow.

The last of the characteristics of a reform social movement identified by MacDonald (1979: 157), 'the routinization of the organizational effort with increasing emphasis on organizational maintenance and decreasing emphasis on philosophical goals', seems to be applicable as well. Perhaps the clearest evidence of this stage is the almost inevitable diminishing of concern and emphasis on educating the people to think and to reason and to learn to solve their own problems, in favour of efforts dedicated to helping them overcome their immediate economic concerns.

It is much easier to proclaim your organization's success by pointing to such quantifiable changes as the number of credit unions formed, the new membership numbers in producer or consumer cooperatives, the amount of money saved or loaned over a period of time, or even the number of students registering in a certain course or programme, than it is to identify the changes in the quality of a human being's thinking and living.

It was, perhaps, an understanding of this instinct for institutional self-aggrandizement that inspired Coady's most memorable exhortation:

We have no desire to remain at the beginning, to create a nation of mere shopkeepers, whose thoughts run only to groceries and to dividends. We want our men to look into the sun and into the depths of the sea. We want them to explore the hearts of flowers and the hearts of fellow-men. We want them to live, to love, to play and to pray with all their being. We want them to be men, whole men, eager to explore all the avenues of life and to attain perfection in all their faculties. We want for them the capacity to enjoy all that a generous God and creative men have placed at their disposal. We desire above all that they will discover and develop their own capacities for creation. It is good to appreciate; it is godlike to create. Life for them shall not be in terms of merchandising but in terms of all that is good and beautiful, be it economic, political, social, cultural, or spiritual. They are the heirs of all the ages and of all the riches yet concealed (Coady 1939: 163).

COADY – A MAN BEFORE HIS TIME

In addition to the problem presented by the sheer volume of Coady's work, there is another aspect that makes it difficult to present his thoughts to the satisfaction of today's reader. He was a man ahead of his time. His ideas in so many fields were so advanced that many find it difficult now to credit him with the positions he advocated then. Today's temporal chauvinist finds it easier to spurn the evidence than to believe that over 50 years ago someone could have been put into practice the social and educational reforms they affirmed in the 1980s and 1990s.

But consider a few examples. In an area and at a time when religious divisions were deep, wide and strongly held, Coady and the Antigonish, in daring to be different, anticipated the ecumenism of Vatican II by a generation. While the participation of Protestants is not always apparent even in today's descriptions of St Francis Xavier and the Antigonish Movement, it should be noted that their contributions were significant. As Laidlaw (1961: 75) confirms, 'from the outset Protestants were selected for its staff if they were the right ones for the job'.

In environmentalism, another area that elements of our contemporary society have taken for their own, Coady anticipated today's views. Laidlaw (1961: 12) writes that Coady was 'as a Jeremiah about the waste and destruction of natural resources to a generation that wasted and destroyed with abandon'. He warned of 'poisoning our earth and our waters' at a time when pollution was only a shadowy spectre, visible on the horizon to only a few Rachel Carsons'. Coady spoke of organically fit soil, for Sir Albert Howard's composting methods, of 'devitalized foods like corn flakes' (Coady quoted in Laidlaw, 1961: 159) and in comments that have a tragic significance today for the economically shattered communities so recently dispossessed along with huge, ruthlessly clear-cut areas of Canada's forests, Coady spoke of the inexhaustibility of intelligently handled forest resources. 'We cannot', said a stern Coady (quoted in Laidlaw, 1961: 149), 'sin against nature and hope to win'.

In another place he strikes a chord with today's generation when he spoke out for peace and against the dangers of technology when it is allied to war's demands instead of to humanity's betterment but, being Coady, his mind searches beyond the warnings to suggest a blueprint to achieve peace. 'If we don't put to good use', wrote Coady (quoted in Laidlaw, 1961: 204), 'the scientific knowledge and machinery that the genius of man has discovered and invented, then they will be used for evil ends. Everything of a scientific nature, from botany to bombs, will be turned into the killing business of war. Peace can come only when people are satisfied with their world, when they have (a life) in harmony with their dignity as human beings'.

His blueprint for peace, through unity and brotherhood, listed 'Technological Unity' first, a concept where his thoughts are still ahead of most people even today. He urged the sharing of all technological advances with all the world's people. 'It is the right of all the people of earth', Coady wrote in the December 1952 issue of *The Canadian Messenger*, 'to have access to this knowledge'. Next, after considering 'Economic Unity' and 'Political Unity', Coady moved to 'Social and Educational Unity'.

> All the peoples of the earth should put their faith in the power of ideas and knowledge rather than in the coercion of external force. The whole human race must be lifted out of illiteracy and must have access, not only to the educational institutions that will enlighten their minds, but also to the social and cultural institutions that will look after their souls and bodies (Coady, 1952: 3).

And this concern with men's souls as well as their bodies illustrates a Coady principle mentioned earlier: any ontological ordering of human needs must put the spiritual in a pre-eminent place.

In curriculum terms, Coady's vision of adult education appears to have been far ahead of his time as well. More than a quarter century before the explosion of Romanticism shattered the certainties of the educational world in the mid-1960s, Coady had been advocating principles and implementing practices that were remarkably similar to these 'new' ideas, hopes and expectations. Labelled the 'Romantic Curriculum' in contrast to the traditional or 'Classical' curriculum by those who studied these ideas in the 1970s (see Jenkins, 1972; Lawton 1973; Griffin 1978; and others), the new curriculum echoed Coady's emphasis on the learner instead of the content or material to be learnt. Certainly the whole 'study club' or 'discussion circle' technique that Coady (143: 66) described illustrates the learner centeredness of the Antigonish approach. Similarly, both Coady and the later Romantics were concerned with creativity, originality, discovery, awareness and the value of experience in contrast to the traditional or classical model's concern with skills, conformity, information handling, obedience and the value of instruction.

Coady's achievements were all the more remarkable since they occurred in an era when society's traditional boundaries, their form and structure, were much more dominant, much more firmly in place, than those faced by the later Romantics. In the later era, as Martin writes (1981: 15, 25), there was 'a whole new cultural style, a set of values, assumptions and ways of living… exemplified (by)… a setting of freedom and fluidity against form and structure'.

Coady's technique of beginning the education of his adults with real-life problems and concerns, of involving the learner in his or her own education, and of choosing cooperation as a solution are all forerunners of the 1960s Romantic approaches (see Lawton 1973: 22–24) and contrast sharply with the Classical position. The latter presented traditional subjects to study, offered those didactically and encouraged competition among the students. Even more fundamental are the purposes evident in each of the contrasting curriculum models. For the Classical enthusiast, the acquisition of knowledge appears to be the purpose of education while Coady, and later the Romantics, seem to be saying that the development of attitudes and values that encourage the individual to develop to the utmost limit of his or her capacities must take precedence. This aim, expressing one of the Antigonish Movement's six basic principles, encapsulates, according to Keuscher (1970: 6), the Romantic curriculum philosophy.

While there may well be echoes of the John Dewey and progressive education in the Antigonish Movement and, of course, in the much later Romantic curriculum, Coady's great achievement was that he actually put his ideas, theories and principles into practice. He discovered and acted upon some remarkable insights into the nature of the adult learner.

In areas well beyond education, Coady's mind and tongue ranged widely. 'With prophetic foresight', records Laidlaw (1961: 13), 'he called on sisters in religious orders to come out of their convents, to mix in the workaday world of ordinary men and women – shortly after his death there were nuns marching at Selma'. In another place he had scolded Americans on 'the scandal of believing on the one hand in the equality professed in the Declaration of Independence and on the other denying to blacks the full rights of citizenship' (Coady quoted in Laidlaw, 1961: 189). Further, Coady warned, it was infinitely bad foreign policy to be allied with 'the big boys of business and finance (who) are the real source of trouble' (Laidlaw 1961: 189), 'for in too many cases the powerful vested interests have taken over and exploited for their own advantage the natural resources of other peoples, especially in the undeveloped sectors of earth. If we add to this the arrogant insistence on white supremacy, backed up as it often is by force and supreme contempt for the coloured races, the situation gets still more serious. This cannot go on forever… Some day we will reap dividends of wrath for so stupid a policy. If we were wise we would help the people everywhere to get the good and abundant life by a proper development of their own natural resources' (Coady quoted in Laidlaw 1961:121–22).

Perhaps because Coady had been advocating 'the application of adult education and cooperative organization to the underdeveloped world' as long ago as 1939 (MacEachen, 1979: 12), and perhaps because he had been warning against the excesses of unrestrained capitalism for even longer, there were times, particularly in his final years, when he seemed to succumb to discouragement. Perhaps that is why, just five years before he died, he wrote to a friend of many years in bitter disappointment:

> There is not much hope for the world because the economically and politically powerful people of the Western democracies – and this goes also for the religious leaders of all denominations, at least a great percentage of them – will stop short of doing the whole job. Their philosophy is: we will go far enough with reform to ward off the present danger, but we must not allow reform to interfere with the privileged status quo. That's just it in a nutshell. The rank and file of the world's people have a sixth sense by which they can unerringly detect this fatal duplicity. They are not going to be fooled any longer, and when the right time comes they will put up new guillotines to cut the stupid heads off the leaders in Church and State who are incapable of seeing where the real danger is and who lack the courage to apply an adequate remedy (Coady, quoted in Laidlaw, 1961: 208).

REFLECTION

But it is not as a momentarily embittered idealist conscious of failures that Coady is remembered. Indeed, if Coady is in any sense a failure it is only in that special sense of a man's actual accomplishment falling short of his Utopian dreams. Coady spoke and believed in the millennium, in that special time when all the world would achieve social justice, unity and peace. It is perhaps this poignant sense of the unfulfilled that Tom Lovett (1980: 163) discerned when he wrote that 'Antigonish is now a lost dream'.

For almost all other commentators, Coady and the Antigonish Movement have been a boundless success. 'Recognition came quickly', wrote Laidlaw (1961: 91):

> ... and to an extent that could hardly have been anticipated. The world at that time was feverishly searching for a way out of the Great Depression; here was a program that went from theory to practice in a relatively short time, that struck at the most serious problems of the time – the economic ones, and that still preserved, and indeed fostered, the democratic ideals which peoples in other parts of the world were surrendering for security.

With increasing prosperity the times changed and just as the initial impetus of the movement was slackening, Antigonish was discovered by concerned and thoughtful leaders from the Third World. Increasingly, visitors were drawn from Asia, Latin America, the Caribbean and Africa during the post-war period. As MacEachen (1979) writes, they found at tiny, relatively obscure St Francis Xavier, a proven method of economic self-help allied to adult education that used very minimal resources, mobilized the local population and used straightforward techniques that poor people with limited education could learn readily. 'Moreover, the techniques were... aimed at meeting immediate needs – marketing, credit, housing' (MacEachen, 1979: 13). Further, the philosophy of the movement appealed to these developing countries as they moved to independence. Their 'leaders held high hopes that self-determination could be given real substance through a transformation of political, economic, and social institutions. They remained wary of the competing ideologies of capitalism and statesocialism... The cooperative approach', as formulated by Coady, 'stressed self-reliance, the development of local leadership, broadly based education, and a peaceful redistribution of economic benefits' (MacEachen, 1979: 13).

These requests for help re-invigorated the movement and only a few months after Coady's death in 1959, the Coady International Institute was established to train people from over 100 countries in adult education methods, community development and the philosophy and techniques of cooperative organization.

Those who analyse Coady and the movement's success do have important reservations, however. First, they insist, it is important to distinguish between its philosophy, its programmes and its techniques. 'This differentiation must be made because it is unlikely that the social pattern of a particular social movement can be replicated in different social circumstances and in different time periods' (MacDonald, 1979: 159). It is obvious, then, that techniques have to vary to suit the new circumstances. Indeed, even in Maritime Canada, the movement's birthplace, the old techniques no longer suffice in these days of good communications and relative prosperity, of good roads and reliable vehicles, of satellite television receivers and radios and telephones in every home and office.

While the usefulness and applicability of the Antigonish cooperative programme appears to be more readily accepted by the policy makers in developing countries than does the adult education programme, 'it is not so evident', argues MacDonald (1979: 161), 'that they recognize or accept the human development possibilities of the cooperative program'. They do not appear to realize that the second objective of an Antigonish cooperative programme is the increased development of human capacities through such methods as participation in decision making and choice by the members. Similarly, many in translating the movement into their own terms miss the essential significance of the adult education element. To Coady and the movement, social reform – permanent institutional reform – could only come about through adult education. But in the hearts of many of the policy makers gratefully accepting the Antigonish programme of economic development, there may well be little commitment to 'allowing man's capacities to be released through education on the social institutions which are primarily responsible for underdevelopment' (MacDonald 1979: 159).

Ultimately, the success or failure of Coady and the Antigonish Movement can only be judged in terms of their own philosophy. If the people themselves become preoccupied with things economic and fail to use the opportunity to learn how to master their social and political realms, then Coady, as he would be the first to admit, and the people themselves have failed. Indeed, the people's own economic accomplishments, no matter how substantial, are in jeopardy if they have not learnt how 'to manipulate the forces that control society', if they have not learnt to become 'masters of their own destiny' (Coady quoted in Laidlaw 1961: 109).

REFERENCES

Boyle, G (1953) *Father Tompkins of Nova Scotia*, P J Kenedy & Sons, New York

Campbell, D F (1985) Tompkins, James John, *The Canadian Encyclopedia*, Alberta Hurtig Publishers Ltd, Edmonton

Coady, M M (1939) *Masters of Their Own Destiny*, Harper & Brothers Publishers, New York and London

Coady, M M (1943) *The Antigonish Way*, St Francis Xavier University, Antigonish, Nova Scotia

Coady, M M (1945) *The Social Significance of the Co-operative Movement*, St. Francis Xavier Extension Department, Antigonish

Coady, M M (1952) Unity and Brotherhood, in *The Canadian Messenger*, December

Corbett, E A (1953) Dr M M Coady, in *Pioneers of Adult Education in Canada*, ed Harriet Rouillard, Thomas Nelson & Sons (Canada) Limited, Toronto

Crane, J M (1983) The Antigonish Movement: An historical sketch, *International Journal of Lifelong Education*, **2** (2)

Faris, R (1975) *The Passionate Educators: Voluntary associations and the struggle for control of adult educational broadcasting in Canada 1919-1952*, Peter Martin Associates Limited, Toronto

Freire, P (1972) *Pedagogy of the Oppressed*, Penguin Books Ltd, Harmondsworth

Gordon, K (1979) The Coady in Development, in *Human Development Through Social Change*, J Gremillion, Nova Scotia Formac Publishing Co Limited, Antigonish

Gremillion, J (1979) *Human Development Through Social Change*, Nova Scotia Formac Publishing Co Limited, Antigonish

Griffin, C (1978) *Recurrent and Continuing Education: A curriculum model approach*, University of Nottingham, Nottingham

Hernon, J (1960) The Humble Giants, *The Atlantic Advocate*, (February), pp 67–72

Jenkins, D (1972) Romantic and Classic in Curriculum Landscape, *Curriculum Philosophy and Design*, Open University Press, Milton Keynes

Keuscher, R E (1970) Why Individualize Instruction, in *Individualization of Instruction: A teaching strategy*, ed Virgil M Howes, the Macmillan Company, New York

Kidd, J R (1960) Foreword, in *The Campus and the Community: The global impact of the Antigonish Movement*, A F Laidlaw, Harvest House Limited, Montreal

Laidlaw, A (1961), *The Campus and the Community: The global impact of the Antigonish Movement*, Harvest House Limited, Montreal

Lawton, D (1973) *Social Change, Educational Theory and Curriculum Planning*, Hodder and Stoughton, New York

Lotz, J (1977) *Understanding Canada: Regional and community development in a new nation*, N C Press Ltd, Toronto

Lovett, T (1980) Adult Education and Community Action, in *Adult Education for a Change*, ed Jane L Thompson, Hutchinson & Co, London

MacDonald, A A (1979) A History of the Antigonish Movement, *Human Development Through Social Change*, Nova Scotia Formac Publishing Co Limited, Antigonish

MacEachen, E A (1979) Canadian Approaches to Co-operation, *Human Development Through Social Change*, Nova Scotia Formac Publishing Co Limited, Antigonish

MacPherson, I (1979) *Each for All: A history of the cooperative movement in English Canada, 1900–1945*, the Carleton Library no 116, Macmillan of Canada in association with the Institute of Canadian Studies, Carleton University, Toronto

MacSween, R J (1953), The Little University of the World, *The Universities Review*, **XXV** (2), pp 91–98

Martin, B (1981) *A Sociology of Contemporary Cultural Change*, Basil Blackwell, Oxford

Milner, P (1979) Preface, in *Human Development Through Social Change*, Nova Scotia Formac Publishing Co Limited, Antigonish

Ward, B (1979) I cannot tell you how sad I am, in *Human Development Through Social Change*, ed J Gremillion, Nova Scotia Formac Publishing Co Limited, Antigonish

Wasserstrom, R (1985) *Grassroots Development in Latin America and the Caribbean*, Praeger Publishers, New York

Chapter 15

Horton of Highlander

John M Peters and Brenda Bell

I can't sleep, but there are dreams. What you must do is go back, get a simple place, move in and you are there. The situation is there. You start with this and let it grow. You know your goal. It will build its own structure and take its own form. You can go to school all your life, you'll never figure it out because you are trying to get an answer that can only come from the people in the life situation (Horton, 1983a: 30).

When Myles Horton wrote this note on Christmas night in Copenhagen in 1931, he captured the long and promising future of his work as a radical educator. He had pursued an education by conventional means, studied independently, travelled, and experimented in search of 'something to offer' poor adults in the southern region of the United States. These efforts helped shape his beliefs about adult education and social change and they underpinned the development of what he referred to as 'the only instrument I ever learned to play', the Highlander Folk School – now the Highlander Research and Education Center, New Market, Tennessee. Highlander was to be surrounded by controversy, failures and successes as it became involved in the most important social movements of the 20th century in the United States.

No analysis of Horton's approach to adult education can be made without reference to Highlander, whose history has been ably chronicled by Aimee Horton (1971); Adams (1975); Glen (1985); and others. Horton has not published as much as most adult educators featured in this book. Most of what he has said about adult education was expressed in his 58 years of practice at Highlander. His approach to education and what has come to be known as the 'Highlander Idea' are practically synonymous. We therefore begin this chapter with a brief sketch of Horton's life and development prior to Highlander, then provide an overview of Highlander's activities since its inception in 1932. We finish with our interpretation of the major features of Horton's thinking as it shaped and was shaped by Highlander and the events of the last century. While examples and quotes selected for the first half of the chapter only begin to paint the whole Highlander portrait, they are included for what they reveal about the man and his thinking.

BEFORE HIGHLANDER

Horton's childhood in small West Tennessee towns was shaped by his parents' strong belief in the value of education and by his family's involvement in the Cumberland Presbyterian Church. The church was 'rational rather than revivalist, and placed emphasis on good works in this world rather than salvation in the next' (A Horton, 1971: 13). Both of his parents were school teachers at the time of his birth in 1905, but later became farmers and sharecroppers. They believed that 'The only way to get out of poverty was to be assertive and to go to school, and to be of use in the world without being so poor' (Horton, 1985).

Horton found few challenging educational experiences in school or in church and placed greater value on experiential learning outside these formal institutions. Aimee Horton (1971: 14) wrote:

Working in a grocery store after school, he learned something about the social structure of the small southern community – about the Negro sharecropper families whose crops were 'owned' by the landowner until their bills were paid and who were systematically over charged for inferior goods; about the white business and church leaders who paid the bills for Negro women and their lighter-skinned children. Working in a local box factory in the summer, he learned something about the spoils system in southern industry where several hundred 'grateful workers' were paid two dollars per day for producing thousands of wooden boxes which were sold to farmers for twice what they cost to make. And the cost... was passed along to poor families in town who paid for the boxes with potatoes.

The workers who made potato boxes were eventually organized by Horton to strike for and attain higher wages. Horton (1985) 'didn't know about unions at the time', but his principled attitude toward worker rights even as a teenager was essentially the same framework he followed during his later involvement with unions during the second quarter of the last century. The insights Horton formed through such early work experiences would also help shape a personal philosophy of education and social change that kept company with some of the world's greatest philosophers.

Horton's youthful sense of morality and social justice matured during his college years at Cumberland College in Lebanon, Tennessee, where involvement with the student YMCA brought him into closer contact with other races and nationalities. 'Civil Rights' was not a label or a social issue at the time, but Horton, as a college freshman, demonstrated his opposition to infringement on individual rights by organizing his classmates and successfully resisting the traditional practice of freshman hazing. Later, after hearing a paternalistic, anti-union speech by the owner of a local woollen mill, Horton responded by going to the mill to talk to the workers about their rights. The mill owner was on the board of the college, and Horton felt his wrath. Horton recalls that he was not thinking in terms of labour unions; he was responding to the mill owner's suggestion that, because he owned the factory, he could make determinations about people's lives. 'That just hit me as an immoral way of thinking – such a crude, crass way of thinking. The arrogance. I'd always been on the worker's side. I knew only working people' (Horton, 1985). His sense of justice was accompanied by a strategy that came to typify much of his later active involvement in labour and civil rights activities. He set up the meeting at the mill under the pretence of holding a religious service. 'The real purpose was to get the people together. It took a religious form, because that was something I was familiar with' (Horton, 1985). It was also a bit of competitiveness on Horton's part.

In the years that followed, Horton was to reflect upon that experience and begin an extensive and largely self-directed study of unions and unionism, especially the British labour union movement, which proved influential in his formulation of the Highlander idea. The writings of the Fabian Socialists broadened his conception of trade unionism to include elements of a social movement. The Fabian vision of a political democracy in which 'economic power and privileges of individuals and classes (will be) abolished through collective ownership and democratic control of the economic resources of the community' (Cole, 1961: 338), motivated Horton to envisage an educational programme that would individually and collectively empower poor adults in the South.

THE OZONE EXPERIENCE

Under the auspices of the Presbyterian Church and during the summer prior to his senior year in college, Horton organized vacation bible schools in Ozone, a small village in rural east Tennessee. The experience led him to conclude that the church and other organizations were not helping people deal with their problems of poverty and unemployment, as they lived in a countryside devastated by logging and mining practices. Without a formal plan, he asked parents of bible school students to come to the church to talk about their concerns. They came and talked and to his amazement, they were not disappointed in his inability to answer their questions or to 'teach them' something they did not know. He discovered that these adults could articulate their problems and look for answers in their own experiences. Adams (1975: 4) later wrote:

> He had learned that the teacher's job was to get them talking about those problems, to raise and sharpen questions, and to trust people to come up with the answers. Yet, he could not wholly trust the people or this way of learning.

In spite of appeals by his 'students' for his further work with them, Horton decided not to return to the area after graduating from Cumberland because he wanted to come back only when he 'had something to offer' the mountain people. He was to realize six years later that his first experience with community education in Ozone would provide the anchor for the Highlander idea.

A SEARCH FOR SOMETHING TO OFFER

Following graduation and while serving as YMCA field secretary, Horton began to read widely, searching for a model of a community school for adults. A Congregationalist minister, sympathetic to Horton's interests, gave him a copy of Harry Ward's *Our Economic Morality* (1929), and encouraged him to go to Union Theological Seminary to study with Ward, a professor of Christian ethics.

Union Seminary in the late 1920s was a place of great intellectual ferment. Encounters with the religious thinkers at Union and the progressive educators nearby at Columbia challenged Horton's thinking. The ideas of the Christian Socialists aided in uniting his sense of morality and justice with his concern for economic problems. Ward, a founder and first chairman of the Board of the American Civil Liberties Union, staunch union advocate, and a supporter of Marxist thought (Link, 1984), challenged Horton to think in terms of integrating theory with practice. Reinhold Niebuhr, professor and socialist, became a mentor for Horton and a later a strong proponent of his idea of a community school. Niebuhr's most widely-known book, *Moral Man and Immoral Society* (1932), was written while Horton was at Union under his tutelage. Horton (Horton and Freire, 1990) said this about his encounter with Niebuhr and his book:

> I was in his class when he was working on it, and he practiced his values on us. So I was influenced by the thinking, the clarification that went into the book – that it's the structures of society that we've got to change. We don't change men's hearts. So it was in Niebuhr's class that I first really clarified in my own mind, my own thinking, the idea that it doesn't make a great deal of difference what the people are; if they're in the system, they're going to function like the system dictates that they function. From then on I've been more concerned with structural changes than I have with changing hearts of people (p 103).

While in New York, Horton also talked with Dewey and Eduard Lindeman. Horton found Lindeman to be a 'fresh breeze', as he 'made sense out of adult education, and I was moving more in that direction without knowing it. I saw adult education, through Lindeman, as a way of dealing with some of the problems (of working with poor southerners)' (1985).

Horton left Union in 1930 to study at the University of Chicago under sociologist Robert Park, whose theories of conflict and of mass movements added to his growing understanding of the processes of social change. Concurrently, he was influenced by Lester Ward's *Dynamic Sociology* (1883), which argued that education is action and that dynamic action is the foundation of social progress

(A Horton, 1971). While in Chicago, Horton spent time at Hull House, learning from Jane Addams, and was encouraged by a Danish-born Lutheran minister to visit the folk schools of Denmark. That recommendation was to become another major phase in Horton's search for meaning, bringing him even closer to Highlander.

DENMARK

Horton's study of Danish folk schools produced mixed results. He was disappointed in the 'newer' folk schools for their lack of spirit and their loss of earlier vitality, but found in the history of the older schools some examples that were to become useful to his vision of a community school in the US. According to Adams (1975: 22–23):

> He found that many of the directors were unconventional educators. They were men on fire to correct injustice, to awaken the peasants to the misery restricting their lives. The schools, each (had)… a distinct purpose… made wide use of poetry and song… and sought to develop feelings and will more than memory and logic.

Hart (1926: 23) had written earlier:

> A folk school in America, as in Denmark, would probably center about a personality of some real teacher, a man who is capable of learning, and who can teach, not so much by his teaching, as by his capacity to learn… we have very few (people) who can teach their own capacity to learn (emphasis ours).

Purpose, a personality, a capacity to learn, song, feelings and will versus memory and logic – these were elements of Horton's idea, in terms of which he began to shape his approach to adult education. These were among the ideas that Horton identified with the work of Bishop Grundtvig and the founders of the Danish Folk High School movement. Social interaction in non-formal settings, freedom from state regulation, and peer learning were other features of the Grundtvig approach with which Horton identified. (Horton, 1983: 29). While Horton '… did not slavishly copy the Danish Folk School – the present needs (in the Southern US) were totally different from those of Denmark's' (1983: 30), Highlander was to feature many of the same concepts and activities as the early Grundtvig schools. The note written on Christmas night at the end of Horton's study in Denmark tied Grundtvig to Ozone.

HIGHLANDER

At the time Horton and Don West (a graduate of Vanderbilt Divinity School) started Highlander in 1932, Horton was one of many young Southern intellectuals deeply affected by the political, economic and social climate of the time. As Richard Pells (1973: 44) observed, for many 'the depression exposed for all time the fundamental unreality of the American dream, especially the fact that the quality of human life in a system dedicated to profit offered people no feeling of community or common vision'. The call for a new social order was widespread and political movements for change had strong appeal. Horton and a few of his fellow students at Union and other young Southerners studying at Vanderbilt Divinity School in Nashville were not espousing new ideas, but it was their insistence on putting the ideas into practice that was significant (Dunbar, 1981).

It is important to begin an overview of the history of Highlander with the understanding that it was not a series of schools, each marked by a major social movement, but a continuous and comprehensive single idea put into practice. 'I've always thought of each ("school") as a part of a larger whole, instead of being a labor school, a civil rights school, a school for mountain people' (Horton, 1985). While education is at the heart of Highlander's programme, it reaches into all forms of movements for a democratic society.

Horton knew for years that he wanted to work within the framework of education, but sought a broader focus for his efforts. He had studied the works of Dewey, Lindeman, Niebuhr, Marx, the Fabians, Grundtvig, Shelly and Park. Ideas from these and other sources enriched his thinking, as did values shaped during his formative years, but it was not focused thinking. Highlander provided the focus needed. Horton said that he was forced by the advent of Highlander to 'make a formulation' of his beliefs. He recalled that, by the time Highlander started, he was very clear on at least two matters (Horton, 1985). First:

> There is no such thing as neutrality. Neutrality is for the status quo. (The educator) can't be objective. You have to decide what you want to do and who you want to work with. You have to have a purpose.

The second came from his religious background. Horton grew up:

> ... knowing that all the great religions judged nations by how they treated their poor. I accepted that. I wanted to work on the side of society that didn't live by owning. If you're going to have a democracy, that's the kind of people you build it on.

These principles grounded Horton's new focus. 'They synthesized my religious and ethical upbringing and my reading and thinking in terms of an analysis of society' (1985). Horton therefore had a moral and philosophical framework within which to operate and he had ethical motivations. At Highlander, he could combine these and make them a part of the labour movement and other movements that followed.

Highlander was opened in 'one of the eleven poorest counties in the United States' (Adams 1975: 30), in a home donated by a friend of a minister/supporter.

The intent was 'to provide an educational center in the South for the training of rural and industrial leaders, and for the conservation and enrichment of the indigenous cultural values of the mountains' (Highlander Folk School, 1939). The school's first fund-raising letter, sent by Niebuhr, stated that the school proposed 'to use education as one of the instruments for bringing about a new social order' (Aimee Horton, 1971: 44). This purpose involved two central foci of Highlander: 1) the achievement of a democratic movement, initially involving unions and eventually in society as a whole; and 2) leadership training. The latter was not atypical in its time, but the former served to distinguish Highlander from most other US adult education institutions.

Park's conflict/crisis theories were to be tested early, as Horton told of 'being alert for places in the South where contention was rising' (Adams, 1975: 25). A coal miners' strike at nearby Wilder, Tennessee, a bugwood cutters' strike in Grundy County and a shirt factory strike in Knoxville were ready-made arenas for the young activist-educators. Significantly, Horton and staff participated directly in the organizing activities of the strikers. And they began to learn about the reality of conflict, with its attendant threats to the lives of organizers. Horton and others associated with Highlander were to endure physical beatings, failings and a closing of the school itself as a result of their organizing activities.

Horton and his colleagues learnt very quickly that their own academic experiences were a handicap, insofar as their attempts to teach strikers were concerned. 'The staff and I had gone to school. We were motivated to do it. But, we wrongly assumed that poor people would do some of the same things we did. We failed to correctly analyze the fact they weren't motivated by the same things, weren't socialized to go through the formal school system as we' (Horton, 1985). Horton and his colleagues were teaching and attempting to convert the workers to a way of thinking about democracy. But it was not working. The people were paying much more attention to their own informal leaders than to Highlander. During these early years, Horton concluded they would have to 'teach within the experiences' of the local leaders.

While the early Highlander programme looked traditional 'on paper', the content was not. Like labour schools of the era, Highlander's course and workshop topics included labour history, cultural geography, social and economic problems and literature. However, the subject matter at Highlander was determined by problems brought by students, and new learning experiences were integrated into students' lives by the use of such means as improvisational drama, songwriting and singing. Students were given major responsibility for the daily operation of courses and workshops, and were usually involved in teaching other workshop participants before leaving Highlander. These features continue to the present time to characterize Highlander workshops and courses.

A TRANSITION IN MOVEMENTS

Highlanders' labour programme, which grew steadily to include residential education for rank-and-file leaders, continued on a reduced scale through the war years. From 1944 to 1947, Highlander ran the Congress on Industrial Organizations (CIO) schools for union leaders from around the South. But just as it seemed that the relationship with the CIO was solidifying, it was also dissolving. Horton and staff were pursuing their goal of a workers' movement for change by developing a farmer/labour coalition, focusing on the problems of black Americans and seeking to maintain a broad vision of brotherhood and cooperation in Highlander's work with CIO unions. The CIO, however, beset by internal struggles of its own, was losing much of its former militancy and social vision. When the CIO asked Highlander to dissociate itself from any 'Communist-led organizations', the Highlander board drafted a statement of purpose, which declared its intent to 'create leadership for democracy' (Aimee Horton, 1971: 366). The CIO leadership was not satisfied and member unions were instructed not to continue working with Highlander. But some maintained their relationship. For several years into the 1950s, Horton served as the educational director of the United Packinghouse Workers (while maintaining his Highlander staff position), implementing a broad-based education programme with rank and file workers (Glen, 1985).

As their worker education programme waned, Horton and staff began to work with people whose concerns focused on Southern racial problems. As increasing numbers of blacks came to Highlander to participate in labour education programmes, the school became known as an 'affirmation' of the possibility for an integrated society. It was perhaps the only place in its time where people of different races met, ate, learnt and worked together in a residential setting. Highlander's work was being done at an early stage of the civil rights movement.

One of the most successful initiatives in Highlander's history was the development of 'Citizenship Schools' in the 1950s. The schools were started on John's Island, South Carolina, in response to a black community leader's wish to register his fellow Islanders to vote. To qualify to vote, all citizens had to read the State Constitution, but few blacks were able to read or write. Horton's strategy for the schools began with a personal six-month visit to the area to learn from the people involved and extended to teacher training and fund raising for the civic and literacy education programmes. Horton insisted that whites refrain from leading the programme or teaching in the localized classes. Instead, he and the Highlander staff worked through popular black leaders on the Island, and trained black teachers selected on the basis of their acceptance by the students and their interest in teaching (Adams, 1975; Morris, 1984). Leadership of the Citizenship Schools was passed to the Southern Christian Leadership Conference (SCLC), a leading civil rights organization in the 1950s and 1960s. By 1970, the SCLC estimated that approximately 100,000 blacks had learned to read and write through the Citizenship Schools (Adams 1975: 118).

Dozens of meetings and workshops at Highlander were followed by civil rights activities that made major changes in race relations in the South. The Student Non-violent Coordinating Committee (SNCC) was among many civil rights groups to meet at Highlander. Activists involved in sit-ins and demonstrations in the 1950s and 1960s participated in Highlander workshops. Rosa Parks, the black woman who sparked a historical protest when she refused to give up her seat on a bus to a white man, was at Highlander a few months prior to the incident in Montgomery, Alabama. The Montgomery bus boycott that followed led to the early distinction of Martin Luther King, himself a visitor to Highlander. Andrew Young, former United States Ambassador to the United Nations, would say that 'For fifty years the Highlander Center has produced leadership ideas, and a spirit of freedom that changed the course of history' (cited in Horton, 1983: 23).

A new phase

Highlander came under attack by Southern political leaders and was closed by the State of Tennessee in 1960. The school's closing and the transfer of the Citizenship School Program to the SCLC marked another transition point. Horton applied for and received a new charter for the school, this time to be called the Highlander Research and Education Center. While the civil rights movement was in full swing, Horton was again analysing the situation of Southern Appalachian mountain people and beginning to work to build ties between black activists and poor whites. Horton's sights were on the same goal as before: 'He dreamed of a massive social movement that would fundamentally alter America, and genuinely felt that the potential for such a movement existed' (Adams, 1975: 179–80). Horton led Highlander into the Poor People's Campaign, the Community Action Programs of the late 1960s and into a renewed tie with the Council of Southern Mountains, a coalition of organizations concerned with economic and political problems in Appalachia. However, no 'massive social movement' materialized and Highlander found itself for the first time in its history without a movement to contextualize its educational programme. However, it continued to thrive in the absence of a major movement, focusing on issues relating to workplace democracy, land use, control of toxic wastes, occupational safety and health, labour organizing, cultural work in local communities and international issues. As the 21st century dawns, Highlander continues as a gathering place for grassroots leaders and community and worker groups organizing for justice in the South and Appalachia. Building on the strengths of past leadership work and with the focal points of economic justice and democratic participation, the Center launched a collective leadership programme for teams of people from groups organizing among people of colour, low-income workers, immigrant workers, union members, women and those discriminated against because of sexual orientation. True to its original vision, Highlander Center's work seeks to build a broad-based economic and social justice movement, both nationally and internationally, that can reverse the widening gap of wealth and power between rich and poor.

Horton retired in 1973, but remained active in the affairs of Highlander until his death in January, 1990.

UNDERSTANDING HORTON'S IDEAS AND EDUCATIONAL PRACTICE

Horton was stimulated very early in life to make his contribution to society through some form of educational process. He had examined the public schools and colleges in the interest of pursuing teaching as a career but found these institutions lacking in their impact on the conditions of poor people, who in his estimate had problems greater than any other segment of society. Education for social change of the kind Horton had in mind was rarely practised in the USA.

While Horton's lifetime commitment to social reform reflects noble vision and laudable contributions, broad aims do not easily convince the reader in search of specific new educational techniques and pedagogies. However, guides to understanding Horton's approach to education are located at the level of ideas, beliefs and principles that he developed and consistently followed during his 60-year practice.

Two underlying ideas seem foundational to that practice (Horton and Freire, 1990):

First is the fundamental belief in the importance of the freedom of people everywhere. Second is the radical democratic belief in the capacity and right of all people to achieve that freedom through self-emancipation (1990: xxx).

For Horton:

… real liberation is achieved through popular participation. Participation in turn is realized through an educational practice that itself is both liberatory and participatory, that simultaneously creates a new society and involves the people themselves in the creation of their own knowledge (1990: xxx).

Horton's belief in the imperative of people's control over their own lives and the means of production paralleled his belief in control of a learning activity by a circle of learners whose experiences and problems are being discussed. He argued equally convincingly that labourers need to develop confidence in their ability to direct change in their working conditions as well as to learn in a workshop from their own experiences. Dependency on authority was believed by Horton to be antithetical to freedom of thought and expression, whether it is in labour–management relations or in the relationship between student and teacher. Horton's approach to education was a restructuring process that placed more control and responsibility in the hands of the learner, not only for purposes of democratizing the experience, but also as intended practice for learners who were interested in achieving the same ends in other arenas of their lives. It is perhaps for these reasons that Horton cautioned the observer not to think of Highlander in terms of methods or techniques. He regarded these aspects of an educational process transient in nature and far less important than the philosophy and purpose of an educational programme.

NEUTRALITY AND THE STATUS QUO

As mentioned earlier in this chapter, a significant feature of Horton's thinking related to the issue of 'neutrality' in teaching and learning and in educational programming. Horton decided early on that he could not take a neutral stance toward the structure of society or be neutral in his approach to adult education. On the view that adult education must not be neutral, he was aligned closest to Freire and next to Lindeman and probably furthest from Paterson (1979) and Lawson (1975). Horton's view paralleled those of the great philosophers of education who have treated education as a branch of politics, such as Plato in his *Republic*, Aristotle in his *Politics* and Dewey in his *Democracy and Education* (Brubacher, 1977: 14).

Neutrality in education does not necessarily mean that the educator takes an 'objective' versus a 'subjective' content-centred approach to educating adults. The distinction might better be made between positions that actually support the status quo and those that would deliberately alter the social order. On this point, Horton took a critical, analytical approach to changing society.

Horton made an important choice of goals when he paired his aim of contributing to social movement with the aim of leadership development. He decided early that working with one local union or one isolated civil rights group at a time was not the route to broader social change and neither was his work as an organizer of union and civil rights groups. Instead, he concentrated on working with leaders from several organizations or communities at a time. His assumption was that these leaders would take what they learnt at Highlander and work with other actual or potential leaders with help from the staff when needed, and let the influence of Highlander multiply over larger numbers of people. However, few leaders could effectively do that without an understanding of their own social system, larger systems and intended changes in them.

SOCIAL ANALYSIS

Horton believed that the activists need to understand society in order to change it or at least in order to cope with its demands. Two forms of analysis were important to him: 1) a long-range analysis of the overall social and economic structure of society; and 2) an analysis of the local situation facing the learner seeking change. Of participants in Highlander's educational programmes, Horton said:

> They aren't operating in a vacuum. They are operating in a given period in history under a given economic system (eg, capitalism). You have to know where we are in history, in terms of ideas (eg, democratic ideas, authoritarian ideas). You have to know how they have been carried out by politicians and industrialists, for example, and what the system has done in the way of structure to affect the people with whom you are working. You have to know what stage of development the people are in, relative to the situation. If you want to maximize the control people have over their lives then you need to know what control they don't have and why. Therefore, you need to understand the economics, the politics, the culture. This is an objective understanding. Anything you do has to be done in relation to this knowledge of the situation in which you are working. The educator must know this first, in order to know what learners don't know (1985).

Once educators are clear in their analysis and beliefs, they are able to help students carry out their own analyses, which are prerequisite to collective action. Horton did not hide his own analysis from workshop participants, but neither did he impose it. Optimally, the process Horton favoured is a dialogue between equals in which the facilitator and students exchange ideas and learn from one another:

> You get the learners to know about their situation by asking questions. And then you share what you know. You draw information from them and supply information they don't have. You supplement what they need (to complete the analysis). There may be technical things they don't have because they haven't had the opportunity to learn them. The educator doesn't tell the learners what to do or give advice, but just shares facts. The learners decide what to do with the facts (Horton, 1985).

> It's unavoidable that you have some responsibility, regardless of what you teach or what your subject is or what your skill is. Whatever you have to contribute has a social dimension. And I think it's ineffective to try to impose that on anybody. Sharing it with them is one thing, but trying to impose it is another. You honestly say these are my ideas and I have a right to my opinion, and if I have a right to my opinion then you have a right to your opinion. I'm going to try to expose them to some ideas, some learning that was mine, in the hopes that they will see what I believe. I don't see any problem with taking a position. (Horton and Freire, 1990: 105).

Following Hart's admonition, Horton was in this manner 'teaching his own capacity to learn'. There is also in this quote a sense of respect for the learner's own experiences, one of the keystones of Horton's approach to adult education.

THE ROLE OF EXPERIENCE

Like most adult educators, Horton believed that the extent of people's initial understanding of new ideas is in part a function of their own past experiences. He also believed that people's ability to learn from experience is a crucial factor in their subsequent ability to bring about social change. 'I try to get people to understand that they have the makings of solutions to their work or societal problems in their own experiences. But they have to learn how to learn from their experiences and from other people's experiences' (Horton, 1985). Horton's near-term objective was for individuals to develop meaning from their own experiences and from experiences of others in a learning group. His longer-term objective was for the learner to develop 'social meaning' (meaning that generalizes to others' experiences) that will form a basis for social change. Social meaning therefore begins with the learner's own reality.

> Often when I say you start with people's experience, people get the point that you start and stop with that experience, (but) there's a time when people's experience runs out.... You stay within the experience of the people, and the experience is growing right there, in what I call a circle of learners, in a workshop situation. You're not talking about the experience they brought with them. You're talking about the experience that is given them in the workshop, and in a few days time that experience can expand tremendously. But if you break the connection between the starting point, their experience, and what they know themselves... you lose them. Then you reach the outside limits of the possibility of having any relationship to those people's learning. Now, my experience has been that if you do this thing right, carefully, and don't get beyond participants at any one step, you can move very fast to expand their experience very wide in a very short time (Horton and Freire, 1990: 152–53).

In agreement with Freire, reality for Horton was a function of one's own experience, and truth existed as the individual produces it in action. Action becomes the basis of the individual's experience and the precursor of meaning. 'Experience produces knowledge, and knowledge leads to meaning' (Horton, 1985). Action and experience are therefore critical factors in Horton's model of learning and social change, for at least three reasons:

1. past actions and the actor's interpretation of them can serve as the object of reflection and analysis in a learning experience;
2. the act of learning itself can be the focus of an analysis;
3. further action is the goal of learning.

According to Horton, 'one cannot act on learning if he cannot make it his own experience' (1985). This rules out learning by memorizing or other means that are independent of the learner's own experiences.

Community and organizational leaders who come to Highlander with problems to solve and goals to reach bring their action experiences with them (This becomes the 'curriculum' at Highlander.) They engage in another form of action when they share their experiences with other leaders and project further actions on the basis of what they learn from one another. Reflection follows these actions and reflection becomes the basis for further acting. In this way learners begin to theorize about action from acting experience and frame their approach to social change in this context. Theory flows from action toward action.

ORGANIZING VERSUS EDUCATION

Since its inception Highlander has been regularly involved with organizations needing help and with groups organizing to solve local problems. These included labour organizations in the early years and civil rights groups in the middle years. However, Horton was very careful to differentiate between organizing and education. The difference helps to shed light on what he believed about the purpose of education and role of the educator:

> I always said that Highlander was not a school for organizers. It was a school to help people learn to analyze and give people values, and they became the organizers. The reason so many of Highlander's people were successful organizers was because of that. Solving problems can't be the goal of education. It can be the goal of organiza-tions. That's why I don't think organizing and education are the same thing. Organizing implies that there's a specific, limited goal that needs to be achieved, and the purpose is to achieve that goal. Now if that's it, then the easiest way to get that done solves the problem. But if education is to be part of the process, then you may not actually get that problem solved, but you've educated a lot of people….An orga-nizing experience can be educational. But it has to be done with the purpose of having democratic decision-making, having people participate in the action and not just having one authoritative leader. Otherwise it won't work. You have to make that choice. That's why I say there is a difference. The goal is different (Horton and Freire, 1990, pp 119–24).

In essence, Horton believed that the role of an educator is to help people develop the capacity to make decisions and to take responsibility for their actions. 'An organizer's job is not to educate people as a prime consideration. His job is to accomplish a limited, specific goal… An educator should never become an expert, and an organizer quite often finds that's his main strength' (Horton and Freire, 1990: 127–28).

In Horton's model, collective action, essential to social change, begins with the individual and develops through group learning experiences. Individual community leaders develop their collective action skills in a collaborative learning experience (Cunningham, 1983; Peters and Armstrong, 1998), which they begin in a residential workshop setting and continue in their efforts to effect social change in their daily lives. They develop social meaning in the ultimate sense when and if a social action takes place. Horton's aim was to nurture a social movement through widening circles of influence, beginning with the efforts of leaders working at Highlander in a democratic learning environment.

CONCLUSION

The elements of what Horton called a 'good education' are imbedded in the above quotes and analysis. He identified three elements of good education during a conversation with Paulo Freire at Highlander in 1987: 'First, love people; second, respect people's abilities to learn and to shape their own lives, and third, value people's experiences' (Horton and Freire, 1990: 178). Myles Horton and Paulo Freire, two of the leading exponents of adult education for social change, had come together to 'talk a book'. When that project was finished and a few days before Myles's death in 1990, Paulo said: 'It was an honor to participate with him. He's an incredible man. This history of this man, his individual presence in the world, is something which justifies the world' (1990: xxxiii).

We agree.

REFERENCES

Adams, F (1975) *Unearthing Seeds of Fire: The idea of Highlander*, John F Blair, Winston-Salem, NC

Bell, B and Ansley, F (1974) East Tennessee Coal Mining Battles, *Southern Exposure*, **1**, (3–4)

Brubacher, J (1977) *On the Philosophy of Higher Education*, Jossey-Bass, San Francisco

Cole, M (1961) *The Story of Fabian Socialism*, Stanford University Press, Stanford, Ca

Cunningham, P (1982) Contradictions in the Practice of Non-traditional Continuing Education, in *Linking Philosophy and Practice*, ed S Merriam, Jossey-Bass, San Francisco

Cunningham, P (1983) Helping Students Extract Meaning From Experience, in *New Directions for Continuing Education: Helping adults learn how to learn*, ed R Smith, No 19

Dunbar, A (1981) *Against the Grain: Southern radicals and prophets*, 1929–1959, University of Virginia Press, Charlottesville, Va

Egan, G (1975) *The Skilled Helper: A model for systematic helping and interpersonal relating*, Brooks/Cole, Monterey, Ca

Elias, J (1982) The Theory-practice Split, in *New Directions for Continuing Education: Linking Philosophy and Practice*, no 15, ed S Merriam, Jossey-Bass, San Francisco

Glen, J (1985) *On the Cutting Edge: A history of the Highlander Folk School, 1932–1962*, PhD dissertation, Vanderbilt University

Hart, J (1926) *Light from the North: The Danish folk high schools – Their meanings for America*, Henry Holt & Co, New York

Heaney, T (1982) Power, Learning, and Communication, in *Microcomputers for Adult Learning: Potentials and perils*, ed D Guelette, Follett Publishing Co, Chicago

Highlander Folk School (1939) *Highlander Folk School: The story of an educational center for working people*, pamphlet in Highlander Library

Horton, A (1971) *The Highlander Folk School: A history of the development of its major programs related to social movements in the South, 1932–1961*, PhD dissertation, University of Chicago

Horton, M (1983a) Influences on Highlander Research and Education Center, New Market, Tennessee, USA, in *Grundtvig's Ideas in North America – Influences and parallels*, ed The Danish Institute, The Danish Institute, Denmark

Horton, M (1983b) Bill Moyer's Journal: An interview with Myles Horton, *Appalachian Journal*, **9** (4)

Horton, M (1985) Interviews conducted by the authors

Horton, M and Freire, P (1990) *We Make the Road by Walking: Conversations on education and social change*, eds B Bell, J Gaventa and J Peters, Temple University Press, Philadelphia

Lawson, K (1975) *Philosophical Concepts and Values in Adult Education*, Barnes, Numby Ltd, Nottingham, England

Link, E (1984) *Labor-religion Prophet: The life and times of Harry F Ward*, The Westview Press, Boulder, Co

Merriam, S (1982) *Linking Philosophy and Practice*, Jossey-Bass, San Francisco

Mezirow, J (1985b). Conceptual Action in Adult Education, *Adult Education Quarterly*, **35** (3), pp 142–51

Morris, A (1984) *The Origins of the Civil Rights Movement: Black communities organizing for change*, The Free Press, New York

Paterson, R (1979) *Values, Education, and the Adult*, Routledge and Kegan Paul, Boston

Pells, R (1973) *Radical Visions and American Dreams: Culture and social thought in the depression years*, Harper and Row, New York

Peters, J and Armstrong, J (1998) Collaborative Learning: People laboring together to construct knowledge, in *The Power and Potential of Collaborative Learning Partnerships. New directions for adult and continuing education*, No 79, eds I M Saltiel, A Sgroi and R Brockett, Jossey-Bass, San Francisco

Reed, D (1981) *Education for a People's Movement*, South End Press, Boston

Tjerandsen, C (1980) *Education for Citizenship: A foundation's experience*, Emil Schwarzhaupt Foundation, Inc, Santa Cruz, Ca

Chapter 16

Paulo Freire

Peter Jarvis

Paulo Freire was born into a middle-class family in Recife, Brazil, in 1921 and initially read law and philosophy and qualified at the bar. However, it was during this period that his interests broadened and he began to read sociology and education. Perhaps the latter is no surprise since his first wife, Elza, was a school teacher. Consequently, Freire abandoned law and assumed the position of a welfare officer, later becoming director of the Department of Education and Culture in the state of Pernambuco. It was during this period that he made contact with the urban poor, although it was not until the next phase of his career when, as director of the Cultural Extension Service of the University of Recife, he began to implement his well-known literacy campaign. However, Freire did not act in isolation in Brazil, so that it is necessary to understand something of the historical background in that society during this period.

THE HISTORICAL SITUATION

There was a very important influence upon Freire's intellectual development at this time: the rise of radicalism in the Church of Rome in Brazil. This development has been recorded in the writings of Emanuel de Kadt, and it is from his essay in Landsberger (1970) that this historical background is discussed here. Although de Kadt points out that Freire arrived at his view independently, there can be no denying that working within the same religious and cultural milieu, his own development was in some way related to what was happening in the church. As early as 1929 Catholic Action was founded in Brazil, and it rapidly established its own university groups, Juventude Universitaria Catholica, but initially this was not a radical organization. However, a number of factors in the 1950s contributed to a swing towards radicalism so that by the early 1960s the movement recognized that university reforms in Brazil had to be part of the

Brazilian revolution. Such a move towards a Marxian, rather than a Marxist, radicalism incurred disfavour with many of the ecclesiastical hierarchy, which was a lesson that a second movement, Acao Popular, was to note. This movement began informally during 1961, was officially launched on 1 June 1962, and rapidly gained a middle-class, radical and intellectual following. The movement was explicitly non-Marxist, but neither was it officially bound with any ties to Rome, although a theological position was implicit within it from the outset. Indeed, de Kadt suggests that it was a para-Christian movement and underlying its position are the writings of Teilhard de Chardin, Emanuel Mournier and Pope John XXIII, especially the latter's *Mater and Magistra*.

For this movement, the development of history was not merely a simple evolutionary process but a dialectic one in which human struggle plays a significant part. This dialectic struggle gives rise to a historical consciousness (consciencia historica) which is a critical conscious reflection about the historical process (de Kadt in Landsberger 1970: 210). This consciousness only arises when the individual begins to examine the world in a critical manner in order to act upon it and transform it. Such transformation is called humanization. The end-product of this historical struggle is the creation of Utopia, a concept rather like Christ's 'Kingdom of Heaven' or Marx's 'classless society', but one that must lie outside of historical time. However, in order for the process of humanization to proceed individuals must have the opportunity to develop their potential and this can only occur when the yoke of oppression is removed. Emanuel Mournier claimed that:

> Man must strive in co-operation with others to create a society of persons, a society which will rest on 'a series of original acts which have no equivalent in any part of the universe.' Such acts would include efforts to put one's self in the position of others, to understand them, and to make one's self available to them... (cited in Landsberger 1970: 213).

Mournier was fully aware that for as long as humanity exists there will be a struggle of force rather than a static Utopia and it is within the context of this struggle that the person makes choices. Through these choices the person demonstrates authenticity and becomes edified. Since humanity has no essence apart from existence the person develops in and through these choices. But the restrictive structures of society often prevent the mass of people from making free choices, so that the social structure often inhibits the development of the person. Hence, the movement is faced with a dilemma: Acao Popular must inform the mass of people about the problems involved in building the new society without restricting their freedom. Mournier called the individual realization of these problems conscientization (conscientizacao). Yet in order to help people to realize that they were inhibited by the social structures, the idea of the dominant and the dominated was introduced. This clearly relates to the idea of the human struggle, but it also reflects the Marxist dialectic.

It was these ideas that were being worked out and put into practice in just a few areas of Brazil, such as Pernambuco, before the coup in 1964, after which Freire was arrested and imprisoned; finally he went into exile. Indeed, it was against this background and within this cultural milieu that Freire worked out his own ideas about education. His literacy campaign gained recognition, indeed it was known as 'Metodo Paulo Freire'. But with the overthrow of Goulart's government, these radical activities were halted by the new, dictatorial regime. In his enforced exile Freire wrote *Education: The practice of freedom* in 1967 (English edition published in 1974). Other books followed and were translated into English, so that Freire was able to move from Chile to Harvard and from there to become a consultant to the World Council of Churches in Geneva. It was during this period that he worked with the government of Guinea-Bissau and *Pedagogy in Process* followed in 1978.

By 1980, the regime in Brazil had changed and Freire, who had expressed a longing to return to his native land (Freire, 1978: 67–68), went back and assumed the posts of professor of education in both the state and the Catholic universities in Sao Paulo. In addition, for a short time he acted as secretary of education for the city. During this period Freire re-married, his reputation in the world continued to grow and he added to the output of his writing with a number of substantial books – including what he called 'talking books', which are fundamentally dialogues and interviews. Perhaps the best known of these are *Literacy: Reading the word and the world* (1987), which is a dialogue with Donald Macedo and which contextualizes literacy within cultural politics; and *We Make the Road by Walking* (Horton and Freire, 1990), which was a dialogue with Myles Horton – and which is fully reported in a previous chapter in this book. A broad examination of his thinking is to be found in another of these dialogues, *Mentoring the Mentor* (1997), which records dialogues he had with 16 leading thinkers.

While there is a sense in which Freire's underlying position did not change greatly, he certainly added to the range of his concerns, examining such topics as *Pedagogy for the City* (1993), which reflects his thinking and planning as secretary for education for the schools in Sao Paulo. Freire continued to be active until the end of his life, with some books being published after his death. Among these are *Pedagogy of Hope* (1998a) which is a re-statement of his beliefs and *Pedagogy of Freedom* (1998b) which shows that his beliefs and vision were as alive at the end of his life as they were at the outset of his career. More so: in this latter book there is a wonderful statement of what it means to be a teacher.

In *Letters to Cristina* (1996b), his niece, Freire began to reflect upon his own life and work and perhaps these form the best introduction to his thinking, as well as a personal reflection on his own life as a scholar and as one whose work has influenced perhaps more people than any other adult educator in the last century.

THE CONTEXT OF FREIRE'S WRITING

Freire's ideas were clearly developed within the context of Acao Popular but, as Mackie (1980: 93-119) points out, he has been influenced by a variety of writers, so that he is something of an eclectic. Perhaps he is best understood from within the realms of Christian activism, demonstrating a socially dysfunctional prophetic position, rather than any other. But Freire has also been influenced by Marxism, although no more than by other systems of thought, so that it would be unwise to classify him simply as a Marxist. He was certainly Utopian and looked to a world that could be a lot better than it is.

Even so, it must be recognized that there are similarities between Mournier's struggles between the dominated and the dominant and Marxist dialectics, so that as most of his early writings were written from the context of the oppressed they do appear revolutionary to those who have adopted a dominant perspective. Clearly, Freire (1972b) had adopted a revolutionary perspective in which he saw education as liberating and Utopian. Stanley (1972: 42–46) focused upon this as one of the problems in Freire's thought since he did not really consider the possibility that even the educated may not seek liberation but rather accept a benign authoritarianism, and while this may be a just criticism it was clear that Freire never expected all people to accept the position that he espoused, as will become clear when his educational method is discussed in greater detail. Yet Freire (1972b: 40–1, 71-83) continued to have faith in people to recreate the social world and establish a dynamic society.

The only one of Freire's early works that was not written from the context of the oppressed was *Pedagogy in Process* (1978), produced while he was advisor to the government of Guinea-Bissau in its post-colonial period. Here, Freire (p 14) calls for a radical transformation of the colonial educational system, rather than a mechanical assumption of control over whatever existed prior to independence. Even so, education is still expected to create a critical awareness in the people:

> In the revolutionary perspective, the learners are invited to think. Being conscious, in this sense, is not simply a formula or slogan. It is a radical form of being, of being human… (it) involves a critical comprehension of reality. (p 24).

However, this form of education must be part of the state plan because in the new democratic society all participants should be critically aware of their reality. Education is not politically neutral but rather it always has political implications. Therefore, education must be in accord for this state plan for society, which Freire contrasts to a more traditional society's policy:

> Policies carried out by a rigid bureaucracy in the name of the masses to whom they are transmitted as order are one thing; policies carried out with (his emphasis) the masses are quite another thing – with their critically conscious participation in the reconstruction of society, in which the necessary directions never become slogans (p 101).

Indeed, when he was in a position where he could do something about this when, later in his life, he became secretary for education for the city of Sao Paulo he tried to give schools autonomy. He said that 'the greatest advance with respect to school autonomy was in allowing individual schools to develop their own pedagogical projects that, with the support of the administration, can accelerate the transformation of the school' (1993: 73–74).

THE NATURE OF EDUCATION

Much of Freire's writing concentrated upon literacy education, which is not surprising considering the context within which he wrote. Even so, he (1978: 100) claims that neither literacy nor post-literacy education is a separate process but they are two moments in the same process of lifelong formation. Basically, for Freire education had one major aim, to help the participants to put 'knowledge into practice' and it was this combination of reflection and action that he called 'praxis'. In this relationship between reflection and action lies an understanding of the debate between theory and practice and throughout Freire's work there is a concern for the practical in education and a recognition that only then is it relevant to learners. Hence he was clear that education is a human process (Freire 1972b: 51) and a revolutionary one because its outcome will be that authentic human beings will be able to transform the world and humanize it. He returned to this theme in his later writings and in *Pedagogy of Freedom* he re-emphasized that teaching is a human act. He also returned to the idea that education is ideological in nature, but the humanness of the process also emphasizes its ethical nature.

However, early in his career, it is suggested by Peter Berger (1974: 136) that Freire was more concerned with political revolution than with literacy:

> The political themes are not dragged in to help with literacy training. On the contrary, literacy training is but a useful tool for expansion of political consciousness and for political activation of the individual.

Such a claim, phrased in the way that it was, demonstrated Berger's own unfamiliarity with Freire's writings. It was also somewhat surprising since some of Berger's own significant contributions to knowledge have been in the field of the sociology of religion. Yet in his unsympathetic discussion of Freire, he failed to detect the influence of the Christian prophetic tradition, one which is more concerned with the humanization of the world than with the retention of the status quo and the power of the dominant. Had he read Freire more thoroughly, especially some of the later works, he would no doubt have retracted his position.

Clearly Freire was concerned with creating a better world. He was concerned with the development and liberation of people and he did see education as one means by which individuals could acquire confidence as authentic human beings rather than having knowledge transferred to the learner from the teacher. But these are simultaneous processes rather than separate and discrete ones as implied by Berger.

Freire (1972b: 21) referred to humanization, one of the fundamental doctrines of Acao Popular, when he wrote: 'This, then, is the great humanistic and historical task of the oppressed: to liberate themselves and their oppressors as well'. Hence, Freire recognized that both the dominated and the dominant are in their different ways imprisoned within the structures of society and that both need to be liberated. Clearly the oppressed are apparently more ignorant of the social processes that create for them a culture of silence and through education, by which they can become critically aware of their reality, they can discover themselves and look to the future to play their part in transforming the world. The oppressors also need to be liberated and it is probably harder for them than it is for the oppressed, claimed Freire (1972a: 36–37), so that liberation must begin with the latter. 'Indeed, it would be a contradiction in terms if the oppressors… actually implemented a liberating education' (Freire 1972a: 30).

Freire extended this idea in his later writing (1998: 29–48), pointing out that anger must be appropriate 'otherwise it simply degenerates into rage and even hatred' (p 45).

Among the other aims of education is conscientization, another concept that Freire shared with Acao Popular. For Freire (1972b: 51) conscientization 'refers to the process in which men, not as recipients but as knowing subjects, achieve a deepening awareness both of the socio-cultural reality which shapes their lives and of their capacity to transform that reality'. It is specifically and exclusively a human process and it is one which Rivera (1972: 56) likens to rebirth or religious conversion. It is perhaps one of the concepts more closely associated with Freire than any other and yet he claimed later in his life that it was a term that he no longer employed himself. (This claim was made at a public meeting in Cecil County Community College, Maryland, USA, in 1985.) However, it does occur in most of his publications, including the last ones. In *Pedagogy of Freedom* (1998b: 55) he wrote:

> In the 1960s, when I reflected on these obstacles I called for 'conscientization', not as a panacea but as an attempt at critical awareness of those obstacles and their *raison d'etre*. And, in the face of pragmatic, reactionary and fatalistic neo-liberal philosophizing, I still insist, without falling into the trap of 'idealism' on the absolute necessity of conscientization.

But it was a concept that Berger (1974: 139–45) claimed that Freire was mistaken about on both philosophical and sociological grounds. Berger regarded conscientization as consciousness-raising and then went on to suggest that this related to the Marxist concept of false consciousness, which in turn implied a cognitive hierarchy. While the concept of false consciousness does imply this cognitive hierarchy, the idea of conscientization does not. Berger again demonstrated his unfamiliarity with Freire's work because he failed to understand that Freire's educational method was about problematizing reality rather than imposing another 'superior' reality upon that already held by the learners. Hence, an aim of education is that because individuals become more aware of the social processes they are more able, if they so desire, to transform the world. Hence Freire was basically a Utopian thinker.

Having thus far examined the humanistic aims of education in Freire's writing, it is now necessary to look at the methods through which he suggested that these aims will be achieved. Freire's teaching methods are perhaps best summarized by Goulet (Freire, 1974: viii):

- participant observation of educators 'tuning in' to the vocabular universe of the people;
- (an) arduous search for generative words at two levels: syllabic richness and a high charge of experiential involvement;
- a first codification of these words into visual images which stimulate people 'submerged' in the culture of silence to 'emerge' as conscious makers of their own 'culture';
- the decodification by a 'culture circle' under the self-effacing stimulus of a coordinator who is no 'teacher' in the conventional sense, but who has become an educator-educatee – in dialogue with educatee-educators who are too often treated by formal educators as passive recipients of knowledge;
- a creative new codification, this one explicitly critical and aimed at action, wherein those who were formerly illiterate now begin to reject their role as mere 'objects' in nature and social history and undertake to become 'subjects' of their own destiny.

Goulet (p ix) went on to suggest that 'Paulo Freire's central message is that one can know only to the extent that one "problematizes" the natural, cultural and historical reality in which s/he is immersed. Problematizing is the antithesis of the technocrat's problem solving stance' because within the former the person is totally involved whereas in the latter the problem solver seeks to distance himself or herself from reality in order to try to arrive at a solution. However, a very significant factor in Freire's teaching methodology is the recognition of two cultures, that of the teacher and that of the learner, and the realization that the teacher has to bridge the gulf between the two in order to offer a service to the learner. Freire (1998b) returned to these themes when he re-stated his own humanistic philosophy of teaching.

Theologically, this may be viewed as an incarnational approach in which the teacher seeks to identify him/herself with the learner in order to learn not only the vocabulary but also the thought patterns of the learner. Only when this has been achieved can the teacher help problematize reality with the learner. Freire (1972b: 36) summarized this as:

The educator's role is to propose problems about the codified existential situations in order to help the learners arrive at an increasingly critical view of their reality.

It should be noted that Freire was not suggesting that the teacher's view of reality should be imposed upon the learners, as Berger (1974) implied, but rather that reality itself should be regarded as problematic. Indeed, despite the fact that he had espoused this approach for many years, he records (1996a: 24–27) how he really learnt this lesson many years before when, having given an address, a labourer told him of the pitiful conditions of the people to whom he was talking. When he said to his wife that he did not think they understood him, she responded by asking him whether he understood them. Throughout *Pedagogy of Hope* Freire's understanding that teaching is about giving hope, not telling people that they are wrong, shines through. Clearly this is a lesson that has not been learnt by all the teachers or bureaucrats in Western education. In his last books (1998b: 101–12) he returned to the theme of the dialogue in education, especially to the theme of teachers and students listening to one another and to their own reflective processes, often through moments of silence.

For Freire the teaching and learning transaction is a dialogue between those who are participants in the process. Rather like the ideal society, in Freire's thoughts there must be a human relationship between teacher and learner, so that the traditional teacher-learner relationship is transformed into a relationship of 'teacher-student with students-teachers' (Freire 1972a: 53). Bee (1980: 50) puts it another way when she notes that traditionally in children's education, children are made the object rather than the subject of their learning. For Giroux (1981: 133):

> radical pedagogy requires non-authoritarian social relationships that support dialogue and communication as indispensable for questioning the meaning and nature of knowledge and peeling away the hidden structures of reality.

While Giroux regarded Freire's pedagogy as radical, Griffith (1972: 67) claimed that Freire's 'assumptions about the relationship between teachers and students, were neither new nor particularly useful in bringing about an improvement in the process'. Griffith went on to cite many adult educators who have countenanced similar teaching techniques and he then criticizes Freire for not having examined or cited the works of adult education in which these approaches are discussed. It is perhaps significant that Griffith was an adult educator, since adult education theory has frequently differed from initial education theory on this fact that learners are adult human beings and should always be treated as such. That Freire did not cite those other adult educators who have espoused this approach is a fact but his background must be borne in mind when making such a comment. Freire's concerns were with adult literacy and education in the Third World rather than an academic treatise upon the development of adult education theory. However, the significance of this discussion may perhaps be seen in the contrasting direction of the two sets of relationships. Jarvis (1985: 48–50) suggested that there are two distinctive curricular models in education that relate to these two sets of directions: 'Education from Above' is the more traditional approach whereas 'Education of Equals' reflects that which is more common in adult education, especially that approach adopted by Freire.

However, Freire was also been criticized by Boston (1972: 87–89) for his approach to relationships. Boston claims that Freire is too concerned with the dominant-dominated relationship and that he needed to examine other dimensions of relationship. He suggested that Freire's analysis was one-sided and that there are other styles of relationship in Latin America, one he suggests being intermediary and another which he regards as a bargaining relationship. However, bargains can only be struck within the limitations of power. By contrast, Boston suggested that intermediary relationship is one that the Roman Catholic Church serves in Latin America but it is perhaps significant to recall that it was Acao Popular that recognized the dominant-dominated relationship. That Freire contrasted a vertical with a horizontal relationship and that he wished the teacher-learner relationship to be a horizontal one is in accord with adult education theory and also in accord with the ideal, democratic society for which he aspired. Additionally, in his later work, Freire re-emphasized the significance of the ethical and the personal in the teaching and learning process.

In his early writings, Freire paid little attention to feminist issues, something that feminists brought to his attention. This he readily acknowledged, since his own Christian faith had already made him aware of it:

> Since I was a child, I have never been able to understand how it could be possible to reconcile faith in Christ with discrimination on the basis of race, sex, social class, or national origin. How is it possible to 'walk' with Christ, but refer to the popular classes as 'these stinky people' or 'riffraff' (1998b: 41).

In his condemnation of all forms of discrimination he also wrote:

> It is equally part of right thinking to reject decidedly any form of discrimination. Perceptions of class, race or sex offend the essence of human dignity and constitute a radical negation of democracy (p 41).

While he omitted age from this statement, it introduces one of his firmest criticisms of the so-called democracy of a Western society that kills, beats, destroys property and practises all forms of discrimination. Yet he does so with a poignant statement from the South:

> I feel more pity than rage at the absurd arrogance of this kind of white supremacy, passing itself off to the world as democracy' (p 41).

What, then, is the content of Freire's teaching? To a very great extent the content was closely related to the methods that he employed. Freire was concerned not merely to teach people to read and write but to understand and relate their learning to the reality of their everyday life. Hence, he did not start with meaningless words and phrases but, having attuned himself to the vocabulary and the social world of the learners, he focused upon 'generative themes', that is, themes that allowed them to analyse that which they already understood and which would encourage the development of associated and critical ideas within the discussion in cultural circles (Freire 1974: 157). Yet the presentation of these themes might be through visual, tactile or audio methods, and discussion between learners and learners and teachers should ensue, etc. However, only the theme was to be presented as a problem and never a solution; the theme acts as a problem–posing rather than a problem–solving situation (Freire 1972a: 91–93).

In a sense it may be seen that he was not seeking to transmit either worthwhile or objective knowledge, since 'worthwhileness' by definition is ideological and objective knowledge is a questionable concept. This approach, which Freire rejected, he referred to as the banking concept of education but by contrast he endeavoured to encourage learners to create knowledge and meaning as a result of a constant problematizing of their existential situations. For him, the banking concept ensures that the educator has a major role, but not one of which he approved:

> It follows logically from the banking notion of consciousness that the educator's role is to regulate the way that the world 'enters into' the students. His task is to organize a process which already happens spontaneously, to 'fill' the students by making deposits of information which he considers constitute true knowledge (1972a: 49).

Hence, in traditional education the educator controls the knowledge and, to some extent, the perception of reality with which the student is presented. But the student already has a perception of reality, so that another perception might be rejected whereas through dialogue and problematization new knowledge and new meaning may be created. This is obviously no new debate within either the philosophy or the sociology of education, nor indeed of adult education, although it had been thoroughly reviewed elsewhere (Jarvis 1985: 73–92) when the first edition of this book was published. Even so, Freire's thoughts about teaching are certainly much more widely accepted among many who teach adults in all fields – it will certainly strike chords with those who have introduced problem-based education into medicine and other forms of higher and further education. Suffice to note that through the relaxation of control by the teacher, this approach encourages the creation of knowledge and meaning relevant to the social situation of the learners. Since it does relate to their own reality, which they learn to analyse critically, Freire expected that praxis will occur, ie that having thought about the ideas the learners will act in accord with their conclusions in order to transform the world. But in transforming the world the individual has to make choices that will not automatically produce beneficial results:

> The process of transforming the world, which reveals this presence of man, can lead to his humanization as well as his dehumanization, to his growth or diminution.

These alternatives reveal to man his problematic nature and pose a problem for him, requiring that he choose one path or the other. (Freire 1972b: 55).

It is significant that Freire's own praxis is demonstrated through the publication of his 'talking books', for these are dialogues in which his own ideas are subject to the scrutiny of colleagues and friends and through which new ideas and new knowledge is generated.

But is Freire's approach successful? Certainly learners have become literate in a few weeks, because the topics relate directly to the social experience of the learners. Berger (1974: 136), commenting upon the success rate, claimed, without justification, that for Freire pedagogical results are no real justification for the method since it was only undertaken for political ends. Such a claim demonstrates Berger's inability to see that for Freire the human being and human society were central to his thinking and that the achievement of humanization is both an educational and a political act, so that it is necessary to assess his work not only in literacy but also in human terms. Freire (1972b: 43–47), recording the human success in literacy, makes no mention of political revolution.

Yet politics cannot 'be isolated from the education process', so that it might be asked whether Freire's approach to education, one which came out of a Third World situation, has any validity for the remainder of the world? Boston (1972: 91) was in no doubt, claiming that 'even an indirect translation of Freire is simply folly'. Even Giroux (1981: 139), who is very sympathetic to Freire's approach, suggests that:

It would be misleading as well as dangerous to extend without qualification Freire's theory and methods to the industrialized and urbanized societies of the West.

Yet Griffith (1972: 67) claims that Freire offered nothing new to adult educators and London (1973: 56) suggests that:

Freire's approach to education and social change has important implications for our own country (USA) and for most industrialized societies, as well as for the newly developing world.

Freire himself addressed this question in terms of the contemporary world:

Recently in Bavaria, a German educator friend mentioned having heard a 'leftish' activist say: 'Paulo Freire no longer makes any sense. The education needed today has nothing to do with dreams, utopias, conscientiousness but rather with the technical, scientific, and professional development of learners'. 'Development', here is understood as training. This is exactly what has always interested the dominant classes: the depoliticization of education. In reality, education requires technical, scientific, and professional development as much as it does dreams and utopias.

I reject the notion that nothing can be done about the consequences of economic globalization and refuse to bow my head gently because nothing can be done against the unavoidable (Freire, 1998a: 43).

Indeed, in the United Kingdom, radical community adult educators had no doubts that Freire's approach was applicable (Batten, 1980: 27–38; Alfred, 1984: 105–14). Freire offered a theory of teaching and learning that is at the heart of much adult education theory, even political adult education, so that there is not a great deal with which many adult educators would wish to dispute. However, the context within which he placed his theory and practice caused some educators doubts. He coupled his approach to education to a theory of change that had radical political implications as well as human ones and it is this that have caused some educators unease.

Having reviewed this historical context, it is significant that this approach to teaching and learning is now more widely accepted, except for those with a conservative approach to education, since it is now widely recognized that knowledge is discourse (Foucault, 1972) and that the dominant determine its content and nature. Additionally, there has been a greater emphasis on the autonomy of the learner and some recognition that teaching is an ethical process. Whether Freire's writing has helped change the educational climate or whether it was merely a reflection of the way society has been changing is a much harder question to answer. Certainly since the recognition that education is a lifelong process for many in the knowledge society his methods have been more widely introduced. Even so, the political element has been lost to a great extent in the West although less so in the South, and in this he stands as a reminder that the depoliticization of the process is dangerous when the system within which it functions is immoral. Clearly, it is an approach that was espoused in adult education before Freire wrote but he popularized it and he still serves to remind us of its value.

FREIRE'S CONTRIBUTION TO EDUCATIONAL THEORY

When the first edition of this book was published, the study of the education of adults was beginning to be more widely accepted and I attempted to locate Freire within it. As I pointed out then, citing Griffith (1972: 68), Freire's own intellectual mentors were clearly not to be discovered from within this discipline. But then many of the early educators of adults had their intellectual history in other disciplines and, indeed, adult education *per se* is a mixture of overlapping fields of practice upon which academics from different disciplines can have a perspective. Freire, like many other adult educators of his generation, had this wealth of knowledge from other fields of study, which he used wisely and well to analyse his own and others' practice. His own analyses have been enriched by his understanding of these diverse disciplines. Paradoxically, the success of adult educators in getting adult education accepted as a field of study has probably resulted in much narrower analyses of the field since many practitioners do not have the same breadth of understanding.

Freire, to a very sophisticated extent, has incorporated this wealth of knowledge into his own analyses; sociology, philosophy, ethics, theology are all present. While it is clear that he has added little to the practice of teaching adults, since there have been many adult educators who have espoused techniques similar to those he adopted, there have been few who have contributed to the theory of adult education from such a wide variety of disciplines. However, it is in the areas of sociology, politics and philosophy/theology of adult education that his contribution is perhaps the greatest.

The sociology of education underwent a major change in the West in the early 1970s and it is often equated with the publication of *Knowledge and Control* in 1971. This symposium, edited by Young, highlighted a more radical and phenomenological analysis of education and it is one that is similar to the perspective discovered in Freire's writings, although his are more humanistic and ethical. Clearly many of the issues about both knowledge and power were not new, many being traced back to Mannheim and Marx. Their publication at that time had a profound effect upon sociological studies of education. By contrast, there was no highly developed sociology of adult education, although there were a number of sociological studies of the education of adults, so that Freire's analysis brought the 'new' sociology of education to adult education before it had even established a sociology of adult education. His philosophical and political analyses have added a fundamental new dimension to the study of adult education and continue to serve as a reminder that the educational processes cannot be separated from the social context within which they appear.

Because adult education had wrongly been a predominantly psychological discipline with emphasis upon adults learning, neither the sociological nor the political implications of learning had been developed or analysed; now learning is understood from a much wider context (see Jarvis, 1987, 1992, *inter alia*). However, these were issues quite central to the whole of Freire's work. Indeed, the recognition that knowledge itself is controlled and socially structured, while commonplace in sociology, had not really been developed in adult education, so that some of these radical and different ideas had not been discussed in great detail when Freire's writings became known to Western adult educators. He certainly helped adult educators to extend the breadth of their analyses.

In 1985, Freire (1985) reverted to a theme that had been implicit in much of his writing and in which the history of adult education is rich – that of the involvement of the church. No history of adult education could be written that is true to history without recognition that the church's role has been long and honourable. However, in Freire's work it is the prophetic tradition of the church rather than the missionary one that takes precedence. Such a tradition has frequently been uncomfortable to the elite, so that it is unsurprising that his writings have not always been accepted since the political implications of the prophetic tradition often inhibit unbiased analysis. Yet for Freire the humanization of society must have political, indeed revolutionary, implications and it is this he tried to practise in Brazil and Chile. Indeed, Gutierrez's (1974: 91–92) study of liberation theology views Freire's approach as one of the most creative and fruitful efforts that have been implemented in Latin America. Much of what he has written may be viewed as a theology of adult education. Freire's emphasis upon liberating the learner to become an agent in the world was significant to adult educators in helping to locate adult education within the structure-agency debate in sociology (Giddens, 1979), but it is also important as both a philosophical concept about the development of authenticity and as a theological idea about the development of the human being.

However, Freire's understanding of liberating the oppressor and the teacher was much more new and it is something that pointed to the recognition that people are entrapped in their social context.

Freire's work contains a profound humanistic philosophy of education that requires further analysis in the philosophy of adult education. Perhaps its relationship to some of the ideas expressed by Dewey (1916, 1938) and by Bergevin (1967) need to be discussed. Bergevin (pp 30–31) suggested some of the major goals in adult education in terms of the meaning of life and the provision of conditions and opportunities for adult advancement, although he did not really relate these to a radical sociological analysis in the same manner as Freire.

Freire offers an implicit theology of adult education that has not yet been developed, despite the long history of involvement that the churches have had with the education of adults. This is an area that requires considerable analysis in the future. Even so, Freire has produced profound insight into the philosophy, politics and sociology of education that must not be lost among the debates on lifelong education and the learning society. Indeed, in his latest books, he has also addressed questions relating to globalization and post-modernism, demonstrating how he continued to keep abreast with the academic debates and show that his thinking is still relevant. Indeed, his work epitomizes his own beliefs in a Universal Good and offers a hope and an idealism of what the human being can become and a role that education can play in that process. Because Freire has written from a perspective of the South, he has provided insights and understandings that those from the North would find more difficult to see. These are not only invaluable to educators, they also help us in the North to understand the South and the North's imposition upon it. Hidden within the pages are illustrations of the pain and the suffering he and others like him have suffered in order to be true to their beliefs and fight for their people.

CONCLUSION

Perhaps the measure of Freire's success in influencing the world of adult education may be seen by the fact that at the UNESCO World Assembly on Adult Education, there was a special session remembering the man and his work. Adult educators and administrators of education from all over the world met to remember a man who had helped keep alive human values in adult education and whose work had influenced people from most countries in the world.

Perhaps, however, the best way to conclude this chapter is to let Freire explain his own thinking and philosophy:

> The taste of freedom disappears if its practice becomes scarce, even though it may return in libertarian expressions. The taste of freedom is part of the very nature of men and women, it is part of their orientation toward being more. That is why we talk of the dream of freedom, about the possibility of the taste of freedom when necessity overcomes freedom. Freedom, a sine qua non of being more, is not the finish line but the starting point...
>
> The future is not a province from the present which just waits for us to arrive some day and perform the operation of adding this ready-made tomorrow to today, which both become old and obsolete. The future is born of the present, from possibilities in contradiction, from the battle waged by forces that dialectically oppose each other. For this reason, as I always insist, the future is not a given fact, but a fact in progress... (Freire, 1996b: 151–52).

REFERENCES

Alfred, D (1984) The relevance of the Work of Paulo Freire to Radical Community Education in Britain, *International Journal of Lifelong Education*, **3** (2)

Batten, E (1980) Community Education: A case for radicalism, in *Issues in Community Education*, eds C Fletcher and N Thompson, The Falmer Press, Lewes

Bee, B (1980) The Politics of Literacy, in *Literacy and Revolution: The pedagogy of Paulo Freire*, ed R Mackie, Pluto Press, London

Bell, B, Gaventa, J and Peters, J (1990) *We Make the Road by Walking: Myles Horton and Paulo Freire*, Temple University Press, Philadelphia

Berger, P L (1974) *Pyramids of Sacrifice*, Pelican Harmondsworth

Bergevin, P (1967) *A Philosophy for Adult Education*, Seabury Press, New York

Boston, B O (1972) *Paulo Freire: Notes of a loving critic, in Paulo Freire: A revolutionary dilemma for the adult educator*, ed S M Grabowski, Publications in Continuing Education, Syracuse University

Dewey, J (1916) *Democracy and Education*, The Free Press, New York

Dewey, J (1938) *Experience and Education*, Collier Books, New York

Fletcher, C and Thompson, N (eds) (1981) *Issues in Community Education*, The Falmer Press, Lewes

Foucault, M (1972) *The Archaeology of Knowledge*, Routledge, London

Freire, P (1972a) *Pedagogy of the Oppressed*, trans M B Ramos, Penguin, Harmondsworth

Freire, P (1972b) *Cultural Action for Freedom*, Penguin, Harmondsworth

Freire, P (1974) *Education: The practice of freedom*, Writers and Readers Cooperative, London, originally published in the United Kingdom as Education for Critical Consciousness, Sheed and Ward, London

Freire, P (1978) *Pedagogy in Process: The letters to Guinea Bissau*, Writers and Readers Cooperative, London

Freire, P (1985) *The Politics of Education*, trans D Macedo, Bergin and Garvey Publishers Inc, Massachusetts

Freire, P (1993) *Pedagogy of the City*, trans D Macedo, Continuum, New York

Freire, P (1996a) *Pedagogy of Hope*, trans R Barr, Continuum, New York

Freire, P (1996b) *Letters to Cristina*, trans D Macedo, Q Macedo and A Oliveira, Routledge, London

Freire, P (1997) *Mentoring the Mentor*, Peter Lang, New York

Freire, P (1998a) *Pedagogy of the Heart*, trans D Macedo and A Oliveira, Continuum, New York

Freire, P (1998b) *Pedagogy of Freedom*, trans P Clark, Rowman and Littlefield, Lanham

Freire, P and Faundez (1989) *Learning to Question: A pedagogy of liberation*, trans T Coates, World Council of Churches, Geneva

Freire, P and Macedo, D (1987) *Literacy: Reading the word and the world*, Routledge and Kegan Paul, London

Giddens, A (1979) *Central Problems in Social Theory*, MacMillan, London

Giroux, H A (1981) *Ideology, Culture and the Process of Schooling*, The Falmer Press, Lewes

Giroux, H A (1985) Introduction, in *The Politics of Education*, P Freire, trans D Macedo, Bergin and Garvey Publishers Inc, Massachusetts

Goulet, D (1974) Introduction, in Education: *The practice of freedom*, P Freire, Writers and Readers Cooperative, London

Grabowski, S M (1972) *Paulo Freire: A revolutionary dilemma for the adult educator*, Publications in Continuing Education, Syracuse University

Griffith, W S (1972) Paulo Freire: Utopian perspectives in literacy education for revolution, in *Paulo Freire: A revolutionary dilemma for the adult educator*, ed S M Grabowski, Publications in Continuing Education, Syracuse University

Gutierrez, G (1974) *A Theology of Liberation*, SCM Press Ltd, London

Horton, M and Freire, D (1990) *We Make the Road by Walking: Conversations on education and social change*, eds B Bell, J Gaventa and J Peters, Temple University Press, Philadelphia

Jarvis, P (1985) *The Sociology of Adult and Continuing Education*, Croom-Helm, London

Jarvis, P (1987) *Adult Learning in the Social Context*, Croom Helm, London

Jarvis, P (1992) *Paradoxes of Learning*, Jossey Bass, San Francisco

de Kadt, E (1970) J V C and A P: The rise of Catholic radicalism in Brazil, in *The Church and Social Change in Latin America*, ed H A Landsberger, University of Notre Dame Press

Landsberger, H A (1970) *The Church and Social Change in Latin America*, University of Notre Dame Press

London, J (1973) Reflections upon the relevance of Paulo Freire for American Adult Education, *Convergence*, **6** (1)

Mackie, R (1980) Contributions to the Thought of Paulo Freire, in *Literacy and Revolution: The pedagogy of Paulo Freire*, ed R Mackie, Pluto Press, London

Mackie, R (1980) *Literacy and Revolution: The pedagogy of Paulo Freire*, Pluto Press, London

Rivera, D M (1972) The Changers: A new breed of adult educator, in *Paulo Freire: A revolutionary dilemma for the adult educator*, ed S M Grabowski, Publications in Continuing Education, Syracuse University

Stanley, M (1972) Literacy: The crisis of conventional wisdom, in *Paulo Freire: A revolutionary dilemma for the adult educator*, ed S M Grabowski, Publications in Continuing Education, Syracuse University

Young, M F D (1971) *Knowledge and Control*, Collier & Macmillan, London

Chapter 17

Ettore Gelpi

Colin Griffin

It could be said that since the first edition of this book, Gelpi's analysis of lifelong education has been more than borne out during the last years of the 20th century. Developments in what he called the international division of labour and what we now refer to as economic and cultural globalization, together with new technologies that have transformed the conditions of employment, all go to make his analysis as relevant now as it was then. The struggles, conflicts and divisions that characterize his approach to education are with us still and the trends towards global inequality and exclusion have, if anything, gathered even greater strength.

Together with the growth of inequality on a local and global scale there is a rhetoric of equal opportunity and social inclusion, which almost inevitably accompanies statements of lifelong learning policy. The rhetoric of 'for all' in the titles of policy documents, such as *Lifelong Learning for All* (OECD, 1996), or routinely incorporated into policy discourse (NAGCELL, 1997), is exposed by Gelpi as just that. As he himself said, much earlier: 'Education for all, and at all ages; but with what objectives and with what means?' (see below). His own understanding was that lifelong education could serve either to reproduce existing social divisions and inequalities, or to contribute to a fairer and more inclusive society. Being a dialectical thinker, he thought it likely that lifelong learning policies would do both of these things. And so it has proved, with the development of mass education systems alongside the growth in social inequality and exclusion. Gelpi insisted on the primacy of the system of production, not only now globalized but transformed by information systems and communications technologies, in determining the system of education and its policy rhetoric.

In other words, Gelpi always problematized lifelong learning, seeing its capacity for reproducing global inequalities as well as challenging them. Although a critical perspective on lifelong learning has since developed (Coffield,

1997; Elliott, 1999) there can be little doubt that Gelpi was among the earliest to adopt a sceptical position. After quoting Gelpi, a recent writer on lifelong learning puts precisely the issues he raised:

> When governments put large amounts of money into lifelong learning it is not a subversive question to ask 'Why?' If a government invests more than might reasonably be expected in lifelong learning, it may be for the enhanced creativity of the individual citizen, or it may be to serve the interests of the state; or of course, it may be for a combination of both types of benefit. (Oliver, 1999: 4).

This is certainly a way of reflecting upon Gelpi's problematization of lifelong learning, although Gelpi himself provides a much more complex analysis of the relation of the individual and the state, by way of the relations of production and the division of labour in society. In any case, it is increasingly clear to many what was always clear to Gelpi, namely, that there are various possible beneficiaries of lifelong learning, not only the state and the individual, but families, communities and, above all for some, employers.

Although Gelpi's work includes many scattered papers arising from the nature of his educational work with international agencies such as UNESCO, the themes he consistently addresses can all be shown to have been justified in the event. In many cases he has anticipated the kinds of global trends we are witnessing at the beginning of the 21st century and which throw light on global policies of lifelong learning and education.

In the first place, Gelpi has emphasized the policy dimension, rather than focusing, as much of the literature had done, upon the unique characteristics of adult learning and education. For one thing, the social divisions represented by adulthood are contingent in many ways and in relation to production, culture and struggles for emancipation, it amounts to adding yet another social division to the overwhelming number that already exist. The absorption of adult education into lifelong learning has come about as a result of education policies, rather than any philosophical, sociological, psychological or even methodological accounts of adulthood or childhood.

Secondly, Gelpi's view is nothing if not global: much of his work is constructed around an analysis of the international division of labour and production. The movement of capital and production around the world, together with the consequent migration of workers, have become ever more significant for global relations of East and West, North and South. At the same time, the collapse of communist regimes in the face of what Gelpi calls 'multinational hegemony' has posed issues of local and national identity that are for the most part yet to be resolved. The example of eastern Europe is but one example of the way in which new identities are being forged against the background of economic and cultural globalization.

Thirdly, Gelpi's focus upon the consequences of globalization for social divisions and struggles remains at the heart of his analysis still. The failure of traditional adult education and training systems to mitigate or resolve these struggles is one of the reasons for his sceptical vision of the emergence of the learning society. Now that learning in the context of globalization and risk management is established as the context for analysing lifelong learning policies worldwide, Gelpi's earlier analysis has been more than vindicated.

Similarly, and fourthly, the threat posed by these developments to identity continues to constitute a major theme of his writings. Identity is conceived in every possible context, personal, cultural, economic and national. In the face of global conflicts and the global movement of people, the re-establishment of identity becomes a central concern of education. It enters into Gelpi's vision in the form of what he calls 'identite terrienne', or the possibility of creating a universal sense of belonging to place or land, which transcends the kinds of divisions that have historically been the source of alienation and anomie, and which globalization is now exacerbating

The fifth consistent focus of Gelpi's work is that of production in relation to education and culture. In particular, the threat to popular cultures posed by postmodern conditions is one he has increasingly addressed. The system of production associated with global capitalism being both divisive and hegemonic, a major function of education systems becomes one of reasserting identities through popular cultural struggles. With his own vast international experience of cultures and education systems, no one is better equipped than Gelpi to observe the consequences for identity and popular cultures of the new regime of production. But he is also aware of the possibilities for resistance and creativity in the face of the hegemony of the market in both education and culture. The fundamentally dialectical perspective that he has always adopted makes resistance an inevitable consequence of oppression, and his writings provide many examples of ways in which workers, women, communities and cultural identities struggle to maintain themselves against the consequences of the global marketplace. In particular, the changing nature of employment in every country of the world has remained a major preoccupation of his writings and he continues to understand identity, culture, education and employment as existing in dialectical relations. This is what has marked off the originality of his work from the beginning and it is still the case that few writers on adult education or lifelong learning attain the kind of scope and vision which he brings to his own analysis.

Despite his scepticism, and his dark and critical view of the possibilities for lifelong learning and the learning society in the face of developments in production, Gelpi's vision remains one in which human creativity triumphs over threats to freedom and identity. In addition to poetry, Gelpi even includes the libretto of an operetta in three acts for bureaucrats, migrant workers and trainers, including some of the musical score (Gelpi 1992a: 57–69). He is nothing if not creative in his own style of writing, but this just reflects a profound faith in the power of human creativity to overcome difficulties and problems, the necessary utopianism of his approach, which should always be remembered when contemplating the sceptical analysis that underpins it. It is precisely the failure of traditional adult education to embrace this degree of creativity which, in Gelpi's eyes, has constituted its failure in the face of the current situation.

Finally, there is the theme of science and technology and the part these play in shaping the forms which production now takes and which, because he accepts a material analysis, Gelpi sees as containing both the possibilities of repression and transformation. He has consistently stressed the need for science and technology to address universal human needs, rather than those of capital accumulation and has argued for the role of human values in development (Gelpi, 1992b). This, in turn, entails the central role of such values in cultural development and educational strategies.

These are the kind of themes that Gelpi has consistently addressed and that have proved to be of enduring importance during the 1990s. Some, indeed, are even more significant in popular awareness than they were when he first addressed them: globalization, local identities, migrant workers and so on. But his fundamental theoretical analysis has remained consistent and is therefore reproduced in its original form below. The chapter will then conclude with a brief account of the kinds of issues he has since addressed in the large number of scattered and largely unpublished papers since the first edition of this book, many untranslated into English.

Until the publication in 1985 of *Lifelong Education and International Relations* (1885) Gelpi's his work was best known in the two volumes called *A Future for Lifelong Education*, published in 1979 by the Department of Adult and Higher Education of Manchester University, translated and introduced by Ralph Ruddock. Here are contained papers on diverse topics with a bearing upon the development of his thought, rather than a systematic exposition of the concept of lifelong education. The reader will not discover in Gelpi any conventionally academic discourse upon adult learning. Instead, he offers a powerfully suggestive analysis of the significance of education in the international division of labour and in the struggles of workers and all marginalized groups in society against the forms which this division takes. However, as Ruddock says in his sympathetic and perceptive introduction, Gelpi is not to be labelled or identified with any single ideological position: his concern for popular struggles and for the dialectical possibilities that lifelong education opens up, reflects a turn of mind unfamiliar perhaps to the Anglo-Saxon way of thinking. To this way of thinking his work may appear unduly abstract and generalized. In terms of his own experience of the consequences of the international division of labour and wealth such criticism may be dismissed out of hand. Nevertheless, it is particularly necessary to impose some sort of framework upon Gelpi's writing, even at the expense of betraying its authenticity.

It is appropriate, therefore, to think of Gelpi's contribution not in terms of a theory of adult learning and teaching, but rather as a policy model according to which lifelong education becomes an integral feature of the struggle against the international division of labour and its consequences for all those people who are in some way 'marginalised' by it. In his study of Gelpi, for example, Timothy Ireland identified three areas of special concern, which either run through Gelpi's writing or else represent a typical consequence of his social and political analysis. These are workers' education and the role of trade unions in it, with special reference to migrant workers and the training of young workers; the linguistic and cultural needs of migrants and their children, and other linguistic and cultural minorities; and finally the lifelong education needs of the elderly, especially in industrial society (Ireland, 1978: 66–84). Gelpi is not, of course, the first to have considered these areas from a standpoint of educational policy, but what distinguishes his particular contribution is the range and consistency of the underlying analysis, together with a vast practical experience of what he is talking about. Much of his writing, in fact, is concerned with specific lifelong education projects and applications, rather than with the systematic exposition of the underlying analysis around the concept of the international division of labour.

The opening chapters of *A Future for Lifelong Education* do provide an indication of Gelpi's conceptual framework, as well as of the difficulties of expressing it in the conventional categories of Anglo-Saxon adult education discourse. For example, a dialectical conception of theory and practice: education for all, and at all ages; but with what objectives and with what means? 'Lifelong education' could result in the reinforcement of the established order, increased productivity and subordination; but a different option could enable us to become more and more committed to the struggle against those who oppress mankind in work and in leisure, in social and emotional life (Gelpi, 1979, vol 1: 1).

Lifelong education is not one option but many: in societies of whatever ideological order. Its potential is both for liberation and repression. It is at the same time both progressive and reactionary. According to our more familiar categories of reasoning, as the philosophical Bishop Butler said, 'everything is what it is, and not another thing'. But this is not the logic of the continental tradition of philosophy in which Gelpi was educated and he sees lifelong education as a universal potential for the autonomy of individuals and groups that is contradicted in practice.

The paradox of adult education in a climate both of developmental activities and financial constraint is easily understood in Gelpi's terms: what is being developed and what constrained? Lifelong education policies are not neutral. This statement, says Gelpi, is 'the point of departure for all consideration of it'. Why should there be an almost total international consensus on lifelong education policy alongside what he calls 'a progressive reduction of self-directed learning'? The paradox is resolved:

> The repressive forces of our contemporary society are ready to increase the time and space given to education, but only on the condition that it does not bring about a reinforcement of the struggle of men and of peoples for their autonomy.
> (Gelpi, 1979, vol 1: 2).

Policies for lifelong education which have the whole-hearted backing of the state are not likely to be advancing human freedom, in that they are unlikely to advance the cause of self-directed learning. The thoroughgoing application of the principles of andragogy, Gelpi seems to be saying, would actually threaten the social order. In our society, he argues, 'it is found necessary to teach and to learn in order to protect the established order'. It is also necessary to 'adapt people to change' in consequence of the application of science and technology: It is easy to imagine governments of whatever ideology eager to embrace lifelong education on these terms.

And of course, from a global perspective, the application of science and technology is hardly a neutral process. Rather, it is a process deeply implicated in the exploitation of the poor countries of the world by the rich. Lifelong education as self-directed learning therefore becomes an actual obstacle to lifelong education as 'education for adaptation' because it means 'individual control of the ends, contents, and methods of education'.

The struggle for lifelong education is the struggle for control, which far transcends the boundaries of pedagogy and is concerned with far more than the psychological obstacles to adult learning. Its aim is nothing less than transformation, social change, a crisis of values and of authority in productive and educational life. Gelpi is critical of any educational progressivism that is not directed towards genuinely political objectives and consistently distances his concept of lifelong education from alternative educational strategies such as deschooling, non-formal education, the OECD's version of recurrent education and so on (see Ireland, 1978: 11–13). Gelpi has developed his own concept along very different lines from that of lifelong education as conceived at the UNESCO Institute for Education, Hamburg (Dave, 1976), which has continued to be dominated by traditional pedagogic categories. For Gelpi, education transcends not only educational institutions but local and national frameworks and one of his most characteristic contributions had been to relate lifelong education to international organization and cooperation. But given what he calls 'the planetary scale of the economic system' lifelong education may be an instrument of cultural liberation or dependency, of autonomous development or of new colonialism.

It is clear, then, that Gelpi's view of lifelong education is essentially one of a social and political process whose objective is to achieve individual and cultural autonomy. He sees lifelong education as an integral aspect of the struggle of marginalized people in all societies against the oppressive structures of the international division of labour. It is an attractive feature of Gelpi's writing that his concept of struggle is not a dourly political one but incorporates creativity itself: 'Happily,' he says, 'the exploration of educational reality is always full of promise'. This holds true because such reality is 'composed of both control and creativity'. Not many writers on education celebrate its creative potential by breaking into poetry. Gelpi does not offer the kind of systematic and largely negative critique associated with much political writing on education and he cannot be associated with any particular ideological camp. Believing that education systems are relatively autonomous in any social system, he never loses sight of creative opportunities for development towards individual and collective autonomy.

Nevertheless, he consistently argues that in all social and political systems education is inextricably linked with the structures and processes of production.

Work and education cannot be other than clearly tied together. The discovery in Britain and elsewhere of a so-called 'new vocationalism' should not lead us to suppose that education has not always, in some way or other, been a reflection of the realities of the work system. Education policies of industrialized and developing countries alike are aimed at problems of unemployment and underemployment. Whatever ideological form they take, such policies are concerned as much with containing social conflict as with experimenting with new educational ideas such as lifelong education. The very fact that countries with very diverse political systems may adopt such a strategy suggests its ambiguous character. Fundamental conceptions of work and production do not change much as a result, any more than do judgements about the value of academic work (Gelpi and Beraho-Beri, 1983). As an expression of the relations of work and education, then, lifelong education may be a progressive strategy for human liberation or a repressive agency of state control. No one has expressed the dialectical potential of lifelong education better than Gelpi. Most writers on the subject simply and simplistically assume that it could only be a necessarily desirable thing. As was earlier suggested, this is not so much a matter of ideology as a way of thinking philosophically about education: a way of thinking about the contradictory possibilities of things rather than of their analytic categories. To subscribe to a view that lifelong education could only be a good thing is to neglect its truly contradictory possibilities:

> A lifelong education policy which reinforces the division of labour, a partial schooling which is in contradiction with itself, encouraging urbanisation and the unemployment that goes with it, impoverishes the natural resources of some Third World countries even to the point of exhaustion... These effects cannot be objectives for educational strategies designed to favour the interests of exploited groups, classes and countries (Gelpi, 1979, vol 2: 10).

These kinds of considerations hold true, though, for all societies, and not only the neo-colonized countries of the Third World. In industrialized countries too, access to an education system does not of itself constitute a system of lifelong education aimed at liberation. In Gelpi's terms a genuinely progressive strategy of lifelong education would be an exercise in the politics of knowledge and production itself, one which asks who should acquire knowledge and for what purposes or control and how should knowledge be organized in society? These tend to be neglected issues in educational debate. In his discussion of political and social factors (Gelpi, 1979, vol 1: ch 3) he argues that educators and policy makers prefer to deal in generalities 'rather than face conflicts and contradictions, or to attempt significant utopian projects'. The need for an analysis of the political, social and institutional framework at the community, national and international level is therefore urgent. This means, in effect, that educationists need to address problems of class oppression, rural and urban conflicts, the exploitation of the countries of the Third World.

'For too long', says Gelpi, 'too many progressive educators have failed to take into account the world of production, which is in all reality so significant for personal and social development.' A progressive strategy of lifelong education needs to be addressed to the kind of educational inequality arising from what he describes as the dualism of elite systems: 'In all truth, the problems of quality in mass education is the first problem to be resolved in lifelong education'. The second is that of participation in the educational enterprise:

> If the extinction of the social and international division of labour and the achievement of participation by all individuals in decision-making within the economic, political, social and cultural fields are seen as the grand objectives for modern man, an active role for all within the educational process and in cultural activity is one of the conditions for the realisation of these objectives (Gelpi, 1979, vol 1: 31).

To understand what is meant by the international division of labour is to understand the political origins of global divisions. In his earlier work Gelpi has brought out the main features of this idea:

> … the international division of labour which is developing today is based on the exchange of popular consumer goods manufactured by abundant and cheap manpower in developing countries with more sophisticated goods mainly incorporating capital and an advanced technology from the older industrialized countries (Gelpi, 1985: 25).

This reflects an economist's categories of countries and regions of the world, to which must be added the specific social, cultural, scientific and technological conditions obtaining in different countries at different stages of development. Gelpi would fill out such categories further therefore with a sociological analysis of the distribution of power and the different forms taken by the struggles of groups, countries and regions for social transformation. The international division of labour is imposed upon countries and the international labour market conditions economic policies for reform and development, not to speak of the global military necessities which determine the fate of 'marginal' nations. In short, the international division of labour reflects the international balance of power. Its consequences can be described in terms of massive migrations of people and the transformation of processes of production and technology, together with the nature and possibilities of employment for children, youths and adults. The division between industrialized and developing countries is made manifest in these terms. Great disparities exist between these countries in terms of gross domestic product, rates of economic growth and so on. 'The general conclusion is inescapable that much of the world's output is produced and consumed by relatively few of its people.' The growth of world trade, as determined by the multinationals, will not benefit the majority of the peoples of the world and the industrialized countries will experience greater and greater competition. In all countries, however, education will come to have greater and greater significance, reproducing in its functions for production and technology the international division of labour in new forms.

In order to transform the division of labour and bring about what Gelpi describes as a new world order, it is necessary for lifelong education to take the form of a struggle for cultural identity. This is particularly the case where, as in most Third World countries, the productive system itself is defenceless in the face of the global movement of investment, technology and workers as a result of the operations of multinational corporations. Nor could the rich and industrialized countries of the OECD, the EEC and COMECON escape the competitive logic of the international division of labour, as planners, industrialists and trade unions strive to defend ever narrower categories of economic interest, and more and more vulnerable groups in society are pushed to the margins of affluence. In his writings Gelpi has paid much attention to the analysis of the situation of people who are, in some sense or other, marginalized by the international division of labour. In particular, therefore, he has addressed issues of trade union education and workers' education, of peasant culture and working-class culture and the problems of cultural identity, and of the significance of language teaching for migrant workers and their children (Gelpi, 1979, vol 2). In later work he addressed problems of urban and rural culture in comparative contexts of migration and international relations (Gelpi, 1985: Part 3) and the role of education in international relations between the countries and blocs and regions of the world (Gelpi, 1985: Part 4).

Clearly, the concept of lifelong education as developed in these scattered papers emerges sometimes as more easy to grasp in its abstract and dialectical nature than in its practice, despite the fact that Gelpi spent his life practising it worldwide. The practice asks for lifelong education that he envisages as follows:

1. The involvement of the widest possible representation of the people in the management of educational systems with open access to all the necessary information in order to perform the function effectively. The widest possible education of the entire population with the opportunity for them to acquire information about the most complex tasks of contemporary societies regarding production, social and cultural life.
2. The realization of educational reforms centred on new relationships between the social system, the production system and social and cultural movements.
3. The experimentation and development of educational structures capable of satisfying the demands both of particular publics and of the whole of the population, and capable of being a meeting place between traditional and modern education, formal and non-formal education, institutional education and self-directed learning.
4. The utilization of 'space' in, for example, educational institutions, workplaces, daily social life, and time and leisure, to encourage individual and collective self-directed learning and the creation of new knowledge and understanding.
5. The association of creative workers in different aspects of educational activity, from the perfection of educational methods and contents to their diffusion by means of mass media and teaching.

6. Initial and continuing education of educators in liaison with research, creative and productive activities.
7. The definition of methods and contents aiming at individual and collective fulfilment; full intellectual, manual, sensory, aesthetic, linguistic expression; psychological self and interpersonal equilibrium; identification with living, creative culture.
8. Establishment of schemes for the evaluation (chiefly educational) of knowledge acquisition, with more attention to the development of individuals and societies than to the mere internal coherence of educational institutions (Gelpi, 1985: 14).

In considering the practical tasks, however, the dialectical nature of lifelong education needs always to be borne in mind:

> The new world order, as well as the new international order of education, is at once a concrete objective and an ideal to be attained. The transition from the old to the new order appears to be both difficult and contradictory since the development toward the new world order is not strictly a linear one (Gelpi, 1985: 41).

The international context is as inescapable in terms of knowledge as it is in terms of production itself. 'The production and transfer of knowledge are among the most powerful instruments of new relations of domination or equality.' The contribution of education systems to the production of knowledge is diminishing in relation to other sources, such as the media. And broader conceptions of education itself, especially as linked to productive and cultural life, are emerging. Countries and populations are beginning to 'reappropriate' their educational and cultural histories and cultural creativity is becoming a major source of strength in the struggle against the national and international social hierarchies that the division of labour creates. At the same time, education systems continue to function to reproduce such hierarchies in both industrialized and developing countries. In the end, Gelpi trusts to what he describes as dynamic human creativity to frustrate the forces of oppression. As he says, 'history is full of surprises which enable men to be confident in their future'. Above all, Gelpi subscribes to a humanist belief for a new world order, envisaging a humanism that is 'anti-racist; sensitive to the different forms of human creativity; concerned with the individual and collective rights of men with respect to their objective and subjective existences; and, above all, active in the creation of an international society' (Gelpi, 1985: 43).

Gelpi's writings are, it has been said, a scattered and cumulative achievement rather than a systematic elaboration of the concept of lifelong education. The main features of his contribution to our thinking about education are, however, easy to identify:

1. He is a dialectical rather than an analytic thinker, concerned with the contradictory potential of policies rather than with abstract distinctions of theory

and practice, which tend to characterize Anglo-Saxon thinking about these things. Lifelong education is at the same time both a source of liberation and oppression. From Gelpi's point of view it is useless to talk of progressivism in pursuit of freedom without taking into account the social, political and cultural realities of people's lives.

2. Gelpi is consistent in his insistence upon the link between education and production. There is no point in talking about progressive education except in relation to systems of work and production, which constitute the basis of the social, political and cultural realities of people's lives and are at the heart of their experience of powerlessness and inequality.

3. There is no point in talking about systems of work and production without regard to the new forms being taken by the international division of labour. Thus educational work in relation to unemployment or underemployment, or in relation to workers' struggles, cannot be adequately conceptualized in national or regional terms alone.

4. In relation to adult education, lifelong education is obviously very much concerned with adult learning projects. Equally obviously, Gelpi does not see much resemblance between lifelong education and adult education as it generally exists. For one thing, as it exists, adult education continues to reproduce social hierarchies as well as offering opportunities for liberation. 'Adult education can play an important role', he says, 'only if it is not content to be merely a compensatory instrument' (Gelpi, 1979: vol 1:47).

5. Against the backdrop of the international division of labour, and the realities of work and production, it is unhelpful to conceptualize education in the narrow, age-specific categories of traditional adult education theory, which all too often projects ethnocentric concepts of adulthood and individual need. In Gelpi's terms, progressive education theory is as likely as not to contribute to the kind of cultural imperialism against which lifelong education, properly conceived, is an instrument of struggle.

6. Adult education as social policy, rather than as theory, is also challenged by Gelpi's concept of lifelong education. Such policies, as addressed to national issues, such as unemployment or poverty, are transformed by the realities of the international division of labour. In Britain, for example, adult education as a form of social policy is dissipating into forms of special provision for the special needs of special target groups of people. All such groups, according to Gelpi's way of thinking, experience the common effects of the division of labour and their common experience of marginalization must constitute the heart of any adult education policy if it is to be really effective in meeting their needs, rather than simply another officially inspired strategy to contain social conflict.

7. Ettore Gelpi is a humanist and a utopian. The struggle that he finds at the heart of the lifelong education project is not revolutionary but one arising out of the contradictory possibilities for freedom that exist in the repressive structures of the international division of labour. Self-directed learning alone could never bring into existence the new, humanistic world order that he

anticipates; only the analysis of the social and political realities of people's lives and the possibilities these present for transformation.

During the years when this analysis was being developed, Gelpi was already assuming that adult education, having failed to achieve its humanistic project as he saw it, needed to be subsumed under a wider category such as lifelong learning. Although he was not among the first to talk in terms of lifelong learning or the learning society, he was certainly one of the first to take a view of adult education as a failed project of modernity, with its narrow technicalities and its focus on adulthood at the expense of society. Only now are such dimensions as culture, production and consumption becoming central to the analysis of lifelong learning. In these respects he was a pioneer and since events have largely borne out his analysis his subsequent writings have consisted mostly of its development in new or emergent contexts.

One of the most important developments has been the issue of migrant workers and their contribution to cultural and economic production. Global conflicts and the global economy have between them created the conditions for the rather distinct but related issues of migrant labour, refugees and immigration. Gelpi's approach is to expose the underlying myths and realities behind these issues, stressing the positive aspects in terms of cultural identity and diversity that accompany such movements of people.

At the same time, in cases such as that of eastern Europe for example, he addresses the ideology of nationalism and the ways in which nationalist responses to immigration may mask other social conflicts. The role of all workers in economic and cultural production, the changing nature of work and above all the changing significance of employment and unemployment are all addressed in recent writings. The stress on culture remains very important for Gelpi and he continues to see cultural development as a function of production, technology and the organization of work.

Culture also remains at the heart of the struggle for identity and for democratic education systems. This is also the only basis for the struggle against social exclusion, which will not be obtained simply through the expansion of educational opportunities or guaranteed by a learning society. It could be said that the relation between production, culture and education remains the master concept of all of Gelpi's accounts of lifelong learning. Out of this relationship comes all he has to say about the importance of culture in the struggles for identity, which have become so prominent in recent years.

Gelpi has also addressed issues of peace and environmental issues in recent writings, considering the possibilities of non-violent resistance to the environmental damage that global capitalism inflicts on the world. Threats of global militarism continue to challenge the possibilities of Gelpi's one-world vision. The concept of what is now described as an ethical foreign policy has long been central to such a vision. It remains one of a moralized international community. There is, he says, an international economic community, but no international civil community.

Otherwise, he has continued to analyse another current concern, namely that of the meaning of citizenship in conditions of cultural pluralism, diversity, minorities and migration (Gelpi, 1996) as well as issues of human and social development, literacy, gender divisions, educational research and so on. Development, for example, he describes as 'a choice and as an action of the people', asserting the kind of rights of people to control over their own lives, which now seem under threat. Science and technology, for example, while in principle a potentially liberating force, may in practice contribute to new forms of social exclusion in society and in the world unless human values remain at the heart of development. Again, literacy is seen by Gelpi as strongly related to social and global inequalities rather than simply as a problem of national education systems.

These issues and analyses constitute the background against which Gelpi continues to formulate his own account of lifelong education policy. Undogmatic, sceptical, experiential, dialectical, humanistic, visionary and creative, it could be described as a progressivism for the postmodern age.

REFERENCES

Most of Gelpi's work is written in languages other than English. The following references are to all of his writings and writings about him that have so far appeared in English.

The three main references cited in the text and from which all the quotations are taken are as follows:

Gelpi, E (1979) *Future for Lifelong Education, vol 1: Principles, policies and practices*, trans R Ruddock, Department of Adult and Higher Education, University of Manchester, Manchester
Gelpi, E (1979) *Future for Lifelong Education, vol 2: Work and education*, trans R Ruddock, Department of Adult and Higher Education, University of Manchester, Manchester
Gelpi, E (1985) *Lifelong Education and International Relations*, Croom-Helm, London

By Gelpi:
Gelpi, E (1969) Structure and Functions of Italian Universities, Education in Europe, *Proceedings of the European Seminar on Sociology of Education*, pp 241–246, Mouton
Gelpi, E (1973) General and Vocational Education for Workers, General and Vocational Education, *Report of an international seminar*, Sankelmark/Flensburg, pp 72–76, German Commission for UNESCO, Cologne
Gelpi, E (1974) European Renaissance and Reformation, History of Education, *Encyclopaedia Britannica*, pp 343–348
Gelpi, E (1976) *Human Settlements and Education*, UNESCO, Paris
Gelpi, E (1977) Science Education and Society, in *Education in a Changing Society*, eds A Kloskowska and G Martinotti, pp 109–117, Sage, London
Gelpi, E (1979) Creativity, Contemporary Civilization, the Future of Mankind, *Dialectics and Humanism*, No 1, pp 99–103

Gelpi, E (1979) Lifelong Education Policies in Western and Eastern Europe: Similarities and differences, Recurrent Education and Lifelong Learning, *World Yearbook of Education 1979*, ed Tom Schuller, pp 167–76, Kogan Page, London

Gelpi, E (1979) *A Future for Lifelong Education: Principles, policies and practices*, Manchester Monographs 13, 1, Department of Adult and Higher Education, University of Manchester, Manchester

Gelpi, E (1979) *A Future for Lifelong Education: Work and education*, Manchester Monographs 13, 2, Department of Adult and Higher Education, University of Manchester, Manchester

Gelpi, E (1979) Lifelong Education: Suggestions for an evaluation of experiences, in *Lifelong Education: A stocktaking*, ed A J Cropley, pp 50–62, UNESCO Institute for Education, Hamburg

Gelpi, E (1980) Politics and Lifelong Education Policies and Practices, in *Towards a System of Lifelong Education: Some practical considerations*, ed A J Cropley, pp 16–31, UNESCO Institute for Education and Pergamon Press, Hamburg

Gelpi, E (1981) The Meaning of Life and the Meaning of History in Some Contemporary Cultures, *Dialectics and Humanism*, **VIII**, (3), pp 21–25

Gelpi, E (1981) Emerging Cultural and Educational Needs of Young Adult Learners, *Policy and Research in Adult Education*, pp 98–107, first Nottingham International Colloquium, Department of Adult Education, University of Nottingham

Gelpi, E (1982) International Division of Labour and Educational Policies, *Dialectics and Humanism*, **IX** (2), pp 5–10

Gelpi, E (1982) International Division of Labour and Educational Policies, *Education with Production*, **1**, (2), pp 64–76

Gelpi, E (1982) Education and Work: Preliminary thoughts on the encouragement of productive work in the educational process, *International Journal of Lifelong Education*, **1** (1), pp 53–63

Gelpi, E (1983) Teaching, *Encyclopedia of Occupational Health and Safety*, ILO, Geneva

Gelpi, E (1983) Learning for a Lifetime, *UNESCO Courier*, pp 4–7

Gelpi, E (1983) (with I Beraho-Beri) Work and Education: Ideological impasse or hope for an educational alternative? *Education with Production*, **2** (2), pp 49–53

Gelpi, E (1983) Culture in the City, *Dialectics and Humanism*, **X** (1), pp 183–88

Gelpi, E (1983) Intercultural Cooperation in Higher Education, Higher Education by the Year 2000, *Proceedings of the IVth International Congress of the European Association for Research and Development in Higher Education*, pp 138–152, Frankfurt am Main

Gelpi, E (1984) *Educational and Cultural Realities: Creative struggles for development*, mimeo, Department of Educational Studies, University of Surrey

Gelpi, E (1984) Lifelong Education: Opportunities and obstacles, *International Journal of Lifelong Education, 3 (2), pp 79–89*

Gelpi, E (1984) Encounters and Confrontation in Education, Scottish Journal of Adult Education, **6** (3), pp 5–12

Gelpi, E (1984) International Relationship, Lifelong Education and Adult Education, *Education and Society: Focus on Asia and the Pacific*, pp 92–100, Asian Students Association, Kowloon, Hong Kong

Gelpi, E (1985) Lifelong Education: Trends and issues, *Encyclopedia of Education*, Pergamon Press, Oxford

Gelpi, E (1985) Lifelong Education and International Relations, Lifelong Education and Participation, *papers presented at the Conference on Lifelong Education Initiatives in Mediterranean Countries*, pp 16–29, University of Malta Press, Malta

Gelpi, E (1985) *Lifelong Education and International Relations*, London, Croom-Helm

Gelpi, E (1985) Education, Work and the Young: Creativity and hopes, *Vocational Training*, No 17, pp 20–23

Gelpi, E (1985) Problems of Educational Research, *International Social Science Journal*, No 104, pp 149–156

Gelpi, E (1992a) *Conscience Terrienne : Recherche et formation*, McColl Publisher, Firenze

Gelpi, E (1992b) Scientific and Technological Change and Lifelong Education, *International Journal of Lifelong Education*, **11** (4), pp 329–34

Gelpi, E and Belanger, P (1994) Lifelong Education, reprinted from *International Review of Education*, **4** (3–5), Dordrecht, Kluwer

Gelpi, E (no date) *Towards a Democratic Citizenship: Adult education, democracy and development*, Council for Cultural Co-operation, Strasbourg

On Gelpi:

Cross, J (1981) A rediscovered unity, *Times Educational Supplement*, 5th June

Griffin, C (1983) Gelpi's View of Lifelong Education, *Curriculum Theory in Adult and Lifelong Education*, pp 172–200, Croom-Helm, London

Ireland, T D (1978) Gelpi's View of Lifelong Education, Manchester, *Manchester Monographs 14*, Department of Adult and Higher Education, University of Manchester

Ruddock, R (1981) A Trilogy of Extracts: The material issues (Ettore Gelpi), Evaluation: A consideration of principles and methods, *Manchester Monographs 18*, pp 94–101, Department of Adult and Higher Education, University of Manchester, Manchester

Suchodolski, B (1980) Ettore Gelpi on Lifelong Education, *Dialectics and Humanism*, No 1, pp 155–60

Other references:

Bates, L *et al* (1984) *Schooling for the Dole? The new vocationalism*, Macmillan, London

Coffield, F (1997) *A National Strategy for Lifelong Learning*, Department of Education, University of Newcastle, Newcastle upon Tyne

Dave, R H (1976) *Foundations of Lifelong Education*, Pergamon Press for UNESCO Institute for Education, Oxford

Elliott, G (1999) *Lifelong Learning: The politics of the new learning environment*, Jessica Kingsley, London

Gerhardt, Paul, Howard, Stuart and Parmar, Pratibha (1985) *The People Trade: An IBT study guide*, International Broadcasting Trust, London

Oliver, P (ed) (1999) *Lifelong and Continuing Education: What is the learning society?*, Ashgate, Aldershot

Trades Union Congress and United Nations Children's Fund (1985) *All Work and No Play*, Trades Union Congress, London

Chapter 18

Women in adult education – second rate or second class?

Mal Leicester

In contrast to the first collection of *Twentieth Century Thinkers in Adult Education* (Jarvis, 1987) this second collection includes attention to the contribution of women. In contrast to the rest of the second collection, however, in which, as before, we find a single 'great male' thinker, such as Paulo Freire or Robert Peers, separately celebrated in each paper, in this paper (with the exception of Pat Cross) all the females are gathered together. Where are the single, prominent 'great female' thinkers? Do they not exist? Are female theorists so few and so minor that they can readily be crammed together?

There are many reasons, of course, why female contributors to theorizing in adult education are fewer in number. There have been, and continues to be, educational barriers for women. Numerous studies at school level have shown how lower expectations, less teacher attention, parental bias, lack of social role models and so on combine to produce educational inequality (Sharpe, 1994). Fewer but sufficient studies at post-school level reveal a similar picture of unequal opportunity. (Benn *et al*, 1998).

Moreover, at the level of higher education, the universities, those very institutions whose *raison d'etre* is research and reflection, preserve male privilege. In addition to direct gender prejudice, the weighty forces of indirect institutional discrimination not only hold women back from entry, but once in, from promotions and power. Cronyism and the inflexibility of an inherent conservatism take their toll. The very structure of the university is that of a patriarchal Victorian household, with the father figure (the vice-chancellor) the older brothers (heads of department) and the children (male academics and their rather alarming, bookish sisters, the female academics). These 'children' are looked after by nannies (secretaries) while the housemaids (cleaners) go about their invisible work (Kelley and Leicester, 1995). In short, even when women overcome the barriers to becoming adult students to take their place, at last, as theorists in the academy, they continue to meet forms of structural discrimination, which reduce the scope and impact of their work. As Kelly and Slaughter document and explore:

> Women, even when academics, are in marginalised positions in higher education, hired as part-time teachers and as junior faculty. In many countries like the United States, they are hired to teach disproportionately in junior colleges and clustered in female fields like the Humanities, Education and Nursing. Higher education may incorporate women as students, but the institutions remain dominated by men who serve as professors and administrators and hold power and authority in the institution. (Kelly and Slaughter, 1990: 9).

Not that we should conclude that structural sexism is the only reason for the relative lack of great female thinkers. Some women make significant contributions against these odds. But who evaluates and elevates an individual to guru status or influential prominence? Mainly men!

Some feminists would argue that women's ways of working tend to be less individualistic and competitive. In general, it is claimed, women are more collaborative and put less time into self-promotion.

For these reasons, among others, it is not surprising that women's names are absent from the usual guru pantheon. Rather one thinks of a whole galaxy of able female thinkers who have quietly and collegially added to our collective understandings of our field: Acker, Thompson, Benn, Keddie, Westwood, Coates, Weil, McLaren, Whaley, to name but a few. Let us acknowledge that women like these who, against the odds, have also contributed to the achievement of putting gender on the post-school agenda.

In what follows I have divided contributions into two categories. First I cover, briefly, women whose work has added to our knowledge about women as adult students and teachers, and second turn to ideas that have enriched feminist understandings of the theory and practice of adult education.

WOMEN IN ADULT EDUCATION

The invisibility of female 'great thinkers' was, for a long time, matched by the invisibility of women within the category 'mature students' because large-scale studies of such students treated them as a homogeneous group (eg Woodley *et al*, 1987). Thanks to a number of female researchers, (eg Benn *et al*, 1998; McLaren, 1985; Merrill, 1999; Edwards, 1993; Hughes and Kennedy, 1985; etc) understandings of women's experiences and perspectives are beginning to emerge.

Some of this research investigates non-university adult education, including women on Access programmes and women taking women's studies courses. Some empirical studies investigate university women students (eg Acker, 1994;

Pascall and Cox, 1993) and some focus on female academics (Davies *et al*, 1994; Moreley and Walsh, 1995) and in international perspective (Kelly and Slaughter, 1991). Barbara Merrill (1999) documents the research that has been undertaken on mature women students, particularly in higher education. She begins with the pioneering study by McLaren (1985) because, although this is not about universities, her longitudinal study provided a full account of mature women's experiences in a residential adult education colleges and showed how studying impacted on their family life. Within higher education, Edwards also explored the way in which the public and private lives of women students impinge upon each other (Edwards, 1993). Merrill also mentions McGivney (1992) who has comprehensively researched non-university adult education and Benn *et al* (1998) who research the experiences of women in a wide range of continuing education. She describes Pascall and Cox's (1993) 'optimistic' study in which education is seen as potentially empowering for women and Usher's (1982) more pessimistic view that university adult education contributes to the sexual division of labour, which undermines genuine equality of opportunity for women. Sperling (1991) finds gender inequality in mature students' access to higher education, detailing structural and attitudinal barriers. Most admission tutors are male, for example, and view women as less reliable than male adult students because of domestic commitments.

Weil (1986, 1989) is concerned with learning experiences from the perspectives of the students. Class, gender and ethnicity shape these experiences, experiences that are not taken account of by the institution. Another recent study explores the experiences of mature women studying by distance learning with the Open University (Lunnebourg, 1994).

Merrill concludes from her survey that though research is growing, it is by no means extensive. How do the experiences of mature female students on various modes of degree compare to those of adult male students? She asks whether it is possible to combine macro and micro sociological approaches to understanding this experience, and it is to these more theoretical female contributions to our understanding of adult education that I now turn.

WOMEN ON ADULT EDUCATION

Jane Thompson has been an influential feminist theorist in adult education over a long period from the 1980s into the new millennium. I will mainly focus on Thompson's ideas – because of her merit, influence and challenge – while recognizing that there have been many other important female thinkers. In a way I think of her as representing these others (eg Acker, 1994; Westwood, 1980; Mayo and Thompson, 1995).

I have always admired the close interrelation of theory and practice in Thompson's work. Her theoretical writing has been grounded in the practice with which she has been simultaneously engaged. Thus in the 1980s her pioneering work in second chance education for women inspired both the practice of others and her own reflection. This grounding remains the case as is testified by the paper that is included in a collection on lifelong learning (Field and Leicester, 2000). In this paper she illustrates her concern that the lifelong learning agenda often omits reference to collective learning with an example of such useful learning through collective action at the Rosemount Resources Centre in Derry.

Back in 1980 her collection *Adult Education for a Change* was influential and has remained so. (Incidentally, it was this influence that led me to title my own book, on anti-racist continuing and higher education, *Race for a Change*). This book exemplifies Thompson's tendency to include both theory and practice. The first section (Perspectives) is grounded in theory and the second (Selected Studies) provides focus on a range of actual initiatives. The purpose of the collection was to look beyond the accepted orthodoxy and to initiate a serious debate. Sally Westwood's opening chapter sets the tone. She is concerned with the middle-class bias of adult education and the need to understand it in order to reconstruct and radicalize it.

Nell Keddie, another important female thinker on adult education, also contributed a paper to this collection. She questions the distinctiveness of adult education. Like primary education, adult education emphasizes the importance of individuals, claiming a student-centred concern with individual needs. She points out that this 'individualism' actually produces uniformity and encourages competitiveness. To radicalize adult education will not be possible if 'meeting individual need' is understood in terms of individual achievement and middle-class lifestyles. In what is almost an early communitarianism, Keddie ends with the claim that:

> Adult education responds to the collective voice of individualism, but it has in a large measure failed to identify or to identify with the needs of those who reject the premises on which individualism is based (Keddie, 1980: 64).

In Thompson's own paper in this section, on the disadvantaged, she too is concerned about the devaluing and marginalization of the working class and, just as she will later argue about women's education and the women's movement, she argues that there is a need for working-class consciousness raising through adult education linked to social change. In the final paper of the collection she reinforces this message. She reminds us of the link between knowledge and social control and argues that education should provide working men and women with a cultural and political tool. Adult education should be a radical force, part of the struggle for socialism 'to provide, for all those who have had least in the past, adult education for a change' (Thompson, 1980). In 1981 Thompson established the Women's Education Centre as the first of its kind. It was funded by Southampton University, the WEA and Hampshire LEA but was organized for the 10 years of its existence by the women who were its members. In 1983 she wrote directly about *Women and Adult Education* (Tight, 1983) claiming that sexism characterized adult education organization and policy. Local authority and university extramural provision was dominated by men's ideas about what was appropriate for women: not 'really useful knowledge' but leisure activities and domestic skills.

These criticisms were of a sector whose self-image was that of offering a student-centred, democratic service contrasting with the 'mainstream' education system. It was easy for male adult educators to be complacent about provision that had grown out of a working-class movement while failing to consider the position of women. Although adult education was the only sector of the education system in which women students were a significant majority, 'an essentially female past-time is none the less managed and orchestrated by men within a system of female subordination. There assumptions and experience are constructed within a context of male values, male definitions and male authority and are then generalised to represent human assumptions and experience and indicted with universal validity and objective truth!' (Thompson, 1983: 45).

Such provision had largely abandoned a concern with social change, except for women's studies, which were helping to 'consolidate the growing rejection of patriarchal authority by increasing numbers of women' (Thompson, 1983). Thompson illustrates this contention by reference to the establishment and work of the Women's Education Centre. Here women defined their own concerns (child care, male violence, equal opportunities at work, health issues, the women's peace movement) and took collective decisions about centre policies and activities. This female control, Thompson argued, was crucial.

> In the education system generally men control 97 per cent of the government of education. The distribution in adult education is not radically different. Only when this is shared on a fifty-fifty basis with women, and when the cultural heritage and validity of women's experience is reflected in the curriculum, shall we begin to imagine an education system which serves both sexes equally. (Thompson, 1983: 51).

In the same year Thompson also published *Learning Liberation: Women's response to men's education*. This was one of the first publications in adult education to explore the domination of women's education by male authorities. It can therefore be seen as one of the first influences to encourage a feminist stance, in several countries, to adult education theory and practice.

One of Thompson's main arguments was that women's education should be part of the struggle for women's liberation. Radical learning can assist in the consciousness raising necessary to collective action for social change. In the course of such argument she often draws on insights from a more general feminist literature to illustrate sexism in adult education, insights such as the gendered nature of the English language and the marginalization of women. She disseminates the words of particular women, which carry the collective wisdom of countless women who have lived and shared a similar experience.

Living on an estate has shown me the feeling of hopelessness that so many working-class women feel. Trapped by bad education, early marriage and children.

The kind of liberation we were being pushed into was sexual liberation. Sexual liberation was merely about removing even more of the barriers that prevented us being readily available to men.

I felt there was something wrong in the reality that the person who was the wage earner, was also, almost by that fact, the main decision maker; that the wage-earner's time was seen as more valuable, and his opinion better informed and of greater insight than the homemakers; that his outside commitments, however many hours they occupied, were almost always awarded first priority. (Thompson, 1993b: 31–34).

Thompson points out the contradiction between the view that women should find fulfilment in their families and the dissatisfactions that confuse, anger and depress so many women. She argues that relationships between men and women have to change and that education has an important part to play – education that will have to be of women's making.

In 1988 Thompson explicitly connects adult education and the women's movement (Lovett, 1988). She continues to argue the need for separate education for women within the direction and control of women, not as a confidence building exercise, but as part of women's liberation.

In her edited collection with Mayo (Thompson and Mayo, 1995) she explores the contribution made by the women's movement to adult education, considering that it has been of tremendous importance in the recognition and creation of what counts as 'really useful knowledge'. Not simply in the recent past, in relation to second-wave feminism, but also in relation to the educational imperatives of the suffragettes and suffragists, the cooperative women's guilds and the early struggles to establish women's trade unions. Knowledge that is 'really useful' raises critical awareness and understanding of how oppressions are structured and sustained.

The dominant liberal tradition in adult education excluded the voices of 'working class, women-centred and black consciousness'. Personal knowledge and commitment to collectivism were more important than the traditional forms of authority and wisdom as represented, for example, by the male gurus such as Illich and Freire. Such feminist knowledge gained ground through academic women's studies programmes.

In this particular paper she also notes the relativistic dangers of postmodernism, its danger to structural explanation of social inequality, to collective action and to political will. At this time Thompson was teaching at Ruskin and she describes the development of the women's studies programme there, as usual interrelating her theoretical perspectives and her practical experiences at a given time.

THE INFLUENCE OF FEMINIST THOUGHT

Women thinkers in the field of adult education have been influenced by feminist theorists in the academic world beyond that field. These feminist theorists are many and have contributed much to our understanding of women's experience and our understanding of the many structural forms of sexist oppression. To illustrate this I again want to include a thinker whose influential work I admire as a kind of representative of many others.

Carol Gilligan has enriched our understanding of women's ethical thought and in doing so has provided an illuminating example of how women can be negatively evaluated. The influential (male) thinker, Lawrence Kohlberg, had established a sequence of stages of moral reasoning about moral dilemmas. His work had seemed to show that on the whole men tended to reach higher stages of such reasoning than do women. Men seemed, relative to women, to have higher levels of understanding about justice and the application of moral principles. Gilligan, working with women, established that women on the whole, more than men on the whole, incorporate a concern with care, with special relationships and with context, as distinct from (Kohlbergian) justice and the application of abstract 'universal' principles. It is not the case that women are less able than are men to produce higher stages of reasoning about moral dilemmas so much as that they bring a different and equally important set of moral values to the resolution of such dilemmas.

WOMEN'S WAYS OF KNOWING

This distinct moral perspective, researched by Gilligan, could be seen as a particular instance of the general, feminist contention that women's ways of knowing are often invisible, or, when visible, undervalued. Since education is considered to be concerned with the development of worthwhile knowledge and understanding, for educators, including adult educators, epistemological questions about the nature of knowledge (and if and how it makes sense to claim that knowledge is gendered) are crucial ones.

Such discourse about women's ways of knowing has, traditionally, emphasized knowledge that is generated by reflection on personal experience. The claim is that we have insufficiently recognized the epistemological potential of autobiography and story. Though we recognize the power of 'the great writer' to generate fruitful, valid insight, a kind of truth through fiction, we have devalued this form of knowledge in the anecdotes and narratives of 'ordinary' lives. Where social science research has dealt with personal experience, there is a scientistic/positivistic obsession with the quantity of such qualitative material. Yet recognition of the general 'truth' within its necessary particularity and locatedness adds to our understanding in ways that the 'universal', abstract academic disciplines, such as philosophy, by their very nature, fail to capture.

Similarly, the academic disciplines sift out human emotion and the particularity of human relationships leaving an epistemological undervaluing of emotional intelligence and insights. Moreover, whereas the paradigm changes that occur, from time to time, for the traditional disciplines (forms of knowledge) rely on fundamental shifts in framework assumptions, for 'women's ways of knowing' such fundamental shifts in perspective, gestalt switches, tend to occur through lateral thinking or change of metaphor or reflexive attention, in the knowledge making, to the knower herself.

The idea that knowledge can be gendered is more fundamental than the idea that there is much data still to be found out about women and their lives, their participation in adult education or their position in the labour market, etc. It is the idea that knowledge is a social construct and, therefore, influenced in the construction by the shared experiences, values and perspectives of the constructors. If women do not play a significant part in the constructing of knowledge, knowledge itself is impoverished. In other words, if women's shared experiences, values, interests, etc, are part of the social construction of knowledge, new insights, understandings, concepts, paradigms, etc, will emerge and enrich our shared human forms of understanding. (As I have indicated, I refer here not to new information, but to new ways of knowing).

Thus have feminists rightly challenged bias in the established academic disciplines and developed interdisciplinary research agendas. In so doing they have generated new areas of knowledge. And in women's studies not only do we see that a new area of knowledge has been constructed, but, in a sense, we see in action the epistemological assumptions which these developments presuppose.

In a recent and very interesting book, feminist adult educator Jean Barr (1999) has engaged with these fascinating epistemological questions. This book, *Liberating Knowledge: Research, feminism and adult education*, is underpinned by the kind of epistemological constructivism to which I have referred, but in the service of a radical and feminist adult education agenda. Barr means, by 'liberating knowledge', both that knowledge can be liberating and that what counts as knowledge can be contested.

> Women's education as it developed in adult education thus challenged, in concrete, practical ways, the notion of disembodied knowledge, recognizing that knowledge is not neutral, but always socially situated: there is no 'God's eye view', no 'knowledge from nowhere.' (p 40).

In keeping with this epistemological position, Barr begins with a brief preface in which she provides information about her Glasgow childhood. It seems to me that if all thinkers were to provide such a succinct, interesting and pertinent foreword to indicate their formative values, experiences and social background this would indeed add to our insight into the general thesis that the work which follows cannot be 'neutral'. Moreover, we will have a deeper understanding of the particular research/theorizing in question. She maintains that we over-privilege academic and abstract knowledge and undervalue knowledge generated by personal experience or derived from narrative modes, metaphor, emotional understandings. Her final word is that:

> A failure to transgress by being far too deferential to academic, abstract knowledge, for example, all too frequently goes hand in hand with a failure to produce really useful knowledge, that is, knowledge which enables an understanding of human experience, enhances self-respect and helps people to deal critically and creatively with the world in order to change it. (p 163).

I suggested at the beginning of this chapter that the prominent 'male thinker' approach to adult education is at odds with these feminist ways of knowing and working. Barr makes a similar point.

> If we are to develop more inclusive practices of knowledge development we need to abandon once and for all the prevalent individualistic and heroic notion (and myth) of knowledge development which is enshrined in our education system. We need, in other words, to acknowledge the part played by social processes and collective change in the development of knowledge (Evans, 1995). This goes as much for adult education as a field of study as any other. In the adult education literature, certain figures – like Paulo Freire, Antonio Gramsci and Raymond Williams, for instance (but especially Freire) – have huge symbolic significance as 'radical heroes'. 'The trouble with the radical heroes story is that once individuals are fetishised, their ideas cease to be open and productive of new insights, challenge is disallowed and debate dies' (Coben, 1998) (p 154).

CONCLUSION

In this chapter I have suggested that the lack of female guru figures in adult education tells us more about sexism in adult education than about a genuine lack of important female contributions to theory and practice. We have seen that many women have contributed to our knowledge about women and adult education and to our understanding of related theoretical issues.

Of course, women have also contributed, alongside men, to non-gendered aspects of adult education. I have focused on the gendered aspects because almost all the contributors to these aspects are women. In the course of my discussions I have effortlessly made more than 20 references to significant work of female adult educators.

These women researchers and theorists are high achievers. They have put gender on the agenda and dented sexism. However, because male power remains dominant, these first-rate female thinkers remain second-class citizens in the academic male stream.

REFERENCES

Acker, S (1994) *Gendered Education*, Open University Press, Buckingham

Barr, J (1999) *Liberating Knowledge: Research, feminism and adult education*, NIACE, Leicester

Benn, R *et al* (1998) *Educating Rita*, NIACE, Leicester

Coates, M (1994) *Women's Education*, Society for Research in Higher Education, Open University Press, Buckingham

Coben, D (1998) Radical Heroes: Gramsci, Friere and the politics of adult education, *Studies in the History of Education*, 6, Garland Publishing Inc, New York

Davies, S *et al* (1994) *Women in Higher Education*, Taylor & Francis, London

Edwards, R (1993) *Mature Women Students: Separating or connecting family and education*, Taylor and Francis, London

Evans, M (1995) Ivory Towers: Life in the mind, in Morley, L and Walsh, V (eds) *Feminist Agents for Change*, Taylor and Francis, London

Field, J and Leicester, M (2000) *Perspectives on Lifelong Education*, Falmer Press, London

Gilligan, C (1982) *In a Different Voice: Psychological theory and women's development*, Harvard University Press, Cambridge, MA

Hughes, M and Kennedy, M (1985) *New Futures Changing Women's Education*, Routledge & Kegan Paul, London

Jarvis, P (1987) *Twentieth Century Thinkers in Adult Education*, Croom-Helm Ltd, London

Keddie, N (1980) Adult Education: An ideology of individualism, in *Adult Education for a Change*, ed Jane L Thompson, Hutchinson, London

Kelley, E and Leicester, M (1995) Upstairs, downstairs: Universities as Victorian households, in *Women and Higher Education Past, Present and Future*, Aberdeen University Press, Aberdeen

Kelly, G P and Slaughter, S (1991) *Women's Higher Education in Comparative Perspective*, Kluwer, Boston

Kohlberg, L (1981) *The Philosophy of Moral Development*, Harper & Row, San Francisco

Leicester, M (1993) *Race for a Change in Continuing and Higher Education*, Society for Research in Higher Education, Open University Press, Buckingham

Lovett, T (1988) *Radical Approaches to Adult Education: A reader*, Routledge, London

Lunnebourg, F (1994) *Undoing Educational Obstacles*, Cassell, London

Mayo, M and Thompson, J (1995) *Adult Learning, Critical Intelligence and Social Change*, pp 124–136, NIACE, Leicester

McGivney, V (1992) *Tracking Adult Learning Routes*, NIACE, Leicester

McLaren, A (1985) *Ambitions and Realisations: Women in adult education*, Peter Owen, London

Merrill, B (1999) *Gender, Change and Identity: Mature women students in universities*, Ashgate Publishing Ltd, Aldershot

Morley, L and Walsh, V (1995) *Feminist Academics*, Taylor & Francis, London

Pascall, G and Cox, R (1993) *Women Returning to HE*, Society for Research in Higher Education, Open University Press, Buckingham

Sharpe, S (1994) *Just Like a Girl*, Penguin, Harmondsworth

Sperling, L (1991) Can the Barriers be Breached? Mature women's access to higher education, *Gender and Education*, **3** (2), pp 199–213

Thompson, Jane L (1980) *Adult Education for a Change*, Hutchinson & Co Ltd, London

Thompson, Jane L (1980) Adult Education and the Disadvantaged, in *Adult Education for a Change*, ed Jane L Thompson, Hutchinson & Co Ltd, London

Thompson, Jane L (1980) Adult Education for a Change, in *Adult Education for a Change*, ed Jane L Thompson, Hutchinson & Co Ltd, London

Thompson, Jane L (1980) Introduction, in *Adult Education for a Change*, ed Jane L Thompson, Hutchinson & Co Ltd, London

Thompson, Jane L (1982) *Women, Class and Adult Education*, Department of Continuing Education, University of Southampton, Southampton

Thompson, Jane L (1983) Women and Adult Education, in *Opportunities for Adult Education*, ed M Tight, Croom-Helm, London

Thompson, Jane L (1983) *Learning Liberation: Women's response to men's education*, Croom-Helm, London

Thompson, Jane L (1993) Learning, Liberation and Maturity: An open letter to whoever's left, *Adults Learning*, **4** (9), p 244

Thompson, J (1988) Adult Education and the Women's Movement, in *Radical Approaches to Adult Education: A reader*, ed T Lovett, Routledge, London

Thompson, Jane L (1995) Feminism and Women's Education in *Adult Learning Critical Intelligence and Social Change*, eds M Mayo and J Thompson, pp 124–36, NIACE, Leicester

Tight, M, *Opportunities for Adult Education*, Croom-Helm, London

Usher, P (1982) Women and University Extension, in *Women, Class and Adult Education*, University of Southampton, Southampton

Weil, S (1986) Non-traditional Learners within HE institutions: Discovery and disappointment, *Studies in Higher Education*, **11** (3), pp 219–35

Weil, S (1989) From a Language of Observation to a Language of Experience: Studying the prospectives of diverse adults in higher education, *Journal of Access Studies*, **3** (1), pp 17–43

Westwood, S (1980) Adult Education and the Sociology of Education: An exploration, in *Adult Education for a Change*, ed Jane L Thompson, Hutchinson, London

Woodley, A *et al* (1987) *Choosing to Learn*, Society for Research in Higher Education, Open University Press, Buckingham

Conclusion: Adult education at the end of the twentieth century

Peter Jarvis

This book commenced with a thesis about adult education as a social movement and highlighted the way that it has been changed over the century. In this chapter we shall return to this theme, first of all by establishing that adult education was a social movement and then by illustrating how some of the values became less significant as adult education gained social acceptability and became a field of study, as well as a field of practice. Finally, it will be argued that as adult education has become subsumed in the lifelong learning market, these values need to be rediscovered. The values underlying the adult education movement in the West were basically Christian, although those whose work was primarily scholarship, rather than activism, do not display the same religious values so overtly in their work. This distinction illustrates the difference between the movement and the profession and both are equally important to our considerations. We shall return to this when we examine lifelong learning and the learning society in the final part of this chapter.

PART 1: ADULT EDUCATION AS A SOCIAL MOVEMENT

Initially, we need to establish that adult education was a social movement during the period that we now know as modernity and in this section I have relied quite a lot on my previous writing on adult education as a social movement (Jarvis, 1997). Within the sociological literature, there is a broad general agreement as to a definition of social movement. For instance:

> The term covers various forms of collective action aimed at social reorganization. In general, social movements are not highly institutionalized, but arise from spontaneous social protest directed at specific or widespread grievances. (Abercrombie, Hill and Turner, 1984: 227).

In Smelser's classic study of collective behaviour (1962: 23), it is defined as 'a collective redefinition of an unstructured situation'. He outlines a variety of types of collective behaviour – two of which are especially applicable to the adult education movement – norm-oriented and value-oriented movements. Adult education was a norm-oriented movement since it sought to change the way that education was structured so that it catered for adults as well as children. It was a value-oriented movement because underlying its activities has been the belief that all human beings have equal rights to education, irrespective of their class, gender or age. Indeed, we shall return to this in the following sections of this chapter.

More recently, Scott (1992: 139) also made a similar distinction between structural and social action movements – both of which may also be related to adult education in a similar manner since adult education has both sought to change social structures and adult educators have endeavoured at times to act as a force in the polity debate.

Social movements, according to Scott (1992: 132) have the following five characteristics:

1. occasional mass mobilisation;
2. loose organizational structure;
3. spasmodic activity;
4. working at least in part outside the established frameworks;
5. seeking to bring about (or prevent) social change.

Scott does not emphasize here the values underlying the movement but it is these that drive individuals to be active and either to create or to inhibit social change. It will be clear in the opening section of this chapter that many of the characteristics regarded as intrinsic to social movements have been exhibited by adult education.

Tilly (1984) actually argues that social movements are themselves a product of modernity, which arise because societies have developed some of the following characteristics:

- a nationalization of politics;
- a greatly increased role in special purpose organizations;
- a decline in the importance of shared interest communities;
- a growing importance of organized capital and organized labour as participants in the power struggle.

While Tilly is mainly right, adult education began as a movement before the Enlightenment because Protestantism (a 'special purpose' organization in Tilly's terms) sought to exercise both an evangelical and an adult literacy mission so that many people could be taught to read the bible. Kelly (1970) recognized Protestantism as one of the earliest forms of adult education – indeed, the Methodists actually called their midweek meetings 'class meetings'. By the start of the Enlightenment, there was already an adult education movement within a larger social movement in Britain and the USA. Nevertheless, Protestantism has not had a monopoly in social activism in adult education since both Freire and Coady were members of the Church of Rome.

PART 2: THE INFLUENCE OF RELIGIOUS BELIEF UPON THE GROWTH OF ADULT EDUCATION

A recurring theme in many of the above chapters has been the religious belief of the thinkers whose work has been discussed; this is as true for the thinkers in Britain as it is for those in the Americas. Indeed, this influence is still to be found among educators, especially adult educators, as was demonstrated by the book *Adult Education and Theological Interpretations* (Jarvis and Walters, 1993)

Perhaps the most significant thing about this commitment is that its out-workings are totally social; it is an element of the social gospel of Christianity and a highly sophisticated doctrine of the human being. From Mansbridge to Coady and from Tawney to Freire, there is a consistent pattern of religious belief being a motivating factor in the lives of these adult educators. At the same time, it must be recognized that the way that the belief is put into practice varies from one thinker to another. Mansbridge, for instance, enlisted the help of the establishment in order to propagate his ideas, while Freire was much more revolutionary, adopting the prophetic role and confronting the power structures of his country, although he was finally accepted and adopted by them. But this difference should not be regarded as surprising since the Christian religion has always produced a variety of different responses to social inequality. Yet, in different ways, there are a number of recurring themes that may be discovered in these chapters:

- concern for the poor and the working classes coupled with indignation at social inequality;
- idealism and the belief that the education of adults can help provide a base for a better world;
- belief that people can learn throughout their lives and that education should, therefore, be a lifelong provision.

Each of these themes will now be briefly discussed individually.

Social inequality

A recurring theme in nearly all of the writers is that the poor and the working classes have not had sufficient opportunity to be educated and to enjoy the fruits of knowledge. This is not something that is new to the 20th century, as is well known, and may be illustrated from the work of the Christian Socialists in Britain in the previous century (Gibson, 1986). Even so, Christian socialism may be found in the ideas of many of the thinkers discussed in this book: Mansbridge founded the Workers' Educational Association, Coady and Horton were both involved in workers' movements, Horton was also involved in civil rights and Tawney was concerned about the conditions of the poor. Freire, however, may be located within the liberation theological movement that emerged in South America in the 1950s and 1960s. In addition, both Knowles and Kidd had a period in their adult education careers working with the Young Men's Christian Association and much of Lindeman's academic career was in social work. It is perhaps not surprising that in the light of the above that some of these writers expressed their Christian belief in their philosophies of adult education.

There was also a great concern that adult education is a democratic process with adult learners owning their own knowledge and experience. Consequently, the relationship between teachers and learners had to be democratic – something that has become a fundamental tenet of some philosophies of teaching in adult education. Knowles epitomized it in his understanding of andragogy but Freire took the argument even further by pointing out that the teaching and learning interaction is not a teacher-student relationship but a teacher/student-student/teacher relationship where each learns from and teaches the other. This democratic relationship certainly reflects the Christian beliefs of many of the authors but it is also significant that in many situations it has become recognized as being fundamental to adult learning.

However, the Christian churches have been slow to recognize the inequality experienced by women; the reason for this is that many Christians wrongly believed that the social structures of the world were inspired by God and that the women's place was in the home. Consequently, it is clear that feminism in adult education is a secular crusade as was evident in the work of Thompson, discussed in the previous chapter. However, Hart and Horton (1992) have interpreted this from a spiritual, but not Christian, perspective. In addition, the learning needs of the elderly were not considered by the early adult education thinkers and it is only in the latter half of the last century that educational gerontology has become a major sub-discipline of education.

Religion is not the only driving force underlying the social concerns of adult education. In Gelpi's work, for instance, there are the recurrent themes of social justice, the right to work and the relationship between education and work. In a sense, Gelpi's focus is on the relationship between education and work rather than just the right to education per se since he wrote at a later period. Even so, the early thinkers were not unaware of the economic benefits to the nation of an educated workforce, for the 1919 Report on Adult Education in Britain specifies that the sound economic recovery of the nation, after the 1914–18 war, was dependent upon an educated workforce (HMSO, 1919, para 7).

The majority of these writers were concerned that social inequality should be overcome without too great a disruption to the social structures of society. They were clearly reformist rather than radical (Jarvis, 1985: 8–14), but others were

liberal rather than reformist since they viewed education as the force for development of the individual, who was then empowered to act as an individual
agent. It is perhaps significant that few of the early writers on adult education in
the last century actually regarded adult education as constraining people and
perhaps acting as a hegemonic force, something which also reflects the liberal and
reformist ideologies that they espoused.

Freire, in contrast, proclaimed a more revolutionary perspective based on the
idea that people's thought processes are ensnared in the hegemonic culture into
which they are born and socialized, so that liberation through conscientization
became part of his message. It is significant that he is the only writer from the
South included in this collection and had other such writers been included here
there is little doubt that they would have also portrayed a more radical perspective than those from the North. However, liberation is meaningless unless those
people who have been freed seek to recreate the social world in which they live.
Freire recognized that the oppressors were also trapped within their world and
few would lay down the reins of power voluntarily, so that his revolutionary
perspective culminates in the need for reconciliation between the oppressed and
the oppressors.

Adult education for a better world

One of the major themes of Christian theology is that in the fullness of time the
world will be re-created into a more perfect place. In a sense this was also a major
concern in Marxist thought, where the outcome of the class struggle was to be a
classless society. Whether religious or secular, looking forward to a time when
the world is a better place than it is today has been a constant hope and thinkers
from both persuasions, and a combination of the two, have seen education as a
means to creating this better world, often through the creation of more active
citizens. Education should not, therefore, be the prerogative of the wealthy and
the leisured classes but open to all. Perhaps the claim in the famous 1919 Report
summarizes this belief:

> That the necessary conclusion is that adult education must not be regarded as a
> luxury for the few exceptional persons here and there, nor as a thing which concerns
> only a short span of early manhood, but that adult education is a permanent national
> necessity, an inseparable aspect of citizenship, and therefore should be universal and
> lifelong (HMSO, 1919: para 5).

Mansbridge, Yeaxlee and Tawney all served on that committee, so that it is
hardly surprising that these words do reflect these early thinkers' beliefs. Clearly,
Kidd's work in both the Canadian Association and in founding the International
Council was because he believed that adult education could help create a more
democratic and a better world for all people. More recently, Ranson's (1994)
work on the creation of a learning society also falls into this tradition, in which
education is seen as a means to achieve a better, more egalitarian society.

Horton, working in slightly different conditions, also embraced the cause of the exploited black population through the civil rights movement in the southern United States. Sharing the vision of Martin Luther King, the adult educator has to assist those whose education has not already equipped them to assert themselves, negotiate with their oppressors and, if necessary, to use the peaceful forces at their disposal – such as the withdrawal of labour and public demonstration – in order to create better working and living conditions for and with the people.

Other thinkers, like Gelpi, have taught that people have the right to work, so that their lives may be enriched, and that they have the right to be educated for work throughout their lives. Nearly every thinker included in this book has claimed that the provision of education throughout the lifetime can result in an enriched life and some have argued that education is a means to create a better society for all. In a real sense, most of the thinkers would see education as a significant means to a desirable end, rather than as an end in itself (Dewey, 1916: 50). But Giddens (1998: 109–10) reminds us that the idea that education can reduce inequalities directly should be regarded with some scepticism since it has tended to serve as a reproductive mechanism in many cases, especially in its institutionalized form.

It is perhaps significant to note that adult education has long regarded itself as a movement and outside of the educational institution. However, its early protagonists endeavoured to get it accepted within the institution, but its values, as a movement, tend to become less significant in the process of institutionalization. It is perhaps this commitment above all that has been quite crucial to the development of adult education. Even so, many of its practitioners still regard it as a service to others and as a moral process, so that they can still work to extend participation and work with the socially excluded. Paradoxically, it is the capitalist system that has ultimately been responsible for many of the changes that have helped institutionalize the education of adults that, when functioning efficiently, creates social exclusion. It was this recognition that led to Illich and Verne to write *Imprisoned in a Global Classroom* in 1976.

Not all thinkers included in this book were activists but their contribution is just as important to the development of the field. They were not among the early thinkers but as adult education became more established and gained a foothold within universities they became very significant to its development. Peers, as the first professor of adult education, pointed the way in the United Kingdom and many others were to follow. Houle did the same in USA and his legacy is still with the field in the form of Houle scholars and Houle Awards. Cross's research has also played an important role in the development of the theory and practice of education, especially in helping people understand the adult learner. As adult education has embraced the world of work, the scholarship of Schon and Argyris has developed the field in many ways, enhancing learning theory and helping our understanding of learning in work situations.

There is a sense in which adult education was coming of age and there was less need for the activism of the past as professors in the 1960s and 1970s struggled for academic recognition. But as we pointed out in the first chapter some of the changes that were occurring in education, and especially in adult education, were happening not only because of the high quality of these thinkers; social and economic forces were at work helping to create lifelong education in Western societies – something many of these early activists had hoped for. But what occurred was not quite what they wanted.

PART 3: LIFELONG LEARNING AND LIFELONG EDUCATION:

It was suggested in the opening chapter of this book that adult education has been subsumed within lifelong education and lifelong learning. Clearly the concern with lifelong education did not just arise 'out of the blue', as it were. Throughout the chapters in this book, the theme of lifelong education has been recurrent. Many of the thinkers looked to a time when lifelong education would be the order of the day. They were more concerned with lifelong education than lifelong learning, since they did not quite envisage all the changes that were to occur. However, there is now a confusion between the two terms, with lifelong education being subsumed within lifelong learning and the two treated as synonymous, as government policy documents have tended to do (DfEE, 1998). Education may be regarded as the institutionalisation of learning (Jarvis, 1986) but the institutionalisation of lifelong learning did cause some radicals considerable concern. Illich and Verne (1976), for instance, suggested that the new knowledge produced would not necessarily be for the good of individuals but would be for the benefit of the capitalist system and that workers would be forced to continue learning so that they could continue working.

Yeaxlee (1929) was the first scholar to examine the idea of lifelong education in depth and many of the problems upon which he focused are as significant now as they were at the time when he wrote about them. But it is also important to recognize that these thinkers were in a small minority at this time, since many people still believed that adults could not continue to learn throughout their lives. Part of their vision was that there should be lifelong education opportunities for all adults. Although it was Yeaxlee who was the first to offer a developed treatise on lifelong education, it has been shown here that Dewey's work implicitly presupposes such a theory. For Dewey (1916), however, education was to be life long and to have no end beyond itself.

But lifelong education did not emerge is such a manner. The global forces of advanced capitalism needed adult learners to form part of its highly educated workforce. The workforce, with a decline in manufacturing jobs and an increased demand for knowledge-based workers in the West, but with new industrial workers in others, needed more knowledge-based workers who could keep abreast with the changes in knowledge throughout their work lives.

Among the first thinkers to see what was happening were Kerr and his colleagues. The logic of industrialization thesis was first published at the beginning of the 1960s in *Industrialism and Industrial Man* (Kerr, *et al*, 1973). In it the authors argued that the industrializing processes at the heart of society would have a worldwide impact, producing a convergence in the social structures in the different countries of the world, a more open and global society. Like Marx, but from an entirely different viewpoint, they implied that each society has a substructure and a superstructure. The substructural driving force of change was the industrialization process itself and, not surprisingly, education was part of the superstructure – responding to the needs of the infrastructure and being forced to change according to its demands. However, it was the identification of the substructural forces that was a major weakness; they did not foresee the global changes that were to occur in the 1970s and alter the face of industry and commerce itself.

But another aspect of their argument is important here: they located education in the superstructure responsive to the demands of the substructure. They were only really concerned about higher education, which they regarded as the handmaiden of industrialism, but their thesis is relevant to the education of adults in general. They wrote of it, thus:

> The higher educational system of the industrial society stresses the natural sciences, engineering, medicine, managerial training – whether private or public – and administrative law. It must steadily adapt to new disciplines and fields of specialization. There is a relatively smaller place for the humanities and the arts, while the social sciences are strongly related to the training of the managerial groups and technicians for the enterprise and for government. The increased leisure time, however, can afford a broader public appreciation of the humanities and the arts. (Kerr *et al*, 1973: 47).

They claimed that the educational system would have to expand to meet the needs of industrialization and this process would create an increasing level of education for all citizens, albeit there would be greater emphasis on those subjects relevant to the substructural demands. The process about which they wrote has occurred – it is not just higher education that has expanded but the whole of the education for adults. We have lifelong education but it is not quite in the form nor with the human values that those early thinkers had hoped for. Adult education has been subsumed in lifelong learning but it is now a function of the global market. Indeed, it almost appears as if lifelong education has become work-life education and that people are now educated, not because they are human beings, but because they are potential employees. The values of adult education have been lost and the movement has become part of the market.

Clearly this is not true in much of the non-Western world, although the whole world is being affected by these changes. The market is secular and values in education have become much less apparent. But global capitalism continues to produce inequalities. This is not just a matter of the people of the underdeveloped world – this is a matter of global capitalism itself. Indeed, inequality is a symbol of successful capitalism – as Bauman (1998: 79), quoting Jeremy Seabrook (1988: 15), reminds us:

> Poverty cannot be 'cured', for it is not a symptom of the disease of capitalism. Quite the reverse: it is evidence of its robust good health, its spur to even great accumulation and effort…

Perhaps the values of the movement are as necessary today as they were when those early adult educators began to develop adult education in the West.

CONCLUSIONS

This book has attempted to demonstrate how adult education has changed from a social movement to an accepted field of study and been incorporated within a lifelong learning market. It has illustrated how those who had embraced it as a social movement in the West were frequently driven by their own religious beliefs. But it has also shown how, as adult education gained wider social acceptance, leading scholars gave it academic respectability. Without their pioneering work, we would have known less about learning, less about different ways of teaching adults, and it would have been even more difficult to see the education of adults, as a field fit for university study. There is a sense in which they gave it an academic identity. The movement became an important field of study during the 20th century and its leading thinkers embraced both – but as the century drew to a close further changes occurred. Scholarship about the education of adults is still to be found in the universities but perhaps, as Schon argued, technical rationality is insufficient, but we now have to rediscover the rationality of values.

REFERENCES

Abercrombie, N, Hill, S and Turner, B (1984) *The Penguin Dictionary of Sociology*, Penguin, Harmondsworth

Allen, J, Braham, P and Lewis, P *Political and Economic Forms of Modernity*, Polity, Cambridge

Bauman, Z (1998) *Globalization: The human consequences*, Polity, Cambridge

Department for Education and Employment (DfEE) (1998) *The Age of Learning*, DfEE, London

Dewey, J (1916) *Democracy and Education*, Free Press, New York

Gibson, G (1986) Thought and Action in the Life of F D Maurice, with particular reference to the London Working Men's College, *The International Journal of Lifelong Education*, **5** (4)

Giddens, A (1998) *The Third Way*, Polity, Cambridge

Hart, M and Horton, D (1993) Beyond God the father and God the Mother: Adult education and spirituality, in *Adult Education and Theological Interpretations*, eds P Jarvis and N Walters, Krieger, Malabar, Fl

HMSO (1919) *The Final Report of the Adult Education Committee of the Ministry of Reconstruction*, Department of Adult Education, University of Nottingham, Nottingham

Illich, I and Verne, E (1976) *Imprisoned in the Global Classroom*, Writers and Readers Publishing, London

Jarvis, P (1985) *The Sociology of Adult and Continuing Education*, Croom-Helm, London

Jarvis, P (1986) *Sociological Perspectives on Lifelong Education and Lifelong Learning*, Department of Adult Education Monographs, University of Georgia

Jarvis, P (1997) *Ethics and the Education of Adults in a Late Modern Society*, NIACE, Leicester

Jarvis, P and Walters, N (1993) *Adult Education and Theological Interpretations*, Krieger, Malabar, Fl

Kelly, T (1970) *A History of Adult Education in Great Britain*, University of Liverpool Press, Liverpool

Kerr, C et al (1973) *Industrialism and Industrial Man*, 2nd rev edn, Penguin, Harmondsworth

Ranson, S (1994) *Towards the Learning Society*, Cassell, London

Scott, A (1992) Political Culture and Social Movements, in *Political and Economic Forms of Modernity*, eds J Allen, P Braham. and P Lewis, Polity, Cambridge

Seabrook, J (1988) *The Race for Riches: The human cost of wealth*, Marshall Pickering, Basingstoke

Smelser, N (1962) *Theory of Collective Behaviour*, Routledge and Kegan Paul, London

Tilly, C (1984) Social Movements and National Politics, in *Statemaking and Social Movements*, eds C Wright and S Harding, University of Michigan Press, Ann Arbor

Wright, C and Harding, S (1984) *Statemaking and Social Movements*, University of Michigan Press, Ann Arbor

Yeaxlee, B (1929) *Lifelong Education*, Cassell, London

Index